Multiculturalism in Latin America

D0005664

Institute of Latin American Studies Series

General Editor: **James Dunkerley**, Director, Institute of Latin American Studies, University of London

The Institute of Latin American Studies, a member of the School of Advanced Study of the University of London, was founded in 1965. The Institute is dedicated to research on Latin America in the social sciences and humanities. The purpose of this series is to disseminate to a wide audience the new work based on the research programmes and projects organised by academic staff and Associate Fellows of the Institute of Latin American Studies.

Titles include:

Victor Bulmer-Thomas (*editor*)
THE NEW ECONOMIC MODEL IN LATIN AMERICA AND ITS IMPACT ON INCOME DISTRIBUTION AND POVERTY

Victor Bulmer-Thomas, Nikki Craske and Mónica Serrano (*editors*)
MEXICO AND THE NORTH AMERICAN FREE TRADE AGREEMENT: WHO WILL BENEFIT?

Elizabeth Joyce and Carlos Malamud (*editors*)
LATIN AMERICA AND THE MULTINATIONAL DRUG TRADE

Walter Little and Eduardo Posada-Carbó (*editors*)
POLITICAL CORRUPTION IN EUROPE AND LATIN AMERICA

John Lynch
LATIN AMERICA BETWEEN COLONY AND NATION
Selected Essays

Oliver Marshall (*editor*)
ENGLISH-SPEAKING COMMUNITIES IN LATIN AMERICA

Maxine Molyneux
WOMEN'S MOVEMENTS IN INTERNATIONAL PERSPECTIVE
Latin America and Beyond

Eduardo Posada-Carbó (*editor*)
COLOMBIA
The Politics of Reforming the State
ELECTIONS BEFORE DEMOCRACY
The History of Elections in Europe and Latin America

Rachel Sieder (*editor*)
CENTRAL AMERICA: Fragile Transition
MULTICULTURALISM IN LATIN AMERICA
Indigenous Rights, Diversity and Democracy

John Weeks (*editor*)
STRUCTURAL ADJUSTMENT AND THE AGRICULTURAL SECTOR IN LATIN AMERICA AND THE CARIBBEAN

Institute of Latin American Studies
Series Standing Order ISBN 0–333–71476–8
(*outside North America only*)

You can receive future titles in this series as they are published by placing a standing order. Please contact your bookseller or, in case of difficulty, write to us at the address below with your name and address, the title of the series and one of the ISBNs quoted above.

Customer Services Department, Macmillan Distribution Ltd, Houndmills, Basingstoke, Hampshire RG21 6XS, England

Multiculturalism in Latin America

Indigenous Rights, Diversity and Democracy

Edited by

Rachel Sieder
Senior Lecturer in Politics
Institute of Latin American Studies
London

First published 2002 by
PALGRAVE MACMILLAN
Houndmills, Basingstoke, Hampshire RG21 6XS and
175 Fifth Avenue, New York, N.Y. 10010
Companies and representatives throughout the world

PALGRAVE MACMILLAN is the new global academic imprint of St Martin's Press LLC Scholarly and Reference Division and Palgrave Macmillan Ltd (formerly Macmillan Press Ltd).

ISBN 0–333–99870–7 hardback
ISBN 0–333–99871–5 paperback

This book is printed on paper suitable for recycling and made from fully managed and sustained forest sources.

A catalogue record for this book is available from the British Library.

Library of Congress Cataloging-in-Publication Data
Multiculturalism in Latin America : indigenous rights, diversity, and democracy / edited by Rachel Sieder.
         p. cm. — (Institute of Latin American Studies series)
    Includes bibliographical references and index.
    ISBN 0–333–99870–7 — ISBN 0–333–99871–5 (pbk.)
        1. Multiculturalism—Latin America—Case studies. 2. Latin America—Politics and government—1980– 3. Indians—Social conditions. 4. Latin America—Economic conditions. 5. Latin America—Social conditions. I. Sieder, Rachel. II. Series.

HM1271 .M8432 2002
305.8'0098—dc21

                                                              2002025212

10   9   8   7   6   5   4   3   2   1
11   10   09   08   07   06   05   04   03   02

Printed and bound in Great Britain by
Antony Rowe Ltd, Chippenham and Eastbourne

Contents

List of Figures, Tables and Appendices

Figures

Tables

Appendices

Notes on Contributors

Xavier Albó is a Jesuit priest, anthropologist and one of the most prolific scholars of Andean society. He is a researcher at CIPCA (the Centre for the Research and Promotion of the Campesino) in La Paz, of which he was a founder member. He is the author of some 20 books and over 200 articles on linguistics, social and rural issues in Bolivia and the Andean region. His publications include *La paradoja aymara: solidaridad y faccionalismo* (1975); *Desafíos de la solidaridad aymara* (1985); *Raíces de América: El mundo aymara* (1988); 'El retorno del indio', in *Revista Andina* (1991); 'Alcaldes y concejales campesinos/indígenas: La lógica tras las cifras' in Secretaría Nacional de Participación Popular; *Indígenas en el poder local* (1997) and *Ojotas en el poder local, cuatro años después* (1999).

Robert Andolina is Assistant Professor of Political Science at Bates College in Maine, USA. Previously he was Postdoctoral Research Associate in Geography at Cambridge and Newcastle Universities in the UK, and Instructor in Political Science at the University of Minnesota, USA. He has worked on indigenous social movement and development politics in Ecuador and Bolivia, and has publications in Ecuador on indigenous movement ideology and political discourse, including 'El Proyecto Político de la CONAIE como Lucha Anticolonial: Una (otra) Reconsideración de Nación y Ciudadanía en el Ecuador', in Ileana Almeida and Nidia Arrobo (eds) *En Defensa del Pluralismo y la Igualdad: Los Derechos de los Pueblos Indígenas y el Estado* (1998).

Demetrio Cojtí Cuxil is one of the foremost Mayan intellectuals in Guatemala. He is currently Vice-Minister for Education and was previously at the Educational Programme of the United Nations Children's Fund (UNICEF) in Guatemala. He received his doctorate in social communication at Louvaine University in Belgium and during the 1980s he taught at the San Carlos and Rafael Landívar universities in Guatemala. He has written widely on ethnic politics and social communication and has worked as an advisor to many indigenous organisations, NGOs and international institutions. His publications include *Políticas para la reivindicación de los mayas de hoy* (1994), *El movimiento Maya (en Guatemala)* (1997), and 'The Politics of Maya Revindication', in Edward F. Fischer and R. McKenna Brown (eds), *Maya Cultural Activism in Guatemala*.

Shelton H. Davis is Sector Manager in the Social Development Unit, Environmentally and Socially Sustainable Development, Latin America and

Caribbean Region (LCSES) at the World Bank in Washington, D.C. where he is responsible for the Bank's work on social development, including tribal and indigenous peoples, civil society, resettlement, etc. He has written extensively on indigenous peoples, environment and development issues in Latin America. His books include *Victims of the Miracle: Development and the Indians of Brazil* (1977) and *Land Rights and Indigenous Peoples: The Role of the Inter-American Commission on Human Rights* (1988). He is the editor of the World Bank publications *Indigenous Views of Land and Environment* (1993) and *Traditional Knowledge and Sustainable Development* (1995). Davis has taught at the Federal University of Rio de Janeiro in Brazil, Harvard University, University of California at Davis, Massachusetts Institute of Technology, Boston University, Clark University, the University of Massachusetts and most recently at Georgetown University.

Nina Laurie is Senior Lecturer in the Department of Geography at Newcastle University, UK. She has worked on issues of social development in Latin America for more than ten years, with specific interests in gender and development, indigenous issues and social exclusion in the Andes. She also focuses on regional development, participation and decentralisation through research on informal employment and water privatisation. She works collaboratively with colleagues at CESU, San Simón University, Bolivia and in the Postgraduate Centre in San Marcos University, Peru through DFID/British Council Higher Education Links. She is co-author of *Geographies of New Femininity* (1999). She is an affiliated Research Fellow at the Latin America and Caribbean Studies Centre at the University of Illinois, USA.

Guillermo de la Peña is Research Professor at the Centro de Investigaciones y Estudios Superiores en Antropología Social (CIESAS) (Guadalajara, Mexico), where he directs a project on changes in the relationships among indigenous peoples, the state and civil society in Mexico. During the last 30 years, he has done extensive fieldwork in Central and Western Mexico, both in rural and urban areas. He has been a Visiting Scholar at the University of Cambridge, a Tinker Professor at the Universities of Chicago and Texas, and a Bolívar Professor at the University of Paris III. Among his publications are *A Legacy of Promises: Agriculture, Politics and Ritual in the Morelos Highlands of Mexico* (1982); *Antropología Social de la Región Purhépecha* (1987); 'Populism, Regional Power, and Political Mediation: Southern Jalisco, 1900–1980', in Eric Van Young (ed.) *Mexico's Regions: Comparative History and Development* (1992); 'Rural Mobilizations in Latin America since c. 1920', in Leslie Bethell (ed.) *The Cambridge History of Latin America*, Vol. 6, Part II (1994); *El Cambio Social en la Región de Guadalajara* (1995); 'Los Desafíos de la Clase Incomoda: El Campesinado frente a la Antropología Americanista', in Miguel de León-Portilla (ed.) *Motivos de la Antropología Americanista* (2001). He has also edited several books, the most recent of which (in collaboration with Luis Vazquez León) is *La Antropología Sociocultural en el México del Milenio: Búsquedas, Encuentros y Transiciones* (2002).

Roger Plant is a specialist on social policy, land rights and indigenous issues and currently heads the Special Action Programme against Forced Labour at the International Labour Organisation (ILO), Geneva. He has worked for several UN agencies, including the ILO (where he worked in preparation of the ILO's Indigenous Peoples' Convention) and the UN Mission to Guatemala, where he served first as special advisor on indigenous issues and subsequently as head of the socioeconomic area. He has also worked as a consultant for the Interamerican Development Bank and Asian Development Bank on issues of indigenous poverty and development, where his recent publications include *Issues in Indigenous Poverty and Development* (1998), *Indigenous Peoples and Poverty Reduction: A Case Study of Guatemala* (1998), *Land Titling and Indigenous Peoples* (2001) and *Indigenous Peoples, Ethnic Minorities and Poverty Reduction in South-East Asia* (2002). Other recent publications include 'The Rule of Law and the Underprivileged in Latin America: A Rural Perspective'; in Juan Mendez, Guillermo O'Donnell and Paulo Sérgio Pinheiro (eds), *The (Un)Rule of Law and the Underprivileged in Latin America* (1999); and 'Indigenous Identity and Rights in the Guatemalan Peace Process', in Cynthia Arnson (ed.), *Comparative Peace Processes in Latin America* (1999).

Sarah Radcliffe is a Fellow of New Hall, and Senior Lecturer in the Department of Geography, University of Cambridge. Her research interests include social and political restructuring, and socio-cultural identities in the Andes. Her recent projects include work on popular national identities, the intersections of gender and race, political transnationalism among indigenous people, and the spatial formation of states. She is also starting work on Ecuadorian migrants to Europe. Recent publications include a piece in *Global Networks*, while her book *Remaking the Nation: Place, Politics and Identity in Latin America* (with S. Westwood) was published in Spanish (Quito, 1999). She is currently Co-Editor of the *Bulletin of Latin American Research*.

Rachel Sieder is Senior Lecturer in Politics at the Institute of Latin American Studies, University of London. She has been a visiting fellow at FLACSO Guatemala and a visiting lecturer at the Centro de Investigaciones y Estudios Superiores en Antropología Social (CIESAS) in Chiapas, Mexico. Her research focuses on legal reform, indigenous rights and human rights. Her recent publications include 'The Politics of Remembering and Forgetting in Central America', in Alexandra de Brito et al. (eds), *The Politics of Memory and Democratization* (2001); with Jessica Witchell, 'Advancing Indigenous Claims through the Law: Reflections on the Guatemalan Peace Process', in Jane

Cowan, Marie Dembour and Richard Wilson (eds), *Culture and Rights* (2001); and 'Revisioning Citizenship: Reforming the Law in Post-Conflict Guatemala' in Thomas Blum Hansen and Finn Stepputat (eds), *States of Imagination: Explorations of the Post-Colonial State* (2001). Her articles have appeared in the *Journal of Latin American Studies, The Bulletin of Latin American Research, Democratization* and *Citizenship Studies* and her edited books include *Guatemala After the Peace Accords* (1998) and (with Pilar Domingo) *Promoting the Rule of Law: Perspectives on Latin America* (2001). She is Associate Editor of the *Journal of Latin American Studies*.

Rodolfo Stavenhagen, research-professor in sociology at El Colegio de México (Mexico), is currently United Nations Special Rapporteur for the Human Rights of Indigenous People. He is Vice-President of the Inter-American Institute of Human Rights and member of the Council of the United Nations University for Peace. He is a former Assistant-Director General for Social Sciences at UNESCO. In Mexico, he has been General Director for Popular Cultures in the Ministry of Public Education, and worked for several years in the National Indianist Institute. He was founding president of the Mexican Academy for Human Rights and a member for ten years of the Council of the National Commission of Human Rights. He is currently a member of the Commission on the Monitoring and Follow-up of the San Andrés Peace Accords between the federal government and the Zapatista National Liberation Army. In 1997 he was awarded the National Prize of Sciences and Arts by the Mexican government. He has been visiting professor at Harvard and Stanford universities. His research interests include social development, agrarian problems, ethnic conflicts, indigenous peoples and human rights. His recent books include: *Derechos humanos de los pueblos indígenas* (2000), *Ethnic Conflicts and the Nation-State* (1996), *The Ethnic Question: Development, Conflict and Human Rights* (1990) and *Entre la ley y la costumbre: el derecho consuetudinario indígena en América Latina* (1990).

Donna Lee Van Cott is assistant professor of political science at the University of Tennessee, Knoxville. She is editor of *Indigenous Peoples and Democracy in Latin America* (1994) and author of *The Friendly Liquidation of the Past: The Politics of Diversity in Latin America* (2000). Van Cott has published articles on diverse aspects of indigenous peoples' politics, most recently, in the *Journal of Latin American Studies, Studies in Comparative International Development*, and *Latin American Perspectives*. She is currently working on a book that explains the emergence and success of indigenous political parties in South America.

Raquel Yrigoyen Fajardo is a Peruvian lawyer, PhD candidate in law, with a Master's degree in criminology, and post-graduate studies in Anthropology and Indigenous Law. She has worked on human rights, justice, multiculturalism and indigenous rights in several countries in Latin America, for various branches of the United Nations (the High Commissioner for Human Rights, MINUGUA, UNOPS, UNICRI, UNDP) and other human rights organisations. She is author of two books and more than 40 articles related to indigenous law, legal reform, legal pluralism and human rights. She has been guest lecturer in more than 20 universities of Latin America and Europe. Currently she is editor of the web site Alertanet – Portal on Law and Society for the Latin American Network of Law and Society, www.alertanet.org

Acknowledgements

This volume originated in a conference and workshop convened at the Institute of Latin American Studies in March 1999 entitled *Pluri-Cultural and Multi-Ethnic: Evaluating the implications for state and society in Mesoamerica and the Andes*. Thanks are due to the administrative staff of the Institute for facilitating that event, especially to Olga Jiménez and Tony Bell for their skilful and seamless organising of everything and everyone involved. The contributions made by the participants and discussants at the workshop immeasurably enriched the contents of the final volume and I am enormously grateful to Deborah Yashar, Olivia Harris, Maxine Molyneux and James Dunkerley for their critical observations and collegial input and support. John Gledhill took time out from a busy schedule to provide insightful comments and helpful suggestions on an initial draft of the book. Donna Lee Van Cott and Raquel Yrigoyen were an important source of inspiration and encouragement and completed their revisions in record time. The Institute of Latin American Studies provided me with a six-month sabbatical during which the introduction to the volume and editing were completed and my thanks are due to all my colleagues, but particularly to James Dunkerley and Pilar Domingo, for making that possible. John Maher, my editor at ILAS, and Alison Howson and Guy Edwards at Palgrave made the editorial process a painless one. I also gratefully acknowledge the financial support of the European Commission.

Rachel Sieder

This book has been produced with the financial assistance of the European Community. The views expressed herein are those of the authors and can therefore in no way be taken to reflect the official opinion of the European Community.

Introduction

Rachel Sieder

Latin American societies have long been multicultural in their composition, yet until recently ethnic difference did not feature explicitly in the region's politics or legal and administrative arrangements. However, during the last decade of the twentieth century ethnicity became a key focus of political concern, as demands for reform of the state to accommodate indigenous peoples' demands gathered pace. This development was prompted by three interrelated factors. The first of these was the emergence of indigenous political movements onto the national and international political stage during the 1980s and 1990s. The second was a developing international jurisprudence, which increasingly characterised the rights of indigenous peoples as human rights. The third factor of signal importance was the constitutional reform process that took place in many Latin American countries during the last 15 years of the century, and which recognised – at least in principle – the multicultural and multi-ethnic nature of those societies. Ethnic claims were propelled centre-stage, at least in part, by the radical changes in economic and social relations engendered by the twin processes of economic and legal globalisation. These ongoing transformations also provide the context within which the politico-juridical recognition of difference across the continent is taking place. At the start of the twenty-first century, this new 'politics of difference' is profoundly challenging accepted notions of democracy, citizenship and development. This volume examines some of the key features of this unfolding process and explores the analytical and policy questions it raises.

Most estimates concur that indigenous people now number approximately 40 million people in Latin America – roughly 8 to 10 per cent of the region's overall population. The vast majority, some 85 per cent, is concentrated in Mesoamerica and the central Andes. In Bolivia and Guatemala indigenous people constitute over 50 per cent of the population, in Ecuador and Peru between 30 and 40 per cent, and in Mexico between 10 and 15 per cent (this last, at approximately 11 million individuals, is the numerically largest

1

indigenous population in Latin America). The question of precisely who is defined as indigenous remains a question of some controversy. Under international law, the broad criteria remain threefold: self-definition as a person belonging to an indigenous community, subordination to dominant society, and historical continuity with pre-colonial societies.[1] Indigenous identity, though evidently fluid and constantly changing, is linked to a prevailing sense of cultural difference and to discrimination by dominant society: in other words to a complex dynamic of self-identification and ascription.[2] In the majority of cases, poverty is a defining feature of indigenous identity – according to all social indicators indigenous people are among the poorest sectors of Latin American society and, in many cases, are getting poorer.[3]

Indigenous livelihoods remain dependent on access to land, albeit far from exclusively so. During the twentieth century indigenous people in Mesoamerica and the central Andes organised as peasants, or *campesinos*, to defend and secure land resources. They were mobilised by civilian and military elites in favour of nationalist modernising projects, guided by a developmentalist ethos, which varied from revolutionary to counterrevolutionary in intent, depending on the country in question. Where agrarian reforms were implemented, indigenous communal authority structures were reorganised around inalienable and collective land holdings, for example the *ejido* in Mexico after the 1930s, and the *comunidades campesinas* or *comunidades nativas* in Peru after the 1969 agrarian reform of the Velasco Alvarado government.[4] In effect these *agrarista* structures provided some protection for a subordinated communal autonomy and group rights to land, although in many cases these rights were weakly enforced. However, during the 1970s and 1980s land poverty increased as a consequence of population growth, sub-division and encroachment by commercial agriculture. This, together with civil conflict (in the cases of Peru and Guatemala), stimulated rural out-migration and the flight of many indigenous people to the cities. Less and less tied to a spatially located 'indigenous community', the vast majority of these migrants were integrated into an increasingly globalised market on highly disadvantageous terms. Huge numbers ceased to be rural inhabitants, forced instead by rural impoverishment to scrape a living within the informal sector of Latin America's cities.

The decade of the 1980s witnessed an upsurge of ethnic organising and indigenous protagonism, as the transition from authoritarian rule across the continent allowed for new forms of protest and organisation.[5] Many democratising reforms – such as, for example, the enfranchisement of illiterates in Peru and Ecuador, which occurred in 1979 and 1980, respectively – directly incorporated indigenous people for the first time into national politics. In addition, since the 1970s the formation of indigenous grass-roots organisations was supported across the region by domestic and international NGOs and by the Catholic Church (Van Cott 1994; Brysk 2000). Following the transition to electoral democracy, specifically indigenous demands emerged within a broader context of economic structural adjustment and democratic deficits across the continent (Yashar 1998). The rollback of state services and the exigencies of debt-servicing payments, which forced governments to ever-greater exploitation of natural resources, negatively affected indigenous peoples and propelled them into the national – and international – sphere. In addition, neoliberal economic policies prescribed by international donors advanced the reform of land markets through the promotion of individual titling and the abolition of collective entitlements previously afforded through agrarian reform legislation. Whether they lived in the countryside or the cities, indigenous people's economic – and thus social and cultural – vulnerability increased rapidly during the 1980s, contributing in turn to greater indigenous organising and protest. Domestic and international allies also played a vital role in promoting their demands: by the 1990s indigenous rights issues had become increasingly regionalised and transnationalised by various non-governmental and inter-governmental networks concerned with advancing indigenous platforms (Brysk 2000).

Indigenous activism also reflected profound changes in the international legal environment. Indigenous rights are now increasingly recognised by the international community as a form of human rights. Whilst some analysts continue to insist that human rights pertain exclusively to the individual, in recent years the idea has gained ground that certain collective rights are necessary for the full enjoyment of individual human rights (Donnelly 1989; Stavenhagen 2000). Indigenous activists have long fought to be recognised as 'peoples' under international law, a status that, it was hoped, would secure them the right to self-determination. However, international conventions and draft declarations referring to indigenous peoples have specified that the use of the term 'peoples' does not confer conventional rights of self-determination under international law; that is the right to separate statehood. Nonetheless, indigenous peoples' rights to internal – as opposed to external – self-determination, understood as rights to greater participation and autonomy *within* the nation-state, are clearly recognised. Autonomy regimes, comprising a combination of group rights, territorial ambit, indigenous institutions and specific politico-administrative competencies vis-à-vis the central state, are increasingly advanced as the most appropriate formulae.

Indigenous 'peoples' are now firmly established as subjects of rights in the international legal order.[6] As a consequence, the claims that individuals and groups can make against the state and the resources they have to contest its impositions have increased greatly. Undoubtedly the most important international instrument in this respect is the International Labour Organisation's (ILO) Convention 169, the only existing international legislation referring to indigenous rights. Once ratified, the Convention has the force of domestic law in signatory states. Its fundamental points are the following: indigenous people are defined according to the criteria of self-identification and signatory governments commit to ensure equality of social, economic and cultural rights of all indigenous peoples within their jurisdiction. Indigenous peoples are to be guaranteed full participation in the formulation of all policies that affect them. Governments are to ensure respect for indigenous norms, practices, customary law and institutions. They are also bound to guarantee indigenous peoples' traditional lands and territories, and to ensure their right to be consulted about and participate in the formulation of development policies affecting their territories and subsoil resources. Lastly, governments must provide indigenous peoples with labour rights guarantees and adequate education and health provision. By the year 2000 ILO Convention 169 had been ratified by the majority of Latin American states, although it remained far from fully implemented in most cases.[7] Other international instruments were also of significant influence, although none is legally binding as yet (as ILO Convention 169 is). Most notable were the United Nations' draft Declaration on Indigenous Rights, drawn up in a lengthy consultative process during the 1990s, and the Organisation of American States (OAS) Draft Declaration, completed in 1998 (Stavenhagen 2000; Plant 1998a; Van Cott 2000a).[8]

As Donna Lee Van Cott has observed (2000a: 262), ILO Convention 169 had an enormous impact on the process of constitutional reform in Latin America. Since 1986 new constitutions, or amendments to existing charters have been passed in Bolivia (1994), Colombia (1991), Ecuador (1998), Mexico (1992), Nicaragua (1986), Paraguay (1992), Peru (1993) and Venezuela (1999) recognising the multi-ethnic and pluricultural nature of those societies.[9] Some of these reforms, though not all, explicitly acknowledged indigenous *peoples* as subjects of rights. For example, the revised constitutions of Colombia, Peru, Bolivia and Ecuador all recognise indigenous authorities, customary law and special indigenous jurisdictions. As Van Cott has signalled, such changes evidenced an 'emerging regional model of multicultural constitutionalism' (2000a: 17).

These reforms, although by their very nature declaratory, held out the promise of a new social pact involving a different relationship between indigenous peoples and the state. Potentially, at least, this constituted a radical break with the past. In Europe the legal existence of distinct ethnic and religious communities preceded the formation of the modern, liberal state and continued to exist alongside it, in the form of minority rights for certain populations, federalist arrangements and tolerance of pluralism during the nineteenth century. In Latin America, by contrast, dominant *criollo* elites took up the emancipatory discourse of liberalism during the nineteenth century, and used it to legally erase difference, associated with the corporatist colonial regime, which had afforded limited protections for 'subordinate' indigenous populations. Forging the post-colonial state involved homogenising the nation and the consolidation of an enduring political centralism. Society remained characterised by sharp racial, ethnic and class discrimination, yet the hegemonic discourse was of universal and undifferentiated citizenship, shared national identity and equality before the law. This discursive egalitarianism, however, was sharply at odds with the political and economic vision of the nineteenth century liberal modernisers: liberalism was not a common emancipatory project and was in practice anything but 'difference blind'. Property and literacy qualifications on the franchise meant that indigenous people were effectively excluded from national politics. At the same time, the abolition of corporatist protections meant that many were despoiled of their historic lands to facilitate the expansion of agro-exports. As Rodolfo Stavenhagen discusses in his contribution to this volume, during the twentieth century the nationalist paradigms of modernisation and developmentalism advanced a vision of a homogenous, mono-ethnic, mestizo state, premised on the assimilation of indigenous identity. Indigenous people were seen as 'backward', a brake on development in need of modernisation and integration into wider society and the market. It was supposed that this would eventually lead to their disappearance, as indigenous groups became culturally and ethnically absorbed by mestizo society. By the 1990s this model was increasing denounced as discriminatory and unacceptable. Instead, various sectors began to advocate a multicultural, pluralist and ethnically heterogeneous state, based on tolerance, respect for cultural differences and intercultural dialogue. Evidently ethnic claims are central to the redefinition and reconstitution of the state in Latin America. What is being advanced is, at least potentially, a radically new politico-legal order and conception of citizenship.

In a recent volume focusing on indigenous claims and reform of the state in Latin America, Willem Assies called for 'further study on the relations between new legislation and concrete practices' (2000: ix). The essays in this volume aim to contribute to this debate, exploring what recent constitutional and legal changes have meant in practice for indigenous peoples and their demands, the state and the prospects for democracy and social justice in Latin America. Much discussion of the recent successes of indigenous organisation has focused on the numerically minority indigenous populations, such as those in Nicaragua and Colombia, and lowland populations, who made significant gains in terms of territorial recognition during the 1990s, particularly in Bolivia, Brazil and Ecuador.[10] However, the contributors here focus particularly on Mesoamerica and the central Andes, the areas where the majority of indigenous people, historically defined as *campesino*, reside. In particular, they consider the ways in which new legal frameworks have been implemented, appropriated and contested on the ground, assessing the broader implications of these processes. The questions raised by recent developments are challenging and multiple, and can only be briefly signalled here, in the hope of encouraging further comparative and case-specific research. They fall into three broad areas or sets of issues, explored below: first, *representation and autonomy*; secondly, *legal pluralism and human rights*; and thirdly, *poverty and social justice*.

Representation and autonomy

The politico-legal recognition of multiculturalism has profound implications for governance and democracy in Latin America. The recognition of different ethnic groups by the state implies, at least potentially, a new *national* project. Yet the tensions between the incorporation and participation of formerly excluded groups within the nation-state on new terms, on the one hand, and ethnic separatism, isolation and new forms of exclusion on the other are inherent in any such experiment. Although greater inter-ethnic compromise is the preferred outcome and stated objective of recent moves to reform in Latin America, increased inter-ethnic tensions cannot be ruled out, depending on how the process unfolds. One of the overriding concerns of indigenous activists in Latin America and their supporters is to democratise the state. Yet multi-ethnic states are not, in and of themselves, necessarily democratic. Multiculturalist reforms could contribute to the strengthening of the state and democratic deepening, or conversely to the weakening of the state and the strengthening of authoritarian forces. A key question that must therefore be posed to recent developments is the extent to which they contribute to an increase or a decrease in overall democratic accountability and guarantees.

Electoral democracy alone has plainly been unable to guarantee indigenous peoples' rights, or indeed the basic citizenship rights of the majority of the region's population. Following the transition from authoritarian rule, Latin American governments experienced a crisis of legitimacy as they introduced structural adjustment programmes and dismantled the corporatist and welfare arrangements that had undergirded the 'national-popular' state. The recognition of ethnic difference through the process of constitutional reform can be understood, in part, as a response to that legitimacy crisis. However, the challenge of 'deepening democracy' ultimately involves rethinking the existing terms of political participation. Alan Cairns has referred to the vertical and horizontal dimensions of citizenship, the former linking individuals to the state and the latter entailing the 'positive identification of citizens with each other as valued members of the same civic community' (1997: 4). Both dimensions are weak in Latin America, where acute socio-economic inequalities and de facto ethnic stratification have impeded the development of mutual understanding and cooperation. Indigenous peoples in particular, historically excluded, subjugated and stigmatised, often feel little solidarity and identification either with the rest of the population or with political parties and the state. Recognising the historic injustices against indigenous populations and taking measures to secure their greater equality *in practice* could advance a common civic identification, based on the principle of fair treatment of all citizens. However, it cannot be assumed, prima facie, that such an outcome would prevail. In a forceful recent critique of multiculturalist policies, Brian Barry has rejected the legal and political recognition of cultural differences, charging that 'a situation in which groups live in parallel universes is not one well calculated to advance mutual understanding or encourage the cultivation of habits of cooperation and sentiments of trust' (Barry 2001: 88).[11] Such critiques of multiculturalist policies – which analyse practice in established Western democracies – are not easily transferable to debates concerning indigenous peoples' rights in the Latin American context.[12] However, they do raise a central question: to what extent do recent multicultural initiatives and reforms support or impede the development of a shared citizenship or civic identification in the countries of the region? Answering this question necessarily involves an empirically grounded examination of the policies themselves and the specific political and economic contexts in which they are implemented.

Different models of political participation have been advocated by indigenous activists during the last two decades, most involving some kind of autonomy regime at local or regional level. This is an unprecedented development. While the colonial state in Latin America recognised subordinate autonomies, the guiding ethos of the republican state was the negation of difference and the unity of political and legal jurisdiction. Even under federal constitutions – in Argentina, Brazil, Mexico and Venezuela – the power of the political centre over state governments has remained overwhelming until very recently. In contrast with other regions of the world, Latin America has little or no experience of political structures that grant autonomy to culturally distinct communities. At present, considerable controversy continues throughout the region regarding the units, competencies and mandates of the autonomy regimes proposed by indigenous movements. For indigenous activists, the notion of 'autonomy' generally implies a combination of land, resources and normative and administrative space, what has been referred to in some contexts as '*territorio étnico*'. Yet dispute persists between organisations over the precise nature of territorial autonomy, some advancing positions favouring community-based and municipal-based autonomy, others preferring regionally centred arrangements.[13] During the last decade, state recognition of indigenous autonomy has tended to be restricted to community or municipal level. However, as Willem Assies has noted '[c]laims to autonomy ... tend to go beyond the circumscribed community level that states now seem to be prepared to concede but to which "autonomy" has historically tended to be reduced' (2000: 12). Such was the experience, for example, of Chiapas between 1996 and 2001. The federal government manoeuvred to reduce the scope of indigenous autonomy set out in the 1996 San Andrés peace accords with the Ejército Zapatista de Liberación Nacional (EZLN), alleging that the original proposals would conflict with the existing federal model and the rights to property guaranteed by the Constitution. The state government of Chiapas subsequently advanced a number of initiatives aimed at limiting autonomy claims and undermining support for the EZLN.[14] An indigenous rights law was eventually approved by Congress in 2001 within the framework of the peace negotiations. However, in contrast to the law drawn up by the consultative peace commission (Comisión de Concordia y Pacificación, COCOPA) on the basis of the 1996 agreements, this was a unilateral initiative of the executive that effectively restated the restrictive municipalisation approach to indigenous autonomy, falling far short of activists' demands.[15]

Securing the effective recognition of indigenous rights and greater social justice will entail more than localised autonomies – or, in effect, legal recognition of the de facto autonomy which already exists in many places as a consequence of marginalisation, official neglect and ethnic resistance. What it in fact requires is a new political arrangement, implying a profound redefinition of national political, administrative and legal space. Yet issues of participation and representation remain largely unresolved in those countries where indigenous people constitute a sizeable proportion or majority of the overall population. Consociational arrangements such as proportional representation for indigenous peoples in national congresses and senates have been ruled out by dominant elites, but little consensus exists on alternative mechanisms to articulate the local to the national.[16]

In some countries, most notably Bolivia after 1994, governments have combined constitutional recognition of multiculturalism with processes of political and fiscal decentralisation of the state, aimed in principle at securing greater local participation and governmental accountability. Decentralisation was favoured as a new development rubric during the 1990s and was supported by a wide range of international donors. It is a multi-faceted process, involving municipalisation – strengthening municipal government and granting it greater autonomy, the privatisation and decentralisation of service provision, and the much vaunted 'strengthening of civil society' and local participatory mechanisms. This last element often involved an increased role for NGOs in the provision of services that were previously the responsibility of the state. All of these processes strengthened the spaces and opportunities for indigenous movements. Yet recent experience has often shown that the discourse of 'participation' has not translated into effective oversight mechanisms in practice.[17] In some cases, decentralisation has mitigated against democratisation, reinforcing local power elites, clientelist politics and unequal access to power. In others, the increased penetration of the logic of political parties into rural areas has increased the fragmentation and division of indigenous authorities (see Calla 2000; Albó in this volume). In an important sense, contemporary policies such as the recognition of legal pluralism (see Sieder in this volume; Van Cott 2000b) and municipalisation have actually *extended* the territorial outreach of the state. In this manner they have increased its power, or the ability of local elites, to intervene in what in many areas were previously semi-autonomous indigenous spheres. This can be understood as a reorganisation of authority, territory and space according to a statist logic. Yet at the same time this is no unidirectional, top down process: national polities are also undoubtedly being rebuilt 'from the bottom up' as local actors engage in a dialectic relationship with national level state reform.

While indigenous movements have been highly successful in articulating indigenous peoples' claims during the last two decades, political parties continue to dominate as the main form for pursuing and implementing them, particularly at regional and national level. The development of specifically indigenist parties and of alliances between indigenous movements and other non-indigenous political actors has been most consolidated in Bolivia, Colombia and Ecuador and was critical to ensuring constitutional recognition of indigenous rights in all three cases (Albó 1994; Van Cott 2000c). However, in the wake of constitutional recognition, indigenous peoples have been faced with the need to increase their political influence in order to pursue the promulgation and implementation of adequate secondary legislation. The dangers of the co-option of leaders and the fragmentation of indigenous movements in the post-constitutional phase of reform are high. In part this explains why many indigenous activists have rejected political parties altogether. Local indigenous representation independent of political parties has increased in recent years, for example through reforms such as that passed in 1995 by the state government of Oaxaca, Mexico, which allowed for the election of municipal authorities according to indigenous *usos y costumbres* (Hernández Navarro 1999). However, the dynamic between participation through different types of local autonomy and the national politics of representation is currently a key area of concern for indigenous activists. Linked to this, what makes certain alliances between indigenous movements and parties possible in some contexts at certain conjunctures and not in others should continue to be a central focus of enquiry.

Legal pluralism and human rights

Since independence, official doctrine in Latin America has traditionally stressed the unitary nature of the law. However, in practice a situation of legal pluralism – the overlapping coexistence of different legal and regulatory orders – has prevailed across the continent (Santos 1995). In part this derives from the legacy of colonial rule, when a separate, subordinate legal system for indigenous subjects – *la República de Indios* – existed alongside the colonists' law. During the nineteenth and twentieth centuries, the lack of coverage of state judicial systems across huge swathes of national territory, combined with the cultural and social marginalisation of indigenous people, meant that indigenous communities continued to use their own local authorities, norms and practices to resolve disputes. While no neat division exists between 'state law' and 'indigenous law', indigenous people invariably resorting to both in order to resolve their conflicts, the official judicial system throughout the region discriminates against indigenous people and remains largely inaccessible in terms of cost, language and geographical and cultural distance. ILO Convention 169 and many of the constitutional reforms passed in the 1990s recognised indigenous peoples' right to use their 'traditional' or 'customary' law. In effect, what this implies is the formal incorporation of indigenous authorities, norms and practices into the state legal system.

However, the course of recognition to date has been far from smooth. On the whole, governments have tended to incorporate indigenous communities' legal practices as a form of alternative dispute resolution mechanisms (ADR) within overall processes of judicial reform, but they have failed fully to recognise indigenous peoples' rights to their authorities, legal norms and practices as stipulated by ILO Convention 169.[18] Conflicts revolve around the appropriate limits to indigenous legal autonomy. ILO Convention 169 specifies that customary law should be respected when it does not conflict with universal human rights. Such a stipulation, or limiting clause, was incorporated into those constitutional amendments that recognised indigenous customary law in the 1990s. In addition, most states continue to insist that customary law should not conflict with national laws, such as the right to due process. In practice this means that governments reserve for themselves the right to decide which aspects of 'custom' are acceptable and which are not. Certain practices and procedures have been condemned as abuses of human rights, and in some cases indigenous authorities have been imprisoned for 'exceeding their functions' (Mexico and Peru are cases in point).[19] Yet precisely what constitutes a violation of human rights in such contexts is far from clear cut. Those state officials who make such judgements may have actively discriminated against indigenous people in the past and have little empathy with or understanding of cultural differences; for many Latin American jurists, 'custom' remains associated with barbarism. Officials may also have political reasons for suppressing certain indigenous authorities. Sticking strictly to definitions of 'due legal process' as set down in national legal systems invariably invalidates indigenous forms of conflict resolution. This is because these generally concentrate on reconciling the parties and re-establishing relations, rather than adhering to occidental norms of evidentiary proof, which arguably belong to a different conceptual framework (Speed and Collier 2000). Evidently the full recognition of indigenous peoples' right to customary law requires an intercultural interpretation of 'human rights'. Although human rights are, by definition, universal, there is no single and universally valid means of respecting them – 'due process', for example, is defined differently in different Western legal systems. Many different forms of respecting human rights exist according to different circumstances and cultural frames of understanding. Indigenous norms invariably involve a profound and complex conception of human dignity, even though – as in all communitarian systems – the ideal balance between the rights of the individual and their obligations to the community are weighted more heavily toward the latter.

Constitutional amendments passed to recognise indigenous customary law generally stated that the coordination between state law and customary law would be regulated by secondary legislation. However, such legislation was not promulgated during the 1990s and little intercultural legal dialogue has occurred in practice. Only in Colombia have decisions by the Constitutional Court regarding cases concerning alleged conflicts between indigenous justice and human rights established an emerging jurisprudence which attempts to develop a new balance between indigenous autonomy and human rights. In cases of alleged conflict between indigenous practices and universal human rights, the Court has attempted to understand and interpret the latter in their cultural context, and to reach judgments through intercultural negotiations and compromises. In broad terms, the human rights enforced by the Court are reserved for fundamental human rights – the right to life and protection against enslavement and torture. The Court established that other rights must be weighed against the right of ethnic groups to cultural self-preservation (Sánchez Botero 1998; Van Cott 2000b). In effect such an approach allows for the possibility of cultural mediation of core values and for different interpretations of certain acts. For example, public whipping as a sanction may be defined as an act of degradation or torture, but may equally be defined within the cultural community as an act of purification and reintegration to the community, which maintains respect for human worth and dignity (Sánchez Botero 1998). Respect for cultural difference then, ultimately entails interpreting actions and conduct in terms of culturally distinct systems of meaning. However, these advances have been easier to achieve in Colombia, where the indigenous population constitutes less than 3 per cent of the population. In countries such as Guatemala, where indigenous people constitute the majority, the question of deciding over competing jurisdictions and conflicts is inevitably more complicated.[20] Similarly, in contexts where indigenous peoples are highly urbanised and/or transnationalised through migration, discerning 'culturally distinct systems of meaning' becomes a highly complex and controversial task.

Even when dominant political and legal authorities are open to intercultural dialogue, the balance between guaranteeing the group rights of the collectivity and ensuring the individual human rights of its members is highly complex. This is because the legitimacy and nature of 'customary law' or 'traditional dispute resolution practices' is not only contested by non-indigenous authorities, but also often *within* indigenous communities themselves. In an increasingly globalised legal context, people on the ground make appeals to the idea of 'human rights' in order to contest what they consider to be discriminatory or authoritarian practices within their communities, and – increasingly – within their private, domestic space. Indigenous communities are not homogeneous, but – like any society – are divided by age, class, gender, wealth and so on. The 'communal logic' may be an expression of the superior bargaining power of those within the community with the power to enforce their will. As Bithu Parekh and others have noted, 'far from being a transparent and univocal system of meaning claiming the spontaneous allegiance of its members, every culture is subject to contestation, and its dominant meaning tends to reflect the balance of power between its different groups' (2000: 79). Three issues are particularly contentious for the balance between communal rights and individual rights in this respect: gender equality, religious freedom and property rights.

Very real problems of gender equality and discrimination exist within indigenous communities, just as they do within society as a whole.[21] In some countries, lengthy debate has taken place within indigenous communities and organisations on this question. For example, in Mexico indigenous women organised in the Zapatista movement in Chiapas have reframed 'autonomy' claims to include demands for the personal and individual autonomy of women to make decisions about their own bodies, education, marriage partners, and so on (Eber 2001). Yet concerns have been raised that in other contexts, guaranteeing autonomy for communal legal structures and practices may continue to deny equal rights to justice for women. On the question of religious freedom and the right of the individual to apostasy, examined in this volume by Guillermo de la Peña, much controversy exists. The widespread process of conversion to Protestantism experienced across Latin America in the last decades has posed serious threats to indigenous communal cohesion. The refusal of certain individuals to carry out ritual duties considered necessary for community coexistence has led to much conflict and, in extreme cases, to forced expulsions. Widespread inter-communal religious conflict is not a prominent feature in Latin America and the right to freedom of religion is generally not denied within indigenous communities. However, tensions undoubtedly exist and might conceivably increase with the strengthening of communal autonomies. Lastly, with regard to property rights, the rollback of communal land entitlements associated with the agrarian reforms has raised the thorny issue of whether individuals within indigenous communities have the right to sell their land to outsiders. Many indigenous leaders assert their right to protect the integrity of the community by prohibiting the sale, mortgage or alienation of communal land. Such claims are supported by ILO Convention 169, yet they fly in the face of the current neoliberal economic logic. Advocates of liberal theories of multiculturalism have argued that as long as an individual has a right of exit from the cultural community, then certain restrictions on individual freedoms within the community are justifiable (Kymlicka 1995; Young 1990, 1995). This usually refers to situations where the exercise of those individual freedoms would threaten the cultural integrity of the group as a whole, such as sale of community land to outsiders. Differential treatment for historically discriminated and marginalised groups is thus viewed as necessary in order to give substance to the principle of equal citizenship. However, it is generally argued that the individual exiting the collective should be financially compensated for the loss so entailed; for example, by receiving some restitution for their share of communal land. Evidently this is a highly contentious question, conflicts over which are likely to increase in future – particularly given the prevailing neoliberal orthodoxy, which encourages the individualisation of economic assets.

What is ultimately required in Latin America, as elsewhere, is a legal and political framework that appreciates the diversity between cultures, but also allows for diversity and difference *within* different cultural groups themselves. Ideally legal systems in multicultural societies should be informed by certain basic principles of justice, such as, for example, gender equality, while allowing for differences in cultural interpretation of socio-legal concepts, such as transgression, punishment, due process, and so on. An intermediary path must be found between dogmatic adherence to liberal principles of equality before the law followed to the last detail, and cultural relativist positions that exoticise and essentialise the indigenous 'other', arguing that they do not share conceptions of individual rights. (What such positions do in effect is deny the enjoyment of human rights to culturally distinct individuals.)[22] The evolution of appropriate principles of justice for a multicultural society requires an open, equal intercultural dialogue. Establishing the balance between general principles of law and the issues posed by individual cases demands a sensitive, intercultural approach that pays careful attention to the circumstances and context of each case. In short, the full recognition of indigenous legal norms and practices will involve a profound adjustment of legal thinking and practice in the continent and the tackling of deep-seated racist attitudes.

Poverty and social justice

The relationship between the legal recognition of indigenous rights and the prospects for poverty alleviation and greater social justice is a key area of concern signalled in this volume, and is explored in greater detail in the chapters by Shelton Davis and Roger Plant. As the chapter by Nina Laurie, Robert Andolina and Sarah Radcliffe illustrates, tensions clearly exist between the neoliberal economic policies pursued in Latin America during the last two decades and the claims of indigenous peoples, particularly with regard to territorial and natural resources. However, the implications of recognising indigenous rights for development policies are far from self-evident. While the critique of neoliberal policies by the indigenous movement has been particularly vocal in recent years, controversy persists over which alternative national policies are the most appropriate to alleviate indigenous poverty. This is particularly the case given that indigenous people in Latin America are increasingly part of urban populations, dependent on highly globalised patterns of economic production and trade. In such a context, talk of 'indigenous models of development' may be of limited utility and arguably even counterproductive.

The constitutional recognition of multi-ethnicity during the 1990s opened up the possibility of greater indigenous participation in development programmes, albeit mostly at municipal level. However, in most cases, state recognition of multi-ethnicity has gone hand in hand with measures to strengthen economic deregulation and the opening up of land markets (the case of Bolivia since the 1996 INRA Law being the notable exception). That is to say, state recognition of indigenous claims as formulated to date has not fundamentally contradicted the neoliberal reform of the state. Neoliberal prescriptions for dynamising markets in land are premised on an individualist notion of ownership and stewardship. These invariably negate the logic of complex indigenous resource management strategies, which often combine collective logic and protection with individual usufruct rights. In practice recognition of collective land and resource management rights for indigenous peoples has tended to be limited to the lowland and Amazon regions (Assies 2000; Brysk 2000). The demarcation and titling of indigenous lands is more problematic in highland areas, particularly where indigenous people live side by side with non-indigenous as they do in much of the continent. And even in the lowlands the granting of rights to collective property has not necessarily implied recognition of indigenous peoples' right to exercise full politico-administrative authority; conflicts persist over rights to subsoil resources within titled indigenous territories.

In recent years, multilateral donors such as the World Bank have increasingly favoured an approach known as 'ethno-development', aimed at alleviating indigenous poverty at community and sub-regional level. Within this broad paradigm, proposals have been advanced by local NGOs and multilateral donors for integral development plans based on strengthening indigenous grass-roots organisation and knowledge and aimed at improving indigenous peoples' life chances.[23] Such schemes generally encompass subsistence production, basic infrastructure and the promotion of traditional and non-traditional commercial products. These development initiatives can have significant and positive local impacts. However, given their reliance on external donors and their failure to address the wider structural causes of poverty, it is open to question whether they can resolve the economic and social needs of the indigenous poor in countries where they constitute the majority or a sizeable proportion of the population. Fears have also been raised that the preferential targeting of development resources to indigenous groups may increase inter-ethnic tensions. Attempts to implement bilingual education policies, examined in this volume by Demetrio Cojtí for the case of Guatemala, have been particularly controversial throughout the region. Targeting resources at indigenous people inevitably raises the difficult issue of definition. International norms dictate that self-identification as indigenous provide the determining criteria. Yet, as Nina Laurie, Robert Andolina and

Sarah Radcliffe indicate in their examination of water reform policies in Bolivia, if economic and social resources are distributed according to ethnicity, this encourages a 'strategic essentialising', inevitably influencing which sectors of the poor define and present themselves as indigenous.

Few indigenous individuals and families today rely exclusively on subsistence agriculture, the land base for which was systematically eroded throughout the late twentieth century. Rather they have developed diverse and multiple economic survival strategies, including commerce, out-migration to urban areas or to rural areas to work on seasonal cash crop harvests, and transnational migration. In some areas a small indigenous elite is also making inroads to the professions and NGOs. Thus indigenous families straddle urban and rural economies in their search for economic survival. In both contexts, they still constitute a disproportionate percentage of the poor and extremely poor. In order to address indigenous marginalisation and poverty, alternative, nationally focused approaches to development are required, policies that address the poverty of urban as well as rural indigenous, and which are not simply posited on a notion of territorially bounded, rural indigenous communities (Plant 1998b). Yet controversy over appropriate macroeconomic policies persists. Some argue that indigenous poverty is due to the effects of economic globalisation and market penetration on indigenous communities, while others point to *lack* of access to the market as an underlying cause.[24] The central and unresolved question remains that of how to develop a multicultural state that can effectively tackle social exclusion.

The growing recognition of ethnicity and indigenous rights has opened up profound challenges for Latin American polities, economies and societies. Latin American states have never been liberal democracies, in the sense of ensuring a rule of law that secures rights and enforces obligations on all citizens. For this reason they have been described by many as 'low intensity democracies' (O'Donnell 1996), 'illiberal democracies' (Fakaria 1997), or some other variant of 'democracy with adjectives'. Nonetheless, the doctrine of liberalism is intimately bound up with the formation of Latin American nation-states and is deeply rooted in the region's historical trajectory. The model of the unitary, sovereign, liberal state remains a powerful symbol, a promise of modernity. Yet the challenges of adjusting political, economic and legal arrangements to the multicultural nature of Latin American societies imply potentially profound challenges to liberalism. Tenets such as individuals as the sole bearers of rights and obligations, the rule of law and equality of citizens, and the direct and unmediated relationship between the citizen and the state (and between citizen and market) are held up to question. Achieving a balance between communitarian and liberal conceptions of rights and obligations will inevitably be a complex and testing process, particularly in a context where the 'rights claiming' encouraged by globalisation is an ever more ubiquitous feature.

Whether the effective recognition of multicultural demands will constitute a reconstitution of the liberal state in Latin America, or whether it points towards its eventual replacement by another, non-liberal (ethno-nationalist?) variant remains an open question. At present, indigenous activists continue to call on the emancipatory claims of liberalism, but insist that a reformed liberalism should guarantee their collective rights, including their cultural and economic survival. The platform of indigenous movements, most notably in Mexico and Ecuador, represent national proposals for an inclusive, multicultural state respectful of individual and collective differences. The direction in which identity-based platforms develop in the future will depend, in large degree, on the ways in which they are accommodated or contested by dominant groups, within and beyond the frontiers of the nation-state. As Bhikhu Parekh has observed, '[w]hile acceptance of differences calls for changes in the legal arrangements of society, respect for them requires changes in its attitudes and ways of thought' (2000: 2). This will involve challenging deep-seated prejudices based on class and race, which continue to predominate in Latin American societies. The abandonment of the civilising mission by the holders of power, and its replacement by respect and understanding of different cultural forms, values and institutions may take generations to achieve. In addition, changes in the prevailing paradigm will not result from indigenous demands and government responses alone, but also from profound shifts in global and local political economies. Ultimately the challenge is to find ways of pluralising the state in Latin America at the same time as increasing its ability to act in pursuit of the collective interest. Cementing the basis of a new pact for common citizenship involves the twin dimensions of celebrating difference and heterogeneity, but also addressing indigenous poverty and social marginalisation. In this sense the politics of difference in the region cannot be separated from the politics of social justice.

In the following chapters the contributors to this volume explore the implementation of multicultural frameworks by Latin American states since 1986. Together they signal the gap between constitutional subscription to a multicultural society and its implementation, analyse the difficulties of delivering indigenous rights in practice and examine some of the dilemmas raised by implementing indigenous rights legislation.

In an introductory overview, Rodolfo Stavenhagen charts the changing relationship between nation-states and indigenous people in Latin America. He underlines continuities between the positivist state-building of the nineteenth century, which viewed indigenous people as backward and anti-modern, and the populist nationalism of the twentieth century, which posited their integration and assimilation through development. In the late twentieth century indigenous rights movements emerged as part of domestic and international human rights movements to challenge paternalistic approaches on the right and the left, challenging the model of nation-state which has existed to date. However, Stavenhagen cautions that after initial gains via constitutional reform, 'the going will get rough from now on'. Conflicts between autonomous and centralist impulses and between individual and collective rights look set to continue and it is far from clear what kind of 'culture(s)', if any, Latin American states are to promote. Stavenhagen concludes that the fate of multiculturalist policies in the region depends on the broader alliances indigenous rights movements are able to build in the future.

This conclusion is reinforced in the chapter by Donna Lee Van Cott, which provides a detailed comparative analysis of the constitutional reforms to secure indigenous rights that took place in the Andean countries of Colombia, Bolivia and Ecuador during the 1990s. Van Cott examines why and how constitutional reforms were initially secured and what these different attempts to codify autonomy regimes have meant in practice. She argues that two factors were common to all three cases prior to the introduction of the reforms: the crisis of governmental legitimacy and governability and the political maturation of indigenous organisations. However, her analysis indicates that the extent and success of the different autonomy projects in Colombia, Bolivia and Ecuador subsequent to their respective constitutional reforms have depended crucially on the relative strength and leverage of indigenous organisations.

Taking up the issues of representation and autonomy, Xavier Albó examines the experience of indigenous campesino organisations in Bolivia before, during and subsequent to the constitutional and other reforms introduced by the government of Gonzalo Sánchez de Lozada (1993–97). This unique programme for state modernisation heralded recognition of the multicultural nature of Bolivian society and promoted greater participation by grass-roots organisations as part of an overall strategy of administrative decentralisation. Albó analyses the impact of the 1994 Law of Popular Participation (LPP), which effectively extended the outreach of the state and political parties to rural areas by creating or strengthening municipal government. He points to the complex trade-offs involved in increased participation by indigenous campesino organisations in local and national politics and rightly asks to what extent this has in fact benefited the grass-roots constituency of indigenous political leaders.

The trade-offs implied by greater participation of indigenous organisations in state modernisation are also addressed in the chapter by Demetrio Cojtí, which provides an insider's view of the challenges involved in securing multicultural reforms in Guatemala. Cojtí was a civil society delegate to the Parity Commission for Educational Reform (COPARE) and after January 2000 a governmental delegate to the Consultative Commission for Educational Reform (CCRE). Both commissions were created by the 1996 peace accords and charged with devising a reform to make education multicultural, bilingual and decentralised. While emphasising the achievements made to date, Cojtí's fine-grained analysis points to a number of factors that negatively affected indigenous organisations' participation and signals the gap between the peace accords' discursive emphasis on civil society participation and practice on the ground.

The complex questions raised by state recognition of indigenous customary law about the balance between the rights of communities and the rights and obligations of the individuals that make them up are considered in the chapter by Guillermo de la Peña. Adopting an ethnographic approach to examine the issues involved in recognising ethnic citizenship in practice, he analyses the conflicts between 'traditionalists' and 'evangelicals' in the Sierra Huichol over what constitute reasonable obligations for community members. De la Peña locates the conflict within the broader context of transformations in social policy which have reshaped the relationship between indigenous people and the state in Mexico. As he points out, state recognition of cultural rights has provided a new idiom for claims to collective entitlement, in turn encouraging strategic essentialising by indigenous activists and groups, whose appeal to tradition and community resonates with neoliberal discourses on community solidarity and social capital. He concludes that the recognition of cultural rights implies the recognition of cultural communities and greater intercultural dialogue and tolerance to determine appropriate balances of rights and obligations.

Raquel Yrigoyen analyses the challenges of securing recognition of legal pluralism in Peru since the approval of the 1993 Constitution and the ratification of ILO Convention 169. A special indigenous jurisdiction was formally recognised in the new constitution, yet Yrigoyen shows how political authoritarianism, judicial conservatism and the counter-insurgency war against Sendero Luminoso made for contradictory dynamics on the ground. Focusing on relations between state authorities and *rondas campesinas*, she illustrates how formally recognised indigenous rights to customary law have been disregarded by the judiciary, who penalise the *rondas* for exceeding their functions and abusing human rights. Her chapter points to one of the central dilemmas inherent in recognising indigenous customary law – how to determine what constitutes an acceptable sanction or a violation of human rights, an issue also addressed in the chapters by de la Peña and Sieder.

Rachel Sieder's chapter compares state responses to indigenous demands for the recognition of legal pluralism in Chiapas, Mexico and Guatemala. Her focus is on how and why states take up multiculturalist discourses, contrasting Mexico, where the neoliberal state espoused the recognition of difference in the 1990s, with Guatemala, where elites rejected such constitutional reform in 1999. Through a comparative historical analysis, she emphasises the importance of changing patterns of state-indigenous interaction and points to the ways these shape both the opportunities for oppositional movements and the different ideological and political resources states can mobilise to contain, co-opt or absorb challenges from below. Sieder contrasts Mexico, where the official adoption of multiculturalist discourse can be understood as an attempt to reimpose hegemony on challenges to traditions of inclusive authoritarianism, with Guatemala, where traditions of exclusive authoritarianism have precluded such a response by governing elites.

Roger Plant focuses on the economic and agrarian dimensions of the multicultural challenge in Latin America, considering the economic implications of differentiated citizenship and development approaches targeted at indigenous people. Questioning approaches based on an idea of separate indigenous space, he emphasises the fact that most of Latin America's indigenous people inhabit unequally shared territorial, legal and political spaces. Plant considers the experience of indigenous land titling to date and the problems encountered. He underlines the central tension in multicultural reforms between participation and autonomy and cautions against romantic, outdated views of localised, rural and self-sufficient indigenous economies. Instead he advocates a focus on tackling discrimination in land and labour markets and securing indigenous participation on equal terms in national and international economies.

Shelton Davis's chapter provides an overview of the World Bank's recent experience in addressing the socio-economic exclusion and poverty of indigenous people in Latin America and the Caribbean. Davis explains prevailing donor thinking, which views indigenous exclusion as a lost opportunity for development and advances a twin-track approach focused on improving human and social capital as a means to improve indigenous peoples' comparative advantage. Davis describes the new models of participatory development advanced by the World Bank in line with ILO Convention 169. Premised on respect for indigenous cultures, these aim to strengthen indigenous organisations and include indigenous people in project planning, implementation and evaluation. Davis concludes that such approaches can have a significant impact, but that they must take account of the political context in which they are implemented.

Nina Laurie, Robert Andolina and Sarah Radcliffe's chapter examines the implementation and outcomes of multicultural laws for the case of Bolivia. They emphasise the ways in which the identification and self-representation of people as indigenous is bound up with the logic of development projects and processes, and particularly with discourses of 'indigenous-ness' produced by transnational actors. Acute tensions exist between collective claims to entitlement and neoliberal policy prescriptions of private, individual ownership. However, as Laurie, Andolina and Radcliffe illustrate, donor conceptions of indigenous people as 'social capital' have favoured greater grass-roots participation in development planning, opening spaces to challenge neoliberal policy prescriptions. Yet they caution that the framing of claims to entitlement in terms of cultural identities and rights is constrained by national and international policy frameworks and can also exclude other marginalised groups not able to lay claim to indigenous identity.

Notes

1. The United Nations Sub-Commission on the Prevention of Discrimination and Protection of Minorities defines indigenous peoples in the following terms: 'Indigenous communities, peoples and nations are those which, having a historical continuity with pre-invasion and pre-colonial societies that developed on their territories, considered themselves distinct from other sectors of the societies now prevailing in those territories, or parts of them. They form at present non-dominant sectors of society and are determined to preserve, develop and transmit to future generations their ancestral territories, and their ethnic identity, as the basis of their continued existence as peoples, in accordance with their own cultural patterns, social institutions and legal systems'. Cited in Van Cott (2000b: 208).

2. William Assies argues for an understanding of indigenous identity that takes into account both 'strategic essentialising' by movements and 'forced redefinitions' by states, dominant elites and markets (Assies 2000: 4–6). For a useful discussion on indigenous identity construction see Koonings and Silva (1999).

3. See Psacharopoulos and Patrinos (1994), the chapter by Shelton Davis in this volume and Plant (1998b).

4. The conspicuous exception to this regional trend was Guatemala, where the *comités agrarios locales*, the organisational structures of the short-lived agrarian reform promoted by the Arbenz government, were forcibly dissolved following the 1954 coup.

5. This process has been well documented elsewhere. See for example Van Cott (1994).

6. For a detailed analysis of the evolution of international law with respect to indigenous peoples see Anaya (1996).

7. Argentina, Bolivia, Colombia, Costa Rica, Ecuador, Guatemala, Honduras, Mexico, Paraguay and Peru had all ratified ILO Convention 169 by the end of 2000.

8. This is despite the fact that the OAS draft has been criticised by indigenous groups for insufficient participation of indigenous organisations in the drafting process and for not pressing claims for indigenous self-determination.

9. Proposals to reform Guatemala's 1985 Constitution on the basis of the 1996 peace agreements, which included an agreement referring to the rights and identity of indigenous peoples, were defeated in a national referendum in 1999 (see the chapter by Sieder in this volume).

10. Although they do not deal exclusively with lowland indigenous populations, Brysk (2000) and the edited volume by Assies (2000) provide full accounts of these processes.

11. The 'egalitarian liberalism' that Barry advocates also implies that 'any disadvantage for which the victim is not responsible establishes a prima facie claim to remedy or compensation' (2001: 114). Compensatory measures to redress inequality of opportunity are therefore acceptable, although Barry maintains a broadly assimilationist logic, arguing that such measures should exist only for as long as is necessary for the group in question to overcome their disadvantaged status.

12. Such questions of the 'transferability' of critiques of US multiculturalism to other contexts, particularly those where rights are claimed by indigenous groups, have been considered (though not for Latin America) in a recent essay by Will Kymlicka (2000).

13. In addition, disagreement persists over whether autonomous regions should be mono-ethnic or multi-ethnic, although multi-ethnic positions have generally

predominated among all but the most geographically isolated groups. For an argument in favour of multi-ethnic regional autonomy see Díaz Polanco (1997).

14. In March 1999 the interim governor modified the Chiapas constitution to reduce self-determination to communal level and in July 1999 the Chiapas state government announced plans for remunicipalisation aimed at redividing Zapatista strongholds in order to lessen their influence (Mattiace 2001).

15. The law sent by the governing PAN to the national Congress in March 2001 contained elements of the COCOPA draft law, but did not recognise the legal status of indigenous peoples, their rights to land, territory and extensive autonomy, nor their right to extra-municipal association. It remained subject to ratification by a majority of state congresses. For a recent analysis see Díaz Polanco (2001).

16. Such a proposal was accepted in the 1991 constitutional reform in Colombia, a country where indigenous people constitute less than 3 per cent of the overall population. See Van Cott (2000b).

17. See Calla (2000) for an incisive critique of the 1994 Law of Popular Participation in Bolivia.

18. In this sense, incorporating indigenous dispute mechanisms into the lower rungs of the judicial system dovetails neatly with government and donor preferences for decentralising justice administration and promoting resolution of conflicts outside the framework of the courts.

19. On Peru see Yrigoyen in this volume.

20. Van Cott points to two variables accounting for the degree to which legal pluralism has been successfully implemented in Latin America: 'the extent to which multiple legal systems are able to operate without interference, and the extent to which conflicts among legal systems are managed institutionally' (2000b: 209). She notes that jurisdictional conflicts have not occurred in Bolivia, a country with a majority indigenous population. This she attributes largely to the minimal presence of state courts outside urban areas, the tendency to date of indigenous people to support customary law, and the state judiciary's reluctance to intervene in indigenous conflict resolution (2000b: 230–4).

21. For a general discussion of gender inequality and group rights see Okin (1999).

22. If we accept that the values underpinning the UN Declaration of Human Rights are universal, we must also appreciate that different societies may rely on different mechanisms to realise those universal values. As Bhikhu Parekh has observed, 'Some might prefer the language of rights and claims and rely on the state to enforce these. Others might find it too individualist, aggressive, legalistic and state-centred and prefer the language of duty, relying on social conditioning, and moral pressure to ensure that their members respect each other's dignity and refrain from harming each other's fundamental interests.' In other words, the latter might not object to those universal values, 'but think that these are best realized within a communitarian moral framework based on mutual concern, solidarity, loyalty to the wider society, and socially responsible individualism' (2000: 135, 137–8).

23. See Palenzuela (1999) for a discussion of ethno-development in western Guatemala.

24. An alternative approach focuses on tackling discrimination against indigenous people within land and labour markets; see Plant (1998b).

References

Albó, Xavier (1994), 'And from Kataristas to MNRistas? The Surprising and Bold Alliance between Aymaras and Neoliberals in Bolivia', in Donna Lee Van Cott, *Indigenous*

Peoples and Democracy in Latin America, Inter-American Dialogue/St Martin's Press (New York).

Anaya, S. James (1996), *Indigenous Peoples in International Law*, Oxford University Press, (Oxford and New York).

Assies, Willem, Gemma van der Haar and André Hoekema (eds) (2000), *The Challenge of Diversity: Indigenous Peoples and Reform of the State in Latin America*, Thela Thesis (Amsterdam).

Barry, Brian (2001), *Culture and Equality: An Egalitarian Critique of Multiculturalism*, Polity Press (Cambridge).

Brysk, Alison (2000), *From Tribal Village to Global Village: Indian Rights and International Relations in Latin America*, Stanford University Press (Stanford, CA).

Cairns, Alan C. (1997), 'Introduction' in Alan C. Cairns, John C. Courtney, Peter MacKinnon, Hans J. Michelmann and David E. Smith (eds), *Citizenship, Diversity, and Pluralism*, McGill-Queen's University Press (Montreal and Kingston, London).

Calla, Ricardo (2000), 'Indigenous Peoples, the Law of Popular Participation and Changes in Government: Bolivia, 1994–1998', in Assies et al. *The Challenge of Diversity*, pp.77–94.

Cossío Díaz, José Ramón, José Fernando Franco González Salas and José Roldán Xopa (1998), *Derechos y cultura indígenas: los dilemas del debate jurídico*, Grupo Editorial Miguel Angel Porrua (Mexico).

Díaz Polanco, Héctor (1997), *Indigenous Peoples in Latin America: The Quest for Self-Determination*, Westview Press (Boulder and London).

Díaz Polanco, Héctor (2001), 'La autonomía y la reforma constitucional en México', draft paper at http://geocities.com/alertanet/F2b-Hdiaz.Polanco-htm

Donnelly, Jack (1989), *Human Rights in Theory and Practice*, Cornell University Press (Ithaca).

Eber, Christine (2001), '*Buscando una nueva vida*: Liberation Through Autonomy in San Pedro Chenalhó, 1970–1998', *Latin American Perspectives*, Vol. 28 (2), pp.45–72.

Hernández Navarro, Luis (1999), 'Ethnic Identity and Politics in Oaxaca', in Wayne A. Cornelius, Todd A. Eisenstadt and Jane Hindley (eds), *Subnational Politics and Democratisation in Mexico*, Center for US–Mexican Studies, University of California (San Diego), pp.153–73.

Fakaria, Zareed (1997), 'The Rise of Illiberal Democracy', *Foreign Affairs*, Vol. 76 (6), pp.22–43.

Kymlicka, Will (2000), 'American Multiculturalism and the "Nations Within"', in Duncan Ivison, Paul Patton and Will Sanders (eds), *Political Theory and the Rights of Indigenous Peoples*, Cambridge University Press (Cambridge).

Koonings, Kees and Patricio Silva (1999), *Construcciones étnicas y dinámica sociocultural en América Latina*, Ediciones Abya-Yala (Quito).

Kymlicka, Will (1995), *Multicultural Citizenship*, Clarendon Press (Oxford).

Mattiace, Shannan L. (2001), 'Regional Renegotiations of Space: Tojolabal Ethnic Identity in Las Margaritas, Chiapas', *Latin American Perspectives*, Vol. 28 (2), pp.73–97.

O'Donnell, Guillermo (1996), 'The State, Democratization, and Some Conceptual Problems', in William C. Smith, Carlos H. Acuña and Eduardo A. Gamarra (eds), *Latin American Political Economy in the Age of Neoliberal Reform: Theoretical and Comparative Perspectives for the 1990s*, North-South Center, University of Miami (Miami).

Okin, Susan Moller (1999), *Is Multiculturalism Bad for Women?* Princeton University Press (Princeton).

Palenzuela, Pablo (1999), 'Etnicidad y modelos de auto-organización económica en el occidente de Guatemala', in Kees Koonings and Patricio Silva (eds), *Construcciones étnicas y dinámica sociocultural en América Latina*, pp.53–75.

Parekh, Bithu (2000), *Rethinking Multiculturalism: Cultural Diversity and Political Theory*, Macmillan Press (Basingstoke and London).

Plant, Roger (1998a), 'Ethnicity and the Guatemalan Peace Process: Conceptual and Practical Challenges', in Rachel Sieder (ed.), *Guatemala After the Peace Accords*, Institute of Latin American Studies, University of London (London).

—— (1998b), *Issues in Indigenous Poverty and Development*, Inter-American Development Bank Technical Study No. IND–105 (Washington D.C).

Psacharopoulos, George and Harry Patrinos (1994), *Indigenous People and Poverty in Latin America*, World Bank (Washington D.C).

Sánchez Botero, Esther (1998), *Justicia y pueblos indígenas de Colombia. La tutela como medio para la construcción de entendimiento cultural*, Facultad de Derecho, Unibiblos (Bogotá).

Santos, Boaventura de Sousa (1995), *Toward a New Common Sense: Law, Science and Politics in the Paradigmatic Transition*, Routledge (New York).

Sieder, Rachel and Jessica Witchell (2001), 'Advancing Indigenous Claims through the Law: Reflections on the Guatemalan Peace Process', in Jane Cowan, Marie Dembour and Richard Wilson (eds), *Culture and Rights*, Cambridge University Press (Cambridge).

Speed, Shannon and Jane F. Collier (2000), 'Limiting Indigenous Autonomy in Chiapas, Mexico: The State Government's Use of Human Rights', *Human Rights Quarterly*, Vol.22, pp.877–905.

Stavenhagen, Rodolfo (2000), *Derechos humanos de los pueblos indígenas*, Comisión Nacional de los Derechos Humanos (Mexico).

Van Cott, Donna Lee (1994), *Indigenous Peoples and Democracy in Latin America*, Inter-American Dialogue/St Martin's Press (New York).

—— (2000a), *The Friendly Liquidation of the Past: The Politics of Diversity in Latin America*, University of Pittsburgh Press (Pittsburgh).

—— (2000b), 'A Political Analysis of Legal Pluralism in Bolivia and Colombia', *Journal of Latin American Studies*, Vol.32 (1), pp.207–34.

—— (2000c), 'Explaining Ethnic Autonomy Regimes in Latin America', draft paper prepared for XXII Congress of the Latin American Studies Association.

Velásquez Cepeda, María Cristina (2000), 'Frontiers of Municipal Governability in Oaxaca, Mexico: The Legal Recognition of *Usos y Costumbres* in the Election of Indigenous Authorities', in Assies et al. *The Challenge of Diversity*, pp.165–79.

Yashar, Deborah (1998), Contesting Citizenship: Indigenous Movements and Democracy in Latin America', *Comparative Politics*, Vol.31 (1), pp.23–42.

Young, Iris Marion (1990), *Justice and the Politics of Difference*, Princeton University Press (Princeton).

—— (1995), 'Polity and Group Difference: A critique of the Ideal of Universal Citizenship', in Ronald Beiner (ed.), *Theorizing Citizenship*, New York State University Press, Albany (New York).

1
Indigenous Peoples and the State in Latin America: An Ongoing Debate

Rodolfo Stavenhagen

Latin America: nation-states without Indians

One of the more remarkable developments that took place in Latin America during the last two decades of the twentieth century was the emergence of indigenous peoples as new social and political actors and their implantation in the national consciousness of the region's countries. The changing relationship between national states and indigenous peoples in Latin America mirrors to a certain extent the re-emergence of indigenous issues in international legal debates since the early 1980s. However, it is remarkable, considering that throughout most of their modern history the Latin American republics had practically ignored the indigenous component of their national identity.[1]

The colonial history of the dispossession, exploitation and oppression of indigenous peoples is too well known to bear repetition here. When the Spanish-American republics achieved their political independence in the early nineteenth century most of them were populated by a majority of Indians, but the power holders, as is well known, were the *criollo* elites, the direct descendants of the Spanish colonial ruling class. Indians remained, as it were, at the bottom of the heap, where they had been since the European conquest. Independence changed little for them, except that in some cases they were granted formal citizenship rights in the political constitutions, whereas in others such rights would come only decades or even over a century later. Indeed, in some countries Indians were treated as legal minors well into the twentieth century. To be sure, there are differences in the situation of indigenous peoples between the various countries of Latin America. In Brazil and the Southern Cone states, for instance, Indians were for the most part eliminated from areas of colonial and immigrant settlement, pushed into the most inhospitable regions, if not exterminated, in a pattern similar to that which occurred in North America. In contrast, in regions of high-density Indian populations such as the Andean highlands and Mesoamerica, indigenous peoples were forcibly incorporated into the colonial economy and a process of ethnic mixture began during that period leading in later years to the emergence of the *mestizo* population.[2]

Indian oppression in the new republics was twofold. On the one hand, the land-owning oligarchies who consolidated their economic power during the nineteenth century reaped the benefits of the privatisation of crown lands, ecclesiastical estates and traditional collective holdings that the colonial government had allowed Indian communities to keep for their own subsistence. The remaining Indians were pushed into frontier areas, inaccessible mountain ranges, arid wastelands and impenetrable jungles, while the new *latifundistas* and *hacendados* (large estate owners) and, in later years, waves of immigrant settlers, took over the best acreage and pastures. In some areas the land was cleared *manu militari* in genocidal 'pacification' campaigns. Generations of Indian peasants were forced into peonage and servile labour, and eventually into rural migration circuits and emigration, a process that continues today. By the twentieth century, micro-level subsistence holdings and landlessness had become characteristic of the Indian peasantry, leading to agrarian uprisings and revolutions and to multiple experiments with land reforms. These included the Mexican and Bolivian revolutions (1910–20 and 1952, respectively) and land reforms in Guatemala (1952), Peru (1960s and 1970s), the Alliance for Progress of the Kennedy years – designed to stem the appeal of the Cuban revolution, Chile during the Allende years, Nicaragua in the 1980s and so on. Sometimes Indian communities did indeed receive some land and benefits via these reforms, in others such programmes simply passed Indians by. Consequently, access to land has become a major claim of indigenous organisations and the subject of continuous disputes between Indian communities and the state in much of Latin America. In this respect, Indians are not much different from other land-hungry peasants. This prompted numerous analysts during the twentieth century to consider Indians as simply a special type of landless rural labourer whose best interest lay in their class organisation and in forming alliances with other exploited workers. This led to serious and sometimes acrimonious theoretical and political debates since the time of the Mexican revolution at the beginning of the century through to post-Peace Accord Guatemala in the late 1990s.

A second feature that definitively marked the situation of indigenous peoples within the state was the non-recognition of Indian cultural and social identity as part of national society. The founding fathers and intellectual elites of the fledgling Latin American republics grandly ignored demographics and based the projects of their national societies on their self-perception as a Western, Catholic, racially European people, from which Indians and Negroes were excluded.[3] These ruling groups tried hard to be accepted at the court of Western civilisation and to build nations in the image of Western political and economic models. They borrowed their legal systems and public administrations from Spain and France, their political constitutions from the United States, their economic liberalism from Great Britain and their military codes from Prussia. They desired, in true Darwinian fashion, to improve their racial stock and encouraged immigrant settlers from Europe. Indians and blacks (the descendants of former African slaves) were considered a burdensome obstacle to nation building. Wherever it was impossible or too cumbersome to eliminate Indians physically, they were either relegated to the hinterlands to remain as an inexhaustible supply of cheap labour or wither away, or else were forced or encouraged to shed their 'backward' cultural traits and become 'nationalised'; that is, to turn into useful citizens of the state according to the hegemonic cultural model.

Indians, mestizos and state policies

The *criollo* elites were gradually challenged by the growing mestizo population, who came to occupy the ethnic middle ranks and frequently became identified with middle-class political parties and nationalist politics. By the 1940s anthropologists referred to Mestizo-America rather than Indo-America and some of them even foresaw the disappearance of Indians and their cultures by the end of the century. Acculturation and Ladinoisation, terms dear to the social sciences, were seen as inevitable processes, a part of the general tendency towards modernisation in which 'traditional societies' were bound to disappear. Such approaches became official *indigenista* policy during the twentieth century, when governmental programmes stressed assimilation and integration of the indigenous through communications and road building, the market economy, education and community development. Today theorising about the relations between Indians and the nation has come full circle. In the early days of *indigenismo* there was still much talk about racial categories and whether 'Indians' as then conceptualised were apt or not for 'modern civilisation'. Later the literature emphasised the supposed 'cultural backwardness' of indigenous societies. By the 1940s it was clear to many concerned observers that the 'Indian problem' as it was then called, was mainly an issue of social and economic development. Reviewing the stages of *indigenista* thinking, in 1972 Alejandro Marroquín concluded that: 'the Indian was conceptualised as an ethnic category and this was valid for its time, but presently ethnic distinctions take a back seat, and the term Indian becomes a socio-economic category' (Marroquín 1972: 8). During the last two decades of the twentieth century, as we shall see in this chapter, a return to a re-evaluation of cultural and ethnic distinctions and identities took place.

The official launching of continent-wide *indigenismo* took place in 1940 at the First Inter-American Indian Conference, convened by the continent's governments. This conference adopted a declaration of basic principles, comprising the following points:

(a) Respect for indigenous culture and personality
(b) Rejection of legislation and practices originating in concepts of racial differences which are unfavourable to indigenous groups
(c) Equality of rights and opportunities for all population groups of the Americas
(d) Respect for the positive values of indigenous culture
(e) Facilitate the economic elevation and assimilation of the indigenous groups and access to modern technology and universal culture
(f) Every action on indigenous communities should count with the acceptance of the community

According to Marroquín, these points comprised the theoretical framework that underpinned indianist policies on the continent, but few of the signatory states adhered to them fully. The basic objective of *indigenismo* was the integration of indigenous populations into the nation.[4] Although in later years, at other inter-American Indianist Conferences, participating governments began to recognise the demands of indigenous peoples in terms of human rights, by the end of the century official indianist institutions had become less relevant to the issues increasingly raised by the indigenous movement. Indian organisations have justly claimed control over these institutions and others that were created later – an objective they have achieved in some cases. However, more often than not they have called for them to be dismantled.

Other international agencies became interested in indigenous issues in later years, and, more recently, the emerging Indian movement has appropriated these international concerns. Thus Convention 169 of the International Labour Organisation, which was one of the first multilateral agencies to concern itself with indigenous populations in independent countries, has been ratified by most Latin American states, and its main principles have been incorporated by some of them into their national legislation. The UN Sub-Commission on the Promotion and Protection of Human Rights drafted a Universal Declaration of Indigenous Rights which is currently under review in the UN Human Rights Commission, and the Organisation of American States is considering the adoption of a similar regional instrument. Indigenous organisations have been active over the years in these international debates.[5]

During the twentieth century *indigenismo* became the domestic expression of assertive nationalism and populism in many Latin American countries. During the early decades it was a generous, inspiring and progressive ideology. Its proponents, mainly mestizo anthropologists, were convinced that they were not only serving their countries well, but also helping the indigenous overcome their many limitations on the way to becoming modern useful citizens. Directed cultural change and applied anthropology were the conceptual tools that were to facilitate this grandiose enterprise: soon Latin American countries would become modern and Indians would be only relics of a picturesque past (indeed, magnificent museums – such as the one in Mexico City – were built to pay homage to the great dead civilisations of the past and to symbolise the strong roots of the contemporary mestizo nation). In Mexico and some other countries, the mestizo myth was based on the idea of the biological and cultural mixture of Indians and Europeans (the African root was usually ignored), and for some the myth maintains all of its mobilising power to this day. To be sure, the notion of a mestizo nation was quite revolutionary in the 1930s and 1940s when racialist doctrines continued to inspire many a political discourse and not a few governmental policies. Yet, surprisingly, some of the traditional *criollo* elites who had ignored the Indian presence in their countries – and would still like to ignore it to this day – were equally contemptuous of the emerging mestizo population who threatened their status and self-esteem even as it challenged their political and economic pre-eminence.

Assimilation and incorporation of Indians into the national mainstream was a many-pronged affair. The front line of this battle was occupied by the school system. Even prior to the nineteenth century missionary schools had taken upon themselves the task of 'civilising' Indians. Today their overall efforts are deemed as 'ethnocidal', even though they produced some individual success stories. In the twentieth century the official public schools in which Spanish was the sole language of instruction took up the challenge and hispanicisation (*castellanización*) became the desired policy objective. Again, there is no doubt that these efforts were successful to a point, but many indigenous children dropped out of school or were marginalised because the official curriculum was more or less irrelevant to their cultural and social context. Another objective of *indigenista* policy was the destruction of the Indians' closed subsistence economy, which to be sure was more fiction than fact to the extent that ever since colonial times indigenous peoples had become integrated into the world economy. Development planners were convinced that the expansion of the market economy would greatly benefit Indian communities, and thus they promoted the introduction of new commercial crops and stimulated the creation of new productive activities, such as handicrafts.

To sum up, Latin America's ruling classes, unable to wish Indians away, were quite happy to build nations without Indians, and this they have been trying to do for almost two centuries. To their chagrin, as the new millennium dawns, not only are indigenous peoples still present – and their numbers are rising, but they are actually challenging the very model of the nation-state that ruling groups have tried so conscientiously to build up.

Social conflicts and intellectual debates

Many of the intellectual and political debates of the twentieth century in Latin America related, albeit indirectly, to indigenous populations to the extent that they focused on the long-simmering agrarian question. Peasant uprisings and agrarian unrest marked the modern history of numerous countries, from Mexico early in the century to the Andean and Central American states in later decades. Students of economic development, international aid agencies and leaders of social movements all agreed that the break-up of the large estates and the elimination of 'feudal' labour relations on the land was a necessary step for modernisation and economic growth to take place. Militant peasant movements and agricultural workers unions emerged during the 1960s, only to be repressed by the police and the military, or co-opted by middle-class political parties. Some of these movements became the breeding ground for military-political insurrections, armed defence and extended guerrilla warfare, in league with revolutionary students and other urban-based political movements, many of them of Marxist persuasion. To some extent, these movements spawned the military dictatorships and repressive authoritarian regimes that became the bane of Latin America for several decades. Scholars who have focused on this period generally agree that the violent repression of social organisations, such as labour unions and peasant leagues, and of oppositional political groups led to the formation of Marxist-oriented guerrilla movements. These, in turn, provoked more state violence and terrorism within the framework of the Cold War ideological struggle. Indian populations were generally not involved in these conflicts at the outset, but they soon became their victims.[6]

Mainstream sociological approaches during this period had little to say about indigenous populations except to predict their necessary disappearance and to try to help this process along by promoting different kinds of modernisation strategies. In Mexico, progressive government anthropologists considered that Indians were kept down by a 'pre-modern caste structure' and that the task of *indigenismo* was to facilitate the emergence of a 'modern social class system', in which Indians would find their logical place as workers, shoulder to shoulder with the non-Indian working class. This position was increasingly echoed by the numerous exponents of Marxism in Latin America, who since the days of José Carlos Mariátegui in 1920s and 1930s Peru had debated the most likely roads to socialist revolution on the continent. These debates heated up considerably after the victory of the Cuban revolution and various guerrilla experiences in other Latin American countries. For many

Marxists, indigenous populations did not exist as such, they were rather considered as part of the exploited peasantry, and political strategists propounded that Indians, if mobilised at all, should be incorporated into the 'class struggle' whenever possible. Some Marxists felt that Indians were 'too backward' culturally to be of any use in the revolutionary struggle, and their specific problems – if any – should await solution until after the victory of the revolution. Such neglect of the 'Indian question' backfired at a high political cost during the Sandinista revolution in Nicaragua and the early stages of the guerrilla resistance in Guatemala. The emerging Indian intellectuals of this period felt alienated from functionalist and Marxist approaches, rejecting both of them as Western constructs that could neither understand nor do justice to Indian cultures and demands. Some guerrilla organisations and ideologues explicitly condemned Indian claims for rights and recognition as petit-bourgeois romanticism, when not downright counter-revolutionary. In official *indigenista* circles, by contrast, claims for the recognition of indigenous identities and collective cultural rights were decried as conservative utopianism, dysfunctional to modernisation and progress, when not actually intended to dismember the nation.

These discussions were usually held within two distinct but interrelated frameworks. On the one hand, at the theoretical-conceptual level proper to the academic environment, scholars debated the relationship between class and ethnie. Does the class analysis of an underdeveloped country take sufficient account of ethnic and cultural differences? Can ethnic relations be subsumed under class relations? Is class analysis at all relevant to corporate, bounded, isolated Indian peasant communities? And how isolated and bounded are these in the first place? Can inter-ethnic relations be understood at all without reference to dependent, underdeveloped capitalism and its class structure? Can class and ethnie be better understood within the conceptual framework of internal colonialism? Are not both class and ethnie artificial constructs that ignore the self-identification and cultural dynamics of Indian communities? A clear answer to these and other questions has not emerged over the years, and the debates continue, today clothed in the fashionable wording of post-modernism.

At another, more practical level the debate involved questions of strategy of political and revolutionary movements. These questions were debated in the press, in restricted documents and position papers of the various organisations, as well as at party congresses and workshops. Do Indians mobilise and organise themselves qua Indians, or are they mobilised and organised as members of the exploited classes? Can Indian demands be subsumed under wider class-based social demands, or are they specific to Indian cultures? Can Indians form alliances with non-Indians in national popular movements, or do they pursue their own political agendas? Do they have a political agenda at all, or are they simply part of those faceless 'masses' whose mobilising potential can be tapped by the right kind of 'revolutionary vanguard'? If

Indians are exploited by the existing power structure, why is it that they are so often co-opted and side with this power structure against the challenge of subversive movements? Most parties of the left were unable to provide a clear answer to these questions and to propose political alternatives that Indian peoples were eager or willing to accept. In consequence they often became isolated and ended up as prisoners of their own twisted ideological logic, such as happened during the 1980s and 1990s to the Shining Path movement in Peru.

Human rights: a contested space

Beginning in the 1980s, a number of processes and tendencies began to change the nature of the debates. At the international level, Cold War ideological confrontation in Latin America came to a virtual end with the break-up of the communist world, though the US government still actively pursued it when it suited its interests (for example in Cuba and Nicaragua). Secondly, the global economy, which had never been absent from Latin America since colonial times, reaffirmed its impact on the rural areas, including indigenous territories, as in the Amazon basin, Central America, southern Chile and elsewhere, generating tensions and conflicts between Indian peasantries, state institutions and transnational corporations. Thirdly, a cycle of authoritarian military interventions in politics – which had been linked to the 'national security ideology' of the Cold War era – came to an end and a number of Latin American polities began what has been grandly, and perhaps somewhat over-optimistically, called a democratic transition. This liberated the forces of civil society for electoral competition and opened a formerly restricted political space to new or re-emerging social actors.

Thus arose in Latin America an articulate and militant human rights movement, which soon became deeply involved in the issues of indigenous peoples. The Inter-American Commission and Court of Human Rights were increasingly besieged by complaints concerning human rights abuses against indigenous people, and relevant UN committees received reports and complaints on the situation of indigenous human rights. But even more significant has been the emergence of indigenous peoples themselves as new social and political actors, through their own organised activities. While the first faltering steps at indigenous organisation had taken place sporadically since the 1960s, and even before, it was not until the 1970s and 1980s that indigenous peoples' movements really took off. It is almost impossible to chronicle the many associations, caucuses, committees, councils, congresses, conferences, symposia, workshops and meetings that activated Indian agency where none or little had previously existed. Many such organisations have not survived, others changed over the years, and still others grew and developed true to the stages and cycles of the various theories of social movements. What is particularly striking in this process is the formation of an indigenous intelligentsia, the emergence into the public sphere of an increasingly articulate and assertive class of Indian 'organic intellectuals'. They have come from many sources. Some, like Mario Juruna (a federal deputy in the early 1980s) and Davi Yanomami in Brazil, were born in the daily struggle of resistance to encroachment and for the survival of their people. Others were coaxed along by friends and colleagues to produce a personal testimony of the painful process of 'awareness building', resulting, as in the case of Rigoberta Menchú, in a world-wide bestseller and the Nobel Peace Prize for Menchú herself.[7] Still others, who graduated from colleges and universities, used their degrees and expertise in the service of their people, and by entering politics directly have become active spokespersons of indigenous causes in their countries.

The new Indian movement in Latin America has not yet produced a specific coherent ideology, and perhaps it has no need for it. But it is developing a new discourse, which has changed the way the wider society views Indians and the way they see themselves. Most of all, the movement and its various expressions are changing the relations between indigenous peoples and the state in Latin America. In this context must be placed the constitutional and legislative changes that were made in the last two decades of the twentieth century in a number of countries in the region, legally enshrining indigenous rights, in many cases for the first time. In a wave of constitutionalist activity, indigenous rights have become one of the most hotly debated issues of the turn of the millennium.

Bolivia, where Indians constitute the demographic majority, adopted a new political constitution in 1994 that recognises that the country is multi-ethnic, multicultural and multilingual. A new Law on Popular Participation set out the political and legal framework through which indigenous communities were to become collectively recognised citizens of the country. Observers, however, have noted flaws in the legislation that make effective participation by Indian communities difficult, and a new government which took power in 1997 gave this law much lower priority than had the previous administration which adopted it (Calla 1999; Orellana 1999).

Brazil's 1988 Constitution devotes an entire new chapter to Indians. Earlier constitutions had protected the original lands of the 'forest people', but Indians lacked civil and political rights and were treated legally as minors. While Indians represent less than 0.5 per cent of the country's total population, their situation and claims were widely debated in the constituent assembly and by the press (although Indians were not directly represented in the assembly). Article 231 of the new constitution for the first time recognises Indians' social organisation, customs, languages, beliefs and traditions and the original rights over the lands they have long occupied. Political reaction to the new constitution was not long in coming, however, and for several years private interests attempted, but failed, to revise the text and challenge the Indians' rights to land and resources. Attempts have also been made time and again to get the courts to restrict Indian rights to land. In the mid-1990s a new Indian law stalled in Congress and at the end of the decade more than 100 Indian territories were still waiting for official demarcation and certification (Santos 1998; Sierra 1995).

The 1991 Constitution of Colombia grants important autonomy rights to its indigenous populations as well, and recognises Indians' collective territorial rights over their traditional *resguardos.* New administrative territorial units have been created, known as *Entes Territoriales Indígenas* (ETI). According to Donna Lee Van Cott, 'the recognition of the territoriality of indigenous communities, together with a share of state resource transfers, provides the material basis for the exercise of the Indians' right to difference under the constitution' (Van Cott 2000: 86). Indian representatives were actively involved in the debates of the constituent assembly. The constitution establishes the right to *tutela* (protection) for indigenous communities, and this has generally been interpreted favourably towards Indians by Colombia's Constitutional Court. The Court, argues Esther Sánchez, has established that the principle of ethnic and cultural diversity is not purely rhetorical and that it constitutes the juridical acceptance of 'otherness' linked to a multiplicity of forms of life and world views different to those of Western culture (Sánchez 1999: 393).[8]

Among other constitutional changes in recent years the one in Ecuador stands out in particular. The new Ecuadorian constitution entered into force in 1998, and indigenous organisations were quite active in the drafting process, as they have been since then in trying to achieve the right kind of implementing legislation. As in other countries, the constitution recognises the multicultural and pluri-ethnic nature of the nation,[9] promotes a system of bilingual and bicultural education, ensures the collective ownership of traditional Indian lands and territories, and indicates that indigenous peoples are to participate in decision-making processes affecting their lives. The collective rights of indigenous peoples are recognised, but the special ways in which these are to be exercised will have to be spelled out in further legislation.

In addition to the countries just referred to, similar constitutional changes have been enacted in Guatemala (1985), Nicaragua (1986) and Mexico (1992). Panama (1997), Paraguay (1992) and Peru (1993) have no less important constitutional statements. The most recent constitutional reform that includes references to Indians was approved in a popular referendum in 1999 in Venezuela, after lengthy debates in the constituent assembly. In other countries, such as Argentina and Chile, special legislation concerning Indians was adopted in the post-dictatorship years. While these legal advances are surely important in themselves, the open question is how the new legislation will be implemented and how Indian communities will benefit. The answer is not at all clear. Complaints are increasingly heard that the new laws are not being implemented as they should be, or that secondary legislation has not been adopted after general principles were laid down in the new constitutions.[10]

What do Indians want and what can states provide?

The struggle for indigenous rights is still in its infancy and after the promising beginnings mentioned above, the going will be rough from now on. There are several reasons for this. First, opponents to Indian rights have now been able to organise and mount a counter-offensive. Second, after the first breakthrough on the political scene, Indians and their allies have not been able to set themselves clear short and medium term objectives, nor have they been able to develop an effective political strategy to achieve their aims. This seems to have alienated a number of potential sympathisers in the general population and the political establishments. A case in point is the failed civil-military coup in Ecuador in January 2000, in which the Indian movement played a key role.[11] In Guatemala in 1999, a referendum on the incorporation of indigenous rights into the 1985 Constitution, as agreed upon in the 1996 peace agreement which put an end to over three decades of brutal civil war, did not receive majority approval contrary to widely held expectations. While there are increasing numbers of indigenous parliamentarians in many countries, who represent different political parties, there is no clear pattern of ethnic voting nor can any political party count on the automatic contribution of an indigenous electoral bloc. In general, indigenous demands are channelled in other ways than through traditional electoral party politics, but this may change in the future (Iturralde 1998).[12]

A crucial issue today is the debate concerning demands for indigenous territorial autonomy. There are a number of precedents to claims for autonomy, such as the Spanish colonial regime, which – even as it subordinated Indian peoples into the colonial economy and power structure – allowed Indian communities a measure of local self-government under the concept of the 'Repúblicas de Indios'. It was mainly during the post-colonial period in the nineteenth century that the central state took even these minimal rights away from the Indians, together with their lands. After a series of indigenous uprisings early in the twentieth century – helped along by imperialist interests, it must be added – Panama came to recognise the territorial autonomy of its three Indian peoples, as stated in the 1972 constitution (amended in 1997). During the 1980s Nicaragua went through a bloody civil war, the *contras* having been armed by the CIA against the revolutionary Sandinista government, in which the Indians of the Atlantic Coast became unwilling actors. The new Constitution of 1986 recognised the autonomy of the region and its indigenous communities, but post-Sandinista governments have done little to implement the new legislation. In Colombia the present Constitution recognises the old *resguardos* (Indian reservations) as the nucleus of a new kind of territorial autonomy, but practical implementation has been slow in coming. In fact, the meaning of autonomy is ambiguous and its complexities are many. Most of the issues are not resolved in the new legislation, and specialists cannot seem to agree on the details. What is the unit of autonomy and who is the subject of autonomy rights? How is self-government and decision making to be carried out? What is the resource base of the autonomous units, what are their administrative responsibilities, how do they relate to other levels of public administration and so on?[13]

In fact, most governments in Latin America, permeated by a long-standing centralist tradition of authority are leery of autonomy, especially when related to indigenous peoples. Constitutional lawyers and politicians are usually dead-set against it and feel that indigenous demands for autonomy threaten the unity of the state. Their worries are exacerbated when indigenous organisations insist that the right to autonomy is simply an instance of the larger right of peoples to self-determination, which ILO Convention 169 and the draft UN Declaration on Indigenous Rights have incorporated. Self-determination suggests, to many critics of indigenous autonomy, secession and political statehood, meaning fragmentation of the national state. While no indigenous organisation has gone on record as wanting to secede, observers point to recent events in the Balkans in order to call attention to the dangers of ethnic demands for self-determination. However, these have now become a point of honour for the indigenous movement and self-determination appears at the top of the list of rights claimed in almost every indigenous political document. The ambiguous use of the term 'peoples' claimed by the indigenous and denied them by governments, led to a revealing incident at the World Conference on Human Rights in 1993, whose final document speaks of the rights of indigenous 'people' (leaving out the tell-tale final 's'), while human rights NGOs present at the Conference insisted unsuccessfully on incorporating the 's' in the official text.

It is difficult to understand the rigid resistance of some government officials to indigenous autonomy, particularly in federal states such as Mexico. One of the reasons that peace negotiations between the Zapatistas in Chiapas and the national government stalled in 1999–2000 was that the latter decided it could not accept claims to indigenous autonomy, even after it had originally signed a partial peace agreement with the Zapatistas to this effect. Many observers feel that unless the autonomy issue is resolved there can be no peace accord and no democratic solution to the conflict. The Indian movement in Mexico and elsewhere insists that territorial rights should be part of any autonomy agreement, but central governments are usually reluctant to recognise ethnic homelands distinct from existing territorial administrative units (municipios, districts, provinces, states), because in their view this might weaken the sovereignty of the national state.

Despite some constitutional legislation to the contrary, national and regional power structures in most Latin American countries are usually resistant to greater local autonomy and increased political participation by subaltern groups. Some observers fear that the new legislation is not really meant to be implemented and represents more of a cosmetic tinkering with the constitutional system than a real thorough change of power relations between Indians and the state. Others argue that the dismantling of the socially responsible state through neoliberal policies favours a decentralisation process that may appear to strengthen local territorial units, when in fact, by cutting them loose from the central state to fend for themselves, they are left to their own devices, thus creating challenges for development policy that have not yet been met successfully. Just as in the nineteenth century declaring all citizens as equal left Indian populations unprotected to face the first offensive of capitalist accumulation, so in the late twentieth century the retreat of the state in the name of decentralisation has made local units (including indigenous communities) more rather than less vulnerable in the absence of compensatory mechanisms.

The other side of the story, however, is the opening of new spaces for self-management and self-governance of indigenous political and territorial units. Indigenous movements and advocates increasingly maintain that local and regional autonomy is a necessary instrument for the achievement of full participatory rights in the national state, if a number of conditions are met. These conditions imply the devolution of fiscal and other resources, full democratic participation in the state, the legal recognition of Indian administrative units and full juridical liberty to enter into mutually beneficial arrangements with other similar units, the state at all its levels, private undertakings and – if necessary and convenient – multilateral financial agencies and foreign governments. Rather than being conditions for autonomy, however, these features can be considered as objectives to be achieved through autonomy as a process rather than simply as a legal statute.

Latin American states have long argued over the relative benefits and drawbacks of centralised versus federal political systems. Over the years, the federal idea seems to have won out over more unitary and centralised approaches. During the early republican years, federalism was associated with regional autocratic power structures, whereas centralism became an idea associated with national unity, political liberalism and economic progress. Nowadays, federalism has become identified with the diminishing fortunes of the centralised state in a globalised neoliberal environment and, at the same time, with demands for greater democracy and self-determination by the constituent units of the federalised state. In many countries, however, regional entrenched political interests (*caciquismo, gamonalismo*) who want more power for themselves are not willing to give it up to Indian communities – the traditional source of cheap labour and political supporters in well-oiled systems of client–patron relationships. The current debates over autonomy must be considered within this framework and it is unlikely that easy solutions will be found in the short run.

An even more conflictive issue than the debate over autonomy concerns the controversy over individual versus collective rights. The liberal state assures every human being a package of inalienable individual freedoms and rights, and liberals everywhere acknowledge that indigenous persons have the same universal human rights as everybody else. If they are not in fact enjoying fully all these rights, it is argued, the blame does not lie with the rights themselves, but with flaws in the judiciary, inadequate protection and defence mechanisms, and unjust and unequal distribution of wealth and power. These problems cannot be solved by adding other rights, but rather by consolidating democratic politics and promoting economic development and social welfare. Countering this widespread and hegemonic position, indigenous rights advocates argue that even the most basic of individual rights are hardly enjoyed by ethnic groups and minorities who are systematically discriminated against and excluded by the power structure in the prevailing system of social stratification. They claim that something more is needed, such as a bundle of group rights allowing indigenous to fully live and reproduce their cultures, organise their lives according to their own social norms, maintain and develop their own collective identities, enjoy social, political and legal status as distinct groups in the wider society, and relate to this society and the national state on their own terms as recognised and respected peoples or nations.

To be sure, the recognition of these collective rights requires a complete overhaul of the national state, of this 'imagined community', the nation, which the criollo and mestizo elites built up to serve their own interests. Arguably, individual human rights cannot be fully enjoyed by members of discriminated against subaltern groups unless such groups are acknowledged as equal and full partners in all their distinctiveness and dignity within a nation-state. Thus the recognition of group rights may be seen as a condition for the enjoyment of individual rights, but they are not easily acknowledged in Latin America's legal systems. Some legal scholars reject outright the idea of 'collective' rights, arguing that all universal human rights can only be individual. Political theorists generally feel that the recognition of the rights of specific groups not only goes against the 'universality' of the idea of rights but also endangers the unity of the already fragile nations of the region. The claims of indigenous movements openly challenge these classic positions, and whilst recent constitutional texts have not entirely put the debates to rest, they have indeed opened cracks in the strongholds of liberal individualism. Whereas proponents of indigenous group rights may be said to adopt a progressive position to the extent that such rights are identified with greater autonomy, democracy and freedoms, their critics affirm the contrary. According to them, group rights would mean a return to pre-modern days when individual liberties were limited if not suffocated in the name of community, and only the modern liberal view of the free, unattached person will guarantee individual human rights and well-being. These arguments, which are not purely academic but also legal and political, are frequently expressed in relation to the thorny question of the role of customary law in the framework of national legal systems.

Indeed, beyond the issue of autonomy, already referred to, political debates have also centred on the uses of customary indigenous law as against the positive, legislated legal norms of the state. Whereas indigenous organisations demand respect for their customary legal practices, jurists usually insist that the national legal system should not be broken up and that no particular group in society should receive special legal privileges. This argument has been wielded, for instance, against the approval of the San Andrés Peace Accords in Chiapas. Legal pluralism is not palatable to most Latin American jurists steeped in the Roman and Canonical origins of contemporary national legal systems. Criticism against customary law (*usos y costumbres*) also comes from a liberal human rights perspective, where it is argued that the best if not the only way to overcome discrimination and achieve full equality before the law, is by furthering individual human rights and fundamental liberties. Customary law, it is said, is not usually conducive to the full enjoyment of individual human rights, but rather limits individual freedoms in the name of traditional community solidarity. These restrictions apply mainly to women and young people, who suffer from the heavy authority of their male elders. A liberal state, it is argued, should not tolerate such limitations on human rights, even when their purpose is to preserve cultural identity.

This is a powerful argument that generally holds sway among legislators and makes substantive changes in the legal system difficult. Nonetheless, there has been progress in recent years, to the extent that some national legislation now refers to customary laws to be respected, but Latin America is still a long way from establishing true legal pluralism within its borders. There is no single coherent body of so-called Indian customary law, no indigenous 'Sharia'. It is more likely that judicial practice will evolve various forms of hybrid solutions on particular local issues – for example, disputes over land, punishment and compensation for felonies or crimes committed in indigenous communities by its own members – without formal legal recognition of indigenous customary law. In fact, during colonial times this was common practice, and it is closely related to the concept and functioning of autonomy.

These issues are well illustrated by the Guatemala case. The Accord on the Rights and Identity of Indigenous Peoples, part of a general peace agreement, signed by the government and Unidad Revolucionaria Nacional Guatemalteca (URNG) in March 1995, commits the government to the recognition of customary law of the indigenous communities and to increase their access to the national legal system. Rachel Sieder's case study of Alta Verapaz shows that traditional local norms and practices were severely curtailed during the period of violence and that the transition to a democratic political regime requires the rebuilding of the country's judicial system, including greater recognition of customary norms and practices. However Sieder argues, as have others, that indigenous customary law is not a self-contained separate, parallel legal system to state law. Rather, customary law stands in a dialectical relationship to state law, being constantly re-negotiated according to changing political and economic circumstances. It is a means of counter-hegemonic resistance in an asymmetrical system of power relations, characterised by its flexibility (Sieder 1997).

Ethnic cultures versus national culture?

Behind many of the controversial issues over which indigenous peoples and the state in Latin America disagree, none has raised more polemic than indigenous cultures and identities. The almost bicentenary-old idea of a single national culture has been put to a severe test by indigenous demands for bilingual and intercultural education and by the relatively recent legal recognition in some states that these countries are pluri-ethnic and multi-cultural. The current debate in Guatemala expresses these conflicting views rather well.

During the terrible years of the civil war, in which hundreds of thousands of indigenous people were murdered by the army's counter-insurgency and many more became refugees, one of the few spaces of resistance of the Maya population were local cultural associations. These grew in numbers and activities after the mid-1980s when the military ceded formal power to elected civilian governments. Indigenous intellectuals developed a new discourse of Maya cultural identity, which was strengthened by the signing in 1996 of the negotiated peace settlement between the government and the guerrilla high command, one of the major agreements being on indigenous rights and culture. The Pan-Maya cultural movement spread rapidly and has contributed to changing both official discourse and the demands of political and social organisations. In a *criollo* and ladino dominated state, indigenous people, the country's demographic majority, were always considered outsiders, and were effectively excluded qua Indians from the society and the polity. The civil war and the ensuing peace settlement changed all that. The various indigenous ethnic groups are now coalescing into a newly constructed Maya identity, including the revival of Maya religion (this in a traditional Catholic country in which Protestantism has made considerable inroads in recent years). Maya intellectuals and activists see themselves as opposing the hegemonic mestizo 'national' identity, and claim for their people not only a major cultural role in the redefinition of the nation, but also political representation and access to power.

One of the more articulate spokespersons of the new Maya identity writes that 'Mayas have the right to be respected concretely and permanently in their cultural and ethnic identity. They have the right to reclaim and keep their original ethnic territories. They have the right not to become the victims of massacres, persecutions and living conditions which prevent the expression and development of their identity and their integrity as a people.' Furthermore, 'the Mayas have the right to use, preserve and own as property the artistic, historical and cultural riches of their people. And they have the right to defend themselves from the cultural impositions which are foreign to them.' This is the position of Demetrio Cojtí, currently Vice-Minister for Multicultural Education in Guatemala.[14]

The Maya cultural movement has developed various theoretical and policy perspectives and it speaks through different, sometimes dissonant, voices. For example, there is no agreement as to whether the Maya people are to be considered as only one nationality or many. Cojtí speaks of 20 Maya nationalities in Guatemala alone (there are others in neighbouring countries). Should the new politico-administrative divisions in the country be based solely on Maya ethnic identities, or also include ladinos? Should political representation in congress reflect exactly the ethnic make-up of the country? How many of the Maya dialects should be recognised as official languages, and in what way shall multilingual and intercultural education be implemented in the school system? Cojtí, as many others, insists that not only should indigenous languages be the medium of instruction in local schools, but the educational content of the curriculum must also reflect the culture, traditional knowledge and world-view of the local ethnic group. Bilingual and multicultural teachers do not naturally emerge from this new vision, but must be newly trained in a manner that reflects the changed philosophy of education. Other countries in Latin America are facing similar problems, as for instance Peru and Bolivia. Mexico has had an official bilingual educational policy for its 56 distinct ethno-linguistic groups for several decades, including teachers, school-books and curricular content, but this is limited only to the first few years of schooling at the elementary level, and results have been less than entirely satisfactory.

The search for and the construction of a new Maya identity in Guatemala do not enjoy universal approval. The Maya culturalist positions have been attacked by, among others, a polemical journalist and former political activist, Mario Morales, from the vantagepoint of a self-identified ladino. He argues that Maya 'essentialism' is no more than an artificial construct and suggests, in a rather cavalier fashion, that self-proclaimed Maya intellectuals are being manipulated for commercial reasons by internationally financed NGOs, which have spread like mushrooms since the international community pledged US$2.5 billion to Guatemala for the implementation of the peace agreements. Morales maintains that there is no such thing as a Maya nation or people, that Maya activists are becoming anti-ladino racists in turn, and that the only valid solution to Guatemala's problems is the development of an intercultural *mestizaje* in which Indians and ladinos would learn to co-exist and interact on equal terms.[15]

The indigenous movement has developed fairly rapidly in Latin America over the last two decades of the twentieth century. Many people ask themselves whether this is a permanent or a passing phenomenon. Redress for historical grievances – which is what originally started the movement – is a limited objective in the long run. The struggle for the equal enjoyment of human rights, on the other hand, is an ongoing process that may take many decades to be achieved, and it has to do as much with the abilities of the indigenous organisations and their supporters as with the prospects for democracy at large. Whether, at the end of the day, Latin American countries will become fully plural societies in which indigenous collectivities are legally recognised and cultural diversity is protected and promoted by the state, or whether they will evolve into liberal democracies in which individual liberties are valued over and above community identities and loyalties, is still an open question. At any rate, the answer to such questions is not yet around the corner. The burden of the past is too recent and too heavy in a number of countries, and the magnitude of problems to be solved is too great to be left to the slow drift of societal evolution. Indian organisations have learned through recent struggles, that claims for participation, identity, autonomy, and respect for cultural difference and diversity are powerful instruments to be wielded in negotiations with the state and the hegemonic political system. It has now become clearer that what began as demands for specific rights and compensatory measures has turned into a new view of the nation and the state. It is too early to determine whether other sectors of national society are willing to adopt such wider objectives. Indian activists are becoming increasingly aware that they can get only so far if they try to go it alone. Other social forces, however, are sometimes quite clear that Indian organisations must temper their demands if they want outside support. These tensions have been played out in constituent assemblies, parliaments, political parties and public debates. After the enthusiastic groundswell of the 1990s, the first decades of the twenty-first century may find new and more pragmatic forms of accommodation between Indians and various political and economic forces. This is particularly likely given the framework of market globalisation and the diminishing social role of the state, if not a barefaced retreat from positions which appeared to have been won earlier, such as popular participation, bilingual education and legal pluralism. Whatever the outcome of these debates, Latin American nations, as indeed other parts of the world, must in the end come to terms with their history and memory of oppressions and exclusions, and must be ready to build new societies based on tolerance, mutual recognition, equality and human dignity. This is surely the challenge of the twenty-first century.

Notes

1. For an earlier formulation see Stavenhagen (1992).
2. On Indian policy in the United States and Canada, in contrast to Latin America, Franks writes that 'the historical difference between American and Canadian handling of native populations was that the United States decimated theirs by

war, Canada theirs by starvation and disease' (Franks 2000: 227). On the history of Indian policy in Chile, see Bengoa (1985), on Argentina, Martínez (1992). For a classic account of race mixture in the history of Latin America see Mörner (1967).

3. It should not be forgotten that Simón Bolívar, the liberator of South America, was an acknowledged mulatto, and Mexico's president Benito Juárez, who defeated the French in Mexico in the mid-nineteenth century, a Zapotec Indian.

4. Marroquín (1972).

5. See Brysk (2000), Lâm (2000), Dandler (1999), ILO (1953).

6. Some current revisionist history maintains that the insurrectionary guerrillas themselves are to be held responsible for the repressive violence of the authoritarian state, implying in a quaint turn of logic that if only Indian peasants had not resisted repression they would not have been repressed.

7. Menchú's autobiography (1985) is widely used in university courses, and has aroused some academic debate, particularly in the USA. The US media gave prominence to the publication of an American anthropologist who challenged Menchú's accuracy, and this 'revelation' has fuelled criticism of Menchú's role as a legitimate voice for the cause Indian peoples. Aside from the 'facts' narrated in the document, the debate also refers to the circumstances in which young Rigoberta Menchú gave her oral testimony at a time of great emotional stress, of the 'real' authorship of this testimony, and of the uses that different political groups have since made of this material. (In the first edition of the autobiography the author appears as Elizabeth Burgos, who taped Menchú's original testimony and wrote the definitive text.)

8. Sánchez (1993), Sánchez (1999), Van Cott (2000).

9. The proposal to establish a 'multi-national State', although hotly debated, was not accepted by the constituent assembly (Espinosa 1999).

10. Barié (1998), Clavero (1994).

11. Observatorio Social de América Latina (2000). Iturralde (2000) argues that the indigenous movement has matured enough over the last few years so that, in alliance with other social movements, it can make national-level political demands challenging the hegemonic economic model imposed by successive governments. The Zapatista National Liberation Army in Mexico has made national-level political demands that have been rejected by the government with the argument that such issues are not 'indigenous' demands and will not be discussed with a rag-tag indigenous guerrilla group.

12. For a detailed analysis of Indian voting behaviour in Chiapas see Viqueira and Sonnleitner (2000).

13. For a discussion on Indian autonomy in the Amazon regions of Bolivia and Colombia see Hoekema and Assies (1998). On the situation in Mexico, where the debate on indigenous autonomy is in full swing, see Burguete (1999).

14. Cojtí (1994). See also Bastos (1996) and for an analysis of the implications on the accord on indigenous identity and rights García Ruiz (1997).

15. Morales (1998). For a good analysis of these debates see Warren (1998).

References

Barié Kolb, Cletus Gregor (1998), *Los derechos indígenas en las constituciones latinoamericanas contemporáneas*, unpublished thesis, UNAM (Mexico).

Bastos, Santiago and Manuela Camus (1996), *Quebrando el silencio. Organizaciones del pueblo maya y sus demandas. 1986–1992*, FLACSO (Guatemala).

Bengoa, José (1985), *Historia del Pueblo Mapuche*, Ediciones Sur (Santiago).

Brysk, Alison (2000), *From Tribal Village to Global Village: Indian Rights and International Relations in Latin America*, Stanford University Press (Stanford).

Burguete Cal y Mayor Aracely (ed.) (1999), *México: Experiencias de Autonomía Indígena*, IWGIA (Copenhagen).

Calla, Ricardo (1999), 'Indígenas, Ley de Participación Popular y cambios de gobierno en Bolivia (1994–1998)' in Willem Assies, Gemma van der Haar, André Hoekema (eds), *El reto de la diversidad*, El Colegio de Michoacán (Mexico).

Clavero, Bartolomé (1994), *Derecho indígena y cultura constitucional en América*, Siglo XXI (Mexico).

Cojtí Cuxil, Demetrio (1994), *Políticas para la reivindicación de los mayas de hoy (Fundamento de los Derechos Específicos del Pueblo Maya)*, SPEM-CHOLSAMAJ (Guatemala).

Dandler, Jorge (1999), 'Indigenous Peoples and the Rule of Law in Latin America: Do They have a Chance?' in Juan Méndez, Guillermo O'Donnell and Paulo Sérgio Pinheiro (eds), *The (Un)Rule of Law and the Underprivileged in Latin America*, University of Notre Dame Press (Notre Dame).

Espinosa, María Fernanda (1999), 'Políticas étnicas y reforma del estado en Ecuador' in Willem Assies, Gemma van der Haar, André Hoekema (eds), *El reto de la diversidad*, El Colegio de Michoacán (Mexico).

Franks, C.E.S. (2000), 'Indian Policy: Canada and the United States Compared' in Curtis Cook and Juan D. Lindau (eds), *Aboriginal Rights and Self-Government: The Canadian and Mexican Experience in North American Perspective*, McGill-Queen's University Press (Montreal and Kingston).

García Ruiz, Jesús (1997), *Hacia una Nación Pluricultural en Guatemala. Responsabilidad histórica y viabilidad política*, CEDIM (Guatemala).

Hernández Martín, Ramón (1998), *Francisco de Vitoria y su 'relección sobre los indios'. Los derechos de los hombres y de los pueblos*, EDIBESA (Madrid).

Hoekema, André J. and Willem Assies (1999), 'La administración de recursos: entre autonomía y cogestión' in Willem Assies, Gemma van der Haar, André Hoekema (eds), *El reto de la diversidad*, El Colegio de Michoacán (Mexico).

International Labour Office (1953), *Indigenous Peoples: Living and Working Conditions of Aboriginal Populations in Independent Countries*, ILO (Geneva).

Iturralde, Diego (1998), 'Movimientos indígenas y contiendas electorales (Ecuador y Bolivia)' in Miguel A. Bartolomé and Alicia M. Barabas (eds), *Autonomías étnicas y Estados nacionales*, Conaculta (Mexico).

—— (2000), 'Lucha indígena y reforma neoliberal' (unpublished manuscript).

Lâm, Maivân Clech (2000), *At the Edge of the State: Indigenous Peoples and Self-Determination*, Transnational Publishers (Ardsley NY).

Marroquín, Alejandro D. (1972), *Balance del indigenismo*, Instituto Indigenista Interamericano, Ediciones especiales No. 62 (Mexico).

Martínez Sarasola, Carlos (1992), *Nuestros paisanos los indios*, Emecé (Buenos Aires).

Menchú, Rigoberta (Elizabeth Burgos) (1985), *Me llamo Rigoberta Menchú y así me nació la conciencia*, Siglo XXI (Mexico).

Morales, Mario Roberto (1998), *La articulación de las diferencias o el síndrome de Maximón*, FLACSO (Guatemala).

Mörner, Magnus (1967), *Race Mixture in the History of Latin America*, Little, Brown & Co. (Boston).

Observatorio Social de América Latina (2000), *La revuelta indígena en Ecuador*, Consejo Latinoamericano de Ciencias Sociales (Buenos Aires).

Orellana Halkyer, René (1999), 'Municipalización de pueblos indígenas en Bolivia: Impactos y perspectivas' in Willem Assies, Gemma van der Haar, André Hoekema (eds), *El reto de la diversidad*, El Colegio de Michoacán (Mexico).

Sánchez, Enrique, Roldán Roque and María Fernanda Sánchez (1993), *Derechos e identidad. Los pueblos indígenas y negros en la constitución política de Colombia de 1991*, Disloque (Bogotá).

Sánchez Botero, Esther (1999), 'La tutela como medio de transformación de las relaciones Estado-pueblos indígenas en Colombia' in Willem Assies, Gemma van der Haar, André Hoekema (eds), *El reto de la diversidad*, El Colegio de Michoacán (Mexico).

Santos, Silvio Coelho dos (1998), 'Pueblos indígenas de Brasil: derechos constitucionales, tierras y luchas presentes' in Miguel A. Bartolomé and Alicia M. Barabas (eds), *Autonomías étnicas y Estados nacionales*, Conaculta (Mexico).

Sieder, Rachel (1997), *Customary Law and Democratic Transition in Guatemala*, Institute of Latin American Studies (London).

Sierra, María Teresa (1995), 'Los indios en el Brasil de hoy' in Héctor Díaz Polanco (ed.), *Etnia y nación en América Latina*, Conaculta (Mexico).

Stavenhagen, Rodolfo (1992), 'Challenging the Nation-State in Latin America', *Journal of International Affairs*. Winter, 45 (2), pp.421–40.

—— (1995), 'Indigenous Peoples: Emerging Actors in Latin America' in *Ethnic Conflict and Governance in Comparative Perspective*, Working Paper No. 215, Woodrow Wilson International Center for Scholars (Washington, D.C.), September, pp.1–13.

Van Cott, Donna Lee (2000), *The Friendly Liquidation of the Past: The Politics of Diversity in Latin America*, University of Pittsburgh Press (Pittsburgh).

Viqueira, Juan Pedro and Willibald Sonnleitner (2000), *Democracia en tierras indígenas. Las elecciones en Los Altos de Chiapas (1991–1998)*, El Colegio de México (Mexico).

Warren, Kay B. (1998), *Indigenous Movements and their Critics: Pan-Maya Activism in Guatemala*, Princeton University Press (Princeton).

2
Constitutional Reform in the Andes: Redefining Indigenous–State Relations

Donna Lee Van Cott

In the 1990s most Latin American countries underwent significant constitutional reforms. Almost all of the new constitutions incorporated language that formally recognised the identities and rights of their indigenous populations for the first time. Among the first states to do so were the central Andean countries, following the lead of neighbouring Colombia, which introduced the then-most-extensive constitutional regime of ethnic rights in Latin America in 1991.

These remarkable reforms resulted from the convergence of two phenomena. First, in the early 1990s, the Andean countries experienced acute crises of legitimacy and governability that generated elite and popular movements for radical political change. These crises were rooted in the absence of channels for formal representation and access to the protection of the rule of law for significant sectors of the population. In all three cases constitutional reformers sought to address these problems by expanding channels for political representation and participation, decentralising and rationalising public administration, and strengthening, de-politicising, and widening access to the protection of the rule of law.

Second, by the early 1990s, indigenous peoples' organisations in the region had matured to a level at which they could influence and – sometimes – actively participate in the constitutional reform processes set in motion by elites. Taking advantage of changes in the political opportunity structure (Tarrow 1996: 54) presented by radical constitutional reform and favourable elite and public opinion toward indigenous rights (both nationally and internationally), these organisations asserted their demands in terms of constitutional rights. They framed[1] their claims as the reconstitution of relations between pre-constituted, autonomous indigenous peoples and their authorities and forms of organisation within the territorial and institutional confines of the Western state. Arguing that existing democratic institutions excluded large sectors of the population, including indigenous peoples, the non-indigenous poor and political minorities, they linked the ongoing political crises to the problem of social exclusion and advocated the construction of a non-exclusionary 'pluri-cultural' state as a solution. According to such interpretations, the elite project to construct democracy around a homogeneous ethnic identity based on transplanted European cultures had failed: any viable democratic project in the future had to be constructed around a national identity that reflected and valued the cultural diversity of society. Indigenous rights advocates maintained that one single mode of citizenship based on a uniform set of individual rights was insufficient to ensure the political incorporation of all citizens. Instead, they argued, constitutions should recognise multiple forms of citizenship, including collective forms that link individuals to the state through communities that give citizenship greater meaning and content.

This chapter focuses on Colombia, Bolivia, and Ecuador, all of which incorporated language in their constitutions which purported to grant self-governing powers to indigenous peoples. Considerable cultural and organisational diversity exists among indigenous peoples in the Andes – and in Latin America, more broadly. However, they share a vision of territorial and political autonomy based on the restoration of pre-colonial indigenous self-governing authorities and practices – or, more accurately, contemporary conceptions and adaptations of them – and the free development of indigenous culture unfettered by the intrusions of non-indigenous society, the state, and the market. Indigenous claims to territorial and political autonomy provide the institutional framework for the realisation of indigenous aspirations and the legal and material basis for the exercise of all other rights. For that reason I focus in particular on efforts to codify and implement indigenous aspirations for autonomy. The entire set of rights indigenous organisations secured within national constitutions constitutes their vision of 'indigenous citizenship'. They are listed in the table opposite. The Peruvian case, while not discussed in this chapter, is included as a basis for comparison.[2]

In the sections that follow I review the three cases considered, highlighting the principal themes that convinced elites to undergo radical structural reforms of the state and regime, the mode of reform chosen in each case, and the extent to which indigenous organisations were able to influence those reforms. I then focus on the issue of political-territorial autonomy regimes: the aspirations of indigenous organisations; the nature of the regime codified; and the relationship of the autonomy regime to the larger issue of political and administrative decentralisation and to the expectations of political elites with respect thereto. Finally, I evaluate the efforts of the state and indigenous organisations to implement the new regimes.

Table 2.1   Ethnic constitutional rights in the Andes

	COLOMBIA 1991	BOLIVIA 1994	ECUADOR 1998	PERU 1993
% of population indigenous[a]	2.7%	51% – 71%	25% – 43%	38% – 47%
Mode of reform	Constituent assembly	Executive-driven, approved by congress	Constituent assembly	Constituent assembly, approved by national referendum
ILO Convention 169 ratified[b]	1991	1991	1998	1994
Rhetorical recognition	'The State recognises and protects the ethnic and cultural diversity of the Colombian Nation' (Art. 7)	'Bolivia free, independent, sovereign, multiethnic and pluricultural' (Art. 1)	'Ecuador is a pluricultural and multiethnic state' (Art. 1)	'The State recognises and protects the ethnic and cultural plurality of the Nation' (Art. 2)
Customary law protected	yes, limited by Constitution and laws (courts have allowed more liberal application)	yes, limited by Constitution and laws	yes, limited by Constitution and laws	yes, limited by fundamental rights of the person
Collective property rights protected	yes	yes	yes	yes[c]
Status of indigenous languages	official in indigenous territories	none	official in indigenous territories	official in indigenous territories
State promotes bilingual education	yes	yes	yes	yes
Black rights	some territorial and self-government rights for culturally distinct sector of afro-Colombian population	afro-Bolivians have no constitutional standing, treated as indigenous people by government policy	comparable to indigenous rights to the extent applicable, to be determined by law	no
Autonomy regimes	yes, *Resguardos* comparable to municipalities	Indigenous Municipal Districts and Original Community Lands have no autonomous powers	Indigenous Territorial Circumscriptions have autonomous status to be determined by statutory law	No *constitutional* recognition. A 1984 law enables native and campesino communities to form 'municipalidades delegadas' with the autonomous attributes of municipalities[d]

Notes to Table 2.1

a Estimates of indigenous population vary. The first figure for Bolivia, Ecuador and Peru is from Deruyttere (1997: 1), which cites 1993 data from the Instituto Indigenista Interamericano. The second, higher figure is from the website of the International Labour Organisation, www.oit.or.cr/mdtsanjo/indig/cuadro.htm. Population data for Colombia is from the 1993 national census.

b Ten Latin American states have ratified International Labour Convention 169 (1989) on the rights of indigenous peoples. Space constraints preclude a full discussion of its importance.

c Over the strong objections of Amazonian indigenous organisations, property rights were weakened in the 1993 constitution by allowing for the sale and mortgaging of indigenous communal lands. See Aroca, Ardito and Maury (1993).

d Raquel Yrigoyen, personal communication, 19 April 2000.

Colombia

In 1989, an unprecedented wave of political violence that included the assassination of three presidential candidates forced the convocation of a National Constituent Assembly to the centre of the political agenda in Colombia. The inability of the state to protect its citizens from drug cartels, guerrillas, paramilitaries, and its own armed forces, combined with the failure of the national congress to act in the face of threats and bribes from the drug cartels, caused a sharp decline in public legitimacy for state institutions. The political instability generated by the rising violence exacerbated the crisis of representation caused by the refusal of the two dominant parties to allow underrepresented interests to enter the formal political system. There were four main issues on the constitutional reform agenda. First, establishing a regime of rights to protect all citizens, particularly politically, economically and socially marginalised groups. Second, extending the rule of law throughout the Colombian territory to areas where the state has little presence. Third, opening the political party system to non-traditional actors, and fourth, above all, generating institutional change that would stop the political violence by convincing all actors that they had a stake in the democratic regime. Lesser but significant issues were the elimination of corruption, economic modernisation, and the continuation of the process of administrative and political decentralisation begun in 1986 (Buenahora 1995; Dugas 1993, 1997; Van Cott 2000b: Ch. 2).

A national constituent assembly convened between January and July 1991. Two indigenous candidates finished 19th and 27th against 119 competing lists of candidates for the assembly, despite the minuscule size of the mostly unregistered indigenous population (see Table 2.1) and indigenous organisations' acute lack of resources. The delegates represented two indigenous organisations, both based in the south-western department of Cauca: the Colombian National Indigenous Organisation (ONIC), a group that had traditionally worked with non-indigenous popular organisations, mainly on agrarian issues; and the Southwest Indigenous Authorities (AISO), which emphasised the jurisdiction and rights of traditional ethnic authorities. The two elected and one appointed indigenous delegates managed to insert almost their entire agenda into the new charter.[3] Two factors were most important in explaining this achievement. First, the existence of a significant centre-left bloc in the assembly (which included 27 out of 74 delegates), led by the ADM-19, provided a strategic ally on important issues. Since any decision in the assembly had to be supported by a two-thirds majority, this bloc was sufficient to obstruct proposals for constitutional reform. The ADM-19 consistently supported the indigenous delegates' proposals in exchange for their support for ADM-19 platforms. The existence of the ADM-19-indigenous alliance within the Constituent Assembly was a great boon to a movement that – compared to indigenous movements in other countries – had few important domestic or international allies. Second, President Gaviria's repeated statements emphasising the importance of protecting human rights to establishing a democracy in Colombia and halting the spiralling political violence allowed indigenous delegates to claim that protecting the rights of the most vulnerable and marginalised Colombians was vital to democracy and peace. As delegate Francisco Rojas Birry argued,

> Our ways of life must be respected by the authorities and by all people: if not, the very values proclaimed by the new constitution [peace, liberty, equality] will be nullified. The road to a democratic and pluralistic society requires the recognition and effective respect of ethnic and cultural diversity. (Translation by author; Rojas Birry 1991: 14)

Additional explanations for the indigenous delegates' success lay in their savvy manipulation of their symbolic importance to an assembly which purported to demonstrate a new era of tolerance and inclusion, and the media's disproportionate and favourable coverage of the indigenous delegates. The delegates also benefited from warm relations with Gaviria's Office of Indigenous Affairs, staffed by experienced and sympathetic anthropologists who acted as a bridge between the indigenous delegates and the administration.[4] This office enjoyed a long history of institutional continuity within the Ministry of Government dating back at least to the 1960s and would be the main agency overseeing constitutional implementation with respect to indigenous rights.[5]

The indigenous delegates' most important achievement was the constitutional recognition of the inalienable nature of indigenous *resguardos* (communally held lands) and the public nature of indigenous authorities and legal systems within them. Even before the 1991 reform, about 84 per cent of the indigenous population in Colombia lived on *resguardos* totalling 27.8 million hectares, comprising 24 per cent of the total national territory. The 1991 Constitution recognised the rights of *resguardos* to elect their own authorities according to their own customs, to design and implement development plans, to exercise indigenous customary law to resolve disputes within the community, to raise and administer taxes, and to receive a portion of national income comparable to that allocated to Colombian municipalities. Under the constitution, municipalities receive approximately 20 per cent of national income, each municipality's share calculated on the basis of a formula that incorporates population size, level of poverty, and the capacity to absorb public funds. Indigenous *resguardos* are comparable to Colombia's municipalities in terms of their administrative functions, their political autonomy (mayors have been directly elected since 1988), and their share of national resources. In addition, the constitution provides for the establishment of Indigenous Territorial Entities (ETI) in cases where indigenous *resguardos* are contiguous. This creates the possibility of extensive zones of indigenous authority.

Constitutional recognition of autonomous territories for indigenous peoples, and, to a lesser extent, Pacific Coast black communities, was facilitated by a strong movement for municipal decentralisation among a significant sector of the political elite and non-traditional actors represented in the Constituent Assembly. Decentralisation was a particular interest of Liberal Party representatives from the Pacific and Atlantic coasts who had significant representation – alongside indigenous delegates – on the commission addressing territorial administration. Conservatives, the traditional defenders of centralised government, had only two representatives on that commission. While retaining a unitary framework, the new constitution introduced direct election of departmental governors and the distribution of unprecedented amounts of national resources to municipalities, satisfying local elites' demands for greater political autonomy and access to state resources. Linking indigenous *resguardos* and their authorities to the already existing autonomous municipality generated minimal disruption in the existing territorial and legal framework while ensuring meaningful autonomous powers for indigenous authorities.

Some important achievements may be identified in the implementation of indigenous aspirations for autonomy. First, the Gaviria and Samper governments established approximately 100 additional *resguardos*. Second, indigenous congressional representatives achieved the passage of legislation facilitating the transfer of state resources to *resguardos*. These resources have enabled local *cabildos* (indigenous governments dating to colonial times that correspond to the *resguardos*) to negotiate development policy with municipal governments. Funds began to be disbursed in 1994; by March 1997, each *resguardo* was receiving approximately US$61,000 (Cepeda 1995: 11; Roldán 1998: 52; interview, Raúl Arango, 30 January 1997). Third, indigenous organisations have received strong support from the newly created Constitutional Court for the exercise of indigenous customary law (Van Cott 2000a: 217–21).

There are a number of reasons for these achievements in securing indigenous autonomy in Colombia. First, the Gaviria administration, which presided over the constituent assembly and the first three years of constitutional implementation, when statutory legislation establishing the new regime of constitutional rights was enacted, was favourably disposed toward the indigenous movement. An Indigenous Affairs Office sympathetic to the movement had been established within the executive decades earlier and helped to represent indigenous interests before the government. However, despite the fact that no change in the ruling political party occurred, this productive working relationship ended with the start of the Samper administration, which was markedly more hostile to indigenous demands and whose Director-General for Indigenous Affairs had poor relations with the national indigenous organisations and their congressional representatives (Van Cott 2000b: 94–8, 101–4).

Second, among the new constitutional institutions established by Gaviria was the Constitutional Court, which now ranks among the country's most respected institutions. It has tended to side with indigenous communities against public and private actors seeking to disregard indigenous constitutional rights. This is due partly to the unusual professionalism and tradition of social activism among Colombian judges, who have a long-standing tradition of recognising the duty of the state to protect indigenous communities.[6] In addition, Colombia may be unique in the persistence of colonial laws protecting indigenous rights, a legacy of the strong conservative thrust of Colombian law. Colombian jurisprudence with respect to indigenous rights is strongly influenced by colonial Indian law, which recognises the source of indigenous collective rights – particularly territorial rights – in the existence of indigenous peoples prior to the formation of the state. No other country in the region has such a long history of jurisprudence reflecting this commitment (Correa 1992; Roldán 1998: 54–63; Van Cott 2000a: 224).

Third, despite the small size of the indigenous population and its limited economic resources, indigenous political parties formed after 1991 have steadily increased their representation at the municipal, departmental, and national levels. In the year 2000 there were three indigenous senators, two representatives in the Chamber of Deputies, one departmental governor, twelve mayors, and hundreds of municipal councillors. Fourth, Colombia has a strong, relatively unified indigenous movement with more than 20 years of experience as a social movement. Although entry into electoral politics exacerbated existing institutional divisions, indigenous activists share fundamental goals and have proved capable of forging unity at crucial political junctures. Finally, in contrast to the case of Ecuador discussed below, indigenous organisations in Colombia reached a working consensus on the appropriate unit of indigenous territorial and political autonomy, and on the functions and attributes of that level of authority.

These achievements are balanced by the failure of three successive Colombian governments to establish the Indigenous Territorial Entities, despite almost a decade of campaigning on their behalf by the indigenous movement.[7] This delay is principally attributable to resistance from rural landowners to indigenous territorial rights, particularly in the Cauca. Efforts by indigenous congressional representatives to counter this resistance are undermined by promises to deliver material improvements to their constituents in exchange for them not pushing the territorial issue. They also lacked allies in the administrations that followed Gaviria – the Liberal Samper and Conservative Pastrana governments – which have constitutional authority to establish the Indigenous Territorial Entities without congressional action. The state has also failed to remove non-indigenous mayors as intermediary recipients of the funds, as the constitution requires. Indigenous authorities must petition these mayors for access to their own funds, leading to malfeasance in some regions (*El Tiempo*, 9 March 1997, p. 8A). According to indigenous activists, efforts to ensure that the resources are invested wisely once disbursed, for example by providing intensive training in development planning and management to indigenous authorities, have been insufficient. Indigenous activists also cite the need for more productive economic activities within resguardos in order to reduce their now total dependence upon the Colombian state for resources (Roldán 1997: 238–41; interview, Jesús Avirama, Popayán, 10 March 1997).

Implementation of indigenous autonomy is also impeded by the escalation of a multi-sided civil war between drug dealers, guerrillas, paramilitaries, and the Colombian state in zones of indigenous settlement. Armed groups routinely assassinate and threaten indigenous mayors, severely inhibiting the capacity of indigenous authorities to govern or to undertake economic development projects in zones decimated by war. Massive human rights violations that occur with impunity make indigenous political mobilisation difficult; support from international human rights organisations – domestic ones have been decimated by threats and violent attacks – has had little practical effect (Van Cott 2000b: 251–4; WOLA 1997).

Bolivia

The primary source of political instability and declining public legitimacy for democratic institutions in Bolivia was not violence, but rather the inability of the formal political system either to produce programmatically coherent executives with majority support in congress, or to design and implement necessary structural reforms over the opposition of highly mobilised social groups (principally the weak but disruptive labour movement and regional elites organised into departmental civic committees). The inadequacy of formal political institutions was attributable largely to their exclusion of the majority indigenous population and their lack of connection with Bolivia's predominant forms of political and social organisation (Van Cott 2000b: 133–4, 138–46).

When Movimiento Nacional Revolucionario's (MNR) presidential candidate, Gonzalo Sánchez de Lozada, launched his constitutional reform project in 1991, his main motivation was to reform the constitutional provision (Article 90) that had enabled the second and third place presidential candidates, Hugo Banzer of Acción Democrática Nacional (ADN) and Jaime Paz Zamora of the Movimiento de la Izquierda Revolucionario (MIR), respectively, to usurp his plurality victory in the 1989 elections. He also sought to modernise and 'neoliberalise' relations between the state and the economy.[8] Sánchez de Lozada was also interested in promoting a radical municipal decentralisation in order to promote rural economic development and reduce rural poverty, and to reduce the political dominance of regional elites, who were clamouring for regional decentralisation (Van Cott 2000b: 138). Prior to the 1994 reform, municipalities did not exist outside the most densely populated urban areas, leaving a huge vacuum of political representation and public services.

By the end of the Paz Zamora administration in 1993, the three major party leaders had reached agreement on four issues: reform of Article 90, direct election of half of the lower chamber of congress, judicial reform, and municipal decentralisation. The 1993 Law of Constitutional Reform also contained language recognising a set of indigenous rights adapted from the Colombian constitution. The incorporation of indigenous rights into the constitution at this time resulted from a series of successful mobilisations by indigenous organisations in the early 1990s, in particular a march that took place in 1990 which fundamentally changed elite, urban perceptions of the indigenous population, and the maturation of a decade of debate among intellectuals and the left on the cultural roots of Bolivia's political instability.[9]

The Bolivian constitutional reform is exceptional in the Andes as the only major reform produced in the 1990s without the convocation of a directly elected constituent assembly. Bolivian political elites chose not to convoke a constituent assembly for several reasons. First, the 1967 Bolivian constitution clearly prohibited this mode of reform, requiring that changes to the charter be made through legislation passed by two successive legislatures.[10] Leaders of the major parties believed that the reforms would lack legitimacy if passed through extra-constitutional means. Second, party leaders feared the political turmoil a constituent assembly might unleash, particularly if the majority indigenous and poor population was able to steer the proceedings or block modernising proposals. Third, apart from the proposals of politically impotent intellectuals and the lowland indigenous movement, no popular movement for a constituent assembly existed in Bolivia. Popular organisations feared that constitutional reform in the age of neoliberalism might endanger the social and economic rights gained in the 1952 revolution and codified in the 1967 charter.[11]

As a result, the reform process was closely managed by Sánchez de Lozada, who won the 1993 presidential election in an unprecedented alliance with the party of indigenous leader Víctor Hugo Cárdenas, and a team of personally loyal, politically independent technocrats. Sánchez de Lozada's working majority in Congress enabled him to pass a revised version of the 1993 constitutional reform law, approved at the end of the previous administration, together with a set of statutory laws which had constitutional implications. Indigenous organisations had no formal representation in this process. Instead, their interests were represented by Cárdenas and by social scientists with years of experience working with indigenous peoples who staffed Sánchez de Lozada's new Secretariat of Ethnic, Gender and Generational Affairs. The Secretariat's staff consulted extensively with peasant and lowland indigenous organisations in order to ascertain their aspirations and secure their support.[12]

Despite their formal exclusion from the reform process, indigenous intellectuals had generated a discourse of multiculturalism in the previous decades that strongly influenced the thinking of a key set of reformers.[13] This discourse had been initiated by two distinct sectors of the indigenous movement in Bolivia. The highland-based campesino movement, which emerged in the 1970s and was represented at the national level (albeit weakly in the 1990s) by a campesino union (CSUTCB) formed in 1979, generated a discourse of dual ethnic and class oppression. This discourse was reshaped around the theme of natural resource and territorial rights by lowland indigenous organisations, who formed the Eastern Bolivian Indigenous Confederation (CIDOB) in 1982 to unify their struggle against timber extraction in their traditional territories. The lowland organisations added the central idea of territorial autonomy to the indigenous agenda. Lacking the long history of confrontation with the state that the campesino organisations had, CIDOB proved more amenable to constructive negotiation with the governments that presided over the creation and implementation of the constitutional reform.

After 1985, the idea of ethnic and cultural diversity became increasingly politicised as it was juxtaposed with the homogenising, individualistic thrust of the new neoliberal economic model (Calla 1992: 50–4). It inspired a number of proposals for the reconstruction of Bolivian state institutions around ethnic criteria (Van Cott 2000b: 135–8). By the time of the 1994 constitutional reform, this multiculturalist discourse had permeated the analysis of mainstream social scientists and traditional politicians, who identified the source of Bolivia's crises of representation and legitimacy as the lack of fit between the country's homogeneous, individualising political institutions and an extremely diverse population organised politically and socially by a dense fabric of community organisations (Van Cott 2000b: 134).

Indigenous peoples gained unprecedented recognition of their identities and collective rights in the 1994 constitutional reform and related statutory laws on popular participation, education, and agrarian reform. Article 171 of the constitution recognised the right to exercise customary law in indigenous communities. The 1994 Law of Popular Participation (LPP) established juridical personality and important political participation rights for indigenous and peasant communities. The LPP designed the Indigenous Municipal District (DMI) to respond to indigenous organisations' demands for self-government, and allowed geographically discontinuous *ayllus* (an Andean form of community organisation that allows production of food at different elevations) to register as single DMIs. The DMIs have the right to bilingual education suitable for the district and guaranteed representation on municipal oversight committees. Under the LPP, municipalities receive 20 per cent of state income; a huge boon to rural municipalities that previously had received virtually no state resources for social and economic development (Archondo 1997: 11; Van Cott 2000b: 182).

Nevertheless, the reforms fall far short of indigenous aspirations for territorial and political autonomy.[14] Mayors are not legally required to spend any municipal resources in indigenous districts or to confer any powers on indigenous 'sub-mayors' chosen by the DMIs. In practice, municipalities have ignored indigenous districts, leaving them to obtain funding from international development agencies.[15] The DMIs have no specific functions, autonomous powers or independent access to state resources. The type of participation in which their representatives engage under the LPP is structured by the state and fails to accommodate culturally distinct forms of representation and political decision-making (Assies 2000). There are no clear guidelines for their operation and no resources to pay indigenous sub-mayors a salary or to reimburse their expenses. The DMIs also fail to take into account the territorial extension of lowland groups, which exceeds that of municipalities in some areas. Indigenous social and political collectivities are divided into multiple districts that may lie in different municipalities, resulting in the fragmentation of political representation and organisation. The Guaraní, for example, are settled in three departments, six provinces and twelve municipalities. For these reasons, indigenous organisations have proposed the establishment of 'indigenous municipalities', entities that would confer the autonomous powers and resources of municipalities on ethnically distinct communities with special self-governing powers. However, this conception of Bolivian territorial administration is strongly opposed by traditional elites (Booth, Clisby and Widmark 1996: 53; interviews, Ericka Brockman, La Paz, December 1998; René Orellana, Santa Cruz, 18 July 1997).

In Bolivia, indigenous peoples secured collective property rights under the constitutional reform, a significant achievement. As Paz Patiño argues, it is through secure attachment to a territory that indigenous peoples construct their identities and exercise citizenship (Paz Patiño 1998: 128). Collective property rights are also the basis for the establishment of autonomy. But despite fierce lobbying efforts, indigenous organisations and their allies in the Ethnic Affairs Sub-Secretariat failed to secure constitutional recognition of territorial jurisdiction over indigenous lands (Van Cott 2000b: 162). This issue was reopened in 1996 during the debate on the agrarian reform law (Ley INRA). After protracted negotiations with indigenous and campesino organisations that culminated in a march from the lowland department of Santa Cruz to the capital, the government achieved agreement with indigenous and some campesino organisations on a law that resulted in the distribution of titles for 2.3 million hectares of community lands during the last seven months of the Sánchez de Lozada administration (Van Cott 2000b: 241). Although an additional 10 million hectares were earmarked for distribution, the Banzer administration's (1997–2002) lack of political will has delayed the titling process and indigenous organisations lack allies that are able and willing to apply pressure. The 1996 Ley INRA also fulfilled CIDOB's goal of replacing 'tierras comunitarias de orígen', the constitution's term for indigenous collective lands, with the term 'territory', which at least implies jurisdiction and sovereignty (Van Cott 2000b: 198–9). Nevertheless, the original community lands lack any independent status in the Bolivian administrative structure, since they lie within the jurisdiction of existing municipalities. Municipal governments even receive revenues from the exploitation of forests in 'tierras comunitarias de orígen' (Assies 2000).

Implementation of indigenous rights contained in the 1994 constitutional reform and complementary statutory legislation was more decentralised than in Colombia and often blurred the distinctions between governmental, non-governmental and foreign agencies. The Ethnic Affairs Sub-Secretariat, housed and funded by the United Nations Development Programme (UNDP), was the main policy arm advocating the indigenous view in struggles within the government over implementing legislation and decrees. However, apart from some programmes to disseminate information about the reforms, the Sub-Secretariat lacked a budget to develop programmes working directly with indigenous communities to implement their rights. It had tense relations with the vice-president and the CSUTCB, and worked mainly with the more conciliatory CIDOB, to which it lent crucial institutional support. The purge of the Sub-Secretariat's politically independent director, in a mid-term move to consolidate support within the governing coalition, led to greater technical and administrative reliance upon the UNDP and a preference for working with the highland rather than lowland movements (the new director, a congressional representative from Cárdenas' Movimiento Revolucionario Tupaj Katari de Liberación (MRTKL) party, represented the campesino movement). These relations changed abruptly again with the election of Banzer in 1997. The new regime renamed, reorganised and relocated the indigenous affairs portfolio and transferred control to its coalition partner, the centre-left MIR, which perceived an electoral advantage in working closely with the indigenous population. (As Xavier Albó notes in Chapter 3 of this volume, that perception was proved accurate in the 1999 municipal elections.) Thus, in contrast to the Colombian case, which was characterised by institutional continuity and stability, in Bolivia the institutional channel for indigenous rights claims varied dramatically between presidential administrations, resulting in less continuity in the formulation and implementation of indigenous constitutional rights. Institutional continuity existed to some extent outside the state. The UNDP continued its support of indigenous peoples' development programmes during the Banzer administration, albeit at a reduced level. The Danish government funded programmes that assisted indigenous communities to obtain juridical personality, to undertake indigenous voter registration, to assist in drawing ethnically coherent boundaries for indigenous municipal districts, and to train indigenous leaders in resource and municipal management. These programmes were suspended for a time at the beginning of the Banzer administration in response to Banzer's effort to politicise them and to reduce the saliency of ethnic issues in general. In addition, the multilateral Indigenous Peoples Fund provided US$200,000 to train more than 100 indigenous leaders in resource management (Van Cott 2000b: 194–201).

The Banzer administration proved far less committed than its predecessor to developing indigenous constitutional rights. It has expunged the discourse of multiculturalism espoused during the Sánchez de Lozada administration from its policy pronouncements, preferring instead to focus on an economic approach to poverty alleviation. Collective property rights achieved in the 1994 Constitution and 1996 agrarian reform law are under attack by landed elites in the Amazon region, who enjoy significant representation and influence in the Banzer government. The president himself owns extensive holdings in the lowlands, where indigenous lands restrict the expansion of agribusiness and ranching.[16] The distribution of indigenous-claimed land practically came to a standstill during the Banzer administration (Muñoz and Lavadenz 1997: 25). Where it has proceeded, indigenous territories have been 'archipelagised' (to use Willem Assies' term) by competing claims to forest resources (Assies 2000: 11).

In sum, Bolivian indigenous organisations were unable to link constitutional recognition of their authorities and territories to a meaningful level within the political and territorial administration, that is, a level at which functional powers and state resources would be accessible (the only gains made in this respect related to the exercise of customary law and the administration of bilingual educational programmes). Resurgent local elites, whose interests usually conflict with those of Indians and campesinos, have increased their relative power through access to patronage resources flowing to the municipalities, which they control (Assies 2000). The LPP's prioritisation of representation through atomised, weak community organisations had the effect of weakening regional and national-level indigenous and peasant organisations. Apart from financial support from international donors, indigenous organisations lack allies within or outside the government with whom to press their claims. The political parties most receptive to these claims are currently outside the government (MNR, Movimiento Bolivia Libre (MBL), and Conciencia de Patria (CONDEPA)).

The resultant weakening of indigenous and campesino organisations, exacerbated in turn by internal divisions, was partially offset in 1995 by some initial successes in Bolivia's first-ever nation-wide municipal elections, in which indigenous and campesino candidates won 28.6 per cent of municipal council seats (Albó 1997: 9). This was an astounding achievement given the fact that only 8 per cent of the indigenous population was registered to vote in 1995 (Van Cott 2000b: 196). Whereas in Colombia, the 1991 Constitution permitted candidates from social movement organisations to run for election, in Bolivia only registered political parties may field candidates. Thus, in most cases indigenous and campesino candidates ran on ballots with locally strong traditional political parties. A new political party formed by Quechua coca growers, Asamblea por la Soberanía de los Pueblos (ASP), won more than 54 municipal council seats and ten mayorships, mainly in its base in Cochabamba. The ASP won four seats in the National Congress in 1997. These electoral achievements were, however, diminished by the success of local elites in exerting pressures that removed some indigenous mayors from office (Albó 1997: 13; Iturralde 1997: 356; Van Cott 2000b: 188–9).[17] Continued electoral success at the municipal level may enable indigenous organisations to achieve their goal of greater local autonomy, although in most cases they will still be forced to negotiate this autonomy with non-indigenous elites.[18] The ability of the indigenous population to project its political weight above the municipal level is restricted by the greater resources of the traditional parties and the serious internal divisions and corruption that entry into formal politics has generated within indigenous organisations.

Ecuador

In Ecuador the popular demand to convoke a constituent assembly was expressed at a time when Ecuadorian political institutions had entirely lost their authority. The fragmentation, corruption and lack of representativeness of the political party system and the outrageous behaviour of the president had provoked a demand from civil society for better representation and for the establishment of citizen rights. On 5 February 1997, the powerful national indigenous organisation CONAIE, with whom an estimated 80 per cent of indigenous organisations are affiliated (PRODEPINE 1998), led a mass protest demanding the ousting of President Abdalá Bucaram. In the struggle for succession that ensued, the indigenous-movement based political party Movimiento de Unidad Plurinacional Pachakutik-Nuevo País (MUPP-NP) traded its support for congressional president Fabián Alarcón in exchange for, among other things, a promise to immediately convoke a constituent assembly (Nielsen and Zetterberg 1999: 37–8).[19]

When the Constituent Assembly opened on 20 December 1997, indigenous peoples' organisations were in a far more advantageous position than their counterparts in Bolivia and Colombia on the eve of constitutional reform. This advantage is attributable to the creation in 1995 of the MUPP-NP, a loose electoral alliance of diverse social movement organisations based on a common desire to block the imposition of a neoliberal economic model and offer a political alternative to the corrupt and clientelistic traditional parties (Barrera and Unda 1999: 3). In its first outing (1996) the MUPP-NP gained 10 per cent of the seats in the National Congress. A reduced coalition (now the MUPP) gained seven out of 70 representatives in elections for the Constituent Assembly, in addition to three seats on allied lists, making it the third largest political force. The fragmentation and lack of discipline of Ecuador's party system gives minority parties considerable leverage in the formation of governing alliances and enabled the MUPP to be the senior partner in a centre-left minority bloc in the Constituent Assembly.[20]

A second distinct advantage was that the MUPP was one of few actors to enter the assembly with a concrete, comprehensive reform proposal. In order to pressure the government to stop stalling and convoke the official constituent assembly, CONAIE and other social movement organisations had organised their own 'People's Assembly', which opened in Quito on Columbus Day. CONAIE president Antonio Vargas presided over a 220-member assembly dominated by CONAIE and the petroleum workers union (Andolina 1998: 20–4; Nielsen and Zetterberg 1999: 39–41). In its proposal CONAIE maintained its long-standing demand that the constitution explicitly recognise the 'pluri-national' character of Ecuador, a position that was strikingly similar to that of Catalonia during the Spanish constitutional reform. For both CONAIE and Catalan nationalists, constitutional status as a nationality – an autonomous community within the larger nation – provides the basis for self-government (Edwards 1999: 4). Not surprisingly, the Spanish model was influential among CONAIE intellectuals.[21] The centrepiece of CONAIE's vision of pluri-nationalism is the jurisdictional autonomy of indigenous peoples as collective subjects corresponding to a territory (CONAIE 1997: 13).

The MUPP delegation in the Assembly and CONAIE's team of ten lobbyists, which established a daily presence in the official assembly, promoted the same proposal. This unity and coherence of platform was important, given the lack of consensus among traditional politicians on the main goals of reform, the paucity of broad-based alternative proposals for political reform from within the majority bloc dominated by the centre-right Partido Social Cristiano (PSC) and Democracia Popular (DP), and the lack of effective leadership from President Alarcón – due to the absence of public support or constitutional legitimacy for his interim government, and continuing power struggles among the parties in Congress. Moreover, the contemporaneous occurrence of national election campaigns that involved more than one-third of the Constituent Assembly exacerbated the propensity of delegates to pander to sectoral and regional interests rather than to produce comprehensive proposals for reform (Araníbar 1998: 1; Hurtado 1998: 200–1; Programa de Apoyo al Sistema de Gobernabilidad 1998: 5).[22]

As Nielsen and Zetterberg argue (1999), the Ecuadorian indigenous movement was able to insert its vision of the pluri-national state into the 1998 Constitution because it mobilised on three complementary fronts. It did so, first, through its delegates to the Constituent Assembly, second through its representatives in the National Congress (who secured the ratification of International Labour Organisation Convention 169 on the rights of indigenous peoples during the assembly), and, third, through direct lobbying by CONAIE's leadership. MUPP delegate Nina Pacari, a former CONAIE leader, presided over the Constituent Assembly's first commission, enabling her to control the timing of debate on collective rights and the submission of the commission's proposal to the Assembly. In the absence of elite consensus on many important issues – particularly after the centre-right alliance broke down in mid-April over the issue of privatising the social security system – MUPP exploited opportunities for strategic alliances with centre-left delegates and isolated its opposition: mainly the senior military and PSC. With their mandate set to expire, on 22 April 50 out of 70 delegates voted to extend the Constituent Assembly by an extra week. Furious, the 20 PSC delegates walked out, reducing the indigenous movement's opposition in the Assembly.

The successful insertion of indigenous rights in the constitution is also attributable to growing public acceptance of indigenous rights as an urgent social and political issue. This is due largely to the maturity and consolidation of indigenous organisations in Ecuador, particularly CONAIE, which shifted in 1996 from confrontation and threats to a strategy of negotiation and working through formal political institutions (Nielsen and Zetterberg 1999: 62–3; Verdesoto 1998: 7).[23] Ecuadorian Indians also benefited from the timing of the Constituent Assembly, which followed the highly publicised incorporation of indigenous themes into the Bolivian and Colombian charters. Ecuadorian constitutional reformers studied these two cases closely (in particular the Bolivian popular participation scheme) and adapted their lessons to Ecuador's social and political reality.[24]

Although CONAIE/MUPP ultimately backed down on their demand for incorporation of the term 'pluri-national' in the constitution, they achieved recognition of collective rights that effectively constituted their vision of pluri-nationalism. Indigenous and afro-Ecuadorian authorities may exercise a number of autonomous functions, which include administration of justice and the formulation and execution of economic development plans, within ethnically defined territorial circumscriptions to be established by law. But the constitution's language is ambiguous with respect to whether the ethnic territorial circumscriptions are a separate level of government, whether they correspond to a specific sub-national level, or whether they may correspond to multiple levels. This ambiguity reflects a lack of consensus on territorial organisation in Ecuador and on the concrete expression of indigenous autonomy, as well as the drafters' desire to maintain flexibility in the constitution in order to accommodate diverse patterns of indigenous social organisation and settlement. Such flexibility also was incorporated into the Spanish constitution's language on regional autonomy, with mixed results:

> at worst, it provided ill-defined limitations, which could lead to too many powers from some regions and too few for others. In retrospect, it is an exercise in ambiguity triumphing in the name of consensus, placating everyone and laying the foundations for a number of possible adaptations. (Edwards 1999: 3)

From another angle, however, ambiguity allows for the ongoing negotiation and reconstruction of national identities and group boundaries (Edwards 1999: 7).

A variety of factors impede implementation of the new model of indigenous autonomy in Ecuador. First, the constitution reflects a lack of consensus on the fundamental issues or main goals of the reform. Eliminating corruption was among the most important themes for the public, according to a 14-point referendum prior to the Constituent Assembly (Presencia, La Paz, 25 May 1997). Thirty-seven per cent of Ecuadorians cited eliminating corruption as the most important issue on the reform agenda in an April 1998 poll (Boletín de la reforma constitucional 9, 16 April 1998). Yet this was not the main emphasis of political elites. The main theme trumpeted by the Alarcón government, the political elite, and the Inter-American Development Bank (IDB) – which sponsored a project to provide technical support for the Constituent Assembly – was that of strengthening governability (Associated Press, Quito, 6 January 1998; Hurtado 1998: 14, 80, 174, 183; Programa de Apoyo al Sistema de Gobernabilidad 1997, 1998). Political elites and the IDB sought to establish institutions that would enable the formal political system to produce elected officials with sufficient support to make and execute political and economic reforms and to restore legitimacy to the political system. But there was no consensus on how to achieve governability.[25] Economic modernisation was a priority goal of the IDB and coastal elites. Within the region, Ecuador is a laggard in reducing the size and importance of the state in the economy due to a strong anti-neoliberal, anti-privatisation position among highly mobilised popular organisations and a sector of the Quito-based political elite (Nielsen and Zetterberg 1999: 24). Thus, in contrast to the Bolivian and Colombian cases, there was no consensus within the political elite on the modernisation of the state and the shift to a neoliberal economic model. The constituent assembly commission charged with economic reforms was unable to agree on a single proposal.[26]

As a result, the 1998 Constitution provides no coherent model of the state, particularly with respect to the question of decentralisation, despite widespread acknowledgement of the disorder and inefficiency of local and provincial government (Verdesoto 1998: 7). Ecuador's territorial scheme suffers from a lack of clarity concerning the functions of each level of government and poor articulation among these levels. Duplication of functions exists at the provincial level, where elected representatives vie with presidential appointees for control of resources. In addition, there is a surfeit of municipalities, half of which have fewer than 5000 inhabitants.[27] A rift between the Quito-based political elite and the Guayaquil-based economic elite impedes progress on decentralisation. The latter advocates provincial autonomy in order to keep more of its tax money in the province of Guayas and to counter the political domination of Quito at the national level. Three coastal provinces held popular consultations in late 1999, demonstrating overwhelming support for greater fiscal and administrative autonomy. President Gustavo Noboa pledged to uphold former President Jamil Mahuad's promise to include a *consulta* on autonomy in the ballots for the May 2000 elections, but the Congress failed to approve it, and the *consultas* sponsored by CONAIE and other social movements did not specifically address the issue. In the meantime, Congress is debating a Proyecto de Ley on autonomy and decentralisation and Noboa is formulating another autonomy proposal.[28]

Second, there is no high-level, centralised leadership to implement the reforms as there was in the first two years following the Bolivian and Colombian reforms. In Ecuador the new charter came into effect under a newly elected president who had opposed the constitution during his campaign. Following his inauguration, economic crises and political chaos that continue to impede progress on implementing legislation immediately beset President Mahuad. He faced a current account deficit equivalent to 10 per cent of GDP, a fiscal deficit equal to between 5 and 6 per cent of GDP, the highest inflation rate in Latin America (45 per cent), and a severe banking crisis (Acosta 1999: 8–9; Borja Cornejo 1999: 18; *Boletín de la reforma constitucional* 2: 4). The economy shrank by 7.5 per cent in 1999, 'the biggest contraction since records began in 1927' (Anonymous 1999: 32). In its first year in office the government suffered three major national strikes by labour and indigenous organisations opposing its economic policies. The unpopular measures generated a rift in the governing coalition, which collapsed amid massive protests in the summer of 1999 (Unda 1999: 41–2; *El Comercio*, 19 July 1999: A3; *Hoy*, 22 July 1999). Popular protests led by CONAIE, sparked by Mahuad's decision to 'dollarise' the economy, brought the ignominious Mahuad administration to an unruly close on 21 January 2000.

The conjuncture of extreme economic and political instability distracts attention from the issue of constitutional implementation and impedes potential efforts by Mahuad's successor, Gustavo Noboa, to provide the leadership necessary to achieve it. The fragmentation and fluidity of congressional alliances provides a poor basis for forging a sustainable alliance in favour of constitutional implementation for the foreseeable future, a prospect made more unlikely by CONAIE's call to dissolve the current Congress. Although CONAIE demonstrated a capacity to aggregate broad-based public support behind its leadership, that support proved to be temporary and rested more on frustration with political institutions than on support for CONAIE's political agenda or its leaders. The anti-democratic nature of the brief military-Indian coup in January 2000 generated a backlash in some quarters against CONAIE while deepening rifts within the indigenous movement (Beck and Mijeski 2000: 30–3). Since the Constituent Assembly, in a variety of ways too complex to treat in this brief chapter, CONAIE and Pachakutik have alienated most of the social movement organisations – representing women, afro-Ecuadorians, campesinos – that had been important allies during the constituent assembly, leaving them with few secure domestic allies in the current conjuncture. International donors, such as the World Bank, which operates a multimillion dollar, multi-year development project for indigenous and afro-Ecuadorian communities, or the German development agency GTZ, which is working with the executive on decentralisation, have been reluctant to get involved in the essentially political dispute between the indigenous movement and the government.

Thus, in contrast to the swift implementation of key components of the Colombian and Bolivian constitutions, virtually nothing has been achieved with respect to statutory legislation. In late 1999 various non-governmental and civil society organisations, some government ministries, and several political parties (mainly the Izquierda Democrática (ID), DP and MUPP) were working on proposals for implementing different aspects of the reform.[29] These efforts have been delayed by the political crisis generated by the January 2000 coup attempt.

A third obstacle to the implementation of indigenous autonomy in Ecuador is the absence of consensus within the diverse and divided indigenous movement and a lack of concrete details in the multiple proposals being offered. Such proposals fail to consider a number of factors, including: exactly what competencies each level of government will have, how these will correspond to parallel levels in the non-indigenous administrative framework, what mechanisms will exist for holding indigenous authorities accountable to national norms of public sector management, how ethnic electoral circumscriptions will relate to the remaining administrative and political structure, and what rights and opportunities for representation the non-indigenous living within indigenous circumscriptions will have. There are two main visions in contention: on the one hand, a multicultural vision based on the goal of making the entire political system more democratic, with multi-ethnic spheres of autonomy; and on the other, the mono-ethnic vision of the CONAIE leadership and MUPP deputy Nina Pacari. According to Floresmilo Simbañi, an indigenous leader in ECUARUNARI, the sierra federation within CONAIE, this vision is flawed on a number of counts. It has not been sufficiently vetted within CONAIE or the indigenous movement, it is not well related to a national project of decentralisation and democratisation, and is primarily a rural vision that doesn't contemplate the situation of hundreds of thousands of urban Indians. In addition, it lacks an understanding of economic development, since it posits impoverished indigenous communities as the unit of development isolated from the markets and systems of exchange in which the communities operate, and rejects the necessity of working with other popular sectors.[30]

CONAIE has attempted to marginalise rival national organisations – the Federación Ecuatoriana de Indígenas Evangélicos (FEINE) and the Federación Nacional de Organizaciones Campesinos, Indígenas y Negros (FENOCIN) – by imposing a vision of representation through 'nationalities' and 'peoples' that purports to override the national organisations by linking Indians directly through their traditional authorities. CONAIE's vision is being institutionalised by its allies in the Consejo de Desarrollo de las Nacionalidades y Pueblos del Ecuador (CODENPE), a quasi-governmental agency responsible for indigenous policy established during the Alarcón government. The establishment of CODENPE represents an achievement of greater participation for indigenous organisations – particularly CONAIE – within the state. It replaced a long line of state indigenous affairs agencies created and recreated by successive Ecuadorian governments to, alternately, control, placate, and communicate with the indigenous movement. CODENPE's mission is to participate in the creation and coordination of state indigenous policies, although many within the indigenous movement want to see more resources and powers available to CODENPE so that it can undertake more productive development projects for indigenous peoples.

CONAIE's domination of CODENPE (its director comes from CONAIE) and its new representation scheme has generated further disunity within the movement. The decree establishing CODENPE stipulates that Indians are represented through a representative of each of 11 specified 'nationalities', 12 specified 'peoples', in addition to two representatives of Amazonian Quichuas and a representative for the Manta and Huancavilca 'peoples' (Executive Decree 386 of December 1998, Art. 2). The semantic distinction between 'peoples' and 'nationalities' enables the Quichua nationality, by far the most numerous, to be divided into 12 distinct 'peoples', a strategy sierra leaders employed to balance the representation by nationalities favoured by Amazonian organisations.[31] There is no problem with this model in the Amazon, where identities and political boundaries are clear and organisations based upon them long established. But in the central sierra identities and political boundaries are less clear and co-extensive. There, CONAIE is promoting a process of recuperation and construction of identities, authorities, and cultural practices that is resisted by groups that do not fit the official scheme. Much of this population is already organised into multi-ethnic campesino or evangelical organisations, which are marginalised by the mono-ethnic model, and there are discrepancies in some areas over the nature of local identity and the geographic boundaries associated with it. CODENPE's model privileges certain identities while discriminating against others that may be equally valid. Observers within and outside the movement consider CONAIE's emphasis on asserting the most 'pure' identities to be dangerous, since it seems to suggest a primordialist or essentialist view of indigenous identity while denigrating 'non-pure' identities that may be more meaningful for those who hold them. Tempelman notes that this type of 'strategic primordialism' is a tactic of groups that feel discriminated against in their struggle for status as a 'cognisable and politically relevant group by others', a tactic that often leads to pressure on group members to conform for the sake of larger group goals (Tempelman 1999: 25). CONAIE's project has already generated tensions between newly constituted indigenous 'peoples' and their neighbours, who do not see how they will fit in the new scheme of indigenous territorial circumscriptions. Because CONAIE's plan for implementing collective constitutional rights is based on this represen-tational model, the organisation is pushing to impose it quickly, rushing a process that should, ideally, take a generation. The struggle over representa-tion among CONAIE, FENOCIN and FEINE is exacerbated by a battle over management of $50 million in development funds for indigenous and afro-Ecuadorian communities promised by the IDB and World Bank (*El Universal*, 22 June 1998).[32]

Disunity within the indigenous movement extends to its electoral arm, the MUPP, which experienced an 'internal decomposition' in 1999, detonated by the acceptance by Pacari of the second vice-presidency of the National Congress which implied to many within the party an alliance with the neoliberal governing coalition. Major differences among the MUPP's diverse components and internal disputes regarding its identity and mission persist and make it difficult to articulate short or long-term goals, or to expand upon its limited territorial base (Barrera and Unda 1999: 7).[33] Nevertheless, the severe erosion of popular support for and fragmentation within the traditional parties enabled the MUPP and other social movement-based parties to make unprecedented advances in the 21 May 2000 elections. The MUPP won more prefectures (five of 22, including Ecuador's first indigenous prefect) and *juntas parroquiales* (more than 60 per cent of the total) than any other political party in the country, as well as 27 mayorships.[34] The MUPP's greatest strength occurred in the Sierra and Oriente provinces that had been most supportive of January's indigenous uprising.

Internal disputes are reflected in the multiplicity of legislative proposals for implementing the constitutional right to autonomy. CODENPE's 11 January 1999 draft contemplates indigenous territorial circumscriptions at all levels of sub-national government (province, canton and *parroquias*) as a characteristic that applies to these levels, rather than a distinct level with distinct functions. Based on CODENPE's draft, Nina Pacari's congressional office prepared a draft Ley Orgánica de las Nacionalidades, Pueblos y Circunscripciones de las Indígenas that is currently being vetted by indigenous organisations. An important component of the law is the distribution of state resources to *parroquias* – the lowest level in the hierarchy – that currently do not directly receive resources, since many circumscriptions are likely to be drawn at this level. If MUPP militants can agree on a consensus proposal they should be very influential in passing it, since they currently control 50 per cent of *juntas parroquiales*. They also contemplate allowing the recognition of cantons or *parroquias* composed of discontinuous indigenous territories that have been broken up by colonisation and non-indigenous settlement. They are also working on a separate legislative project to implement the constitutional right to exercise customary law. In July 1999, Pacari's legislative aide estimated that it would take approximately two years to complete diagnostic studies of existing territories and legal practices, to fully vet the new laws among indigenous organisations, and to pass them in congress, with full implementation to be completed within five years following passage.[35] Nevertheless, Pacari presented a proposed Ley de Nacionalidades y Pueblos Indígenas immediately following the brief CONAIE-military coup that rocked Ecuador on 21 January 2000, perhaps in an attempt to take advantage of the political chaos and media attention generated by the startling event.[36] No progress has been made on this law as the country deals with more urgent matters.

MUPP deputy Valerio Grefa, president of the Congressional Commission on Indigenous Affairs, developed a separate statutory project, a reform of the 1937 Ley de Comunas, which legally recognised indigenous communities.[37] Because 60 per cent of the country's *comunas* are indigenous, Grefa adapted the law to the constitution's new collective rights regime, although it is intended to apply to all communities more generally. Grefa says that the Ley de Comunas must be reformed prior to establishing the territorial circumscriptions, but it is unclear how the two projects are related. Frictions within the MUPP congressional delegation on legislation can be expected since MUPP deputies do not work together, particularly with Grefa, who is out of favour with the national leadership for having accepted a position in the Bucaram government. Pacari presented to Congress her own proposed re-write of the Ley de Comunas together with the Ley de Nacionalidades mentioned above. Meanwhile, FENOCIN is working on its own draft law implementing the indigenous and black territorial circumscriptions and its own diagnostic of customary law practices. The organisation envisions creating electoral circumscriptions in multi-ethnic sierra communities. Even though FENOCIN is attempting to include afro-Ecuadorian rights in its proposal (the 'N' in FENOCIN stands for 'Negros'), the newly constituted afro-Ecuadorian organisation Confederación Nacional Afroecuatoriana (COADE) is drafting its own proposal modelled after

Colombian statutory legislation (Law 70 of 1993) implementing afro-Colombian constitutional rights.[38]

Fourth, as in Bolivia, and in contrast to Colombia, judicial institutions have been slow to act with respect to implementation of indigenous collective rights. The Ombudsman's office established prior to constitutional reform, one of CONAIE's achievements following the 1997 mobilisation to oust Bucaram, has launched no initiatives in this area, and the courts considered no cases involving indigenous constitutional rights during the constitution's first year in force. However, this changed on 24 August 1999, when the Civil Judge of the city of Macas ruled that the ARCO Petroleum Company could not approach any Shuar individual or organisation without authorisation from the Shuar Federation. This effectively confirmed the Federation's claim to collective rights under Article 46 of the constitution and Article 95 of ILO Convention 169, which has constitutional rank (*Amazon Update* No. 51, 15 October 1999).

It is unlikely that progress on implementing the new constitution will be made until the economic and political crises that grip the country are at least partially resolved and a consensus is formed within the indigenous movement on the issue of autonomy. The current conjuncture may provide an opportunity for indigenous organisations to express a coherent, consensus vision of autonomy and negotiate with the government, since the government is weak and needs political allies. In so doing, CONAIE must overcome a decline in public support, as well as a loss of international resources and prestige, generated by its role in the undemocratic seizure of power on 21 January 2000.

Conclusions

In the three countries considered indigenous organisations proposed the constitutional recognition of autonomy regimes in which their own authorities would exercise the maximum possible amount of autonomous functions within their territorial jurisdiction. The regimes obtained in the three constitutional reforms, however, are quite different:

In Colombia autonomy corresponds to a single level of the existing territorial-administrative scheme (the municipality), a level at which administrative and political autonomy and access to resources exists.

In Bolivia recognition is located at a level that lacks access to resources and autonomous powers, apart from the exercise of indigenous customary law.

In Ecuador the potential for autonomy is great but it is unclear at what level autonomy will be located and what functions indigenous territorial units will have.

The variation among the regimes is attributable to a number of factors, including the relative strength of indigenous peoples' organisations and their advocates during the constitutional conjuncture, their capacity to enlist powerful allies and convert their public support and the perceived legitimacy of indigenous rights claims into political leverage, and their ability to link their goals with those of elites seeking to resolve crises of representation, legitimacy and governability. In Colombia and Ecuador, indigenous Constituent Assembly delegates allied with centre-left blocs of sufficient size and unity to insist upon recognition of indigenous territorial rights. In Bolivia, indigenous organisations had no formal representatives in a process dominated by a president with no need to negotiate with any group opposing his vision.

In all three cases indigenous organisations tried to exploit elite desires to decentralise administrative and political power. In Colombia, a coalition of coastal Liberal Party delegates, the ADM-19 bloc, and indigenous delegates designed a coherent scheme of departmental and municipal decentralisation into which they inserted a relatively homogeneous indigenous territorial scheme. In Bolivia, President Sánchez de Lozada overrode the department-based decentralisation scheme preferred by regional elites and imposed a far-reaching scheme of municipal decentralisation to which the weaker indigenous movement's self-government aspirations were subordinated. A key factor here must be the far more radical implications of recognising explicitly 'ethnic' units of government in a country with a majority indigenous population, as opposed to a country such as Colombia where the indigenous population is minuscule (albeit associated with 25 per cent of the national territory). Nevertheless, the size of the indigenous population in Bolivia provides an opportunity for Indians to fulfil their autonomy aspirations through electoral victories at the local level if they can overcome the extreme imbalance in organisational and financial resources relative to those of local elites. In Ecuador, intense regionalism inhibits both the creation of a national consensus on decentralisation and the imposition of a dominant elite vision in which the fractious indigenous movement could insert a coherent vision of territorial autonomy.

Despite the importance of the proportional size of the indigenous population to the practical implications of incorporating ethnic political autonomy in each case, in general it is difficult to discern any systematic way in which the proportional size of the indigenous population influenced the scope of ethnic autonomy rights recognised and their successful implementation. Whereas the most minuscule population achieved perhaps the most secure and coherent recognition of autonomy rights, their territories extend throughout more than one-quarter of Colombia and the full implementation of their territorial rights has been blocked by regional elites. Interviews with participants in those reforms reveal that many delegates voting in favour of indigenous rights were unfamiliar with their territorial implications and felt pressured by the impending closure of the Constituent Assembly to gain the signatures of the indigenous delegates on the constitution (Van Cott 2000b: Ch. 4). Securing territorial autonomy rights was extremely difficult and controversial in all three cases: the relative success of the Colombian and Ecuadorian delegations is attributable, in my estimation, to the factors enumerated above, rather than to the size of the populations they represented.

In all three cases, the most difficult constitutional rights to implement have been those concerning the exploitation of natural resources on indigenous lands, particularly sub-soil resources such as oil, which in all cases belong to the state. Apart from constitutional provisions in some cases requiring consultations with indigenous authorities in decisions concerning this exploitation and its impact on indigenous populations, all three countries are signatories of ILO Convention 169, which requires that state policies affecting indigenous peoples be devised through a process of consultation and participation. In no case has 'consultation' and 'participation' been defined in a way that gives indigenous authorities the power to veto or control natural resource exploitation. Even Colombia's Constitutional Court – by far the most important ally of indigenous constitutional rights in any of the cases – had its ruling in favour of the U'wa, who are fighting a government concession to a foreign oil company to explore in its territories, overturned by the Council of State. The future development of this right to consultation and participation concerning resource exploitation in indigenous territorial spaces is crucial to the practical and symbolic meaning of political autonomy and indigenous citizenship in the Andes. The state's continued denial and erosion of this right is a clear and highly public challenge to indigenous authorities, while failure to share with indigenous communities the economic benefits of this exploitation deprives them of resources for establishing economic independence as a foundation for political autonomy.

Notes

1. McAdam, McCarthy and Zald define framing as 'the conscious strategic efforts by groups of people to fashion shared understandings of the world and of themselves that legitimate and motivate collective action' (1996: 6).
2. On indigenous rights in Peru's 1993 constitution, see Fernandez Segado (1994) and Aroca, Ardito and Maury (1993). A more comprehensive table of indigenous rights in Latin American constitutions may be found at: http://web.utk.edu/~dvancott
3. All demobilising armed groups were allowed representation in the Constituent Assembly as a condition for demobilisation, although some only received 'voice' and no vote. An indigenous armed group, the Quintin Lame, received such representation.
4. Interviews conducted in Bogotá: Luis José Azcárate, 22 January 1997; Manuel José Cepeda, 28 January 1997; Humberto de la Calle, 20 February 1997; Lorenzo Muelas, 4 March 1997; Francisco Rojas Birry, 24 February 1997.
5. On the history of Colombian indigenous law and indigenist institutions see Correa (1992).

6. Interview, Manuel José Cepeda, 30 April 1999.
7. Interviews in Bogotá: Luis José Azcárate, 22 January 1997; Manuel José Cepeda, 28 January 1997; Lorenzo Muelas, 4 March 1997; Hector Riveros, 27 January 1997; in Washington: César Gaviria, December 1996.
8. Interviews in Washington: Arturo Valenzuela, 15 October 1996; in La Paz: Juan Cristóbal Urioste, 25 April 1997, 2 May 1997.
9. Interviews in La Paz: Iván Arias, 3 June 1997; Gustavo Fernández, 9 June 1997; Juan Cristóbal Urioste, 2 May 1997.
10. This was also the case in Colombia. However, a well-organised student movement was able to launch a petition drive for the convocation of a constituent assembly that enabled Presidents Barco and Gaviria to argue successfully before the Supreme Court that the people themselves had convoked an assembly.
11. Interviews in La Paz: Fernando Aguirre, 8 May 1997; Gustavo Fernández, 9 June 1997; Juan Cristóbal Urioste, 25 April 1997, 2 May 1997; Miguel Urioste, 11 July 1997.
12. Interviews in La Paz: Rubén Ardaya, 12 May 1997; Luz María Calvo, 9 May 1997; Carlos Camargo, 16 June 1997; Marcial Fabricano, July 1997; Ramiro Molina, 28 April 1997; Alcides Vadillo, 20 May 1997.
13. We can include here MBL leader Miguel Urioste, Sánchez de Lozada's constitutional reform advisor Juan Cristóbal Urioste, as well as Cárdenas and anthropologists in the Sub-Secretariat of Ethnic Affairs.
14. Interview, La Paz, Marcial Fabricano, July 1997.
15. Interviews with staff of National Popular Participation Secretariat, June 1997.
16. Interview, Ricardo Calla, La Paz, 16 December 1998; Diego Iturralde, La Paz, 18 December 1998.
17. Information about the ethnic composition of municipal officials elected in 2000 has not yet been compiled.
18. Interviews in La Paz: Xavier Albó, 28 May 1997; Iván Arias, 3 June 1997; Wigberto Rivero, 5 May 1997.
19. Interviews in Quito: Jorge León, 17 July 1999; Luis Verdesoto, 3 August 1999.
20. Since the transition to democracy in 1979, the number of parties in congress has fluctuated between 10 and 14, with no force capable of aggregating more than 30 per cent of the vote, making Ecuador, together with Bolivia, among the most fragmented party systems in the region (Mainwaring and Scully 1995: 30).
21. Personal communication, José Antonio Lucero, 4 February 2000.
22. Interview, Luis Verdesoto, Quito, 3 August 1999.
23. Interviews in Quito: María Fernanda Espinosa, 19 July 1999; Osvaldo Hurtado, 2 August 1999; Jorge León, 17 July 1999; Luis Verdesoto, 3 August 1999.
24. Interviews in Quito: Ampam Karakras, 23 July 1999; Jorge León, 17 July 1999; Luis Verdesoto, 3 August 1999. Bolivian ex-vice president Víctor Hugo Cárdenas participated in several sessions with Assembly delegates and presided over the Inter-American Development Bank-sponsored forum on indigenous rights.
25. Interviews in Quito, Jorge León, 17 July 1999; Jonas Frank, 27 July 1999; Luis Verdesoto, 3 August 1999.
26. The major sticking points were the rights of public sector workers and the privatisation of 'strategic' industries. 'La incertidumbre *ronda* a la reforma económica', *Boletín de la reforma constitucional*, 6 (13 March 1998): 1, 7.
27. Since 1997 municipalities have been entitled to 10 per cent of national income, which creates incentives for their creation (Carrión and Chiriboga 1997: 230). Interview, Jonas Frank, 27 July 1997; 'Nicanor Merchán: Consejos Provinciales

deben cambiar o desaparecer', *Boletín de la reforma constitucional,* 2 (30 January 1998): 7.
28. CONAIE's *consulta* addressed questions including dollarisation, amnesty for participants in the January coup attempt, and the dissolution of congress. Internet communications from Robert Andolina, 15 and 17 April 2000.
29. Interviews in Quito: María Fernanda Espinosa, 19 July 1999; Jorge León, 17 July 1999.
30. Interview, Floresmilo Simbañi, Quito, July 1999.
31. Oral presentation by José Antonio Lucero, Quito, 22 July 1999.
32. Interviews in Quito: Juan Aulestia, 28 July 1999; Pedro de la Cruz, 21 July 1999; María Fernanda Espinosa, 19 July 1999; Ampam Karakras, 23 July 1999; Miguel Lluco, 2 August 1999; Luis Macas, 28 July 1999; Paulina Palacios, 19 July 1999; Floresmilo Simbañi, July 1999; oral presentation by José Antonio Lucero, Quito, 22 July 1999.
33. Interviews in Quito: Miguel Lluco, 2 August 1999; Luis Macas, 28 July 1999; Floresmilo Simbañi, July 1999.
34. Boletín ICCI no. 15, Rimay Instituto Cientifico de Culturas Indígenas, junio 2000, via internet, available at http:.//icci.nativeweb.org.
35. Interviews in Quito: Bolivar Beltrán, 19 July 1999; Julio César Trujillo, 22 July 1999. CONAIE leaders are observing the experience of the municipalities in the highlands with majority indigenous populations and indigenous mayors, which are experimenting with more participatory democratic practices purportedly derived from ancestral forms of democracy. Interview, Juan Aulestia, 28 July 1999. 'Desafíos de los municipios inovadores', *Pachakutik: Revista de debate político* 1 (julio de 1999): 66.
36. Internet communication from Pablo Davalos, via Marc Becker, received 3 February 2000.
37. See Becker (1999: 535–44) for a discussion of this law.
38. Interviews in Quito: Pedro de la Cruz, 21 July 1999; Pablo de la Torre, 28 July 1999; Valerio Grefa, 27 July 1999; Internet communication from Pablo Davalos, via Marc Becker, received on 3 February 2000. I have been unable to determine how Pacari's proposed Ley de Comunas is related to Grefa's proposal.

References

Acosta, Alberto (1999), 'Ecuador: otro coletazo del ajuste neoliberal', *Pachakutik: Revista de debate político* 1 (July), pp.8–12.
Albó, Xavier (1997), 'Alcaldes y concejales campesinos/indígenas: La lógica tras las cifras' *Indígenas en el poder local,* 7–26, Ministerio de Desarrollo Humano, SNPP (La Paz).
Amazon Update No. 51, 15 October 1999.
Andolina, Robert (1998), 'CONAIE (and others) in the Ambiguous Spaces of Democracy: Positioning for the 1997–8 Asamblea Nacional Constituyente in Ecuador', paper prepared for delivery at the 1998 meeting of the Latin American Studies Association, Chicago, Illinois, 24–26 September 1998.
Anonymous (1999), 'The Americas: Under the Volcano', *The Economist* (27 November), p.32.
Aranibar, Antonio (1998), 'Evaluación de la Asamblea hasta el 17 de abril', *Boletín de la reforma constitucional* 10 (April), p.1.

Archondo, Rafael (1997), *Tres años de participación popular: Memoria de un proceso*, Ministerio de Desarrollo Humano (La Paz).

Aroca, Javier, Wilfredo Ardito, and Luis Maury (1993), *Nueva Constitución. El Problema de la Tierra*, Centro Amazónico de Antropología y Aplicación Práctica (Lima).

Assies, Willem (2000), 'El Constitucionalismo multiétnico en América Latina: El Caso de Bolivia', paper prepared for delivery at the XII Congreso Internacional 'Derecho Consuetudinario y Pluralismo Legal: Desafíos en el Tercer Milenio', Arica, Chile. 13–17 March 2000.

Barrera, Augusto y Mario Unda (1999), 'Elementos para discutir la situación actual del MUPP–NP', *Pachakutik: Revista de debate político* 1 (julio), pp.3–7.

Beck, Scott H. and Kenneth J. Mijeski (2000), 'The Electoral Performance of Ecuador's Pachakutik Political Movement, 1996–1998', unpublished manuscript.

Becker, Marc (1999), 'Comunas and Indigenous Protest in Cayambe, Ecuador', *The Americas* 55 (4) (April), pp.531–59.

Booth, David, Suzanne Clisby, and Charlotta Widmark (1996), 'Empowering the Poor through Institutional Reform? An Initial Appraisal of the Bolivian Experience', Working Paper No. 32. Development Studies Unit, Department of Social Anthropology, Stockholm University.

Borja Cornejo, Diego (1999), 'La economía sin rumbo', *Iconos* 7 (April), pp.18–26.

Buenahora Febres-Cordero, Jaime (1995), *La Democracia en Colombia. Un proyecto en construcción*, Controlaria General de la República (Bogotá).

Calla, Ricardo (1992), 'Introducción al tema', in Carlos Toranzo (comp.), *Diversidad étnica y cultural*, ILDIS (La Paz).

Carrión, Fernando and Galo Chiriboga (1997), 'Descentralización y participación social', in *Los Grandes temas de la reforma constitucional. 1 Colección Reforma Política*. Programa de Apoyo al sistema de Gobernabilidad/IDB/Gobierno del Ecuador (Quito).

Cepeda, Manuel José (1995), 'Democracy, State and Society in the Colombian Constitution: The Role of the Constitutional Court', unpublished manuscript.

CONAIE (1997), 'Planteamiento de Reformas Constitucionales', Comisión de Reformas Constitucionales para la Asamblea Nacional Constituyente (Quito).

—— (1998), *Proyecto de Constitución del Estado Plurinacional del Ecuador*, CONAIE (Quito).

Correa Rubio, Francois (1992), 'El Indígena ante el Estado Colombiano', in Esther Sánchez Botero (ed.), *Antropología Jurídica. Normas formales – costumbres legales*, Sociedad Antropológica de Colombia, Comité Internacional para el Desarrollo de los Pueblos (Bogotá).

Deruyterre, Anne (1997), *Indigenous Peoples and Sustainable Development: The Role of the Inter-American Development Bank*, Inter-American Development Bank (Washington DC).

Dugas, John C. (1997), 'Explaining Democratic Reform in Colombia: The Origins of the 1991 Constitution', unpublished PhD dissertation, Indiana University.

—— (comp.) (1993), *La Constitución de 1991: Un Pacto Político Viable?* Universidad de los Andes (Bogotá).

Edwards, Sian (1999) 'Reconstructing the Nation: The Process of Establishing Catalan Autonomy', *Parliamentary Affairs* (October), web version.

Fernandez Segado, Francisco (1994), 'El nuevo ordenamiento constitucional del Perú: aproximación a la constitución de 1993', *Revista de Estudios Políticos*, Vol. 84, pp.27–67.

Hurtado, Osvaldo (1998), *Una Constitución para el Futuro*, Fundación ecuatoriana de estudios sociales (Quito).

Iturralde Guerrero, Diego A. (1997), 'Comentario de Diego Iturralde' in Magdalena Gómez (coord.) *Derecho Indígena*, La Jornada/UNAM (Mexico).

McAdam, Doug, John D. McCarthy and Mayer N. Zald (eds) (1996), *Comparative Perspectives on Social Movements: Political Opportunities, Mobilizing Structures, and Cultural Framings*, Cambridge University Press (New York).

Mainwaring, Scott and Timothy Scully (eds) (1995), *Building Democratic Institutions: Party Systems in Latin America*, Stanford University Press (Stanford).

Muñoz, Jorge A. and Isabel Lavadenz (1997), 'Reforming the Agrarian Reform in Bolivia', paper prepared for the Harvard Institute for International Development seminar on the Bolivian reforms, Cambridge, Mass., 30 April.

Nielsen, Anna and Par Zetterberg (1999), *The Significance of Political Parties for Civil Society: How the Creation of Pachakutik has Influenced CONAIE's Struggle in Ecuadorian National Politics*, Uppsala University (Uppsala).

Paz Patiño, Sarela (1998), 'Los territorios indígenas como reivindicación y práctica discursiva', *Nueva Sociedad*, Vol. 153, pp.120–9.

PRODEPINE (1998), *Censo Nacional de organizaciones indígenas negras e indice de fortalecimiento institucional*, PRODEPINE (Quito).

Programa de Apoyo al Sistema de Gobernabilidad (1997), *Los Grandes temas de la reforma constitucional. 1 Colección Reforma Política*, Banco Interamericano de Desarrollo, Gobierno del Ecuador (Quito).

—— (1998), *Recapitulando la Reforma Política. Informe del estado de ejecución del Programa de Apoyo al Sistema de Gobernabilidad Democrático*, Banco Interamericano de Desarrollo, Gobierno del Ecuador (Quito).

Rojas Birry, Francisco (1991), 'Los Derechos de los Grupos Etnicos', *Gaceta Constitucional* No.67, 4 May, pp.14–21.

Roldán, Roque (1997), 'El régimen constitucional indígena en Colombia: Fundamentos y Perspectivas', in Magdalena Gómez (coord.), *Derecho Indígena*, Instituto Nacional Indigenista (Mexico), pp.233–51.

Roldán, Roque (1998), 'Los convenios de la OIT y los derechos territoriales indígenas, en las políticas de gobierno y en la administración de justicia en Colombia', in *Seminario Internacional de Administración de Justicia y Pueblos Indígenas*, República de Bolivia (La Paz).

Sánchez, Enrique, Roque Roldán and María Fernanda Sánchez (1993), *Derechos e Identidad. Los Pueblos Indígenas y Negros en la Constitución Política de Colombia de 1991*, Disloque Editores (Bogotá).

Tarrow, Sidney (1996), 'States and Opportunities: The Political Structuring of Social Movements' in Doug McAdam, John D. McCarthy and Mayer N. Zald (eds), *Comparative Perspectives on Social Movements: Political Opportunities, Mobilizing Structures, and Cultural Framings*, Cambridge University Press (New York).

Tempelman, Sasja (1999), 'Constructions of Cultural Identity: Multiculturalism and Exclusion', *Political Studies* XLVII, pp.17–31.

Unda, Mario (1999), 'En primer plano: la disputa alrededor del neoliberalism', *Pachakutik: Revista de debate político* 1 (July), pp.41–4.

Van Cott, Donna Lee (2000a), 'A Political Analysis of Legal Pluralism', *Journal of Latin American Studies* 32, I (February), pp.207–34.

—— (2000b), *The Friendly Liquidation of the Past: The Politics of Diversity in Latin America*, University of Pittsburgh Press (Pittsburgh).

Verdesoto Custode, Luis (1998), 'Apuntes sobre la negociación de los pueblos indígenas y negros', prepared for CONAIE (Quito).

WOLA (1997), *Losing Ground: Human Rights Advocates Under Attack in Colombia*, Washington Office on Latin America (Washington).

3
Bolivia: From Indian and Campesino Leaders to Councillors and Parliamentary Deputies

Xavier Albó

In 1994 a package of measures aimed at modernising the state was approved in Bolivia. These reforms, in turn, affected the traditional functions and role of indigenous campesino organisations. An examination of the Bolivian experience allows us to analyse the extent to which the rhetoric of multi-culturalism and multi-ethnicity on the part of popular organisations is able to adapt to a new scenario. The policy shift which began in 1994 and its impact on the indigenous campesino movement is analysed here from two opposite poles: the new local municipal governments and the legal restructuring which took place at national level. The first section briefly maps out the historical context leading up to 1994, followed by an analysis of the principal changes that were introduced thereafter. The second half of the chapter examines the reactions and adjustments made by the indigenous campesino sector in response to the new municipal context and the role of popular struggle and of indigenous campesino parliamentarians in drafting new laws.

A preliminary word is required on the terminology employed here: in theoretical terms a clear distinction exists between the terms 'campesino' and 'indigenous'. However, in Bolivia both terms are equally applicable in the countryside – the overwhelming majority of the rural population is indigenous, in terms of its identity and ethnic and cultural origins, and at the same time campesino, because of its means of subsistence or social class. In addition, following the 1952 Revolution both public and popular discourses were permeated by a pseudo-modernising tendency which restricted the use of the term 'indigenous' to describe only the most isolated groups, in particular ethnic minorities in the lowlands. The rest of the indigenous population was referred to only as 'campesino'. However, with the resurgence of ethnic pluralism and legislation more favourable to indigenous people throughout the world, this trend is currently in decline. Nonetheless, in order to underscore the overlapping of both identities within a large part of the rural Bolivian population, the sole term 'indigenous campesinos' is employed here.

Historical context[1]

With the advent of the 1952 Revolution and the agrarian reform implemented by the first Movimiento Nacional Revolucionario (MNR) administrations (Víctor Paz Estenssoro 1952–56 and 1960–64; Hernán Siles 1956–60), those people who had previously been 'Indians' began to call themselves 'campesinos' and formed a unitary and national 'trade union' organisation called the Confederación Nacional de Trabajadores Campesinos de Bolivia (CNTCB). This was particularly strong amongst Quechuas (who constituted approximately 35 per cent of the national population) and Aymaras (approximately 25 per cent). The CNTCB was closely linked to the governing MNR and its leadership was controlled by Quechua campesinos from Cochabamba, who had been among the first to expel the former landowners and take over their haciendas, even before the Agrarian Reform Law was decreed in August 1953. Once the hacienda lands were recovered, these 'campesino unions' – although they kept the name and the class rhetoric of the powerful miners and workers' organisations (who had set up the Central Obrera Boliviana, COB) – functioned in practice as a modernised version of traditional communal organisations. Any adult *comunario*, including former workers on the expropriated haciendas, was automatically affiliated to the CNTCB merely because they enjoyed relatively stable access to land.

At the same time the MNR began its 'march towards the East', the vast and rich sub-tropical lowland region, up to this point disconnected from the rest of the country. The occupation of this new space took two forms: on the one hand, the agricultural frontier was opened up for colonisation as an escape valve for small-scale producers from the impoverished Andean region; on the other hand, capitalist agro-industrial enterprise expanded rapidly throughout the region, permitting a new Eastern agricultural bourgeoisie to take over huge extensions of the best land. This effectively nullified the Agrarian Reform Law in this highly desirable region by generating a highly unequal distribution of land and capital.

Following the overthrow of the MNR in a coup led by General Barrientos in 1964, the link between the CNTCB and the new military regime (1964–69) became even closer through the so-called 'military campesino pact'. This was particularly effective in the Quechua valleys of Cochabamba from where

General Barrientos – self-styled 'maximum leader of the campesinos' – hailed. However, the honeymoon between the armed forces and campesinos ended in 1969 when Barrientos died in a helicopter-crash in one of his frequent visits to the countryside. The relationship between the two groups worsened under subsequent military regimes, especially after 1974 when the armed forces carried out a massacre under the regime of General Banzer (1971–78) to repress protesting Quechua campesinos from Cochabamba. As one campesino leader commented, a pact imposed through the barrel of a gun had little legitimacy. However, the military–campesino pact finally broke down in 1978 because of the emergence of a new protagonist.

After 1970, the Katarista movement developed among Aymaras in La Paz and Oruro and, without rejecting the 'trade unionist' ticket of the 1950s, put ethnic demands at the top of the agenda.[2] This was signalled not only by the movement's name, inspired by Tupaj Katari, the hero of the 1781 anti-colonialist movement, but also expressed in many other symbols and demands, such as the use of its own flag – the Aymara *wiphala* – and the great importance afforded to Aymara language and culture in popular radio programmes and in educational demands. By 1971 the Kataristas had gained control of the CNTCB leadership, but they were almost immediately forced to go underground when Colonel Banzer took power. Nonetheless, they reappeared, albeit clandestinely, after the Valle Massacre (having reached more radical conclusions about the government's intentions than the Quechuas from Cochabamba who had been the direct targets of government repression).

Towards the end of 1977 Katarismo went public under the banner of ending the military–campesino pact and grew in strength throughout the entire Andean region. In 1978 Banzer called elections but was overthrown by his protégé and former Interior Minister, beginning a confusing period of elections, coups and counter-coups which gave way to the first period of democratic government (Hernán Siles, of the Unión Democrática y Popular, UDP, 1982–85), in itself equally confusing because of parliamentary opposition to the regime, the continued adherence of the COB to a radical socialist platform, and – above all – an acute economic crisis, inflation having risen so fast since the end of the 1970s that elections were eventually brought forward by a year. The next democratic government was led by the veteran politician Víctor Paz Estenssoro (1985–89) and his 'new' MNR. With the assessment of 'Harvard boy' Jeffrey Sachs, the administration stabilised the devalued currency and opened the country up to transnational capital at the cost of dismantling state enterprises, sacking thousands of workers and liberalising labour laws. Together these measures produced the shock that initiated the current neoliberal model, already in place in other Latin American countries, more acceptable at this point in Bolivia because of the accumulated frustrations and disappointments of the preceding years. This model has continued in some shape or form until the present.

During this period (1978–85), the Kataristas, together with the entire Andean indigenous campesino movement, achieved their objective of ending the military–campesino pact. The Kataristas remained at the head of the national organisation, the Confederación Sindical Unica de Trabajadores Campesinos de Bolivia (CSUTCB), a restructured version of the CNTCB which was much more autonomous than its predecessor. The CSUTCB joined the COB and a number of its tendencies created the first indigenous or Indianist political parties which put several indigenous deputies in parliament. Above all the Kataristas promoted a number of activities which ranged from the occupation of various state development institutions, timed to coincide with national protests blocking the roads, to the elaboration – with intense grass-roots participation – of an innovative proposal for a Fundamental Agrarian Reform (which was ultimately never considered by parliament). In the process the entire movement, with its different tendencies and expressions, generated a new awareness of the multi-ethnic nature of the country and of the need to overcome neo-colonial structures, developed new concepts and approaches – such as viewing problems from the dual perspective of an exploited campesino class and oppressed native indigenous peoples, and advanced a new utopian project of a 'multinational state'. This was the golden age of the indigenous campesino Andean movement.

In 1982 the Confederación Indígena del Oriente Boliviano (CIDOB) was formed and began to bring together the numerous minority indigenous groups in the tropical lowlands (who comprised 2 per cent of the national population). In 1987 the Asamblea del Pueblo Guaraní (APG) was set up and quickly affiliated to CIDOB. In 1990 an historic 'march for territory and dignity' took place with the participation of various indigenous groups who walked for 70 days from the lowland jungle regions to a warm encounter with their Aymara counterparts in the Andean mountains, full of rich symbolic ritual exchanges. The march then advanced to La Paz and extracted the first official recognition of indigenous territories from the then government of Jaime Paz (a coalition of the Movimiento de Izquierda Revolucionaria, MIR, and the Acción Democrática Nacionalista, ADN, 1989–93; Contreras 1991). A short while afterwards Bolivia became one the of the first Latin American countries to ratify ILO Convention 169 on Indigenous and Tribal Peoples in Independent Countries.

The exchanges between eastern 'indigenous' and Andean 'campesinos' also generated an intense theoretical discussion about their common identity. This challenged the framework in place since 1952 and resulted in the recognition of both groups as part of *originario* peoples or 'nations' of the country, thereby adopting a concept similar to that of 'first nations' used by North American indigenous groups or that of *adivasi* used by indigenous peoples in India.

The lowland indigenous movement continued to grow in subsequent years. By contrast, the Andean indigenous movement, born almost a decade earlier, began to run out of steam during the first democratic government. The economic collapse meant that indigenous mobilisations only secured worthless paper guarantees, which were never implemented in practice and, as a consequence, interest in mass mobilisations waned. The movement later experienced difficulties in adapting to the new political and economic scenario in place since 1985 – reformulated in 1994 – which demanded proposals and negotiation rather than oppositional tactics.

This brief overview would not be complete without some mention of the expansion of the alternative and complementary economy of coca-cocaine in the lowlands. This took off in the 1970s, when influential military officers and businessmen began to divert economic resources intended for agricultural development in the Eastern lowlands towards this much more lucrative enterprise. Their indispensable counterpart was household production of coca leaf, a hitherto innocuous shrub that had been a central part of Andean peoples' diet, medicine and ritual life since time immemorial. With the expansion of the market for cocaine in the USA and other first-world countries and the acute economic crisis affecting the rural and urban working class, the coca-cocaine economy grew rapidly. In order to cut their risks, the large drug-traffickers opted to maintain production of the raw material – coca leaf – in the hands of small producers, above all in the new areas of land colonisation. In this way coca production became one of the few viable economic options open to many Andean campesinos who had been forced to abandon their exhausted lands in the highlands. These campesinos were subsequently trapped between a struggle for economic survival and being identified as 'the enemy' in the absurd 'war against drugs'. Within this context a powerful movement of campesino coca-producers emerged in the 1980s which, rather than representing narco-traffickers as its opponents alleged, in fact represented the proletarians of the cocaine economy (CEDIB 1993).

The shift of 1994

Within this context a new electoral campaign began, the favourite and eventual winner of which was the mining entrepreneur Gonzalo Sánchez de Lozada (1993–97), of the MNR. Sánchez de Lozada, who never lost his 'gringo' accent, consequence of many years spent in the USA, had been one of the principal proponents of the economic shift begun in 1985. Following a number of opinion polls, he surprised allies and opponents alike by selecting the Aymara activist Víctor Hugo Cárdenas as his vice-president. Cárdenas had been a Katarista leader since the 1970s and did not even belong to Sánchez de Lozada's party. The marked cultural, social and ideological differences between the two men created synergy instead of conflict, above all in the joint search for a new political and social order, expressed in a series of laws which aimed to humanise the neoliberal model without, however, questioning its basic precepts (Albó 1993).

These legal changes were not solely the idea of Sánchez de Lozada and Cárdenas, but rather part of a long and inconclusive process of state modernisation backed by international donor organisations and partially initiated under previous governments. Yet the laws passed between 1993 and 1997 were undoubtedly also moulded by their proponents. The least controversial aspect was the economic model, which remained unchallenged and was indeed consolidated through the process of 'capitalisation' (read privatisation) of state enterprises. However, in terms of social and political policies a significant package of legal and administrative changes was introduced, of which the following are of particular relevance to our discussion.[3]

In 1994 a series of constitutional reforms was approved, the culmination of a process begun under the previous administration. As occurred in other Latin American countries, a significant change, introduced in Article 1, was the recognition of the 'multi-ethnic and pluri-cultural' nature of the country. This was further strengthened in Article 171, which referred specifically to indigenous peoples, decreeing recognition of their 'communal lands of origin' (TCOs) (although falling short of referring to their 'territories'), together with their culture, languages, authorities, and customary law (*'usos y costumbres'*). The main drawback of the new Magna Carta is that it did not allow independent candidates to stand for elected office, its drafters having rejected breaking the monopoly of political parties on presenting candidates at municipal and national levels.

The Law of Popular Participation (LPP) was also passed in 1994. This represented the final stage in the reconstitution of the system of municipal governance and administration, above all in the rural areas, which had been practically ignored by the political parties up to this point. The law recognised traditional organisations in the countryside (unions, *ayllus, cabildos,* and so on) and the neighbourhood councils in the cities. These were all given the generic name 'territorial base organisation' (OTB). This served to consolidate a total of 311 municipalities, the majority of them rural, which were assigned new responsibilities and allocated resources from the national budget according to the size of their population. The municipal councils and mayors were to be elected every five years, and the OTB of each municipality was to name a 'vigilance committee' on an annual basis. This committee was to function as a bridge between the OTBs and the municipal authorities and also act as a check on the latter.

Shortly prior to this, also in 1994, a Law of Educational Reform was approved. Among many pedagogic and structural reforms this introduced two central elements: the generalisation of 'intercultural bilingual education' (with different pedagogic mechanisms for different languages, designed on a case by case basis), and a system whereby grass-roots organisations could participate in the design and execution of the educational reform and oversight of the educational system. This law was the precursor of the more global approach of the LPP.

In October 1996 a Law of the National Agrarian Reform Service, better known as the 'INRA Law' (because of its main Spanish acronym), was passed. This aimed both to stimulate capitalist agricultural production by halting speculative accumulation on idle lands (or at least ensuring that taxes were paid on them), and to guarantee indigenous properties, which were offered a new legal mechanism for collective title, the Tierra Comunitaria de Origen (TCO). For the first time indigenous lands were referred to as 'territories' including natural resources. The TCOs, together with other smallholdings, enjoyed a series of legal protections, such as tax exemptions and the right to indivisible and inalienable title, except in cases of 'works of public benefit'.

A few months previously a new Forestry Law had been passed, in line with the INRA Law, and at the start of 1997 a Mineral Code was approved which, apart from a single and largely rhetorical reference to ILO Convention 169, largely ignored the views of those indigenous campesinos potentially affected by it.

Other reforms were never completed. For example, a proposal for a Law of Community Justice was drawn up, to put into effect Article 171 of the constitution, which recognised *'usos y costumbres'* as an alternative source of law. However, this was never even presented to parliament.

In order to implement the new measures, the government set up the National Sub-Secretariat of Ethnic Affairs, which was promoted to the status of Vice-Ministry under the following administration. This began life simply as a regulatory body and aimed to guarantee a positive intercultural and inter-ethnic approach in all legislation. Over time it acquired executive responsibilities related to a range of activities and projects with indigenous peoples throughout the country, particularly those related to ethnic minorities in the tropical lowlands, which tended to attract more international support.

All these laws remain in force today without notable changes or amendments, although they have been applied differently in practice since the advent of the new government of General Banzer (now a democrat) in 1997. The following section focuses on the ways in which these new laws have affected the behaviour and evolution of the indigenous campesino movement, which had demonstrated such strength and dynamism in previous years.

New municipal power

Of all the laws mentioned above, it is undoubtedly the Law of Popular Participation that has had most impact on indigenous campesino organisations. This should perhaps better have been called the Law of Municipalisation – this would have reflected more accurately its content and subsequent implementation. Initially many urban and rural organisations were wary of the LPP and some even referred to it as one of the 'three damned laws' imposed by the World Bank.[4] There was particularly strong opposition in the countryside to the OTBs, due to fears that these would be a new organisation imposed by the state to replace those which already existed in each locality. A number of assurances had to be given, and the original text of the law was eventually modified to make it explicit that the law only intended to recognise already existing organisations. This was necessary in order to overcome deep-rooted suspicions on the part of indigenous campesino organisations that this was yet another attempt by government to trick and manipulate them. There were indeed a number of cases in which the local authorities tried, against the spirit of the law, to create more compliant parallel organisations through the figure of the OTB. Ultimately, however, as the first results of the LPP became evident, the indigenous campesino organisations gradually changed their attitude, to the extent that some leaders who had previously stridently opposed it began to call it 'the blessed law'.[5]

The factor which most influenced this change of attitude was the so-called 'co-participation funds', which represented approximately 20 per cent of the national budget, previously disbursed to departmental development corporations or other bodies. These funds were now divided up equally between all the municipalities according to the size of their population.[6] This meant that many rural municipalities that in the past had not had any of their own resources, effectively existing in name only, now became financially viable. Before the LPP was passed, 183 municipalities (59 per cent of the total) did not receive a single cent from central government; in 1995 they received nearly 160 million bolivianos, at a rate of just over 1000 bolivianos (about US$ 200) per inhabitant (Ramírez 1995).

The only official instrument that permitted an estimate of the size of each municipality's population was the 1992 national census. In that year many campesino organisations had opposed the census and had even instructed their members not to complete the forms, due to the ancestral fear that a registered increase in the population would result in higher taxes (as occurred with the colonial population registers). With the new law this time-honoured opposition back-fired, those municipalities which had under-registered their population receiving less co-participation funds.

These changes undoubtedly modified the pre-existing tendency for voter abstentionism to be much higher in municipal elections than in presidential elections. This had particularly been the case in the rural areas where the municipalities were concentrated in urban centres and meant little to many rural voters. Due to a series of other factors, abstention levels continue to be high,[7] particularly in the rural areas, but there is generally now much more interest on the part of community members in who their municipal authorities should be, and more active participation in putting forward candidates. In the 1993 municipal elections, prior to the Law of Popular Participation, rural abstentionism stood at 55 per cent, but two years later, in December 1995, this dropped to 40 per cent during the first municipal elections to take place under the new law (Rojas and Zuazo 1996: 22). The next section concentrates on candidates for municipal office of indigenous campesino origin and analyses how their participation in local government has affected traditional indigenous campesino organisation.[8]

Indigenous campesino candidates and councillors

In 1997 at least 464 indigenous and campesino authorities were elected to the new local municipal office for the first time ever.[9] This represented 29 per cent of the total number of councillors elected throughout the country, and in the department of Oruro, the heartland of the Aymara and Quechua altiplano, reached some 62 per cent of all councillors elected. These figures were still low if one takes into account that the rural population represented some 43 per cent of the national total and that 85 per cent of the municipalities were overwhelmingly rural, many of them even without an urban centre. Nonetheless, it was a marked change compared to previous experience.

A number of strategies were pursued to secure the election of indigenous campesinos to local office. The main political parties, whose organisational networks already extended throughout the whole country, tended to ignore this sector. On the whole they sought out reliable party candidates, most of whom were inhabitants of the main towns or even immigrants now resident in the cities, although some indigenous campesino militants were also named by their parties without any grass-roots participation in their selection. Other smaller parties whose apparatus was not as well distributed throughout the country adopted different tactics. In areas where they had militants and sympathisers they favoured them as candidates, but in many parts of the country they offered space on their party lists to local figures, who, by law, had to be presented as candidates by legally registered political parties. A third mechanism was even more important: in a number of areas it was the grass-roots indigenous and campesino organisations who decided in joint assemblies who they wanted to present as their candidates. In some cases, the person selected was already a militant or at least a sympathiser of a particular political party, which could accept them onto their list. But in other cases candidates chosen by the grass-roots organisations negotiated with various political parties to see which would offer them better terms. On the whole it was the smaller or medium sized parties which most easily accepted such arrangements.

Whichever one of the three mechanisms was utilised, negotiations subsequently took place to ensure that the candidates would appear high enough up on the party lists to give them a real chance of being elected. There was no shortage of complaints that the parties presented changes to their lists to the Electoral Court at the last minute in order to favour their members. But one way or another, some 500 indigenous campesinos became municipal councillors, and more than a quarter of these occupied the office of mayor, at least for a part of their term in office. So what happened to these indigenous campesino councillors?

According to our 1999 study (which did not include the Eastern region), 48 per cent of the indigenous campesinos who became councillors in 1995 were directly nominated by their party, and of these some 89 per cent had previously been active in a political party. But a significant 36 per cent were elected after being nominated by their grass-roots organisations, and of these 69 per cent were also party activists in the 1995 elections. We suspect that in many cases this was a case of an initial sympathy for a political party in 1995 and that only during the following four years did they become card-carrying party members, thanks to the closer contacts established throughout their term of office.

Often the leaders of the grass-roots organisations had initially argued that the only thing they were interested in was in having their own people in the municipal government, and that the link with one or other political party was of relatively minor concern because their candidates, together with the grass-roots organisations, would 'manipulate' the party for their own benefit. But four years on it seems that this has not been the case. For better or worse, the logic and interests of the political parties have generally been stronger than the solidarity between those elected and their indigenous campesino grass-roots supporters. Money and other material personal benefits provide some explanation for this phenomenon, particularly in the larger parties.

Table 3.1 summarises party membership for indigenous campesino councillors in 1995 and 1999, and ranks the parties by the number of indigenous campesino councillors they had according to our 1999 survey. The five parties which gained the highest percentage share of the national vote in the 1995 municipal elections (between 11 and 21 per cent) were those which also gained the highest number of indigenous campesino councillors and the highest rates of party membership among these councillors by the end of their term in office, together with the ten indigenous campesino councillors of the small Movimiento Revolucionario Tupaj Katari de Liberación party (MRTKL), allied with the MNR. The MIR, of whose few councillors in 1995 only 67 per cent were party members, had gained a rate of party membership of 89 per cent by 1999.

All of these parties are predominantly urban and, with one exception, selected many more councillors of urban than rural origin. This was particularly significant in the case of CONDEPA (Conciencia de Patria), a populist party with a discourse high in Aymara ethnic content, which – when push came to shove – sought the great majority of its candidates in the urban sector and only trusted indigenous campesino candidates when they were proven party members. The exception was Movimiento Bolivia Libre (MBL), a relatively small party which gained a high percentage of the vote in 1995 thanks to the fact that it was then part of the governing coalition (together with the MNR and the MRTKL) and in an alliance with the popular mayor of

Cochabamba, who shortly afterwards set up his own party, Nueva Fuerza Republicana (NFR), and allied himself to the ADN. However, this alliance had little effect in the countryside and it was there that the MBL gained a high number of indigenous campesino councillors, 90 in all, who also represented the majority of the MBL's councillors in national terms.[10] This was because in the 1995 elections the MBL had engaged in the aforementioned strategy of offering nominations and accepting indigenous campesino candidates more than other parties. But in the following years the MBL lost party members and was also the party with the highest number of councillors who switched allegiance to another party. In other words, for some councillors the MBL was effectively a trampoline to gain municipal power, but following election they acted according to their own devices, even rejecting the party which had afforded them the initial opportunity to reach office.

Table 3.1   Previous militancy, according to party list adopted (sample from Albó 1999, does not cover all municipalities)

Acronym	% of militants of total number of i-c councillors[a]			change of party (no.)	% of national vote[b]		
	(total no. i-c)[a]	1995	1999		M95	P97	M99
MBL	(90)	74.4	69.9	(9)	13[c]	3	5
MNR	(71)	87.5	90.7	(1)	21	18	22
UCS	(34)	96.2	88.9	(1)	17	16	13
CONDEPA	(24)	90.9	95.2	–	15	17	4
ADN	(23)	100.0	82.6	(1)	11	22[c]	16
IU (ASP)	(18)	54.5	63.6	(1)	3	4	5[d]
Eje Pachakuti	(14)	57.1	50.0	(2)	2	1	–
MIR	(13)	66.7	88.9	–	9	17	17
MRTKL	(10)	80.0	90.0	–	1	–	–
TOTAL	(267)	80.8	80.9	6.2			

a. Source: Albó 1999; only parties with ten or more indigenous campesino (i-c) councillors were included in this sample. Some 40 did not respond in 1995, 39 did not respond in 1999. The percentage is over the total number of councillors elected for each party, indicated in the second column.
b. Source: National Electoral Court. M = municipal elections; P = presidential elections.
c. In 1995 the MBL was allied with the NFR (who had an absolute majority in the city of Cochabamba), in 1997 it shifted allegiances to the ADN. In 1999, the NFR ran on a solo ticket and achieved 9% of the national vote.
d. Divided into two groups, which ran as the Movimiento Hacia el Socialismo (MAS), which gained 3.5% and the Partido Comunista de Bolivia (PCB), which gained 1.3%.

The new Quechua campesino party, the Asamblea Soberana del Pueblo (ASP), which fielded candidates almost exclusively in Cochabamba, deserves a special mention. It was founded the very same year and had close relations with local indigenous campesino organisations, strongly influenced by the problematic and leadership of the coca leaf producers in the tropical zone. Just one year earlier these organisations had been highly critical of the 'three damned laws', including the Law of Popular Participation. Yet they reacted quickly and decided that the best way of winning power in this new political context was to take part actively in elections. For this reason they decided to set up their own political vehicle, a theme which was already being discussed some two years earlier in the CSUTCB. In a few months they collected the requisite number of signatures and presented their application to the Electoral Court. However, the Court rejected their application because many of the signatures were not backed up by an identity card as required by law. The ASP persisted and formed an alliance with the Izquierda Unida (IU), a left-wing socialist party which had lost nearly all its support and which provided the ASP with the necessary formalities of party registration. The result was significant – the vast majority (75 per cent) of the ASP's 60 elected councillors were of indigenous campesino origin and the flamboyant 'campesino' party (or the 'party of the coca producers', according to its opponents) received the highest share of the rural vote in the department (although it came third in the department overall), gaining 44 indigenous campesino councillors, the first majority in 15 municipalities and 10 mayors.[11] On this occasion success was due not to negotiation between campesino organisations and other political parties (save that necessary to get around the Electoral Court's prohibition), but rather represented a case of indigenous campesinos adopting the logic imposed by the state and forming their own political party almost overnight.

It is still unclear exactly how many indigenous campesinos were elected to local office in the December 1999 municipal elections because the Electoral Court does not register details of ethnic origin. But it appears that on this occasion it was the political parties who opted for indigenous campesino candidates, including female candidates (in 1995 only one in every 20 indigenous campesino councillors was a woman). This was due to a change in the law that required greater female representation on party lists. Along the way changes occurred in the rural party spectrum, which became much more fragmented after the 1997 municipal elections.[12] The MBL maintained a presence but went into political decline after 1997. CONDEPA split and fell apart after to the death of its founder, and was then beset by an endless, almost comic, battle between those who wanted a slice of his economic and political legacy. The ASP also split into two halves because of a fight for hegemony between two leaders (who had also split the CSUTCB a short while earlier), but this division did not lead to the collapse of the ASP as in the case of CONDEPA, it merely slowed down its growth. Those who gained the greatest advantage were the MIR and the NFR (part of the governing coalition), both of whom have presidential ambitions for 2002 and who learnt from the example of the MBL of the advantages to be gained by nominating rural candidates.

A further trend underpinning this national party fragmentation should be signalled. In 1999 indigenous campesino candidates were more dispersed across different parties, largely because they considered that none of them fully represented their interests and that the most important thing was to gain the highest possible number of indigenous campesino councillors in the new municipal governments, regardless of whose party ticket they were elected on. This leads us to examine another aspect of the previous period of municipal government – relations between the political parties and the indigenous campesino councillors themselves.

From indigenous campesino councillors to mayors

In total, approximately one in every four indigenous campesino councillors elected in 1995 reached the office of mayor, albeit temporarily, and two in every four held some kind of executive post in the municipal council. Only one in four remained simply as a councillor with no extra responsibilities. We were able to reconstruct the trajectory of indigenous campesino councillors for 90 municipalities; these results are summarised in Table 3.2.

Table 3.2 Municipalities according to number of indigenous-campesino (i-c) councillors and their term of office as mayors

Proportion of i-c councillors (in 1999)	*(N)*	*Maximum term of office of same i-c as mayor**				*No i-c became mayor*
		4 yrs	*3 yrs*	*2 yrs*	*1 yr*	
Majority (3+/5)	(50)	17	7	14	8	4
%		34	14	28	16	8
Minority (1 or 2)	(35)	2	1	7	7	18
%		6	3	20	20	51
Suplentes only	(5)	–	–	–	1	4
None in 1999	(2)	–	–	2	–	–
Total no. of	(90)	19	8	23	16	26
municipalities	%	21	9	25	18	27

* Time in office estimated to nearest year

As one would expect, it was easier to gain the mayorship in those municipalities where the majority of councillors were indigenous campesinos. Such municipalities represent 75 per cent of all 67 municipalities where an indigenous campesino became mayor and 89 per cent of those where the mayor remained in office for the four years following initial appointment.[13] This was particularly the case when indigenous campesinos were in a majority on the council and also belonged to the same political party; most common in the aforementioned cases of the MBL and IU/ASP. In contrast, where the indigenous campesino councillors were in a minority on the council it proved more difficult for them to gain the office of mayor, although there were some exceptions.

The divisive effect of the political parties was particularly marked within the Aymara municipalities in the departments of La Paz and Oruro, partly because of traditional Aymara factionalism, but above all because of the high number of candidates resident in the cities, where the backroom dealings of Creole politics are common practice. The case of La Paz city itself is a clear example of this, where the election of a mayoress who had obtained nearly 50 per cent of the vote was blocked by her opponents and afterwards each mayor was replaced annually through a vote of censure. It is also possible that in some cases the annual change of Andean mayors may have also been based on the traditional Andean method of rotating authorities: 'Andean democracy' tends to give everyone the same obligations and responsibilities, including the obligation to 'serve' the community once in their lifetime, through spending money on the *fiesta patronal* or time as a local authority. But the fact that municipal office implies access to greater resources tends to place ambition above such notions of service.

On the other hand, in more remote regions, such as the North of Potosí, influential mestizo inhabitants of the principal town, whatever their political affiliation, were not prepared to accept an 'Indian' mayor. If they were unable to avoid this in the elections, they subsequently blocked the mayor and used votes of censure to ensure that he or she abandoned the post as soon as possible. Sometimes in such cases the mayor was unable even to count on the support of their own party or the governing coalition. In other instances, the indigenous campesinos themselves, even when they had a majority on the council, pre-empted such developments by supporting a sympathetic mestizo candidate for mayor, aware as they were of the discrimination that existed against them. We know of at least one case where such tactics resulted in such a disastrous outcome that in the end an indigenous campesino mayor was subsequently appointed who managed to hold onto power.

The vast majority of the indigenous campesino councillors (some 69 per cent) were of the opinion that their experience in municipal government had been positive in that it had broadened their horizons and helped them to better understand legal and administrative complexities, thus making them more adept in political terms. Those who were most aware of this were precisely those individuals who had reached municipal office directly from their communities (78 per cent of this sub-group), those who were named by their grass-roots supporters (80 per cent) and the few women councillors (82 per cent). Those least willing to recognise this achievement – although they did not deny it – were those who already lived in the central town (54 per cent) and those who had reached the office of mayor (58 per cent); both were more interested in showing off their salaries, however nominal these were.[14]

Municipal development and indigenous campesino organisation

If talk of taking power was largely rhetorical in the past, today indigenous campesinos have learnt to exercise power, albeit at a local level. Some of the most successful councillors ran for election again in 1999, but these were only a minority of those elected in 1995 (one in four). The remainder were elected for the first time in 1999, although this does not of course indicate that those indigenous campesino councillors who did not run for office again were a failure. It is possible that the traditional rotation of office also functioned here, including the desire to rest after having complied with their 'duty', those councillors then becoming former authorities (who traditionally play a supervisory role in rural Andean communities).

The central question is whether this exercise of power by indigenous campesinos worked to the benefit of their community grass-roots supporters who encouraged them to stand for office in the first place. In order to answer this question, a number of distinctions must be made: above all, where the indigenous campesino organisation was relatively strong, it ensured that the municipal government, whether or not it had indigenous campesino councillors, devoted a significant part of its budget to the rural communities and not just to embellish the main town, as occurred in the past. If, in addition, the municipality had been restructured into districts or sub-mayoralties it was even easier to ensure that a certain geographic equity prevailed in the distribution of resources. In some municipalities with a majority indigenous population these were even structured as 'indigenous districts' governed by their own customary law. However, up to now the government has not wanted to consider indigenous demands to have their own 'indigenous municipalities' organised according to their cultural norms, similar to those which exist in other Latin American countries.[15]

By contrast, where indigenous campesino organisation was weak, even though indigenous campesinos formed a majority of the population, it was more likely that resources would be concentrated in the urban nucleus to the benefit of mestizos. In one municipality in the North of Potosí, where the *ayllus* are divided and live in extreme poverty, the municipal authorities decided that their first priority was to build an indoor swimming pool! Sometimes the kind of investment made can be the outcome of different kind of arrangements. For example, the Guaraní of Charagua, in the Chaco, won the election but opted to nominate a white person (*karai*) as their mayor, aware as they were of the inter-ethnic conflict that a more radical solution would have occasioned. The mayor responded by immediately dedicating a good part of the municipal budget to public works in the rural communities. Two years later the mayor proposed that it was now the turn of the urban centre – this was accepted and the following year the *karai* dedicated the lion's share of the budget to remodelling the town square so that it would be the most impressive in the countryside of Santa Cruz.

This interest in improving the appearance of towns and rural communities was not difficult to explain – the towns had previously felt almost completely bereft of markers of civic identity. However, it also indicated the diversity of opinions between town dwellers, inhabitants of rural communities and high-level state bureaucrats about what constituted a priority for the municipalities. Yet once a 'presentable' public space was consolidated in the centre of the rural municipality, little by little other concerns came into play. Our 1999 survey showed that the main benefits achieved by the rural indigenous campesino communities, according to their councillors, were the provision of basic services (51 per cent) and infrastructural works (34 per cent), with economic production projects (5 per cent) and other activities trailing behind. In a number of places the prior existence of micro-regional development plans, drawn up in conjunction with one NGO or another, had afforded a greater degree of coherence and outreach to municipal activities. However, in other cases immediate priorities dictated by electoral interests impeded or indeed frustrated the systematic execution of medium- and long-term development plans, despite all the efforts of other local agencies. In any case, in general grass-roots organisations undoubtedly have no desire to return to the status quo ante prior to the Law of Popular Participation. The Banzer government is aware of this and, even though it has deprioritised popular participation, knows it cannot revoke the law because of the popular protests this would provoke.

Who then has been strengthened by these developments? The organisations and their grass-roots members? The municipality? The agencies who carry out these projects? Everyone has tried to gain advantage. Many government bureaucrats and NGOs who were left high and dry by the structural changes of 1994 have converted themselves into consultancy groups and project managers eagerly in search of contracts with each and every municipality (a local version of what in Washington DC is known as 'the belt of bandits'). The national and municipal authorities also know that the co-participation funds provide them with a valuable mechanism to capture votes, and in 1999 many municipal resources were used for campaign purposes through the sponsoring of public works rather than integrated long-term projects. Even the NFR, the party responsible for the national office of popular participation, has taken full advantage of this position for its own electoral advantage, leaving public works half-finished in many parts of the country with the threat that they will only be completed if its members are re-elected.

Within this tussle, the indigenous campesino organisations have been weakened, unless they have special support from local government or other institutions. If this support is in place, then they have grown. For example, this has been the case in some (but not all) of the municipalities controlled by the ASP in the Cochabamba countryside, or in areas where the organisations have had the support of a sympathetic NGO that has not been seduced by the lucrative consultancy boom. But in many parts of the country such circumstances do not exist and it is therefore not unusual to find that potentially valuable leaders lose influence in the face of the superior economic power of municipal government. In a workshop some months before the December 1999 municipal elections, someone commented: 'Now no one wants to be a leader. They only think about becoming councillors and mayors.' Do they do this in order better to serve their supporters or to serve themselves? This is the unanswered question, and the central paradox, of local power.

In many municipalities the so-called Vigilance Committees have also been problematic. As noted above, this is the body established by the law as a link between the territorial base organisations (OTBs) and the municipal government. Committee members are nominated on an annual basis by the OTBs (unions, communities, *ayllus*, and so on in the countryside and neigh-bourhood councils in the urban centres), with one member for each canton or municipal district (or sub-mayoralty). In theory the Vigilance Committee regularly attends meetings of the municipal government in order to represent the grass roots' proposals and present their concerns. They are also supposed to be informed of plans approved by the municipal government and the progress of their implementation. Although those formally charged with oversight functions are the municipal councils themselves, the Vigilance Committees have the power to present complaints and even to demand the freezing of funds in cases of fraud or embezzlement, as has happened in some places.

However, in practice the Vigilance Committees have not functioned effectively due to a shortage of resources and training.[16] Despite a 1997 decree they still lack independent funds of their own. They are therefore either inactive or at the mercy of the mayor and what she or he decides to allocate to them in the way of resources, the result being that they lose their autonomy and gradually become an appendix of the mayor's office. Particularly in the rural sector, those who face most difficulties are those members of the Vigilance Committee who live in remote areas and who have to use their own funds to come to the municipal capital in order to meet their obligations. Even if they do manage to attend on a regular basis, they do not always have the necessary information, knowledge or support to interpret events.

Another unresolved matter for many OTBs is who they should name as their representative on the Vigilance Committee. Some opted to transfer this responsibility to their highest authority within the grass-roots organisation, even at the risk that this might mean they neglect their other duties. Others chose former leaders with more experience, yet others created a specific post or just sought out someone who got on well with the mayor in order not to cause any conflict. In some cases they preferred to delegate the priest, a teacher or another non-indigenous campesino sympathiser resident in the municipal capital who might have some moral authority over the municipality. The Vigilance Committees also worked better where some institution or NGO has lent support and provided training and advice, or in cases where a close relationship already existed between the municipal authorities and the grass-roots organisations, perhaps due to their similar social backgrounds. However, in the first case it is not clear how sustainable the Vigilance Committees will be in the medium term, and in the second case the perceived need for their existence is not so strong.

This problem is not confined to the Vigilance Committees designed by the Popular Participation Law. Another problematic entity in terms of participation are the educational councils established by the Education Reform Law. These were intended to guarantee a grass-roots presence in the entire reform process and, in particular, to play an active role in the development of intercultural bilingual education in each specific place and region. However, in contrast to the daring utopianism of the legislators, the resistance of those charged with implementing the reform has been marked, particularly the local branches of the Ministry of Education and those who fear that the new changes will negatively affect them, such as teachers. From the very beginning the grass-roots organisations supported the creation of these new councils, but it has proved difficult to alter the structure and functions of the old school support committees so that they can make a more active contribution to the educational system. Some progress has recently been made, thanks – again – to external inputs, such as support from UNICEF for the Educational Councils of Indigenous Peoples and, through these, for more local bodies. But the question is whether they will be able to continue when international aid dries up.

The synergy between the municipality and indigenous campesino organisation envisioned by the Law of Popular Participation and other laws also presupposes greater acceptance of municipal authorities on the part of grass-roots indigenous campesino organisations. In some places the latter, through habit or lack of trust, are still unwilling to adapt to the new scenario; if this continues they will end up being marginalised from local power, perhaps their lack of effective input disguised with purely ceremonial activities. But adjustments need to be made not only from the bottom up. The state, which at long last discovered its huge backyard by creating or strengthening the rural municipalities, must also make adjustments, as must the municipalities themselves. To mention just one aspect, many municipal jurisdictions remain unwieldy or inefficient because they are too large or too small, or because the social and cultural units which they cover do not add up to a coherent whole. However, congress has yet to demonstrate any will to solve these problems.

In search of better laws

The advantage of concentrating attention and activity at the level of the municipality is that here indigenous campesinos can really become local power without losing themselves in utopian discourses. But if their political activity is limited only to the municipal level, they also run the risk of losing perspective and forgetting the other significant challenges facing the indigenous campesino movement at national level. One of the main tasks is to achieve favourable legislation, which is subsequently implemented and respected. Although chronic structural problems exist because of poor coordination between the national leadership and grass-roots members and the loss of valuable national leaders once they finish their term in office,[17] evidently it is the higher ranks of the indigenous campesino organisations which can have more influence on such fundamental decision-making processes. This question is examined here from two points of view: grass-roots mobilisation and developments within parliament itself, taking as a paradigmatic example the conflicts which occurred around the National Law of the Agrarian Reform Service (the 'INRA Law'), which was finally approved in October 1996.

The popular mobilisation road

The 1953 Agrarian Reform was carried out by the first MNR government in a context of considerable social upheaval and spontaneous land take-overs in various parts of the Andean region. During subsequent years it gave rise to a situation almost as unjust as that which had preceded it, above all because of the large extensions granted to new landowners and speculators in the eastern plains (Albó 1979; Urioste 1987). So many arbitrary decisions were implemented, above all during the periods of military government, that in the end the National Council for Agrarian Reform was subject to executive intervention in 1992. Since the colonial period, large extensions of the Andean *ayllus* have remained at the margin of processes to legally register land, giving rise to periodic boundary conflicts in the North of Potosí. In addition, new global tendencies have become increasingly evident in Bolivia in recent years, such as growing indigenous and environmental demands for protected territories on the one hand, and powerful globalising pressures for a freer market in land on the other – this last aspect underpinning much international funding aimed at modernising the legal system.

As a result of these joint pressures, in 1995 the government began to propose the drafting of a new agrarian law. The initial idea was merely to develop a code of practice for the National Institute of Agrarian Reform (INRA), which was to replace the discredited National Council for Agrarian Reform, under special administration following the 1992 executive intervention. Little by little the project shifted towards a much more substantive proposal for legal reform, which included other aspects not initially mentioned. In the first instance a rich and intense dialogue took place between the office responsible for administering the National Council for Agrarian Reform and the grass-roots campesino organisations, to the point that by 1995 they began to refer to a 'consensual' project. But as those in government started to add new elements to the law, mistrust on the part of the campesino organisations grew as they came to feel that their earlier efforts had been to no avail. At the same time, government representatives felt that the dialogue was stalled every time the campesino organisations changed leadership. And although they adopted a low profile, large landowners and the business sectors were discreetly and efficiently lobbying their political allies in order to defend their interests.

In any case, indigenous campesino organisations continued to be open to dialogue and eventually a new version of the proposed law, formally referred to as a 'negotiated' proposal, was sent before parliament. But the government continued to pull rabbits out of the proverbial hat, for example by introducing a new supervisory body called the Superintendencia Agraria which, according to campesino leaders, invalidated the previously negotiated proposal for mixed 'agrarian commissions' made up of government and campesino representatives which were supposed to continue negotiating over specific themes related to the future application of the new law. In sum, the law before parliament ended up satisfying neither party because of the concessions it was perceived to have made to the other side.

A campesino indigenous mobilisation then took place on a scale seldom seen since the times of the original Agrarian Reform; at one point it even appeared to have La Paz under siege. However, what in fact occurred was a multiplicity of poorly articulated mobilisations, each with different objectives. One sector linked to organisations close to the MBL, at the time part of the coalition government, mobilised to lobby for the approval of the draft law, considering that in spite of its deficiencies it was the lesser of all evils. Another sector, linked to the ASP and similar groups, mobilised to try and ensure that the new law was not approved, preferring instead to stick with the 1953 legislation, despite its recognised weaknesses. In addition, some indigenous campesino leaders probably had more interest in raising their own political profile than in reaching a negotiated settlement over the content of the law. The coca producers were most concerned with eliminating a series of clauses related to biodiversity and protected areas, considering these to be an indirect means of halting their presence in the tropical region (which was effectively what the government had in mind). Lastly, the organisations of indigenous minorities in the tropical lowlands simply wanted to guarantee their territories, which they had marched to achieve in 1990, and were prepared to cede on all other points related to the new law.

Some of these discrepancies can be explained by the different historical experiences of each sector. The oldest organisations, such as the CSUTCB, which had a greater Andean presence, and the colonisers of the eastern tropics, highly affected by the problematic of coca production, had a long and traumatic experience of unfulfilled promises made by different governments. Since they broke off the military–campesino pact in 1978, their principal approach was one of wariness and systematic opposition to all initiatives of the 'anti-campesino state' or of the 'officialist' sectors of the popular opposition, who they considered to be infiltrated and divided. This first group had much more regular contact with various opposition parties. In contrast, the new indigenous organisations of the lowlands did not share this long history of frustrations and were in fact discovering that their new relationship with the state afforded them a number of opportunities. This made them more disposed to a pragmatic dialogue. In fact they were the only group who broke off their march, patiently giving the state an opportunity to comply with its promise to legalise their lands, something which they achieved at least in the text of the new law.

It is not possible to enter here into the finer details, but at least at this point in time those in favour of negotiation with the government achieved more than those who systematically opposed the legislative proposal, sticking to maximalist approaches without presenting any viable alternatives. The political conjuncture at the end of 1996 and beginning of 1997 was once again dominated by the run-up to national elections and this meant that those who steadfastly opposed the government ended up, albeit unintentionally, opening the door to the new, even more right-wing government which took office in August 1997. In subsequent years the Banzer administration, through frequent appeals to the objections of the indigenous campesino sector, has undone or ignored the minimal gains achieved by the INRA Law approved in 1996.

The parliamentary road

Throughout the entire conflict over the new agrarian law the few indigenous campesino representatives in parliament failed to develop a coordinated strategy with the popular movement from which many of them originated. The one exception was the vice-president of the Republic and president of Congress, the Aymara Víctor Hugo Cárdenas, who obviously played a central role in the debate and the approval of the different laws advanced during his term in office. This was also the case for the much-opposed INRA Law, which Cárdenas coincidentally ended up signing (he was exercising functions as interim president at the time it was approved by the parliament). During the entire process he had to negotiate with the different parties and make suggestions, but could not appear to be the advocate of a unified indigenous campesino position – both because this was not the role of the president of Congress, and also because such a proposal simply did not exist.

What was the role of the indigenous campesino parliamentary representatives in more general terms? The presence of indigenous campesino representatives in parliament was not a new phenomenon, at least in the lower chamber, or Chamber of Deputies.[18] The 'Campesino Parliamentary brigade' famous in the 1960s (a time when the term 'indigenous' was still frowned upon) was formed when General Barrientos sought to legitimise his de facto regime through elections. These he won thanks to the campesino vote, which not only confirmed him as president but also automatically elected a series of deputies (and one senator) of 'campesino' origin.[19] These were leaders of the military–campesino pact, promoted to deputies because of their close relationship to Barrientos who, in many cases, was also their *compadre*. Subsequently, following the return to democratic government in 1978, a few indigenous campesino deputies and senators allied to the traditional parties (particularly the MNR) were elected, as well as various deputies aligned to the different Katarista tendencies, amongst them the future vice-president himself.

In the 1997 elections a change was introduced making it possible to cast a double tied vote. This was achieved through the innovation of a ballot paper divided into two parts: the first, as before, to select the president and – automatically – his senator and possibly some deputies;[20] the second to select a uninominal deputy, each party presenting a single candidate (and their substitute) in each of 65 local constituencies into which the country was divided. Voters could choose whether or not to cast their ballot for the candidate of the same party as their choice for president, making it possible for the first time to vote for a president from one party, and a constituency deputy from another. The uninominal candidate for deputy who gained the most votes in his or her constituency was automatically elected to parliament.

Nine indigenous campesino deputies were elected to parliament in 1997 through this new, more locally tied uninominal vote. Four of these were ASP deputies from Cochabamba, including Román Loayza, leader of the CSUTCB, and Evo Morales, leader of the coca producers. Another four were urban Aymara leaders of CONDEPA, including '*la cholita Remedios*', who had led the party since the death of its founder. Another was the former regional leader of the whole of the North of Potosí, elected for the MBL. The old method of selecting deputies, tied as before to the presidential vote, yielded only one urban Aymara deputy who was linked to the ADN.[21] Not one deputy was elected for the minority lowland indigenous groups, despite the fact that Guaraní deputies had featured in previous administrations.

All of these deputies, and the substitutes or *suplentes* (theirs or others) who were from the indigenous campesino sector, immediately formed the so-called Indigenous Parliamentary Brigade, committing themselves to work together and put aside their party differences for the benefit of the indigenous campesinos they represented. A number of meetings took place and the group appointed their own internal directorate, initially led by Evo Morales, the leader of the coca producers. However, this much-heralded unity failed to function in practice, collapsing under the strain of party differences and personal interests. The lack of a formal structure within parliament which would allow them to function as a 'brigade' on a regular basis, such as their own office and secretarial support similar to that allocated to each party and parliamentary commission, was also a handicap. A further factor was their lack of experience. This had also been a problem for previous indigenous campesino deputies, but the uninominal mechanism had now catapulted a number of deputies from relatively isolated rural areas to the national parliament. They had to spend even more time and effort than their counterparts in the municipal councils getting used to the complex and confusing atmosphere of parliament. At the same time, more seasoned and astute politicians managed to secure their interests and impose their criteria.

Even if this Indigenous Parliamentary Brigade had managed to consolidate a unitary position, what could a minority group of ten out of 130 deputies have achieved without even one indigenous campesino senator out of the 27 senators in the upper chamber, indispensable for the approval of any law? Few allies were available to them in a parliament with a strong officialist majority and a clearly right-wing government presided over by an ex-military dictator. The most they could hope for was to have some national presence. In this respect the role of their main spokesperson, Evo Morales, was notable, not so much as a representative of the Indigenous Brigade per se, but more because of his personality and role as a direct representative of the coca producers.[22] That is not to say that these deputies (and occasionally the senators) did not achieve some things for their regions, in addition to gaining much experience, contacts and – last but not least – a salary that they would never have been able to earn in the *llano* and which on occasion became the main source of income for their small parties.

We must ask again whether this access to power and public office, a legitimate aspiration of the popular movement, ended up working to the benefit of those who voted for them, or only for the few people who ended up in public office. Experiences varied widely, and it would be well worth doing a more detailed, systematic study of the previous histories and backgrounds of the former indigenous campesino deputies. However, up to now – and in contrast to experience in the municipalities – the correlation of political forces in the legislature has been almost permanently against these few honourable indigenous campesino deputies. One can therefore have few illusions about their room for manoeuvre. The question is whether it is worth risking or sacrificing such valuable leaders in a forum which tends to crush ideals.

Final reflections

Of the numerous lessons of these first years, the following, related above all to the current role of the indigenous campesino organisations, should be emphasised. In general terms, it is clear that a huge gulf exists between grandiose rhetorical dreams and the little that can be concretely achieved, even in relatively favourable contexts. But the road to utopia is always a rocky one. At this stage it is possible to signal the following preliminary conclusions:

1. *Despite reforms to promote greater participation in public affairs, grass-roots organisations continue to be essential as more genuine representatives of indigenous campesinos and as more valid counterparts for the state, both at municipal and national level.*

   At local level, they are essential to ensure that the municipality, now better endowed with resources, works effectively for the benefit of the communities. At national level, they continue to be the most effective instrument to lobby for more favourable laws, policies and allocation of resources.

2. *However, if they are to function more efficiently, the indigenous campesino organisations must adapt better to this new scenario, maintaining a dialectical creativity between their traditional roots and their new challenges (albeit not without uncertainties, tests and tensions).*

   This adaptation affects a range of aspects, including the criteria for selecting leaders, longer periods in office, constructive engagement with state authorities, and even adjustments to existing geographic coverage and jurisdictions. For example, the traditional Andean system determines that every member of the community must 'fulfil their duty' as an authority for a year in turn. This may continue to be an effective formula at community level, where the general assembly and former authorities perform a regulatory role. However, at municipal level it is vital that more apt leaders be appointed, probably for a longer term of office and with possibilities of re-election, so that a real capacity for negotiation and oversight can be achieved. Otherwise communal authorities will end up atrophying and be limited to purely ceremonial activities.

3. *Grass-roots organisations need to have a political vision and be politically engaged. It may also be useful for them to have their own political wing, but they should beware of the pitfalls of party divisions.*

   Since the earliest years of the Katarista movement, the main indigenous campesino leaders agreed on the need to have their own 'political wing' or political vehicle separate from the *criollo* parties, which simply utilised the indigenous campesino movement (even though many of these leaders ultimately ended up in the political parties, given that this was the normal way of pursuing political objectives). Nonetheless, attempts to build such a political vehicle ended up committing the same errors as the *criollo* parties the movement so mistrusted; like them, they became characterised by undemocratic practices, authoritarianism, internal divisions and personal interests. Indigenous campesino groups often have a very suggestive and unique discourse, but this often evaporates when it is put into practice. Undoubtedly the chronic lack of financial resources is a problem, but the main bottleneck impeding the achievement of a coordinated and efficient political influence probably lies in the organisational realm.

4. *Indigenous campesino organisations need to improve their capacity to propose initiatives and negotiate.*

Until 1978 the main problem of indigenous campesino organisations was their almost total dependence on the governments of the day, whether civilian or military. In fact they were little more than mere yes-men (*llunk'us*). Subsequently, they were characterised more by their systematic opposition to government, which was overly strident. In a democratic context it is essential to develop the ability to propose initiatives, make alliances and know how to negotiate with groups different from one's own. Such negotiations won't always be peaceful, as different and often opposing visions and interests exist with respect to many issues. Nonetheless, the aim is ultimately to arrive at compromises in which everyone cedes something in order to achieve something.

Recent experience in Bolivia is full of ambiguities on this point. One of the most widely accepted laws, with a huge potential to transform the status quo, was the Law of Popular Participation. Although it had been redrafted many times, the LPP was not the result of any systematic consultation with the popular sectors it was aimed at. By contrast, the INRA Law was the subject of multiple prior consultations and of large-scale popular mobilisations, without this implying that the end result was any more satisfactory. At the same time the government quietly approved the new Mining Code almost overnight, the result of a swift agreement with the mining companies, without any consultation with popular sectors whose interests were hardly taken into account. The same thing happened with the first water law, approved in 1999 at the eleventh hour without any popular participation. This time different political and popular sectors reacted with large-scale mobilisations, creating alliances and platforms to lobby on this issue.[23]

What these examples clearly indicate is that when a democratic opening exists, indigenous campesino organisations should be neither compliant government allies nor an eternal opposition, but rather be open to negotiation and dialogue on matters of national importance. But they need to be wily and astute, rather like the rabbit in Andean and non-Andean stories, who appears defenceless but somehow always manages to beat the powerful fox.

Notes

1. See Albó (1999b) for an overview of the twentieth century. Other works which cover some periods or aspects include Calderón and Dandler (1984), especially Jorge Dandler's work on Cochabamba; Iriarte and the CIPCA team (1980); and Rivera (1984).
2. On the emergence and development of Katarismo, see Rivera (1984), Hurtado (1986) and Albó (1985).

3. The legislation in favour of indigenous peoples carried out during these years was compiled in a publication by the office of the Vice-Presidency of the Republic (1997), occupied at the time by the Aymara Víctor Hugo Cárdenas.

4. The other two were the Law of Educational Reform and the Law of Capitalisation, which transferred 50 per cent of state enterprises to private ownership.

5. The law had less effect in the large cities, which in fact had to be compensated for the loss of resources they had previously monopolised. The present analysis, however, is limited to the rural area.

6. Other complementary criteria, such as the absence of road networks, distance from the municipal centre, or poverty and human development indexes, could have made the distribution of resources more equitable, but these were not included in order to expedite the swift disbursal of funds.

7. For example, the electoral register has not been updated to include deaths or out-migration, meaning that formal abstention rates are higher than real abstentionism. In addition, some municipal jurisdictions are vast and highly dispersed, something which does not facilitate the electoral participation of the most marginal sectors. Lastly, many men and above all women lack the identity documents they need to register as voters. According to the last census in 1992, only 52 per cent of men and 38 per cent of women in the rural sector over 15 years of age had identity documents.

8. On the 1995 elections see Secretaría Nacional de Participación Popular (1997a). For an analysis of what had happened to those elected four years on see Albó (1999a). The present discussion of the December 1999 municipal elections is based on a workshop which took place shortly afterwards, organised by PADEM (Programa de Apoyo a la Democracia Municipal), and the raw data provided by the Electoral Court, which only indicates parties and candidates elected, without detailing their social or ethnic origin.

9. Secretaría Nacional de Participación Popular (1997a). A subsequent partial recal-culation (Albó 1999a: 21–4) shows that initial data underestimated the number of indigenous campesino councillors, although this did not alter overall tendencies. Ultimately any estimate of who does or doesn't belong to the indigenous campesino category is always going to be partly subjective.

10. Up to 110 indigenous campesino councillors, if we include the other muncipal-ities not included in the 1999 study. See Secretaría Nacional de Participación Popular (1997a: 47 and 12).

11. Including municipalities not covered in our 1999 sample. See Calla (1996).

12. Five parties gained almost equal shares of the vote, with percentages ranging between 16 and 22 per cent (see Table 3.1).

13. According to the electoral law in force in 1999, if a given party list gained an absolute majority of the vote, the first name on their list would automatically become the mayor. In cases where an absolute majority was not achieved (the vast majority of municipalities), the mayor is indirectly elected by the councillors, whose total number ranges between five (in nearly all the rural municipalities) and eleven (in the larger cities), depending on the number of inhabitants. When this form of indirect election has occurred, it is also possible to issue a vote of censure against the elected mayor after one year, replacing them with another councillor. However, this mechanism – intended to provide an additional means of oversight – has become the vehicle for all kinds of personal and party-based

ambitions. See Rojas (1998) and Viceministerio de Participación Popular y Fortalecimiento Municipal (1999).

14. Eighteen and 16 per cent, compared to between 3 and 9 per cent for the other sub-groups.

15. For example in the Colombian *resguardos* and in the state of Oaxaca, Mexico. On the municipal districts in Bolivia, see Secretaría Nacional de Participación Popular (1997c) and Balsev (1996).

16. No systematic, up-to-date research has been carried out on this question. The most complete assessment to date remains the Diagnóstico de la Secretaría Nacional de Participación Popular (1997b). See also Ardaya (1998), who interviewed 50 members of 12 vigilance committees, and Guzmán (1999).

17. For an analysis of this issue see Ticona, Rojas and Albó (1995: 121–56).

18. This chapter does not consider the complementary presence of indigenous campesinos in executive posts, such as, for example, the occasional indigenous campesino ministers in matters relating to the agrarian sector, a practice initiated in 1958.

19. Until 1978 people voted by placing a coloured slip in the ballot box for their preferred party for the presidency. Many of these voting slips were distributed well in advance of the poll by the parties themselves. However, this system provided many opportunities for fraud and conflict, for example supporters of a given party could destroy the voting slips of their opponents or block their prior distribution. In 1979 a single multi-coloured, multiple choice ballot paper was introduced which was given to each voter at the moment they actually cast their ballot, so that they could secretly choose their preferred party. However, under both systems one vote alone simultaneously selected president, senator and deputy for the same party; a split vote was not possible; that is, it was not possible to vote for a president from one party and a senator or deputy from another.

20. Only if the percentage achieved by any given party did not reach the amount necessary for the uninominal election of deputies, explained below.

21. One of the factors which affected the internal division of the ASP (and the CSUTCB), which occurred shortly after these elections, was precisely the fact that the second principal leader of the movement was not elected to parliament. He had pursued the more general route, by which deputies are only selected on the winning presidential ticket if there have not been sufficient deputies elected by the uninominal route in a given constituency. The loser accused his colleague Evo Morales of having instructed the grass roots to cast a split vote, in other words to vote for the ASP candidates in the uninominal category, and for another party in the more general category which covers the presidency, senators and other deputies.

22. His main enemies have made many attempts to discredit him, but they have been unable either to provide any solid evidence to back up their accusations or to achieve support from other sectors in parliament.

23. In April 2000 the mobilisation in Cochabamba was such that people referred to the 'water war' between nearly all popular sectors and the Banzer government. The government decreed a state of siege, but was finally forced to give in and modify the 1999 law and overturn a contract with a multinational water company. However, as long as no law exists to govern water resources which is also capable of satisfying the urban population and agricultural sector's demands for water, the conflict is likely to persist.

References

Albó, Xavier (1979), *¿Bodas de plata? O réquiem por una reforma agraria*, CIPCA (La Paz).
—— (1985), 'De MNRistas a kataristas: campesinado, estado y partidos, 1953–1983'. *Historia Boliviana* V/11–2: 87–127. A revised version in English appeared as 'MNRistas to kataristas to Katari', in Steve Stern (ed.), *Resistance, Rebellion, and Consciousness in the Andean Peasant World: 18th to 20th Centuries*, University of Wisconsin Press (Madison, 1987), pp.379–419.
—— (1993), *¿Y de kataristas a MNRistas? La sorprendente y audaz alianza entre aymaras y neoliberales en Bolivia*, CEDOIN and UNITAS (La Paz). An abbreviated English version appeared in Donna L. Van Cott (ed.), *Indigenous Peoples and Democracy in Latin America*, St Martin's Press and Inter-American Dialogue (New York, 1994), pp.55–81.
—— (1997), 'Alcaldes y concejales campesinos/indígenas: La lógica tras las cifras' in Secretaría Nacional de Participación Popular, *Indígenas en el poder local*, pp.7–26.
—— (1999a), *Ojotas en el poder local, cuatro años después*, CIPCA and PADER (La Paz).
—— (1999b), 'Diversidad étnica, cultural y lingüística' in Fernando Campero (ed.), *Bolivia en el siglo XX. La formación de la Bolivia contemporánea*, Harvard Club de Bolivia (La Paz), pp.451–82.
Ardaya, Rubén (1998), *El comité de vigilancia al servicio de la democracia municipal*, ILDIS (La Paz).
Arias, Iván (1991), *COB: La hoz frente al martillo*, Cuarto Intermedio (Cochabamba) 21: 79–102.
Ayo, Diego (1997), 'La elección del tres de diciembre de 1995: Análisis de las 464 autoridades indígenas y campesinas elegidas' in Secretaría Nacional de Participación Popular, *Indígenas en el poder local*, pp.27–40.
—— (1999), 'Los distritos municipales' in Rojas and Thévoz (coords), pp.27–68.
Balsev, Anne (1996), *Distritos municipales indígenas: las primeras experiencias. Hacia una estrategia para el fortalecimiento de los DMI*, Secretaría Nacional de Asuntos Etnicos, de Género y Generacionales (La Paz).
Bolivia (1994), *Constitución Política del Estado*, Gaceta Oficial de Bolivia (La Paz).
—— (1997), Vicepresidencia de la República, *Legislación indígena (compilación 1991–1997)* (Compilación y estudio preliminar de Jorge Vacaflor) (La Paz).
Calderón, Fernando and Jorge Dandler (eds) (1984), *Bolivia: la fuerza histórica del campesinado*, CERES (Cochabamba).
Calla, Ricardo, José Pinelo and Miguel Urioste (1989), *CSUTCB: Debate sobre documentos políticos y asamblea de nacionalidades*, CEDLA (La Paz).
—— and Hernando (1996), *Partidos políticos y municipios. Las elecciones municipales de 1995*, ILDIS (La Paz).
Cárdenas, Víctor Hugo (1987), 'La CSUTCB. Elementos para entender su crisis de crecimiento (1979–1987)' in *Crisis del sindicalismo en Bolivia*, ILDIS and FLACSO (La Paz), pp.223–39.
CEDIB (1993), 'La absurda guerra de la coca' in Xavier Albó and Raúl Barrios (eds), *Violencias encubiertas en Bolivia*, CIPCA (La Paz), vol. II, pp.13–77.
—— (1997), 'Resultado de las elecciones', *30 días* (Cochabamba), junio 1997, pp.4–20.
CIDOB (Confederación Indígena del Oriente Boliviano) (1992), 'Proyecto de ley indígena' (La Paz).
Contreras, Alex (1991), *Etapa de una larga marcha*, Aquí and ERBOL (La Paz).
CSUTCB (Confederación Sindical Unica de Trabajadores Campesinos de Bolivia) (1983), *Tesis política y estatutos* (La Paz).

—— (1984), *Ley fundamental agraria. Aprobada en el Congreso Nacional* [campesino] *de Cochabamba*, 16–20 de enero de 1984 [Anteproyecto de ley] (La Paz).

Guzmán, Román (1999), 'Denuncias del Comité de Vigilancia o cuán efectivo es el control social' in Rojas and Thévoz (eds), pp.135–56.

Hurtado, Javier (1986), *El katarismo*, Hisbol (La Paz).

Iriarte, Gregorio and Equipo CIPCA (1980), *Sindicalismo campesino ayer, hoy, mañana*, CIPCA (3ª ed. ampliada) (La Paz).

Manifiesto de Tiahuanacu (1973), La Paz. (Mimeo, reproduced in Hurtado 1986.)

Mendoza, Eduardo (1992), 'Asamblea del Pueblo Guaraní: nueva organización guaraníchiriguano', Unpublished thesis in Sociology, La Paz and Camiri.

Ministerio de Hacienda y Ministerio de Desarrollo Sostenible y Planificación (1998), *Primer censo de gobiernos municipales* (La Paz).

Pacheco, Diego (1992), *El indianismo y los indios contemporáneos en Bolivia*, Hisbol and MUSEF (La Paz).

Ramírez, Luis F. (1995), 'Del caos territorial al municipio', *Cuarto Intermedio* (Cochabamba) 37: 56–79.

Rivera C., Silvia (1984), *Oprimidos pero no vencidos. Luchas del campesinado aymara y quechua de Bolivia, 1900–1980*, Hisbol and CSUTCB (La Paz).

Rojas O., Gonzalo (1998), *Censura constructiva, inestabilidad y democracia municipal*, ILDIS (La Paz).

—— and Laurent Thévoz (eds) (1998), *Participación popular. Una evaluación-aprendizaje de la Ley, 1994–1997*, Viceministerio de Participación Popular y Fortalecimiento Municipal. Unidad de Investigación y Análisis (La Paz).

—— and Moira Zuazo (1996), *Los problemas de representatividad del sistema democrático boliviano, bajo el signo de la reforma del Estado*, ILDIS (Debate Político, 1) (La Paz).

Secretaría Nacional de Participación Popular (1997a), *Indígenas en el poder local* (La Paz).

—— (1997b), *Diagnóstico de la situación de organizaciones territoriales de base, comités de vigilancia, asociaciones comunitarias y listado de organizaciones funcionales* (La Paz).

—— (1997c), *Distritación municipal o el sueño de un orden municipal* (La Paz).

Ticona, Esteban, Gonzalo Rojas and Xavier Albó (1995), *Votos y wiphalas. Campesinos y pueblos originarios en democracia*, Fundación Milenio and CIPCA (La Paz).

UDAPSO and PNUD (1997), *Índices de desarrollo humano y otros indicadores sociales en 311 municipios de Bolivia* (Coordinación de David Haquim), PNUD (La Paz).

Urioste, Miguel (1987), *Segunda reforma agraria: campesinos, tierra y educación popular*, CEDLA (La Paz).

Viceministerio de Participación Popular y Fortalecimiento Municipal, Unidad de Investigación y Análisis (1999), *Lectura de los datos del voto constructivo de censura* (La Paz).

4
Educational Reform in Guatemala: Lessons from Negotiations between Indigenous Civil Society and the State

Demetrio Cojtí Cuxil[1]

Introduction

This chapter aims to analyse the negotiations which took place between representatives of civil society – both indigenous and non-indigenous – and delegates of the Ministry of Education in Guatemala to design and implement a comprehensive educational reform. This reform was stipulated in two of the Peace Accords signed between the Guatemalan government and the insurgent Unidad Nacional Revolucionaria Guatemalteca (URNG): the Accord on the Rights and Identity of Indigenous Peoples, signed in March 1995, and the Accord on Socio-Economic Issues and the Agrarian Question, signed in September 1996. Focusing on the question of ethnicity, an attempt is made to highlight the imbalances and struggles that occurred in two of the commissions created by the Accords: the Parity Commission for Educational Reform (COPARE) and the Consultative Commission for Educational Reform (CCRE).[2] These difficulties occurred despite the general principles accepted by the parties to the peace negotiations, which included the pacific resolution of differences, tolerance, solidarity and unity in diversity.

The educational reform itself is not analysed in detail here. Neither is it implied that the progress of both commissions for its implementation was not also marked by incidences of communication and coincidence. In COPARE for instance, differences did not always exist between indigenous and governmental delegates – in some issues the differences cut across both groups, with some indigenous and governmental delegates in favour and others opposed to a given proposal. The period examined here runs from 2

April 1997 to 14 January 2000, during which I was an indigenous civil society delegate to both the Parity Commission and the Consultative Commission for Educational Reform. After 14 January 2000 I continued to participate in the CCRE but as a governmental delegate from the Ministry of Education. The chapter is divided into three main sections: the first deals with limitations of the Peace Accords themselves (Section I), another with the negotiating process in COPARE (Section II), and the last with problems in the CCRE (Section III). The chapter concludes by drawing some lessons from these experiences.

Deficiencies of the Guatemalan educational sector and the response of the Peace Accords

Guatemala is a multi-ethnic developing country. Some 24 languages are spoken, but only one – Spanish – is officially recognised. Approximately 60 per cent of the population is indigenous, and approximately 80 per cent of the population lives in poverty or extreme poverty. A wide range of statistics indicates the severe deficiencies of Guatemalan education. A mere 1.8 per cent of the country's GDP is spent on education, only 80 per cent of the population has access to primary education, only 25 per cent to secondary education, and the illiteracy rate stands at between 30 and 40 per cent of the population. In 1999 the United Nations Development Programme (UNDP) underlined the fact that limited advances in primary and secondary education between 1994 and 1998 explained the low contribution of education to the country's Human Development Index (PNUD 1999: 17–19). Because of its multiplier effects, education was prioritised in the 1996 Peace Accords, which set out the case for a comprehensive educational reform.

However, despite various speeches, laws and pilot projects, the Ministry of Education's policy continues to be one of ethnic discrimination and assimilation of non-Spanish speaking communities. At the level of discourse, literature and legislation advances have been made towards the recognition of cultural pluralism. However, these have not yet filtered down to affect policy on the ground and have an impact in the classroom. Apart from a few exceptions, the exclusion of indigenous history and culture (languages, literature, art, and so on) continues to be the norm. Until the peace accords bilingual education – indigenous languages and Spanish – was treated as a marginal or exceptional phenomenon within the educational system. The General Directorate of Bilingual Education was created in 1983, first as a project, subsequently becoming a programme and latterly a general policy directive. However, this nominal increase in importance has not been accompanied by an increase in resources or coverage and in practice it continues to be a pilot project.

Government commitments to educational reform

One of the revolutionary features of the Peace Accords signed between 1994 and 1996 was that they sought to change neo-colonial policies towards ethnicity for positive recognition of multiculturalism within a framework of national unity and stability. The Accord on the Identity and Rights of Indigenous Peoples set out most clearly the government's obligations with respect to the character that the educational system should have in order to respect indigenous rights (chapter III, section G, number 2). Some of the specifications for recognition of multiculturalism within the educational system were:

(a) That education be regionalised and decentralised, with the aim of adapting it to local needs and linguistic and cultural specificities.
(b) That communities and families be given a decisive role in the definition of the curriculum and the school calendar, together with the ability to propose appointments and replacements of school teachers to ensure that they respond to the educational and cultural interests of the communities in question.
(c) That the educational concepts of the Mayas and other indigenous peoples be integrated into the areas of philosophy, science, art and pedagogic techniques, history, languages, etc. as a central feature of a comprehensive educational reform.
(d) Elements should be included within educational plans to strengthen national unity and the respect for cultural diversity.
(e) Bilingual, intercultural education should be extended and promoted and the study and knowledge of indigenous languages valued at all levels. Educational experiments, such as Mayan schools,[3] should be taken into account and the National Programme for Bilingual Education consolidated in order to attend all indigenous people. Instruction in Mayan Languages and Culture should be given to the entire Guatemalan population.
(f) Bilingual teachers and officials should be employed and trained in order to develop education within their communities and institutionalise mechanisms of consultation and participation in the educational process with representatives of indigenous communities and organisations. Indigenous peoples' access to formal and non-formal education should be facilitated by means of a system of grants and educational awards.

In addition, the Accord on Socio-Economic Issues contains a section referring to Education and Training, the emphasis of which is more on social factors than on ethnicity (chapter II, section A). It underlines the need for a coherent and dynamic state policy on education in order to achieve the following objectives:

(g) To affirm and promote the moral and cultural values, concepts and practices which constitute the basis of a democratic arrangement respectful of the cultural diversity of Guatemala.

(h) To avoid the persistence of poverty and social, ethnic, gender and geographical discrimination, in particular those resulting from the urban–rural divide.

Towards a comprehensive educational reform

The above-mentioned accords both specified that the implementation of these commitments should be carried out in a participatory manner through the Parity Commission and the Consultative Commission for Educational Reform (CCRE). They also specified that the reform should be comprehensive and not piecemeal reform or limited to changes to circumscribed areas, such as teaching methods, curricular adjustments, or changes in graduate teachers' profiles, as had occurred in the past. During the first period of democratic government (1985–90) the System for the Improvement of Human Resources and Curricular Adjustment (SIMAC) was created to develop changes in pedagogic methods and course content. This body continues to exist as an institution, but does not serve as a model for education in terms of study plans and teaching methods. In 1987 the application of the model it had developed was blocked by the teachers' unions, who alleged this was an imposition by technocrats and bureaucrats that would mean more work for teachers without any additional pay. As the government of the day refused to accede to their demands for salary increases, teachers reacted by rejecting the new model.

By contrast, the educational reform proposed in the Peace Accords is a *comprehensive* reform – in the Indigenous Rights Accord the government committed itself to an overhaul of the entire educational system (chapter III, section G, clause 2). The Parity and Consultative Commissions, charged with overseeing its implementation, have also understood their remit in these terms. COPARE identified 11 areas for transformation of the educational system, including pedagogic techniques, language, culture, policy, infrastructure, and training of human resources (PREAL-ASIES 1998: 61–81).

I: Limits of the Peace Accords

The indigenous and governmental representatives – the latter almost exclusively ladinos – who negotiated the application of the educational reform were not always clear quite what their task was because of the confusions, contradictions and idealism contained in the Peace Accords themselves.

The Peace Accords were negotiated between the government and the URNG in line with the 1985 Constitution of Guatemala and the country's international human rights commitments. A number of constitutional norms and principles relate to education. For instance, the constitution states that education is a basic human right, that minors have the right and the obligation to attend pre-primary, primary and elementary education within the limits set down by law, that state education is free, and that indigenous groups have the right to their own educational activities, including the right to establish and maintain schools and to use and teach their own languages. Laws referring to education also specify that the educational system should be decentralised and regionalised, bilingual in predominantly indigenous areas of the country and equipped by trained professionals. The Peace Accords were also negotiated in such a way that they did not contradict each other. So when the Indigenous and Socio-Economic Accords refer to the participation of civil society – families, local communities, ethnic communities – this is in line with the terms set out in the Framework Accord on Democratisation and the Search for Peace via Political Means (the Querétaro Accord of January 1994). This stipulated that the democratisation of the country had to guarantee and promote the participation of civil society in the formulation, implementation and evaluation of policies at different administrative levels.

However, the need to ensure that the Peace Accords did not contradict the 1985 Constitution, international treaty obligations or each other meant that they could not go beyond whatever was set out in these instruments and agreements. This ultimately had a negative impact on indigenous people. Indigenous demands for greater autonomy for ethnic or linguistic communities were never considered in the peace negotiations, either because such autonomy arrangements were not included in the 1985 Constitution or because they were an unknown for the negotiators, and therefore perceived as difficult to control. Ultimately what was seen as an advantage from the point of view of coherence and constitutional probity was a disadvantage for the indigenous organisations, which found their demands blocked by such logic.

The two accords that set out the need for a comprehensive educational reform were those referring to Indigenous Rights and the Socio-Economic Issues. The first was signed in 1995 during the government of Ramiro de León Carpio (1993–95), a government that was seen by both liberals and conservatives as being favourable to indigenous demands. In section G, which refers to the educational reform, the Indigenous Rights Accord detailed the characteristics of the reform, the Mayan educational experiences which should be taken into account in its design and the means by which access to formal and non-formal education for indigenous people could be facilitated. The accord also specified the need to create a Parity Commission made up of representatives of indigenous organisations and government whose task it would be to elaborate the design of the educational reform.

The Socio-Economic Accord, on the other hand, was signed in 1996 during the first year of the government of Alvaro Arzú (1996–99), a government dominated by its conservative and neoliberal wing. In chapter II, which dealt with social development, the accord set out the function of education and training, as well as the objectives of the educational reform. It also signalled government commitments in terms of the educational budget, curricular changes, coverage, vocational training, training to facilitate social participation, facilitating interaction between schools and communities and community participation, training of educational administrators, and providing financial support to disadvantaged students. The accord envisaged a multi-sectoral consultative commission linked to the Ministry of Education that would draw up and implement the reform.

However, the educational reform and the question of education were not only addressed in these two accords. An analysis carried out by PNUD in 1997 (PNUD, 1997) set out the different commitments acquired by the government with respect to education contained in other peace agreements. For example, the Accord on Constitutional Reform and Electoral Regulations (signed December 1996) states that in order to increase the level of electoral participation, the civic education of citizens should be increased, as well as their access to information (clause II). The Accord for the Resettlement of Populations Uprooted by the Armed Conflict (signed in June 1994) includes some five commitments relating to education. The Accord on Strengthening of Civil Power and the Role of the Army in a Democratic Society (signed September 1996) contains ten, and the agreement referring to the legalisation and incorporation of the URNG (concluded in December 1996) another ten. This multiplicity of government commitments and their dispersal across various accords has, at least in part, made their implementation and the monitoring of this process more difficult. Some commitments have been forgotten: for example, those referring to the mass media were not taken up by a specific commission, leaving the government a free hand in this area. The Arzú administration privatised the majority of radio channels, flying in the face of its commitment to open spaces in the mass media for indigenous peoples and their cultures. In the event, not even COPMAGUA, the body charged by indigenous organisations with overseeing the implementation of the Indigenous Rights Accord, intervened to protest.

The Peace Accords also contained contradictions, problems with decision-making bodies, and short-time frames to carry out long-term educational processes. The two commissions (Parity and Consultative) should have been set up to work together to advance the reform. However, in their respective mandates the role of 'elaborating the design of the educational reform' was duplicated, pointing to the failure to specify the tasks of each. In order to clarify their doubts each commission consulted the Accompaniment Commission – COPARE in mid-1997, the CCRE at the end of the same year – which was charged with clearing up such confusions and interpreting the content of the accords. This Commission determined that the Parity Commission should draw up the proposal for the educational reform and that the Consultative Committee should oversee its implementation. The explanation for this repetition of functions was that the Arzú administration had feared an 'indigenisation' of the educational system because of the 'excessive' power granted to indigenous people – or to civil society – in the Parity Commission, which was to have equal representation of government and civil society representatives. It therefore took advantage of the Socio-Economic Accord to restrict the decision-making power of civil society and to leave the Consultative Committee with the possibility of 'correcting' any exaggerated indigenous gains made in COPARE.

Another problem which derived from the composition of COPARE and the particular nature of its remit —the implementation of the Indigenous Accord – were doubts concerning the extent of the educational reform to be designed. Some government and international officials were of the opinion that educational reform could not be proposed for the whole country, given that the civil society interlocutors on COPARE were indigenous. According to this view, only indigenous people could deal with indigenous issues, but they could not decide national policy. This doubt was also clarified with the Accompaniment Commission, which confirmed that the educational reform did indeed have national outreach. The explanation for this problem lay in dis-crimination and negative prejudices against indigenous people. Previously it was held that indigenous people could not even decide their own affairs. Now it is increasingly accepted that they can, but not that they can decide matters of national policy which affect the non-indigenous sector of the population.

Another set of problems referred to decision-making mechanisms. The Indigenous Accord stipulated that decisions of the Parity Commission had to be consensual, and the internal rules of that commission specified the same, stating that any decision had to be characterised by the 'absence of opposition'. However, decision-making by consensus has advantages and dis-advantages – it facilitates full participation and allows for shared responsibilities, but it also requires much more time and progress is very difficult if any of the parties have fixed positions (OEA PROPAZ 1997). In practice, deadlocks had to be overcome by means of majority votes. At the same time, consensus was not always understood or implemented properly – in effect it meant whatever the governmental delegates conceded and what, in the light of this, it was possible to achieve. The CCRE also adopted consensus decision-making as its modus operandi, but it was and remains much more difficult to obtain this, given the greater number of people and institutions who have to arrive at a unitary position: 23 delegates from 17 institutions and organisations. For this reason it has also resorted to majority votes in order to overcome deadlocks or to make explicit the nature of the decision taken.

In terms of higher education, the Indigenous Accord envisaged the creation of a Maya University (chapter III, section G, clause 3). However, the Socio-Economic Accord repeated the stipulation of the 1985 Constitution that the 'management, organisation and development of state higher education is the exclusive remit of the University of San Carlos', thereby contradicting the Indigenous Accord, or at least obliging the Maya University to be a private institution. COPARE decided that the Maya University should be a public university, given that the almost universal poverty affecting indigenous people would not permit their access to a private institution. But as long as the University of San Carlos enjoys a monopoly as the only state university it will be difficult to create the Maya University.

Lastly, the question of the time frame for implementation of the accords also proved to be problematic. The Agreement on the Timetable for Implementation envisaged the implementation of the educational reform within four years (1996–2000) (URL 1997: 219–58). However, short-term educational reforms generally take some eight to ten years and long-term reforms some 15 to 20 years, although some analysts argue for permanent and ongoing educational reform. The timetable for the implementation of the educational reform has already been changed twice. The first revision was carried out by COPARE, the commission responsible for drafting the design of the educational reform, which timetabled a ten-year period (1998–2008), contained in the design of the reform itself. The CCRE made a second change, timetabling the reform for a 20-year period, which is in turn reflected in the Long-Term National Plan for Education 2000–20. These changes to the Timetable for Implementation led to criticism from verification agencies, such as MINUGUA, of the slow pace of implementation and eventually led to the readjustment of the time frame. These extensions have meant that indigenous people have to wait even longer for positive change.

II. Implementing the educational reform: the Parity Commission (COPARE), 1997–98

The Indigenous Accord included the requirement that a Parity Commission made up of representatives from indigenous organisations and the government be set up to elaborate the design of the educational reform (chapter III, section G, clauses 2 and 5). COPARE's objective was to negotiate the precise manner in which the commitments acquired on education could be translated into a concrete proposal. The Parity Commission considered two dimensions of the reform process, the technical and the political. The technical dimension referred to the content and pedagogic methods proposed in the design of the reform which were to be drafted by experts in the field. The political dimension referred to the legitimacy of the proposals for society and for different sectors and organised groups. Other experiences in educational reform had confirmed that without the participation of civil society purely technical educational reforms tend to fail or have a limited impact. The decision-making process had to involve the direct or indirect participation of interested civil sectors, awareness of the needs, interests and proposals of those sectors, and the achievement of consensus and compromise. It was this political dimension that would ensure that civil society was informed about the educational reform and ultimately would approve and support it. In order for the educational reform to have a chance of success both aspects – the technical and the political – had to be carefully dealt with. However, it was not always easy to attend to both dimensions to the same degree.

COPARE was created on 2 April 1997. It included five delegates from indigenous organisations and five government delegates designated by the Ministry of Education. According to the timetable it was to finish its remit within nine months, by December 1997. In the event, the reform proposal was some seven months overdue and was finally completed in July 1998. The structure and format of the negotiations were as follows:

The Coordinator of Organisations of the Mayan People, COPMAGUA, and its specific body on education, the Permanent National Commission for Educational Reform (CNPRE), elected five indigenous representatives after agreeing on the number with the governmental Peace Secretariat, SEPAZ. These five, in turn, represented the different umbrella groups that made up COPMAGUA. COPMAGUA was the body charged with organising the elections of indigenous representatives and was composed of two 'culturalist' Mayan organisations (the Academy of Mayan Languages, ALMG, and the Coordinator of Mayan Organisations of Guatemala, COMG) and three 'popular' Mayan organisations (Tukum Uman, the Instance of Mayan Unity and Consensus (IUCM) and the Union of the Mayan People of Guatemala, UPMAG). The National Council for Mayan Education, CNEM, was not originally part of COPMAGUA but was included because it was explicitly cited in the Indigenous Accord. For the government, the Ministry of Education designated three representatives from the Ministry itself, a fourth person was delegated from the teachers' unions and a fifth place filled by an indigenous person who was not a member of the Ministry of Education. These two last-minute adoptions helped the Ministry of Education to appear less 'ladino-centric' and also gave some space to the teachers' organisations (generally teachers' unions are at loggerheads with the educational authorities and indigenous people are excluded from the government). The elected indigenous delegates had to respond to the organisations where they worked, the umbrella organisations they represented and COPMAGUA. The Ministry of Education delegates had to respond essentially to the educational authorities, something that was quite difficult for the teachers' union representative. The government indigenous delegate, who was quite an independent figure, hardly ever stuck to the government position but rather adopted the role of conciliator between the two sides and, occasionally, leaned in favour of the indigenous organisation delegates.

The framework for the negotiations themselves was set out in the peace accords and international conventions such as ILO Convention 169, which had been ratified but not implemented. An attempt was made to hold the negotiations in a neutral space, such as a house rented for the purpose or a borrowed conference room. In general, the Parity Commission met twice a week for a whole morning or afternoon, sometimes this extended to whole days or various consecutive days if required. According to its internal regulations, COPARE did not have a director but rather a coordinator, a post which was alternated between the government and indigenous organisations' representatives. Because it was a parity commission, decision-making power was equally distributed between the two groups. The regulations also specified that decisions be reached by consensus. COPARE also created two internal parity organs: the Technical Secretariat and the 'Petit Comité', together with teams of consultants to research specific areas and problems.

COPARE had a mandatory relationship with the Peace Secretariat, SEPAZ, the governmental body charged with implementation of the peace accords, and with the Accompaniment Commission, principally in the event of problems arising. The UN Verification Mission, MINUGUA, was charged with checking that the educational reform was being complied with. National embassies in Guatemala monitored compliance with the Peace Accords to a limited extent. The relevant civic organisations participated principally in elaborating proposals for the reform, which were then presented to COPARE. Their role in verifying compliance with the educational reform was minimal, apart from those organisations which had a delegate on COPARE. The Civil Society Assembly (ASC), the body set up in 1994 to channel civil society groups' proposals to the negotiating table, played a minor role in monitoring the educational reform. During the period of COPARE's existence opposition to the educational reform was voiced by conservative sectors and non-participating teachers' unions, but they did not pose a serious problem – their opposition was more due to the non-inclusion of their proposals or members.

Problems encountered in COPARE

Despite differences and competition between them, the indigenous organisations managed to elect their five delegates after a series of meetings and assemblies: three 'cultural' delegates and two 'popular' delegates. Inevitably,

Indigenous delegates	Government delegates
CNEM delegate ◯	◯ Ministry of Education
COMG delegate ◯	◯ CONALFA delegate
ALMG delegate ◯	◯ PRONADE delegate[4]
Garífuna delegate ◯	◯ ANM union delegate
CNPRE delegate ◯	◯ PROMEM delegate

Figure 4.1   COPARE: civic and governmental representatives (see also Appendix 4.1)

however, some organisations felt marginalised or unrepresented in these elections. The five representatives chosen by the Ministry of Education, on the other hand, were not elected but appointed. As the government is predominantly ladino in ethnic terms, these were predominantly ladino. In order not to appear completely mono-ethnic, the government appointed one indigenous representative who helped the government side to appear somewhat more plural. However, the different means of selecting the delegates meant that the two sides took decisions at different speeds – the elected indigenous organisation delegates had to consult more extensively than the government representatives – and that each enjoyed different degrees of legitimacy

Delegating power and acting as a delegate for organisations and institutions is a learning process. The hegemonic sector of COPMAGUA's Permanent National Commission for Educational Reform (CNPRE) was made up of institutions directly or indirectly linked to the guerrilla organisations who were unaware or ill-informed about the procedures to be followed in the Parity Commission. This provoked a series of problems, above all at the outset of the negotiations, because the members of the CNPRE maintained that they had not delegated decision-making power. This practically invalidated the role of their delegates to the negotiating table and provoked the suspension of negotiations for a number of weeks. Ultimately the principles, norms and functions of the representatives in COPARE and the delegation of functions and faculties to those representatives had to be established with the member organisations of the CNPRE with the presence of observers from the UN mission, MINUGUA and the Peace Secretariat, SEPAZ. After weeks of suspended talks, the CNPRE leaders were forced to recognise that their indigenous representatives did have decision-making powers, together with the government delegates.

The Indigenous Accord envisaged an equal number of representatives from the government and from indigenous organisations and the equal division of decision-making power between them. Nonetheless, the indigenous delegation was weakened by the lack of professional qualifications, contacts and resources, resulting in technical disadvantages. It also had little or no access to the data and information held in the Ministry of Education or logistical back-up. These technical disadvantages meant that some of their proposals and demands were rejected or defeated because of technicalities, restricted circulation of information and grandiloquent language. On the other hand, the governmental delegation had more leverage for a diverse series of reasons. The Garífuna delegate on the indigenous side was a teacher in a state primary school, and the authorisation to take time off work or be temporarily substituted depended on the Minister of Education or his subordinates. At the same time, the indigenous delegates who worked in NGOs or international organisations and who depended in some way or other on the Ministry of Education (for authorisation of projects, contracts as intermediary providers of educational services, and so on) could be subjected to indirect pressure. Similarly, the members of the Technical Secretariat, while obliged to act with neutrality, were open to pressure from the educational authorities, given the fact that sooner or later they would need to seek employment. Maintaining good relations with the educational authorities was therefore a kind of insurance for the future. The government was able to impose an almost military discipline amongst its negotiating team by threatening cautions or sackings, thus imposing a unitary line among all the delegates (with the exception of the indigenous delegate on the governmental side who considered himself 'independent', and, to a lesser extent, the trade union delegate). However, nobody on the indigenous team had such coercive power and internal dissent was therefore more pronounced than among its governmental counterpart. These differences in leverage and abilities put the indigenous delegates at a disadvantage.

COPARE made a public call for civic sectors to present proposals for changes to the education system. This was carried out via radio announcements, paid advertisements in the newspapers and a poster campaign in Spanish and three indigenous languages. Participation was relatively high and some 30 proposals of differing quality were received. Proposals were also received orally through a series of public meetings that achieved the involvement of significant sectors of Guatemalan society. The educational reform excited considerable interest and contributions were made in the form of forums, debates and various studies from the organised sectors of civil society, supported in part by the international community. Nonetheless, other members of civil society, above all teachers, perceived their participation as weak or non-existent. The enormous difficulties of communication throughout the country, limited access to the media, high levels of illiteracy, weak purchasing power, linguistic diversity and, above all, a political culture of systematic opposition to all public authorities meant it was difficult to ensure the consultation and participation of all groups and sectors. In addition, for most Guatemalans the Peace Accords were never as important as other issues, such as poverty or violent crime.

Problems related to the content of the negotiations

In negotiations over the content of the educational reform, key governmental representatives acted in such a way as to effectively renegotiate the criteria and parameters of the reform, or impose these as the limit for discussions. In contrast, as far as the indigenous delegates were concerned, the Peace Accords had already been negotiated and all that remained was to agree how to implement them. They also considered the accords as a starting point rather than an end-point for discussions. On some issues, such as indigenous educational autonomy, the government delegates did not cede at all or ceded even less than that stipulated by ILO Convention 169 on Indigenous and Tribal Peoples (which states that indigenous people have the right to direct their own educational institutions). However, despite these difficulties, on the whole the governmental delegation was open to accept indigenous proposals, above all when the leadership of the delegation was in the hands of the Vice-Minister of Education during the first half of 1997. This openness decreased when the minister took over towards the end of 1997 and during the first half of 1998. Nonetheless, despite differences, in general terms they always managed to achieve a 'consensus' that led to the elaboration of the design for the reform.

Both the governmental and indigenous delegates in COPARE adopted the categories and language of the Peace Accords which insisted that the country be characterised as 'multi-ethnic, pluri-cultural and multi-lingual'. The accords stated that four peoples made up the Guatemalan nation (ladino, Maya, Xinca and Garífuna), that each has different cultural expressions in the form of distinct ethnic and linguistic communities. However, the concepts of multi-culturalism and interculturalism were 'guatemalanised'; that is they were contextualised according to where they were to be applied, their meaning shifting according to the plans and fears of each side. For the indigenous delegates multiculturalism meant the possibility of obtaining positive recognition of their existence, strengthening their cultures, which had hitherto been discriminated by the state, and obtaining effective rights to equality and difference. Thus they adopted this doctrine as the appropriate formula to meet their cultural needs In contrast, some ladino governmental delegates viewed multiculturalism as a strategy that would result in indigenous separatism, isolation and even 'ethnic cleansing' and for this reason they opposed it. Government delegates preferred instead the notion of 'interculturalism', effectively the maintenance of good relations between the different cultural groups present in Guatemala. Government delegates explicitly argued that interculturalism was the ideal mechanism to construct positive relations between indigenous and non-indigenous people in order to achieve mutual enrichment. Indigenous representatives rejected the idea of interculturalism not because they did not think it necessary, but rather because they perceived it as a state-imposed formula that was difficult to apply equitably among cultural communities which existed in highly unequal conditions. In addition, they found that ladino governmental representatives interpreted interculturalism in such a way as to permit the continued assimilation and control of indigenous people. Faced with these problems in obtaining a consensus, the negotiating parties decided to use both categories simultaneously and for this reason both concepts appear with equal weight in the proposal for the educational reform. The final solution was to define a sequence between the two: acknowledge and recognise one's own culture (multiculturalism), know and respect other cultures (interculturalism), accept and appreciate the differences between one's own and other cultures (multiculturalism and interculturalism).

For indigenous people the means to resolve their traditional subordination and marginalisation in the education system was to have an indigenous Vice-Minister of Education or their own Ministry, as experience had taught them that they would inevitably be marginalised in state institutions controlled by ladinos. In contrast, government representatives argued that indigenous education would not be resolved by the creation of parallel structures, but rather through one unitary system. Given that consensus decision-making was understood in practice as whatever the government ceded or conceded, indigenous delegates were forced to accept the idea of a single structure, but they introduced the idea of 'shared power', which was accepted by the government side. At the highest level of the Ministry of Education this was taken to mean the integration of Mayan authorities with ladino authorities so that it no longer appeared that the Ministry was controlled exclusively by ladinos or that indigenous people were excluded or only participated in a symbolic manner. The idea of 'shared power' is one formula that facilitates unity with equality in multi-ethnic societies (Lijphart 1994: 159–84).

Problems relating to the procedures adopted

The indigenous delegates faced enormous problems in terms of complying with their obligations. Meetings of COPARE usually took place twice a week for a whole morning or afternoon at a sitting. The indigenous delegates also met outside once a week to consult with their grass roots and report on advances. They also held additional regular weekly sessions to prepare their work and strategies for the coming meetings, and then they often had extraordinary or unscheduled meetings. Apart from very few exceptions, indigenous delegates were not relieved of their normal work duties in order to meet these obligations. The same was also true for the government delegates, for whom participation in COPARE was almost always an additional burden. Hardly anyone had enough time to analyse the topics to be discussed in any depth. Of all the delegates, only those who worked as teachers in state schools (one indigenous and one governmental representative) were excused from their regular work duties, but even then they were unable to contribute much in terms of global overviews or analysis of political processes. This problem of scheduling the meetings meant that the design for the educational reform eventually agreed was quite repetitive; indigenous representatives feared that their points had not been included and therefore fought to have their platforms included in each and every aspect of the proposal. This also made the entire process more drawn out than it should have been.

Those interested in changing the educational system were indigenous people, which implied that they would be proactive and draw up proposals for change. The government side only had to reject, accept or partially accept those proposals and did not see it as necessary to elaborate alternatives. This entailed a series of disadvantages for indigenous delegates, who were generally the least well equipped or qualified, above all in drafting technical proposals. At the same time it implied that they had the time and resources to carry out research and develop proposals, which was not the case.

Because of the mutual lack of confidence between government and indigenous delegates, and perhaps also to maintain the rule of parity, COPARE decided that all the teams which supported or implemented the Commission's work, including the Technical Secretariat and the 'Petit Comité', should have equal representation from both sides. The research teams, which carried out 11 studies to support the design for the reform in the areas of language, culture, administration, teaching methods, legal situation, human resources and public policies, were also subject to the parity rule. Yet the indigenous side faced continual problems in finding sufficient qualified indigenous personnel to work with non-indigenous individuals on these teams; they either lacked academic qualifications or professional experience.

Both sides delegated the task of drafting the final proposal to one of their members. However, because of lack of time, experience and political leverage before the Technical Secretariat, the contribution of the indigenous delegate was weak and the government delegate monopolised the task of drafting the final document, according to the decisions of COPARE. In spite of this, and above all because of lack of preparation on both sides, paragraphs and expressions were added between the first and second versions of the document which led to subsequent difficulties which also had to be worked out according to parity arrangements.

In general, negotiations between indigenous and government representatives were characterised by collective differences in the uses of language. For diverse reasons, some of them cultural, indigenous people tended to use language sparingly, while ladinos tended to speak at length. Linguistic competence and familiarity with technical terms was also a factor – Spanish was not the mother tongue of the majority of the indigenous delegates and for some it very much continued to be their second language. In addition, open displays of anger were rare among the indigenous delegates and only occurred in cases of serious divisions or conflicts. Discussions were hardly ever heated, as everyone was aware this could mean long-term divisions. However, angry exchanges were commonplace among the ladinos, even over minor points, and did not lead to long-term conflicts. For indigenous delegates, evidence of participation and agreement depended on the number of participants and the verbal intervention of each and every one. This sometimes worked against them as the different individual organisations they represented revealed differences that the governmental team used to their advantage. For different reasons, the ladinos were able to channel their participation through election of a group spokesperson. This meant the government side generally presented a strong, united front. These differences were most evident in the negotiations between COPMAGUA and SEPAZ.

The major cause of setbacks in the drafting of the proposal was the temporary suspension of negotiations between October and December 1997. Indigenous delegates broke off the talks arguing that they needed to consult with their grass roots, but in fact the real reason for the division was that the then minister was trying to reduce indigenous participation in the Consultative Commission on Educational Reform to three delegates out of 18. On 29 October 1997 President Arzú inaugurated the Consultative Commission in the National Palace, but the indigenous organisations registered their protest at the Commission's composition by not turning up to take their seats. Negotiations recommenced on 18 December, following a series of agreements between the Ministry of Education, COPMAGUA, CNEM and SEPAZ, under the supervision of the Accompaniment Commission and MINUGUA. The Ministry finally accepted the participation of five supplementary indigenous delegates on the Consultative Commission, increasing their number to eight. The government was forced to accept indigenous demands because of its need to demonstrate results in the negotiating process. The final proposal for the educational reform and an explanation of its public and political implications was officially handed over to President Arzú and SEPAZ on 20 July 1998. SEPAZ passed the document to the Consultative Commission for implementation (although the Consultative Commission was officially created on 29 December 1997, it had been unable to begin its task until it received COPARE's proposal).

III. Implementation of the educational reform: the Consultative Commission (CCRE), 1997–98

The Socio-Economic Accord envisaged the creation of a Consultative Commission linked to the Ministry of Education and made up of participants in the educational process, including representation from COPARE. Initially the CCRE was composed of 18 delegates from 17 institutions and organisations, but after the protest of the indigenous organisations it was extended to include 23 delegates of 17 institutions and organisations. The mandate of the Commission was and is to carry out the educational reform.

Civil society institutions and organisations elected and appointed delegates to the CCRE. Some of these bodies were part of groups, such as the universities which were linked in an Inter-University Forum. Others, such as the indigenous organisations (CNEM and CNPRE) set up coordinating bodies among themselves. The Ministry of Education appointed its delegates, who were generally heads of its internal departments. There was only one indigenous member amongst the Ministry's delegation, the director of the Department for Bilingual Education. The civil society delegates were a heterogeneous group and did not constitute a single bloc. However, events dictated that in some instances the civil society delegates clashed with the governmental delegates. As the delegation was comprised of institutions not individuals, there has been some turnover in the committee's membership. Every delegate has to answer to their own institution and use only COPARE's proposal for the educational reform and the peace accords as their points of reference. If existing legislation had been used as a guide, it would have been impossible to implement significant sections of the reform.

Negotiations took place in the Ministry of Education and consisted of an assembly of the 23 delegates from 17 predominantly civic organisations concerned with education: universities, teachers' unions, indigenous organisations, private schools, and so on (see Appendix 4.3). The Minister of Education was responsible for coordinating the CCRE as he was ultimately responsible for implementing the reform. The Consultative Commission is effectively an adjunct or annex of the Ministry; therefore the minister has the final say. The Commission only has powers of assessment, accompaniment, advice and monitoring – it is not an executive organ nor can it take binding decisions on the implementation of the reform. Its decisions must be taken by consensus. The CCRE also has a number of internal bodies, including the Executive Council, Technical Secretariat, sub-commissions and work-groups, plus teams of research consultants. The Commission has a mandatory relationship with SEPAZ and, in the event of problems, must go to the Accompaniment Commission. MINUGUA continues its role in verifying the implementation of the reform. The embassies have been active in monitoring the implementation of the commitments acquired in the Peace Accords. A greater number of civil society organisations have issued statements on the implementation of the educational reform and have tried to lobby on this issue. Some opponents of the reform publicly voiced their opposition, such as some trade unions and teachers' leaders and non-participating private schools, but on the whole opposition has not increased.

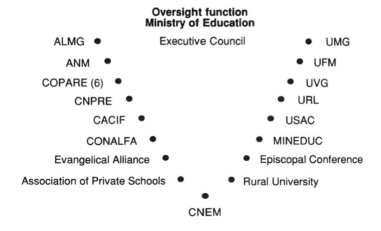

**Oversight function
Ministry of Education**

	Executive Council	
ALMG ●		● UMG
ANM ●		● UFM
COPARE (6) ●		● UVG
CNPRE ●		● URL
CACIF ●		● USAC
CONALFA ●		● MINEDUC
Evangelical Alliance ●		● Episcopal Conference
Association of Private Schools ●	● Rural University	
	● CNEM	

Figure 4.2   Civil and governmental forces represented in the CCRE (see Appendix 4.3)

Problems encountered in the CCRE

One of the aims of including such a range of institutions in the field of education was to ensure as great a participation as possible and to strengthen the Consultative Committee. In order to gain legitimacy, the educational reform needed to integrate as many sectors linked to education as it could, including those that could facilitate or block the reform. But this multi-sectoral approach presented a number of problems. The delegates came from different political trajectories and professional backgrounds and had distinct technical proficiencies and expectations, all of which made collective endeavour difficult. This was evident in the initial elaboration of work plans and the internal rules and regulations of the committee. For example, long discussions took place on whether or not all the representatives had to sign every record of a meeting. Nonetheless, the Consultative Commission is one of the first experiments in multi-sectoral collaboration for education in Guatemala.

Another problem for the CCRE was where to begin. The proposal for educational reform drafted by COPARE did not signal a clear starting point. There was no flow-chart to orient the work of implementation. After a few attempts, the CCRE finally approved a document at the end of 1998 that set out 15 priorities for the Consultative Commission during 1999 (see Appendix 4.2). These included: diffusion and validation of the proposal itself, revision of plans and programmes of the Ministry of Education, the formulation of a National Plan for Education (2000–08), the revision of the legal framework, curricular transformation, and the creation of the Mayan University. Some progress has been made on these different fronts, but coordination between them has been minimal.

After resolving the problem of duplication of functions between COPARE and the CCRE concerning who was to draw up the proposal for the educational reform, the major problem encountered has been the subordinate relationship of the Consultative Committee to government ministers. Until the end of 1997 the then Minister of Education limited the CCRE to assessment and advisory functions. She even expected the CCRE to approve government plans and procedures between 1997 and mid-1998. The CCRE complained that this was not its function and pressed for its right to decide the nature of the educational reform together with the Ministry. At times the Ministry accepted this, but sometimes it acted in such a way as to confirm the subordinate relationship of the CCRE set out in the Socio-Economic Accord. These frictions were at least partly due to lack of experience in managing such relations between government and civil society representatives on a theme of common interest.

Another problem faced by the CCRE was the dual agenda of the Ministry of Education. In one sense, the government had already drawn up its plan and had established targets prior to the final signing of the peace accords on

29 December 1996. The CCRE followed the agenda of the accords and the government stuck to its own agenda. Another factor was the negative attitudes of members of the governing party towards indigenous people in general, and towards bilingual education in particular, which meant that they constantly blocked measures favourable to indigenous people through the Ministry of Education. The minister did little or nothing to try and reconcile both agendas or to subordinate the government agenda to that of the peace accords. The Ministry made the educational reform only one of its eight policy priorities, which meant that the reform received insufficient attention. Nonetheless, the government took advantage of the euphoria and optimism generated by the signing of the peace accords to negotiate large loans with the World Bank and the Inter-American Bank in order to support educational reform. This occasioned conflicts with the CCRE, whose members argued that these loans and the manner in which they were used evidenced the dual agenda of the Ministry. On numerous occasions the Minister of Education at the time made declarations to the press that the educational reform had begun, pointing to the sectoral reforms made under previous administrations and the activities carried out which related to the international loans. However, as far as the members of the CCRE were concerned, the reform had not begun. This dual agenda meant that members of the Consultative Committee felt manipulated and cheated, viewing their participation in the CCRE as a distraction which allowed the Ministry to do what it wanted when it wanted. This tension lessened towards mid-1999 when general elections were on the horizon and the Ministry became much more open to dialogue and criticism. Another problem encountered by the CCRE was its lack of understanding of the political rhythms that dictated the actions of the Executive. Governments were obliged to show results within their four-year term, therefore any suspension or hold-up in the implementation process had potentially dire consequences. In contrast the CCRE was not subject to similar pressures, leading to contradictions between its desire to have a decisive role in the educational reform and its inability to accompany the process at the same pace as the Ministry. This has proved to be a recurring problem.

The CCRE was made up of 17 institutions but included 23 delegates because certain institutions, such as COPARE and the indigenous organisations, had more than one representative. This is a large number of people and does not make for an easy or swift decision-making process. In addition, some institutions rotate their representatives and, in some cases, the level of absenteeism is quite high, making decision-making even slower and more laborious. Because of the time constraints of its members, the CCRE meets every 15 days. This is a long time gap between meetings in terms of providing continuity in the discussions – what effectively happens is that immediate matters are discussed and this has little impact on what has already been discussed or what is yet to be addressed. Indigenous delegates constitute a majority in the CCRE. Although different tendencies exist among them they have managed to work together and ally themselves with non-indigenous popular sectors such as the teachers' unions or ex-members of the guerrillas within COPMAGUA. They have made their weight felt by changing and electing new members of the CCRE's Executive Council. As a result some ladino members of the Commission have complained of a built-in 'Mayan majority'. However, the numerical and political power of the Mayan delegates has been exercised with caution in order not to provoke the unification of the ladino delegates.

In general terms the role of the CCRE's members is more political than technical, although in practice it is difficult to separate these two aspects. Members of the CCRE were unequally prepared to exercise technical functions and make recommendations: few had any pedagogic training, some had formal educational training, others had non-formal educational backgrounds but no experience in teaching. The universities and the churches were perhaps the most qualified delegates to the CCRE. These differences in technical and academic qualifications were made worse by the fact that hardly any of the delegates were relieved of their regular work duties. The sub-commissions therefore produced results slowly and took a considerable time to respond to requests for information.

The Socio-Economic Accord was drafted with the intention of neutralising the possible effects of the Indigenous Accord on the educational system by means of reducing the power of civil society to affect the educational reform. This was achieved by making the Consultative Commission an adjunct to the Ministry of Education and by reducing the focus on ethnic discrimination by widening it to include social, gender and geographical discrimination. Social concerns thus weakened the emphasis on the ethnic question within the CCRE, where the indigenous question was not the central issue (it had not been the central issue either in COPARE, but at least in the Parity Commission the indigenous theme was permanently on the agenda). Attention was focused on the theme by the presence of indigenous delegates, by the need for non-indigenous delegates to accept a multicultural approach, and by the role of the indigenous question in COPARE's draft proposal. The ladino delegates did not champion their ethnic rights, but this relative lack of interest in the ethnic question meant that neither did they focus on the need for ladinos to modify their own believes and attitudes, such as their ethnic chauvinism and negation of their indigenous roots. On occasion Mayan delegates paid less attention to the specific demands of indigenous people in order to focus on general themes related to national education. While this disproves the widespread prejudice that indigenous people can only deal with issues that directly affect them, it has also meant that the Indigenous Accord has not always been respected and many opportunities to advance their demands for culturally and linguistically appropriate education for indigenous peoples have been lost.

A number of changes envisaged by the peace accords were to be approved by Congress and endorsed by a popular referendum. For example, the referendum was to approve the recognition of indigenous customary law, of the nation as multi-ethnic, and the co-officialisation of indigenous languages. In the event, these reforms were not approved in the referendum held in May 1999. The reasons for this were diverse and included racism. Fortuitously, the educational reform was not subject to approval by Congress and public referendum and so was not affected by the fiasco of the rejection of the constitutional reforms. Nonetheless, various opponents of the educational reform, such as some teachers' unions, used the rejection of the constitutional reforms to extend their campaign against the educational changes set out in the peace accords. The general elections at the end of 1999 also had a negative impact on public perceptions of the educational reform. Some opposition parties opposed it as the work of the governing party, the Partido de Avanzada Nacional (PAN). This politicisation of the educational reform was so acute that the Ministry of Education itself, with the backing of the Executive Council of the CCRE, decided to reduce public discussion of the reform while at the same time trying to safeguard the process. It was feared that opposition parties would not support the reform, so the CCRE redoubled its efforts to inform them of the composition of the Commission and the advances made. However, following the defeat of the constitutional reform, opponents of the educational reform gradually increased their profile. Some teachers' unions opposed the reform because it recognised the multicultural nature of the country, which they viewed as a step towards ethnic separatism. They also opposed recognition of the need for parents and civil society to have a greater say in the running of the education system. Some indigenous teachers also rejected the reform because of the 'effect of 500 years of colonialism', viewing the teaching of indigenous languages and cultures as a backward step. Conservative sectors also opposed the reform, arguing it was necessary to prioritise economic growth not education. They additionally alleged that existing laws, not the peace accords – which they maintained had been negotiated with 'criminals' (that is, the guerrillas) – should provide the country's legal framework. Lastly, they opposed multiculturalism and inter-culturalism on the grounds that they would lead to fragmentation and maintained that national unity would only be preserved by uniform policies. Happily, however, the majority of the private sector and a sizeable part of the 15 teachers' unions supported the educational reform, even though they were not enamoured of all of its components or proposals.

Conclusions

The Peace Accords concluded in December 1996 were not perfect, precise or complete. They contained inherent contradictions, limitations, confusions and gaps that negatively affected the task of the negotiating parties responsible for their application. These internal limitations were due to the government and URNG's lack of expertise in the themes negotiated, or to deliberate omissions, authoritarianism, idealism or differences between the projections and plans of different governments involved in the negotiations. These contradictions and inconsistencies, together with the attempt to maintain coherence between the different accords, the 1985 Constitution and existing legislation, limited the development of the negotiations and the recognition of the rights of indigenous peoples. Fortunately the peace negotiators left possibilities open to reinterpret, correct and reschedule the commitments signed, via the mechanisms of the Special and Parity Commissions and the Accompaniment Commission.

Nearly all the problems analysed here negatively affected the negotiations of the Parity Commission, but they most negatively affected the indigenous delegation. Differences in leverage, technical and political inequalities, the unequal responsibilities for drawing up proposals for change and issues of language and different participatory styles all had an impact. The extension of parity to internal teams was perhaps intended to seek justice and equality of opportunity, but in the course of implementation the disadvantages of such arrangements became evident. Despite the institutional parity between the negotiating parties (numerical equality between indigenous and government teams) and the democratic mechanisms employed, the indigenous side was weak or at a disadvantage in nearly all areas.

Both sides suffered from the limited participation of civil society, despite all their efforts, and the fact that they were not relieved of their own work obligations in order to better serve in COPARE. Had they been full time they would have been able to finish the proposal for the reform in four or five months. However, the two teams did manage to reach a reasonably satisfactory 'consensus' which resulted in the completion of the proposal and the construction of good inter-ethnic relations.

With respect to the CCRE, the problems analysed make it clear that external circumstances and factors continue to limit the development of harmonious 'consultation' between the Ministry of Education and the Consultative Commission. This derives from problems that date from the start of the educational reform and frictions between the Ministry and the Commission. The general elections of November 1998 and the defeat of the constitutional reform package also negatively affected the CCRE. However, the most detrimental impact has been on the indigenous representatives and indigenous interests in general.

Multiple lessons can be drawn from this experience. The Consultative Commission demonstrated its coherence and maturity, for example by insisting on its independence from the Ministry of Education, but also proved vulnerable to external events, such as the elections and the referendum. Similarly, it demonstrated its capacity to pursue implementation of educational reform, but was hampered by its slow pace of operation and the difficulties faced in achieving internal consensus. One thing that is clear is that the governmental or ministerial part has always been more powerful than the civil society delegates (indigenous or non-indigenous) in terms of its ability to determine directions and decisions. Civil society delegations have consistently proved to be weaker and less well prepared for negotiations. In general, the elaboration of the proposal and its implementation has not always been a consensual process, but rather has been marked by ongoing struggles. If the government had displayed more political will in complying with the peace accords then this would not have been necessary. For their part, indigenous people have been tenacious in pursuing their linguistic and cultural needs via the educational reform. The Secretariat for Peace, SEPAZ, has identified the indigenous organisations as one of the sectors most interested in ensuring compliance with the Peace Accords. However, their technical, logistical and political disadvantages, together with their focus on general, national themes, meant they lost opportunities to ensure that all their demands which were recognised in the Peace Accords were subsequently respected.

Notes

1. Guatemalan Vice-Minister of Education (1996–). The views expressed here do not necessarily reflect those of the government of Guatemala or the Ministry of Education.
2. COPARE was established on 2 April 1997 and completed its remit on 20 July 1998; the CCRE was set up on 29 October 1997, became operational on 20 July 1998 and was still functioning as of August 2000.
3. 'Mayan schools' refers to non-state schools run either by indigenous communities themselves or by indigenous NGOs which seek to strengthen mechanisms for indigenous cultural self-determination. These schools, which have much more freedom to experiment than the Ministry of Education, have generated a number of culturally and linguistically sensitive pedagogic methods and course materials. In effect, Mayan schools are innovative educational proposals advanced by indigenous civil society.
4. PRONADE stands for National Programme for Educational Self-Development (Programa Nacional de Autogestión Educativa). This highly decentralised programme consists of parents' committees which administer certain funds from the Ministry of Education in order to hire teachers, buy educational materials and carry out repairs to school buildings. It generally operates in inaccessible parts of the country where there are no ordinary schools.

Appendices

Appendix 4.1: COPARE delegates

Indigenous delegates

Demetrio Cojtí for the Consejo Nacional de Educación Maya (National Council for Mayan Education, CNEM)

Obdulio Son Chonay and subsequently Pedro Guoron for the Consejo de Organizaciones del Pueblo Maya (Council of Organisations of the Mayan People, COMG), a member of the Coordinadora de Organizaciones del Pueblo Maya (Coordinator of Organisations of the Mayan People, COPMAGUA)

Ruperto Montejo for the Academia de las Lenguas Mayas de Guatemala (Academy of Mayan Languages of Guatemala, ALMG), also a member of COPMAGUA

Domingo Sánchez, for the Comisión Nacional Permanente de Reforma Educativa (National Permanent Commission for Educational Reform, CNPRE), special organ of COPMAGUA which aims to monitor the Educational Reform

Maura Luz Leiva, state school teacher and delegate of the Garífuna people, represented in the CNPRE

Governmental delegates

María Eugenia Ramírez and later Roberto Moreno, delegates of the Minister of Education, Arabella Castro

Eva Sazo de Méndez, Pedagogic Advisor to the PRONADE educational programme

Floridalma Meza Palma, Executive Secretary to the Comisión Nacional de Alfabetización (National Literacy Commission, CONALFA) and Director of the Peace Secretariat of the Ministry of Education.

Egil Ivan Galindo, trade union leader of the Asamblea Nacional Magisterial (National Teachers' Assembly, ANM)

Santos Virgilio Alvarado Ajanel, indigenous delegate invited by the Ministry of Education, National Coordinator of the Programa de Movilización pro Educación Maya (Pro-Mayan Education Mobilisation Programme)

Appendix 4.2: CCRE's 15-point work plan

Diffusion and validation of the proposal for Educational Reform
Revision of the Ministry of Education's plans, programmes and projects
Formulation of the National Plan for Education, 2000–08
Revision of legislation
Design of a Strategy for Social Participation for the Reform
Strengthen the CCRE
Curricular changes
Mayan University
Promotion of educational research
Private schools
Development of Human Resources
Development of special educational needs programmes
Multicultural and intercultural education
Organisational structures

Appendix 4.3: Member organisations of the CCRE

Academia de Lenguas Mayas de Guatemala (Academy of Mayan Languages of Guatemala, ALMG)
Alianza Evangélica de Guatemala (Evangelical Alliance of Guatemala)
Asamblea Nacional Magisterial (National Teachers' Assembly, ANM)
Association of Private Schools
Comisión Paritaria de Reforma Educativa (Parity Commission for Educational Reform, COPARE)

Comisión Nacional Permanente de Reforma Educativa (National Permanent Commission for Educational Reform, CNPRE) of COPMAGUA
Comité Coordinador de Asociaciones Agrícolas, Comerciales y Financieras (Coordinating Committee of Agricultural, Commercial and Financial Associations, CACIF)
Comisión Nacional de Alfabetización (National Literacy Commission, CONALFA)
Conferencia Episcopal de Guatemala (Episcopal Conference of Guatemala)
Consejo Nacional de Educación Maya (National Council for Mayan Education, CNEM)
Ministry of Education (MINEDUC)
San Carlos University of Guatemala (USAC)
Rafael Landívar University (URL)
Del Valle University of Guatemala (UVG)
Francisco Marroquín University (UFM)
Mariano Gálvez University (UMG)
Rural University of Guatemala

References

CCRE (1999), *Plan Nacional de Largo Plazo (Versión Preliminar)*, Ministry of Education and CCRE (Guatemala).
CNEM (1997), *Reforma Educativa: Síntesis de Propuestas y Comentarios*, CNEM Publications, Litografía Nawal Wuj (Guatemala).
—— (1999), *Segundo Congreso de Educación Maya: Tejiendo la Educación para el Saqarik del Nuevo Ciclo*, CNEM, Litografía Nawal Wuj (Guatemala).
COPARE (1998), *Runuk'ik Jun K'ak'a Tijonik (Diseño de la Reforma Educativa)*, Comisión Paritaria de Reforma Educativa, Editorial Cholsamaj (Guatemala).
Lijphart, Arend (1994), 'El Enfoque del Poder Compartido para Sociedades Multiétnicas', *Autodeterminación*, No.12, July, Editorial Salamandra (La Paz, Bolivia).
Majawil Q'ij (1996), 'Memoria de Trabajo del Programa de Educación de la Coordinadora Nacional Majawil Q'ij (El Nuevo Amanecer)', Majawil Q'ij publications (Guatemala).
OEA PROPAZ (1997), 'Informe del Taller sobre la Toma de Decisiones y el Proceso de Consenso', carried out with members of COPARE, publications of the OAS Culture of Dialogue project (Guatemala).
—— (1999), *Construyendo Consensos: para un Futuro Sostenible*, Centro Editorial Vile, OEA (Guatemala).
PNUD (1997), *Acuerdos de Paz y la Educación en Guatemala*, PNUD publications, restricted circulation (Guatemala).
—— (1999), 'Guatemala: el Rostro Rural del Desarrollo Humano', editorial Magna Terra Editores, 278 páginas.
PREAL-ASIES (1998), *Reforma Educativa en Guatemala*, ASIES publications (Guatemala).
PRODESSA (1998), *Pongamos la Reforma Educativa en Movimiento*, Proyecto de Desarrollo Santiago (Guatemala).
—— (1999), *Transformemos la Educación de Guatemala: Basado en el Diseño de Reforma Educativa*, Proyecto Desarrollo Santiago, Editorial Saqil Tzij (Guatemala).
UNESCO (1995), 'Educación Maya: Experiencias y Expectativas en Guatemala', *Colección Caminos para la Paz*, UNESCO publications, Mayan Peoples Programme, Editorial Cholsamaj (Guatemala).

UNESCO-Fundación Rigoberta Menchú (1997), *Realidad Educativa de Guatemala: Diagnóstico de la Realidad Educativa de los Pueblos Indígenas y otros Pueblos Originarios de Mesoamérica*, Fundación Rigoberta Menchú (Guatemala).

UNESCO PROMEM (1999), *Comunidades Educativas Bilingües Interculturales: Marco Conceptual y Perfiles*, UNESCO, Editorial Cholsamaj (Guatemala).

UNICEF (1996), 'Análisis de Situación de la Educación Maya en Guatemala', UNICEF publications, Editorial Cholsamaj (Guatemala).

URL-IDIES (1997), *Acuerdos de Paz*, Instituto de Estudios Económicos y Sociales, Universidad Rafael Landívar, Industria Litográfica (Guatemala).

Various authors (1998), *Lineamientos Curriculares para la Educación Primaria Bilingüe Intercultural*, joint publication of CNEM, DIGEBI, PEMBI-GTZ, UNICEF, USAID, (Guatemala).

Various authors (1998), *Resumen de Propuestas de las Comisiones Paritarias: Oficialización de los Idiomas Indígenas, Reforma Educativa y Derechos Relativos a la Tierra*, Working document, FRMT, PRODESSA, CNEM, Acción Ciudadana and COPMAGUA, (Guatemala).

5
Social Citizenship, Ethnic Minority Demands, Human Rights and Neoliberal Paradoxes: A Case Study in Western Mexico

Guillermo de la Peña

Social citizenship, understood as the exercise of a body of rights to welfare which the state – in representation of society – grants all human beings as a guarantee of their dignity, has become a key component of modern democracy (Marshall 1964).[1] However, the acceptance of social citizenship was a long and difficult process. As Bryan Turner (1990) has shown, its formal recognition was not achieved merely through the benevolence of enlightened parliamentarians, but was rather a result of the struggles of organisations and parties representing the interests of less privileged classes during different historical periods. Thus, social citizenship has implied the rise and consolidation of class identities vis-à-vis a state which implements certain social policies. Over the last 30 years, in many countries across the world, including those of Latin America, a new struggle has emerged: the struggle for the right to different cultural and ethnic identities, where the latter are understood to be distinct from national identities officially proclaimed by national states. This idea has been defined as *cultural citizenship* (Kymlicka 1996; Pakulski 1997; Rosaldo 1997), or *ethnic citizenship* (de la Peña 1995 and 1999), the search for which also implies the reconfiguration of ethnic subjects themselves in the context of their relationship with the state (Sieder and Witchell 2001). Here I intend to explore some aspects of the relationship between both types of citizenship and both types of identity formation in the case of Mexico.

I will first briefly review the history of social and cultural policies of the Mexican state towards its indigenous peoples. The second part of the chapter relies on ethnographic data collected in the Sierra Huichola (northern Jalisco) dealing with a not uncommon confrontation of indigenous people between 'traditionalists' and 'evangelicals' which highlights conflicting conceptions of different types of rights. The method used is that of situational analysis, which focuses on a particular sequence of interaction (and sometimes confrontation) in a defined scenario, which seeks to understand the motivations of the actors with particular reference to power relations and social and cultural conditioning in a specific time and space (Van Velsen 1967; Garbett 1970). This method is useful when one is not attempting to characterise an ideal social morphology, but rather to understand the contradictions between rival normative frameworks and the discrepancies between norms and their interpretations (Gluckman 1958; Mitchell 1983). Thirdly, I attempt to situate my analysis in the broader context of the changing history of public identities and recent discussions on the political and legal implications of multiculturalism and multi-ethnicity. I should say at this point that I am not persuaded by the essentialist approach which highlights the 'clash between civilisations' (the 'Western' versus the 'indigenous') (Huntington 1996). Rather, I incline towards understanding the process as one of negotiation and repositioning of actors who use symbols and defend diverse cultural values in contexts of domination and resistance (Ong 1999).

From identity in transition to ambiguous identity

The social policies implemented by the post-revolutionary Mexican state have frequently been characterised as populist and corporatist, in that they were directed towards established groups and controlled vertically by an official, hegemonic party (the Institutional Revolutionary Party – Partido Revolucionario Institucional, PRI). These groups have also been used to generate clientelist networks (de la Peña 1986; Cordera Campos 1995; Cordera Campos and González Tiburcio 1999).[2] For example, agrarian policies which granted collective land titles to peasants to guarantee their livelihood involved the formation of groups of *ejidatarios* and *comuneros* organically linked to both the federal government and the rural sector of the governing party.[3] These *ejidatarios* and *comuneros* did not assume an outright peasant class identity, but rather an identity as 'revolutionary peasants'. Similarly, state schools have operated in the context of the hegemony of the Sindicato Nacional de Trabajadores de la Educación (National Teachers Union), equally linked to the PRI, and the political management of parents' associations (Street 1990). Multitudes of similar examples exist. However, one area of social policy was sui generis: Mexican state *indigenista* policies. *Indigenismo* not only sought to secure collective welfare for particularly poor and marginalised regions, but also aimed to unleash a process of 'acculturation' which would convert those groups classified as indigenous into citizen-bearers of a mestizo 'national culture'. The new negotiated identity was not simply a transition to being 'revolutionary peasants or workers', it was also a question of 'indigenous in transition to Mexican-ness' (which in future would take them onto a 'complete Mexican-ness') (Aguirre Beltrán 1958). In principle, the *indigenista* institutions – which were attempting a radical transformation of the socialisation model of children and young people – assumed many of the responsibilities previously shouldered by family and community.

The National Indigenista Institute, Instituto Nacional Indigenista (INI), founded in 1948, concentrated its activities on the indigenous population, creating Centros Coordinadores – Coordinating Centres – in strategic areas to carry out social research (it was assumed that a good percentage of INI employees should be anthropologists or social scientists), formulate regional evaluations, work with state development and welfare agencies (such as the ministries for land reform, education, health, agricultural outreach, communications, and so on) and coordinate activities adapted to the specific characteristics of INI's client population (Aguirre Beltrán and Pozas Arciniega 1954). In education, for example, INI insisted on the need to establish special programmes for literacy and Spanish-teaching ('castellanización'), as well as establishing residential boarding schools for indigenous children. From there the brightest were chosen to be trained as bilingual teachers and cultural promoters. The boarders were explicitly removed from family influences to make their conversion into 'Mexicans' more effective. In political terms, INI encouraged the disappearance of traditional authorities in favour of local involvement in municipal politics and the sectoral organisations of the PRI (Aguirre Beltrán 1953).

INI's institutional growth was slow, its budget limited and its ability to drum up popular support not always effective. Nonetheless, it did achieve substantial legitimacy due to the fact that it operated in the context of expanding state social policies and through its promotion of relatively successful agricultural production projects.[4] However, during the 1970s INI was severely criticised by left-wing academics and intellectuals and even by its own cadre – the young indigenous who had been educated as cultural promoters – who accused the institution of being bureaucratic and culturally repressive. They particularly pointed to its failure to prevent the extreme exploitation and abuse suffered by Indians in many places (see Bonfil et al. 1970; Pozas Arciniega 1976).[5] In 1974 the Indigenous Congress meeting held in San Cristóbal de las Casas, Chiapas, to commemorate Fray Bartolomé de las Casas became the first public stage for this criticism, which was subsequently repeated in many similar congresses (Morales Bermúdez 1992; de la Peña 1995). The government reacted by increasing the INI budget and the number of coordinating centres to more than 100 by 1980. To criticisms of the bureaucratic machine were now added those of waste and corruption. At the same time some officials from INI and other government departments initiated a discussion on the future of *indigenismo* and even promoted indigenous conferences and allowed a say for emerging ethnic organisations demanding respect for indigenous institutions and culture. In INI documents the term 'acculturation' was replaced with that of 'ethno-development' (Durán 1987); in practice, a process of decentralisation was undertaken which took local organisations into account. During the 1970s and 1980s the diffusion of an international discourse on human rights was also important; in Latin America this was used to condemn repressive dictatorship and the massacres of rural and indigenous populations. In Mexico it was deployed specifically to champion democratic values and to protest discrimination against indigenous people (Stavenhagen 1988). A highpoint in the change in *indigenista* policy was the unexpected amendment in 1992 of Article 4 of the 1917 Constitution, which henceforth declared that Mexico is a multicultural country, recognising for the first time the existence of 'indigenous peoples' and guaranteeing respect for their customs (Hindley 1995). This constituted an explicit recognition that people could be both Mexican and indigenous, rather than merely 'in transition' to being Mexican as previously. This subsequently gave rise to the need for a drastic rewrite of INI's role.[6]

It should, however, be noted that this sea change occurred in the context of an equally dramatic change in social policy. After the crisis of public finances sparked off in 1982, the Mexican government, like many others in Latin America, was obliged to follow the neoliberal prescriptions of the International Monetary Fund: opening up to external markets, discipline in public spending and shrinking the state apparatus. This enforced regime particularly affected the major welfare institutions, some of which, such as the land reform bureaucracy, were dismantled. As for INI, its functions of evaluation, planning, coordination and regional development virtually disappeared. Between 1983 and 1989 the *indigenista* budget plummeted in real terms. INI continued its educational role, coordinating the boarding schools together with the Department of Public Education, and prioritised training community leaders and campaigning for the human rights of indigenous people. As of 1990, INI took over the Regional Funds Programme, financing agricultural and commercial production projects run by and for indigenous groups. In its early years this programme enjoyed substantial dividends – not always well deployed – as it received funds from the powerful Programa Nacional de Solidaridad (PRONASOL – National Solidarity Programme), supported by the World Bank and directly promoted by President Salinas (Oehmichen 1999: 113). However, the disastrous economic performance in 1995 and subsequent adjustment measures led to cuts and financing criteria became much stricter.[7] As INI has downsized, state and municipal governments have included indigenous communities in their processes of decentralisation and programmes to support marginalised areas (both indigenous and non-indigenous). However, the funds available for these are limited.[8] Since 1997, the Education, Health and Food Programme

(PROGRESA) has operated in indigenous areas. This is a federal social programme for families in extreme poverty which provides a small payout of between 20 and 40 dollars per month to female-headed households. In return mothers must send their children to school and periodical medical revisions, and attend family planning education.[9] In this context of scarcity, those international and local non-governmental organisations (NGOs) that had been operating in the indigenous world since the 1970s assumed a much greater role as resource providers. NGOs tend to favour work in defence of biodiversity, human rights, minority groups and indigenous cultures.

Given this changing context of Mexican social policy, indigenous communities, organisations and leaders now position themselves vis-à-vis INI and government institutions, but also vis-à-vis civil society, in terms of a discourse which underscores – and exaggerates – cultural difference and ethnic identity. Simply put, it could be said that presenting oneself as a revolutionary peasant in search of land to cultivate or as an indigenous person on the path to acculturation – on the verge of becoming a revolutionary peasant or worker – has lost value in the new arenas of negotiation. There is more advantage in proclaiming oneself the inheritor of an ancestral world, close to nature and with timeless values, even of belonging to a social universe at odds with the Western world. Furthermore, the state's new discourse appears to imply the abdication of its responsibility for social welfare, locating this rather with the community and the family. This, in turn, reinforces the value of community solidarity. At the same time, part of recent, weak social programmes have been labelled 'help for the indigenous'. Given that the recent liberalisation of the state has facilitated the dismantling of corporatism – and therefore the flourishing of formal democracy – the 'indigenous', like many other social groups, enjoy, in principle, a greater ability to lobby for the fulfilment of their genuine demands, often with assistance from NGOs.[10] But one consequence of the essentialisation of community culture and ethnic identity may be the inhibition of indigenous peoples' social and political participation in national society and therefore lack of representation of their citizenship rights and even – paradoxically – of their cultural and ethnic rights. Another consequence is that many state representatives react ambiguously: although they admit that indigenous organisations and even the traditional authorities of Indian communities may be valid interlocutors, they are uncomfortable with and resistant to demands to respect a 'totally different' culture. It is not uncommon for officials to invoke the primacy of human rights in order to reject cultural demands. However, this very reaction often incites even greater insistence by indigenous people of irreconcilable cultural diversity.

The following section describes a conflictive situation between a group of 'evangelicals' of the Huichol people (in northern Jalisco they are also indiscriminately called 'evangelists', 'protestants' or 'pentecostals') and the authorities of their community. The conflict reflects the ambiguities of the changing relationship between indigenous peoples and the state, and also the specific difficulties of practising cultural citizenship, which involves both individual and collective rights. It should be noted that part of the ambiguity derives from the text of the new Article 4 of the constitution, which states:

> Mexico is a multicultural nation based originally upon its indigenous peoples. The law will protect and promote development of their languages, cultures, practices, customs, resources and specific forms of social organisation, and will guarantee its members effective access to state jurisdiction. In legal matters relating to land issues, the legal practices and customs [of the indigenous] will be taken into account, in the terms established by the law.

There is as yet no definition of how the general principle of 'protecting and promoting' is understood and how 'legal practices and customs will be taken into account', which in any case are only relevant in land matters and always 'in the terms established by the law'. In other words, the valid criteria for interpretation are always that of existing state law. Neither is it clear whether indigenous *peoples* as such are legal subjects (Hindley 1995). These and other ambiguities will have to be resolved with new legislation, discussion of which is currently pending in the Mexican Congress.[11]

Evangelicals versus traditional authorities: human rights versus cultural rights?

The tiny municipal assembly hall of Mezquitic, in the extreme north of Jalisco state, was bursting at the seams, with more than 50 people present. It was the morning of 2 February 2000 and the mestizo municipal authority[12] had called a conciliation meeting between two warring parties: the traditional authorities of the Huichol or Wixarika (pl. Wixaritari) community of Santa Catarina Cuexcomatitlán, and an extended family from that community who had converted to the 'evangelical religion'. The dreary decor of the room was offset by the indigenous people present, who were dressed in flamboyant colours.

In attendance, in addition to the Mayor of Mezquitic, the municipal secretary and a Huichol councillor (*regidor*) (who is also an Elder in the ethnic hierarchy), Mauricio, were:

(a) a substantial representation of the ethnic authorities of Santa Catarina Cuexcomatitlán, that is, members of the Elders' Council or *Kawiterutsixi*, the governor (*Tatuwani*), the sheriff (*alguacil*), various ex-governors, various *mara'akate* (shamans), some *Jicareros* (*xukuri'akate*, heads of temples or ceremonial centres) and *Topiles* (their helpers).

(b) The Huichol officials from the Commission for Communal Property (Comisariado de Bienes Comunales), who exercise a dual role as agrarian authorities. They participate in the formal structure of the Mexican state, but at the same time they are acknowledged as part of the system of traditional community offices (*cargos comunitarios*).

(c) A dozen members, both male and female, of the dissident family ('the evangelicals').

(d) A dozen other interested Huichol spectators, both male and female.

(e) The representative of the governmental Sub-Secretariat for Religious Matters of the Interior Ministry (Medardo).

(f) The director of the INI Coordinating Centre (Tania).

(g) The president of the National Confederation of Evangelical Churches (CONFRATERNICE) (Arnulfo, a mestizo lawyer and protestant minister from Mexico City).

(h) The representative of the Jalisco Association for Support to Indigenous Groups (Asociación Jaliscense de Apoyo a Grupos Indígenas, AJAGI), a Guadalajara NGO which has been working for the last 20 years in the Sierra Huichola (Eva).

(i) The evangelical pastor of the neighbouring mestizo village, Huejuquilla (Bibiano, who was dressed as a Huichol).

(j) Three anthropologists (I was one), whom the traditional authorities had allowed to be present as observers.[13]

First the mayor welcomed the participants, explained the reason for the meeting and asked everyone to identify themselves. Then Carlos, the President of the Commission of Communal Property of Santa Catarina, spoke first in Wixarika and then in Spanish, to give the view of the traditional authorities. Speaking up loudly he said:

We demand respect for our culture which has existed since time immemorial and which is maintained through communal obligations, that is through shared community responsibilities. Being a Wixarika means fulfilling the obligations imposed by the Council of Elders and the Community Assembly. Those who do not are punished; those who accept and carry out their duties receive the benefits of being a Huichol, such as using communal lands, living in the communities' villages and hamlets, and receiving help from those government and private associations which work with us. All we Wixaritari are part of a culture, our *costumbre* as we say, which is why it is not possible to accept within the community a religion which goes against *costumbre*.[14] If they leave the community then they can have whatever religion they want. But the leader of the converts, Rufino, who is here, does not want to go, and he condemned himself before the Assembly, as he said that God gave him the freedom to not accept any community offices. The Assembly gave him time to recapitulate, which he ignored, bringing more pentecostals to Los Arbustos[15] [the village where he lives], and giving people presents in order to try and convert them. There was another assembly two months later, when 36 evangelicals turned up, and we again entreated them to rethink, giving them three months notice in the presence of INI and AJAGI. Finally last November we met and offered Rufino and another of them the communal offices of Jicarero and Topil, and a university-educated man from Mexico City told them that these are communal, not religious obligations, and that they should accept them. They did not want to so we gave them a week to leave. At that point they took out a court case against us with the Public Prosecutor's Office, we had another meeting in December and now here we are again. We were very clear with them – you can stay but our conditions are that you must accept communal offices, not proselytise, and not build churches.

Then it was the turn of Rufino, the Huichol evangelical pastor from Santa Catarina. Visibly nervous, he began:

All we want is that the law of our nation [Mexico]) be respected. We cannot accept offices like that of the Jicarero because they do things which are unclean before God. We can do things to serve the community. We are prepared to accept obligations which are not religious. We can pay our financial dues. But we have the right to follow our own religious beliefs. We want there to be mutual respect. We are not forcing anyone and we do not buy people off with presents; but we must follow our hearts.

'We are not against the community', added Rufino's uncle, 'or community work, only the *costumbre.*'

Following these interventions, representatives of the public institutions spoke. Tania, from INI, said she preferred not to intervene directly and asked the parties to listen to each other, to be flexible and to reach an agreement. The official from the Interior Ministry, Medardo, supported her, adding he was pleased that Rufino was prepared to accept some duties and calling on the traditional authorities to cede a little also. The Mayor of Mezquitic simply demanded that they reach an agreement, as he was not going to use his authority to expel anyone from the community as had been requested. However, Raimundo, a Huichol artist linked to some Mexico City-based NGOs, intervened belligerently, calling for an end to the evangelical invasion. He said they had come to the sierra loaded with money and had insulted the Huichol, calling them 'demon worshippers'. At this point Arnulfo, a lawyer and CONFRATERNICE president complained:

This meeting is not for hurling insults: rather it is to build a constructive dialogue. You will not find us aggressive, on the contrary – we are the ones who have been victims of aggression. Rufino was imprisoned and put in the stocks and a young woman was raped. Huichol evangelists are not against culture, they continue to wear traditional clothes and speak the language. They live with you and are part of you. But they do not accept some of the beliefs and practices because they want to be able to respect their wives and give a good example to children. They also respect the legitimate authorities, they just beg you not to oblige them to be Jicareros.

Mauricio, the Huichol Elder and councillor (*regidor*), retorted that the real aggression was that suffered for centuries by the Wixaritari:

We have not got involved with other cultures around us ... and other people who are not our people do not understand our relationship with Mother Earth and what it is to be a *comunero* and how we celebrate Mother Earth in our ceremonies and pilgrimages. Any other way is to trample on Nature, of which we are a part ... What's happening here is manipulation to try and stop us being who we are. Before we were manipulated more easily because we did not understand Spanish, but not any longer.

On Mauricio's request, several members of the Elders' Council gave long speeches in Wixarika, which he translated. Several shed tears. They referred to their gods, who are located in the five cardinal points of the earth;[16] to the first inhabitants of Mexico, their ancestors; to the culture of maize 'which is our life', and to the office of Jicarero, which is a definitive commitment to the community, as that person will not serve anyone else for five years. Two recurrent arguments which evoked murmurs of approval from the other Elders were: first, our culture has been attacked for years and years, but we have maintained it thanks to the *costumbre*, which exists since before the world began; therefore, if we do not follow *costumbre* our culture will disappear. Second, if we begin to allow some young people not to assume these offices then no one will want to do so, because it requires effort and sacrifice and if the young people do not fulfil these obligations then we betray the Earth and Huichol people will cease to exist. If our forefathers who were uneducated were able to resist this onslaught against them, how can we who can read and write not also resist?

The Huichol ex-governor who had ordered Rufino's imprisonment justified his actions, stating that the decision was taken in an assembly, in the presence of the Elders' Council and 564 *comuneros*:

It was not an act of savagery but rather a fulfilment of established procedure with regards to disobedience. I cannot accept criticism for practising our law. The rape was a criminal act which had nothing to do with Rufino being imprisoned and we have already handed over the perpetrator to the competent authorities.

The meeting had lasted for more than three hours. The mestizo officials were looking at their watches and showing signs of impatience. Rufino intervened again (in Wixarika, translating himself for the officials):

> We can forgive. Furthermore we are not asking for other [evangelical] brothers to come and live here. But we cannot be Jicareros, because the *costumbre* is that they hunt deer and there aren't any left: we are finishing them off and that is bad for the environment. Neither do we want to go on pilgrimages to Wirikuta, for [and here he hesitated] for peyote, drugs ... or the drinking parties because it offends the women ... But we do want, for example, to be municipal officers, or members of the school committee, or the health committee ... and maybe Topiles, if we are not asked to kill deer or go on the peyote pilgrimage.

'But being municipal agents or on the committees is not our business, that is what the *tewari* [mestizos] demand', interrupted an angry old man. Others shouted 'Come on, accept to be Jicareros, and we'll leave you alone.' Rufino's father then intervened to explain how they became evangelicals:

> I got married and really loved my family. When my first child was born I made the promise as *costumbre* demands, but my children kept dying. I, my wife and children all fell ill ... Despite the fact I had made sacrifices of cattle and hunted deer and was a Jicarero. I only had two children left alive and the eldest was dying. I took him to Huejuquilla, where he died in a hospital. There I met a Brother [Bibiano, the Huejuquilla pastor] who helped me and brought me back to Los Arbustos, and told me about the true God ... But I took no notice. Another year passed and then Rufino, the only child I had left became ill ... If he had died I did not want to go on living, nothing mattered to me and I also had a bad stomach illness. But the Brother came and he asked me to pray with him and we prayed and I fell asleep and I woke refreshed and well, as did Rufino ... They gave us the Bible and we learnt about the creation of the universe and human beings and that Jesus Christ died for us. Others too have been saved when they left the *costumbre*. They stop drinking and their children are cured ... If they want to kill us, well let them kill us ... We do collaborate, we will carry out the duties which simply involve cooperating.

'We evangelicals respect the Elders a lot', said Arnulfo, taking advantage of the silence which followed Rufino's father's words.

> They are our fellow men who we admire and love. I agree with the Elder who said that for centuries we have been exploited and still are. Some 150 years ago an indigenous man created law for Mexico, bringing stability and justice: Benito Juárez. There are no longer differences of race. The only

difference now is that of faith, of worship, which is a question of conscience. No one has the right to meddle with another man's conscience. That is what the laws of Mexico say. You, respected Elders, if you allow the evangelicals to live in your community you will have better citizens, obedient in everything but matters of conscience. Your habits and customs are worthy of respect, but remember that you are part of a nation which has a Magna Carta, a Constitution, which establishes principles of freedom and justice.

Then Tania requested that both sides try to make specific proposals. The evangelical Huichol withdrew to a corner to consult with Arnulfo and Rufino repeated his offer to serve in civil positions and as Topiles in purely material duties (like cutting firewood for the community). He added that they would pray for God to bless the community and open their hearts, which elicited mocking laughter. Carlos, the president of the Commission for Communal Property, said that they respected freedom of religion but not in the community and that they could accept the offer from Rufino and his people to be Topiles if they did not proselytise, but that being a Topil was not just a question of going for wood but also of being at the service of the Jicareros. This irritated Medardo, the Interior Ministry representative, who burst out 'You are contradicting yourselves: just say once and for all if you accept or not!' Mauricio replied, in the same tone:

This is not an assembly. There is no majority. We cannot pass anything here. Our law, the one that counts for us indigenous, does not permit it: we were never consulted about the Magna Carta [Constitution] anyway. It was made by politicians and is of little or no use to us. As far as freedom of belief ... that is not for people who live in the community. We cannot base ourselves on that. We demand respect for indigenous law, and the government takes no notice of us, they ignore us.

'Perhaps you are right', Medardo attempted to be conciliatory, although then switching to a tougher line:

But we cannot forget that we live in a legal order and are represented by the Congress. We cannot live outside the Constitution. Indigenous ways and customs are respected, but they cannot fly in the face of the Constitution. The Pentecostals are more open than you, who do not accept them because you say that your culture is going to disappear, but culture does not disappear ... all it needs is two people to practise it. The Interior Ministry will guarantee that they will carry out their ceremonies only in specific places, and if the traditional authorities do not permit them to build their churches, then fine. But I would urge you to respect freedom of belief ... because your culture is not going to die out ... Some of you wear jeans and boots and that does not undermine your culture, which is changing anyway. Let us respect difference! This has been dragging on for too long now – it is time to sort it out and accept dialogue. I am the first to want respect for any true Mexican culture. But I have not seen any evangelical group harm a community: quite the contrary.

'Our culture is not changing', shot back Carlos angrily. 'What do you know about it? You should be more respectful. Our customs are not to do with wearing boots or not!'

'You have to give way if you want to win', added Tania. 'You can't just say all or nothing. The Huichol culture must be protected but without repressing others ... For INI you are all Huichols, and we want the two sides to reach agreement.'

The Wixarika governor explained that it was unlikely that the evangelicals would make a commitment as they did not even understand what it meant to be a Topil. Rufino said that they did know – that it was a life-long position: 'very hard work, lots of duties and that is why they are bitter that we don't do it. However we are prepared to do whatever we can to help in civic matters, we are willing'.

'If you were willing', said Carlos, 'you would have withdrawn the legal charges against us. We will believe you when you prove that you have withdrawn them.' Arnulfo withdrew again to talk to Bibiano and the other evangelical Huichols and then he made a final proposal:

All right, when you accept Rufino's offer of service, then at the same time we will drop the legal charges. And we are prepared to go further: the evangelicals will do more communal work and pay higher contributions than the other *comuneros*. But we want to see greater tolerance from you, otherwise the situation will get messy. Of course if you did not violate any human rights you have nothing to worry about ... It is the obligation of the Interior Ministry to demand compliance with our Magna Carta. Although we have the right to proselytise, our brothers may abstain from so doing ... but I want you to know that the indigenous have had enough – they want freedom, and that's why they follow the faith of Jesus Christ. So your assembly should adopt Rufino's proposal, he should withdraw the lawsuit not forgetting that he was unjustly tied up and hung for three days.

He was interrupted by laughter and shouts: 'A pack of lies ... Prove it!' Tania called for order and the meeting was closed after agreeing that a community assembly would be held three weeks later.

What does this dispute mean?

Santa Catarina Cuexcomatitlán, located in the rocky mountains of the western Sierra Madre is sometimes described, even by the Huichols themselves, as 'the most traditional Wixarika community'. To a large extent this is because its approximately 3000 inhabitants, spread over a territory of 760 square kilometres, are bound to rigorous compliance with community offices and obligations.[17] Strict observation of *costumbre* is seen as inseparable from the historical legacy of the community, as the majority of the sacred Wixarika places are located on Santa Catarina's land (Lumholtz 1904, vol. II: 152). The office of Jicarero is central: it is conferred upon a married man (usually in his early thirties), who must devote himself to it for five years, with the unstinting help of his wife, in order to demonstrate his loyalty to the group. His most explicit function is to look after the temple (*tuki*), but the Jicarero is also a fundamental figure in the extended family organisation, involving three or four generations resident in the same village or in nearby hamlets. Under the leadership of a patriarch, the extended family collectively undertakes the task of clearing and burning in preparation for the sowing of maize (*coamil*) and also shares the maize production.[18] This collective labour is viewed as inseparable from ritual and tributes to the earth deities, which should be conducted by the Jicarero and those who have occupied the post of Jicarero previous to him. These are carried out not only in the name of the Jicarero's relatives, but also to fulfil the ceremonial obligations of the entire community (Durin 2000). Equally, the Jicarero is present at the ritual autumn deer hunt, and – under the guidance of a *mara'akate* – on the annual trip at winter's end, to Wirikuta, the sacred place where peyote comes from,[19] or on the pilgrimages to other sanctuaries on the Pacific coast and on Lake Chapala. There are several Jicareros in each community, corresponding to different extended families. They are appointed by the Council of Elders, formed in each community by the most respected *mara'akate* and patriarchs. The Council of Elders also select the governor of the day (one of the patriarchs), who for one year, together with the sheriffs (*alguaciles*) and the justice of the peace (*juez de paz*), maintains law and order and punishes violators of *costumbre*. The Topiles support the Jicareros, both in the material tasks of looking after the *tuki* and in ritual tasks.

However, many aspects of life in Santa Catarina also reflect multiple external relationships and involvement in worlds beyond those of regular, family-based ritual. Although the Wixarika language continues to thrive, all the young men and most of the young women speak Spanish, learnt in the boarding schools set up by INI from 1960 onwards or from their frequent contact with mestizos. A good number of the young people have studied or worked in neighbouring mestizo towns (Mezquitic and Huejuquilla), or in big cities such as Guadalajara and Tepic, and speak, read and write fluently. Many families migrate in the spring to work on the tobacco plantations in Nayarit or to the barley and oat fields in the Colotlán valley, near Mezquitic. Small-scale cattle selling implies frequent travelling. Some craftsmen and artists, particularly those making woollen-yarn paintings and beaded masks, go often to Guadalajara, Tepic, Puerto Vallarta and Mexico City in order to sell their products (often assisted by NGOs). Finally, some Huichols from Santa Catarina and other communities live in mestizo towns or cities without losing contact with their community of origin, although it is difficult to estimate how many (Weigand 1992: 169–70). Thus the discourse of 'defending culture' does not imply insularity; in fact on the contrary, being able to operate in the mestizo world is viewed as a weapon and a resource. As the Elders stated in the Mezquitic meeting: 'we, who can read and write, can resist better than our grandparents who were uneducated'. But they do not look upon mixed marriage kindly, and the offspring (such as Bibiano, whose father is Huichol and whose mother is Yaqui) are not usually recognised as members of the Wixarika people, especially if they are brought up outside the communities.[20]

The first argument wielded by the Mezquitic traditional authorities to oblige the evangelicals to carry out their ritual obligations was based on the national Land Law (Ley Agraria Nacional), which defines Santa Catarina Cuexcomatitlán and the other communities as *agrarian communities* where the land belongs to the communal entity, and therefore individuals and families can only enjoy usufruct rights (not ownership) when the community permits. However, the Wixaritari frequently express their dissatisfaction with the official delimitation of their territory, as according to them it drastically reduces its real size. In the first instance this relates to oral history passed down by their ancestors which speaks of their land stretching to the Pacific coast, but it is also related to the existence of boundary markers from the colonial period which extended far beyond the present territorial borders. In addition, Wixarika place-names persist in areas considered today to be mestizo *ejidos* (Liffman 1996).[21] Furthermore, they know that even if they accept the territorial limits set down by the Secretaría de la Reforma Agraria (Land Reform Secretariat), a part of their land has been invaded by mestizo cattle-ranchers. The Santa Catarina Cuexcomatitlán Huichol specifically cite the invasion of 3000 hectares by members of a family in the neighbouring *ejido* at Tenzompa. After more than a decade of litigation, in 1994 the community achieved a ruling in its favour by the Land Court; but the invaders appealed against the decision and stuck their heels in, refusing to move.[22] (They were finally evicted in June 2000.) Furthermore, in legal terms 'agrarian community' only defines the type of land and administrative faculties of the Commission of Communal Property (Comisariado de Bienes Comunales) – the community is not constituted as a legal subject with rights or as a political entity. Thus, the invocation of the community's legitimacy by the traditional authorities goes beyond state law: it refers above all to the sacred link between the earth, the ancestors and culture. Being a *comunero* means reproducing that link. Together with the right to use the land which the family cultivates, a mythical memory is passed down which gives meaning to the surrounding landscape and knowledge of the sacred places where offerings, prayers and sacrifices are made (Liffman et al. 1997). If the Mexican state is reluctant to enforce the Huichols' rights over the land, then the community does this via their ritual cohesion. This is why the continuity of the system of community offices and obligations (the *cargo* system) is so indispensable. The religious component is not separable from the other aspects of these ritual offices. This is why then – as the Elders said – it is not possible for any *comunero* to be exempt from these obligations: opting out would have a demoralising effect which would lead to the destruction of the Wixarika people.

This community logic clashes with the proselytising thrust of Western religions. In many respects the Huichol religion contains Christian elements derived from the colonial evangelisation; the cult of saints co-exists unproblematically with earthly deities. When the Franciscans set up the Santa Clara Mission in San Andrés Cohamiata in 1950, the Wixaritari accepted baptism of their children and attended mass, but were violently opposed to any interference with their agricultural rituals. The so-called evangelicals or pentecostals, members of diverse denominations (the main one being the Baptists), began to make inroads into the Sierra in the 1980s and stepped up their proselytising following the approval of the 1991 Federal Law which granted legal status to religious groupings. The Wixaritari speak of light aeroplanes dropping propaganda and radios that are permanently tuned in to evangelical radio stations.[23] In the nearby villages and towns, such as Huejuquilla, Jerez and Zacatecas, the evangelical pastors invite indigenous migrant labourers or those travelling on business to stay with them in church premises and give them presents and support, for example in cases of illness (as occurred when Bibiano helped Rufino's family). They have also provided legal help in some cases of problems with mestizo authorities. In fact, some protestant aeroplanes have landed in Huichol territory without requesting permission and on occasion the crew have been imprisoned for a couple of days. But what most irritates the traditional authorities is that the evangelicals are, by definition, diametrically opposed to community obligations and ceremonies. In the February meeting Rufino expressed his feelings of horror with regards to certain ceremonial practices; he then justified his conversion and behaviour by appealing to the freedom of religious belief enshrined in the constitution. Arnulfo, the evangelical pastor from Mexico City, made use of the same justification, although he then adopted an argument in defence of human rights, used to considerable rhetorical effect before the government officials: not only do the traditional authorities violate state law but they also violate the evangelical converts' human rights by denying them personal freedom and subjecting them to torture and rape.

In response to Arnulfo's accusations the Wixarika governor denied torture had occurred, although he admitted the disobedience had been punished.[24] As for the rape, he regarded it as unconnected to the religious conflict. Mauricio caused a stir by not recognising the constitution. But at no time did the traditional authorities question the constitutional principle of religious freedom. Rather, they were defending the cultural aspects of customary law incorporated into the system of communal offices and obligations that have become the basis of their day-to-day relationship with the land.[25] If someone outside of the community practices one or another religion then 'that's their business', as the President of the Commission of Community Property said. Mauricio added; 'we don't interfere with other peoples' cultures', but if a *comunero* who wants to live in the community doesn't participate in the communal offices and obligations then it breaks down the pattern of collective behaviour.[26] None of the officials present – not even the INI representative – indicated any understanding of this position. Rather, they were impatient at how long the discussion took, failing to take into account the fact that in their own assemblies the Wixaritari can take days to come to an agreement. Obviously they were pleased because Rufino had ceded a little with regard to accepting civic duties and some of the Topil functions (in the previous assemblies he had not offered to participate at all), and they hoped that the traditional authorities would also cede ground. They took it for granted that the Huichol position was anti-constitutional, without explaining in detail why. The representative from the Ministry of the Interior even caused offence when he said that culture was changing anyway, that changing religion was like using boots instead of *huaraches* (sandals) and that the evangelicals would be beneficial for the community. In reality, the professions of 'respect for the ways and customs' by the officials and Arnulfo failed to convince anyone. Indeed Arnulfo's invocation of Benito Juárez appeared to be saying that 'good Indians' should imitate him, leaving their communities and forgetting the culture of the community.

The obvious question is: why do the converts insist on staying on Huichol land where they encounter rejection and hostility and where a way of life reigns that they no longer identify with? As Andrew Canessa (2000) has noted, evangelical religious discourse is similar to radical ethnicist discourse in one aspect: both defend the *purity* of their respective beliefs and customs and refuse to accept any modification, eclecticism or *hybridisation*.[27] Despite this, Rufino and his relatives appear to be advocating the creation of a new hybrid identity: 'Huichol evangelicals', that would allow them to maintain their residential and land rights. On the other hand, the evangelical pastors from Huejuquilla, Zacatecas and Mexico City press them to stay in the sierra and act as a spearhead for further evangelisation and even as social and political reformers.

Cultural rights, negotiation and representation

I have attempted to show that the public justification of the demands of the Huichol leaders before the federal and municipal authorities was not formulated simply in terms of the agrarian community as defined by Article 27 of the Mexican Constitution, but above all in terms of a community legitimised by its inextricable link with ancestral culture, where the territorial dimension is not separable from the religious or political. This public debate would have been unthinkable 25 or 30 years ago, when the Mexican government's view was that the traditional authorities lacked legitimacy (see Aguirre Beltrán 1953 and 1986). Furthermore, in pragmatic terms it was easier in the past to frame claims with reference to *agrarista* principles. Today, such explicit resort to the agrarian legacy of the revolution is much less effective, but the new Article 4 of the constitution opens the door to claims being formulated as ethnic demands. In other words, when the traditional authorities speak of culture, their ancestors and their traditional practices and customs, they are doing it within a framework of a *'language of contention'* furnished by the state (Roseberry 1994) and disseminated above all by INI; a language which also links them to the discourse of civil society organisations. It was not by chance that Carlos, the president of the Commission of Communal Property, enumerating the benefits of being a Wixarika, included 'use of the land ..., living in the villages ... and receiving help from the government and private associations ...'.[28] Today the 'traditional authorities' include educated young people who know how to move within a mestizo world. Frequently they are advised by other young Huichol university graduates who live in the city but who have not broken their link with the community and indeed frequently act as consultants for the NGOs who work with the indigenous communities. Thus, ethnic consciousness is expressed and presents itself via concepts that have become common currency in the public domain in Mexico. However, in the situation described, as in many others, the concepts had different meanings for the actors involved. When the Elders used the term *culture*, they meant a complex set of beliefs and symbols substantially and inextricably linked to everyday life practices; whereas for the evangelicals and the mestizo participants *culture* was something adjectival. This is why the evangelicals said that they were against the *costumbre*, but not against the culture – which was a blatant contradiction from the point of view of the ethnic authorities. Therefore, despite the process of appropriation of a public language by the Wixaritari, public manifestations of ethnicity are not able to overcome the ambiguities of current legislation with regard to which cultural or ethnic rights it is legitimate to defend, or who the proper representatives charged with implementing these rights should be.

The problem of representation is particularly acute. While the reform of Article 4 of the constitution means the state has tacitly accepted the existence of traditional authorities, it is not clear what their relationship is with the municipal authorities. (Neither have the individual state legislatures resolved this issue, except in Oaxaca.) The majority of the Huichols in Jalisco live in the municipality of Mezquitic. Although the overwhelming majority of its inhabitants are Huichol, the municipal council has always been controlled by mestizos and, while in recent years it has acted as initiator of some social programmes (see Appendix 5.1), it hardly ever intervenes in indigenous matters – for example, to stop indigenous land being invaded or to entertain individuals complaints, preferring to leave them to INI. In recent years there have been a couple of Huichols on the Mezquitic municipal council who sometimes intervene as mediators (as Mauricio did), but they are not recognised as representatives by the communities. INI has in fact tried to change the relationship with the traditional authorities, via its bilingual promoters and the Commission of Communal Property, but without much success.[29] In 1991 INI set up a supra-community organisation: the Jalisco Union of Huichol Indigenous Communities (Unión de Comunidades Indígenas Huicholas de Jalisco, UCIHJ), which became the conduit through which regional funds tended to be channelled. However, the only way to render it legitimate in the eyes of the Huichol was by appointing the traditional governors to the Management Board. The UCIHJ has increasingly acted as an interlocutor with NGOs and state institutions, although government officials view with a degree of alarm the possibility of it becoming a sort of autonomous tribal government,[30] and are therefore careful to avoid giving it any political recognition. The resulting situation is therefore a kind of limbo.

Conclusion

Appendix 5.1 details 12 government programmes to which the Wixaritari or the Huichol have access. Of these, the first five are exclusively for indigenous people, creating a relational space with the state wherein ethnic identity is explicitly strengthened. Most important for the Huichol are the subsidies for the boarding schools (food and accommodation for 1500 children), full-time employment for 200 bilingual teachers and the easily obtained regional funds, which are all granted to them as indigenous. More limited and not on-going (and therefore less attractive) assistance is conceded to 'indigent peasants' or disbursed as part of specific infrastructural projects or environmental protection initiatives. Furthermore, the latter are notoriously insufficient: the Huichol live in the poorest areas of the states of Jalisco and Nayarit, the vast majority of their houses lack minimal services and there are no paved roads.[31] Thus, the – albeit limited – acknowledgement of the *social citizenship* of the Wixaritari depends, in practice, on a process of negotiation within which the preservation of ethnic identity has taken on a strategic value. Within this context then, the struggle for social rights is not separable from the struggle for the right to cultural difference. This contrasts with the original aims of Mexican state *indigenismo*, which conceived of collective welfare policies as a means to implant the official *national culture* among indigenous groups.

The situation analysed above highlights two different conceptions of the right to cultural difference. For the mestizo authorities and the evangelicals, cultural rights are individual and are exercised voluntarily in the private sphere. However, for the ethnic authorities, the fundamental subject of cultural rights is collective: the community, which is more than the sum of the individuals who make it up and which has predominance over them. In this second view, the discourse of 'natural rights' is understandable and useful not only in terms of the protection of individuals but above all in terms of protection of community life. We find, then, a new version, at local level, of the old dispute between liberalism and communitarianism. Certainly the more radical versions of these positions are incompatible; nevertheless, very interesting attempts to build bridges between them have been made by thinkers such as Charles Taylor (1995), Will Kymlicka (1996) and Luis Villoro (1998) (cf. De la Peña 2000). Following these writers, one may recognise (as liberals do) that the individual is the fundamental bearer of rights, but this does not prevent one accepting that individual fulfilment and exercise of rights are impossible without the insertion of the individual in a specific cultural community which is not an abstraction, but rather something which provides a concrete embodiment of 'us' – that is, a set of roles defining patterns of cooperation, reciprocity and hierarchy. Protection of the cultural community therefore becomes a necessary condition for protection of individuals' rights, and in this sense the community becomes a bearer of rights, as the communitarians assert. These considerations should lead the legislative and judicial authorities of multicultural countries to bear in mind not only generic citizenship rights, but also 'to recognise the particular differences and needs attached to membership of specific cultural groups' (Sánchez Botero 1999: 338; see also Yrigoyen 1999). Thus a modern national constitution might simultaneously recognise, say, the right of the individual to own property and the right of indigenous people to communal ownership of their ancestral lands. Such a constitution would consequently allow that the community prohibit its members from privatising those lands (and might defend them from external invaders), insofar as this would jeopardise the very survival of the community. In the same way, the right to individual freedom of belief would have to be exercised without prejudice to the ability of the community to reproduce its forms of organisation and solidarity.

But, what about the human rights of *individuals*, as such? Would it not be adequate to say that, just as it is inadmissible that individual rights undermine culturally-defined communal solidarity to the extent of endangering the community itself, neither is it acceptable that community rights overrule or wipe out the rights of individuals? (In an agriculturally based society, for example, would it be acceptable to endanger the physical survival of one of its members by excluding them from access to land use in the name of communal ownership?) In this respect, it has to be remembered that inadmissible aggressions to individuals by authorities occur in societies of every kind. Such aggressions do not have to be logically derived from the defence of communal rights. Arnulfo, the mestizo pastor, argued that the *costumbre* was inherently opposed to human rights as a weapon to defend his own proselytising designs; in his turn, Mauricio opposed customary law to the constitution as a means of resistance to specific forms of external domination by upholding the authority of the Elders; in both cases, they were interested in winning positions in a context of confrontation and negotiation – not in winning a philosophical argument per se. Rather than attributing absolute superiority to individual over communal values, or vice versa, what seems to be relevant for the protection of human rights is that reasonable appeals and dialogue should always be present, both within the ethnic worlds and between ethnic peoples and national society represented by the state, which should play a role of promoting and ensuring tolerance.

In Latin America, we are barely at the outset of a long process of negotiation which, if successful, will lead to the normalisation of cultural rights. Some countries, such as Colombia, have achieved not only advanced and clear legislation but also mechanisms of constitutional appeal which, in turn, have generated a growing *corpus* of jurisprudence, where it has already been established that certain individual practices, legal in wider society, may be restricted in indigenous regions because of their harmful effects upon community coexistence.[32] In Mexico, as previously stated, national discussion is currently on hold, but in some regions, in specific communities, and in the myriad new situations confronted by members of ethnic groups, interesting solutions have been worked out. For example, in some municipalities in Chiapas, after decades of violent clashes, it is now accepted that dissident evangelicals will only undertake certain tasks of collective service and in this manner they are able to remain within the community (Ebert 2001). Many Mixteca communities have become disperse networks scattered across central and northern Mexico, and even the United States, and have adapted their *costumbre* to a situation of virtual nomadism, where in addition they have insisted on the importance of their civic, political and social rights – to free movement, free association, public representation, work, fair wages, decent services – without undermining the defence of identity and culture. While the phenomenon which we call globalisation has relativised ethnic and national borders and has created more complex identities, it has also forced a re-examination of the relations between individuals and their relevant collectivities and, likewise, of relations between those collectivities themselves. For many indigenous people this re-examination has been accompanied by a profound reflection on the notion of citizenship.[33]

Full ethnic citizenship – where the state and civil society accept that 'being Wixarika' or 'being Raramuri' and so on is perfectly compatible with 'being Mexican' – will come about through dialogue between participants who are willing to seek a profound understanding of the culture of the other. The Wixaritari have taken great strides towards such a dialogue. Three years ago a group of parents, with the joint support of the traditional authorities and the UCIHJ, and with expert advice from AJAGI and some Huichol graduates, opened a secondary school in San Miguel Huaxtita, in the community of San Andrés Cohamiata (Rojas Cortés 1999).[34] This school, called Centro Educativo Tatutsi Maxakwaxi ('our grandfather Deer's Tail', in honour of the mythic hero who built the first ceremonial centre in the Sierra), has Huichol teachers who impart the national curriculum in Spanish and also teach other subjects, such as Wixarika language and culture in their mother tongue. One of the main aims of these subjects is not just to recover a sense of their traditions, but also to find points of dialogue and interdependence, and of real and potential conflicts, between the Huichols and the national worlds. This is also the guiding principle behind the Unión de Estudiantes Wixarika del Estado de Jalisco (Jalisco State Union of Wixarika Students), set up by 30 university students in Guadalajara. They have opened a social cultural centre which offers support to migrants, whether working or studying, and which functions as a conduit of communication between the city and the sierra. It is these types of communication channels that will foster the growth of an inclusive society which is respectful of otherness.

Notes

1. The tripartite division of citizenship proposed by T.H. Marshall corresponds to three types of rights: civic rights (individual liberties), political rights (participation in public decision-making) and social rights.
2. In the so-called 'Western world' social policies tend to be divided into three ideal types: liberal policies, which seek to equip individuals to compete successfully in the market place; social democratic policies, which seek to create universal welfare standards through public institutions (dealing with education, health, housing, unemployment benefit, and so on); and corporatist policies, which are top-down policies aimed at certain social sectors (Esping-Andersen 1990; Roberts 1998). A fourth ideal type could be added – that of 'neoliberal' or 'post-liberal' policies. This accepts that certain individuals will never be competitive in the market and simply 'compensates' in order that they should not starve to death. Evidently in none of these scenarios is the state the sole welfare provider: it is always expected that other social institutions, particularly the family and the local community, will play a role, although social democratic policies do imply a greater share of responsibility on the part of the state.
3. *Ejidatarios* are members of an *ejido*, a corporation created in an ad hoc fashion which is granted a certain extension of land by the state. *Comuneros*, by contrast, belong to a pre-existing *agrarian community* (a euphemism used to refer to an indigenous community) to which the state restitutes its historic or ancestral lands.
4. During the first 20 years of INI's existence 12 coordinating centres were set up, the first of these in San Cristóbal de las Casas, the former colonial capital of the Altos de Chiapas. Although the detailed history of these centres has yet to be written, available information indicates the existence of multiple projects implemented by their enthusiastic teams (see for example, Plancarte 1954; Villa Rojas 1955; Marzal 1968 and 1993; Sariego 1998).
5. The student movement of 1968 had unmasked the authoritarian face of the revolutionary state. In addition, during those years the documents of the Barbados Meeting generalised the term 'ethnocide', which was later taken up by radical anthropologists (Aguirre Beltrán 1986). (The 1970 Barbados Meeting, under the aegis of the World Council of Churches, brought together anthropologists and indigenous leaders from several countries of the Western Hemisphere.) In an

evaluation of INI which took place in 1971, two well-known intellectuals, Pablo González Casanova and Fernando Benítez, developed damning critiques. For the record of this meeting see *¿Ha fracasado el indigenismo?* (1971).

6. The modification of the constitutional article coincided with Mexico's signature of the International Labour Organisation's Convention 169. However, as indicated below, the wording of Article 4 was weaker than the stipulations of ILO 169.

7. On PRONASOL, which enjoyed considerable support from the World Bank, see Cornelius et al. (1994). A resounding critique of the 'labyrinth of PRONASOL' (an allusion to its clientelist connotations and poor administration) can be found in Díaz Polanco (1997: 104–25). With respect to the current state of the Regional Funds, even INI officials admit that many of these programmes have serious administrative and technical weaknesses.

8. See Appendix 5.1. In practice it is impossible to determine at national level what percentage of these programme funds are destined for indigenous people (personal communication with congressional deputy Felipe Vicencio, member of the Congressional Commission for Indigenous Affairs in the period 1997–2000).

9. PROGRESA has provoked criticisms because it subverts family organisational patterns and subjects mothers to new (sometimes humiliating) forms of control. In addition, the method of selecting beneficiaries is not clear, and it cannot function in the numerous small rural settlements where public medical services are not easily available.

10. The regulation of the use of public funds meant that the PRI lost its capacity for clientelist co-option. It was forced to cede to pressure from civil society to guarantee a 'clean' electoral process and recognise the electoral victories of opposition parties. As a result it lost control of numerous local governments in the 1990s and in July 2000 lost the presidency of the republic.

11. The newly elected president, Vicente Fox, took office on 1 December 2000. A few days later, in fulfilment of one of his campaign promises, he sent a law to Congress to implement the San Andrés Larráinzar Accords, signed in 1996 by representatives of the government and the Zapatista Army for National Liberation (Ejército Zapatista de Liberación Nacional, EZLN). These accords recognise the autonomy of indigenous communities and the validity of customary law. On the characteristics of these accords and the polemic which they provoked see Franco (1999).

12. The term 'mestizo' is used in the region to refer to anyone who is not recognised as a member of an indigenous community.

13. All first names have been changed.

14. *Costumbre* (literally, custom) is the term used by Huichols and other indigenous groups to denote a complex amalgam of beliefs, historical memories, knowledge, religious prescriptions and ethical norms which are transmitted orally and reaffirmed in ritual celebrations.

15. Fictitious name.

16. North, south, east, west and the centre.

17. There are four recognised Wixaritari communities in the state of Jalisco: San Andrés Cohamiata, San Sebastián Teponahuaxtlán, Santa Catarina Cuexcomatitlán and Tuxpan de Bolaños. The first three belong to the municipality of Mezquitic and the fourth to the municipality of Bolaños. A fifth community, Guadalupe Ocotán, is located in the neighbouring state of Nayarit. Each community has its own system of community offices and obligations, although Tuxpan de Bolaños shares agrarian authorities with San Sebastián Teponahuaxtlán. Small hamlets of Huicholes also

exist in the states of Zacatecas and Durango. The Wixarika ethnic collectivity is estimated to comprise some 20,000 people in total.

18. These cooperative groups of relatives vary in size, depending on the extent to which the nature of the terrain concentrates or disperses them. See Weigand (1992: 167–8).

19. Wirikuta is located in the desert sierra of Real de Catorce in the state of San Luis Potosí. In ritual terms, peyote or *jículi* and deer are equivalents (to hunt deer and to 'hunt' peyote is the same thing; for this reason Evangelicals refuse to take part in both activities), and both form a sacred union with maize (which should not be produced without the help of the two other elements; that is, without ritual offerings to the deer-peyote). See Rojas González [1948] (1998); Myerhoff (1974); Torres Contreras (1995); Anaya (1999).

20. Certain mestizos adopted by Wixaritari families can 'become' Huichols, if they subscribe to respect for community norms. A famous case is that of Pedro de Haro, in San Sebastián Teponahuaxtlán, who led an agrarian uprising in the 1950s to reclaim communal land (Weigand 1992: 17–31).

21. Colonial territories were established by Franciscan missionaries, who also named the communities. However, in many places the boundaries were not clearly established, something which has led to recurrent conflicts (Lumholtz 1904, vol. II: 261).

22. Personal communication from Séverine Durin. Unresolved or unenforced agrarian litigation exists in all communities. In all, thanks to repeated claims pursued in the national courts and appeals to the International Labour Organisation, with the active help of the AJAGI and the support of INI, the Huichols have achieved the restitution of 10,320 hectares of a total of 77,000 hectares which they lay claim to. See Rojas (1992); Arcos García (1998); Chávez y Arcos (1999).

23. At present a congregation of Seventh Day Adventists exists in the Huichol community of Tuxpan de Bolaños. The Baptist mission which existed in Nostic, a mestizo town near to the municipal capital of Mezquitic very close to the Huichol territory, disappeared after its North American pastors died in an aeroplane crash.

24. The stocks (*cepo*) are a plank with holes in it to restrain the limbs of the prisoner. This is located in a small, dark and poorly ventilated room. The Huichols do not consider use of the stocks a form of torture but rather as a means to isolate the guilty party from the community (to avoid contamination by their guilt) and to ensure that they do not escape.

25. The entire sierra (known as *Juritzie*, 'the light' in Wixarika) is understood as a sacred space (personal communication from Francisco Talavera).

26. An important Jicarero from Santa Catarina, who has also been appointed president of the recently created Union of Huichol Jicareros, publicly stated – in a forum for discussion of indigenous problems held in Guadalajara ten days prior to the February meeting in Mezquitic – that when he went to the city he visited many churches and shared peoples' religious beliefs, but that when he was in Huichol territory he could not do anything but participate in community beliefs.

27. Evidently Amerindian cultures have undergone a process of hybridisation, at least since the Spanish colonisation. In addition, the lack of written texts and reliance on orality in the majority of these cultures has necessitated continual innovation. However, the explicit commitment to continuity, reiterated and elaborated in discourses and rituals and vigorously promoted by the system of local authorities, conditions the subjective response of many Huichols to change.

28. Interestingly, he would probably not have made this comment in a meeting attended solely by Wixaritari.
29. The ideologues of the new indigenism have doubts about the appropriateness of traditional political structures as a means to defend ethnic rights (Oehmichen 1999: 145).
30. This seems unlikely, given the fierce loyalties of each community to its own jurisdiction. In addition, the UCIHJ is a Jalisco-based organisation and not all Huichols live in the state of Jalisco.
31. It should be noted that the crisis of social policies in Mexico is different from what has been referred to in the European context as 'the crisis of the welfare state'. The latter refers to the success of welfare policies which gave rise to rising demands, the meeting of which would have severe inflationary consequences and would fly in the face of the logic of capitalist accumulation. By contrast, social policies in Mexico were limited in their success and their crisis is directly related to the wider financial crisis of the state.
32. Personal communication from Christian Gros.
33. The reflection about citizenship also feeds into wider discussions about the concept of *indigenous autonomy*, which has become one of the most important political debates in contemporary Mexico. See Díaz Polanco 1997; García Colorado and Sandoval (1998); Burguete (1999).
34. This is an important innovation in education in the region; only 2 per cent of women and 8 per cent of men achieve schooling beyond primary level.

Appendix 5.1: Social and Employment Programmes for Huichol Communities

1) Boarding School Programme (National *Indigenista* Institute – Instituto Nacional Indigenista, INI / Ministry of Public Education – Secretaría de Educación Pública, SEP). There are 14 boarding schools in the sierra, with approximately 1500 children. During the school year (September to June) the pupils receive lodging, bed linen, three meals, medical supervision, school equipment and some pocket money from Monday to Friday. The housemaster, cooks, administration staff and their respective families (who are practically all Wixaritari) live there with the pupils.

2) School Programme (SEP-Dirección de Educación Indígena de Jalisco – Jalisco Indigenous Education Administration). Fifteen primary schools (of which 12 are boarding schools), 46 partial primary or unitary schools and two distance learning secondaries, which in total employ more than 200 bilingual indigenous teachers.

3) Regional Funds (INI/Ministry of Social Development – Secretaría de Desarrollo Social, SEDESOL). One in each community. Providing soft credits for small-scale agricultural production projects (cattle, sheep, pig and hen raising, market garden produce, craft, shops).

4) Support for Indigenous Culture (INI). Small financial grants for research projects (for example, local history or recording of myths and legends), for ceremonies and pilgrimages.

5) Social infrastructure (INI). Community projects; for example, drinking water, electrification (solar panels) using local labour.

6) Community Health (Secretaría de Salud – Ministry of Health). There are nine clinics or health centres in the sierra for basic health care. One full-time nurse and periodical visits from a doctor.

7) Education, Health and Food Programme – Programa de Educación, Salud y Alimentación, PROGRESA (SEDESOL). Provides small amounts of money to a limited number of mothers who must then commit themselves to send their children to school, feed them properly and also visit the health centre for family health care and instruction on contraceptive use.

8) Municipal Integrated Family Development Programmes (Desarrollo Integral de la Familia, DIF). From time to time 'building kits' are distributed (roofing materials and cement) and family dispensaries.

9) Programmes to Help Peasants: Programa de Ayuda al Campo, PROCAMPO and the 'Crédito a la Palabra' programme. (Ministry of Agriculture and Livestock – Secretaría de Agricultura y Ganadería, and SEDESOL.) Small disbursements (soft credits) for maize cultivation.

10) Municipal Development Planning Committee Programmes – Comité de Planeación de Desarrollo Municipal, COPLADE-MUN, and the State Sub-Committee for Support to Ethnic and Priority Areas. Support for small infrastructure works, such as unpaved roads, suspension bridges, drinking water, solar energy plants, latrines, where Huichols are occasionally employed.

11) Jalisco State Development Secretariat's Forest Protection Programme. In collaboration with the municipal government, brigades are organised in the spring, the driest season, to watch for and fight forest fires. Equipment and seasonal work for some 20 Huichols.

12) Federal Programme to Fight Forest Plagues of the Ministry for Environmental, Natural Resources and Fisheries (Secretaría de Protección al Medio Ambiente, Recursos Naturales y Pesca). Casual work for 60 Huichol organised in brigades.

Source: Field work and interviews with state officials.

Acknowledgements

Research was carried out as part of a collective project entitled 'Social Policy towards Indigenous People in Mexico: Actors, Mediations and Niches of Identity', supported by the Centro de Investigaciones y Estudios Superiores en Antropología Social (Centre for Research and Advanced Studies in Social Anthropology, CIESAS), the Consejo Nacional de Ciencia y Tecnología (National Council for Science and Technology, CONACYT) and the Ford Foundation. I wish to thank all the contributions, comments and criticisms of my colleagues in this project, particularly Séverine Durin, Regina Martínez Casas, Angélica Rojas and Francisco Talavera Durón, as well as Rachel Sieder and the other participants in the seminar 'Pluri-Cultural and Multi-Ethnic: Evaluating the Implications for State and Society in Mesoamerica and the Andes' (Institute of Latin American Studies, University of London, March 2000). I also benefited from a discussion of the project in a seminar at the Department of Rural Sociology, University of Wageningen (December 2000).

References

Aguirre Beltrán, Gonzalo (1953), *Formas de gobierno indígena*, Imprenta Universitaria (Mexico).
—— (1958), *El proceso de aculturación*, Universidad Nacional Autónoma de México (Mexico).

—— (1986), *Obra polémica*, edition prepared by Angel Palerm, Centro de Investigaciones Superiores del Instituto Nacional de Antropología e Historia (Mexico).

—— and Ricardo Pozas Arciniega (1954), 'Instituciones indígenas en el México actual', in Alfonso Caso et al. *Métodos y resultados de la política indigenista en México*, Instituto Nacional Indigenista (Mexico).

Anaya Corona, María del Carmen (1999), 'Wilikuta: paraíso terrenal de los wixaritari', *Mexicoa. Revista de divulgación científica*, University of Guadalajara, I, 1, pp.110–20.

Arcos García, María de los Angeles (1998), 'Las vetas Tateikietari: Invocando la lluvia y la lucha de un pueblo', Masters thesis in Rural Development: Universidad Autónoma Metropolitana-Xochimilco.

Barrera Rodríguez, Rosier Omar et al. (1997), 'Monografía III. Santa Catarina Cuexcomatitlán', in Rosa Rojas and Rafael Guzmán (coords) *Rasgos biofísicos, socio-culturales y de sistemas productivos para el ordenamiento territorial de la nación Wixarika*, University of Guadalajara/INI/CONACYT (Guadalajara).

Bonfil, Guillermo et al. (1970), *De eso que llaman antropología mexicana*, Nueva Imagen (Mexico).

Burguete, Araceli (ed.) (1999), *Experiencias de autonomía indígena*, IWGIA (Copenhagen).

Canessa, Andrew (2000), 'Contesting Hybridity: *Evangelistas* and *Kataristas* in Highland Bolivia', *Journal of Latin American Studies*, Vol. 32, Part I, pp.115–44.

Chávez, Carlos y Angeles Arcos (1999), 'The Wixaritari Today', *Cultural Survival Quarterly*, Vol. 23 (1), pp.56–7.

Cordera Campos, Rolando (1995), 'Mercado y equidad. De la crisis del Estado a la política social', *Revista Internacional de Filosofía Política* (Madrid: Anthropos), pp.31–51.

—— and Enrique González Tiburcio (1999), 'La sociedad desigual: El desafío del futuro', *El Mercado de Valores*, Nacional Financiera, 12/99, pp.107–16.

Cornelius, Wayne A., Ann L. Craig and Jonathan Fox (1994), *Transforming state–society relations in Mexico. The National Solidarity Strategy*, Center for US–Mexican Studies, UCSD (La Jolla).

de la Peña, Guillermo (1986), 'Poder local, poder regional: perspectivas socioantropológicas', in J. Padua and A. Vanneph (eds) *Poder local, poder regional*, El Colegio de México\CEMCA (Mexico).

—— (1995), 'La ciudadanía étnica y la construcción de "los indios" en el México contemporáneo', *Revista Internacional de Filosofía Política* (Madrid: Anthropos), 6, pp.116–40.

—— (1999), 'Reflexiones preliminares sobre la "ciudadanía étnica". (El caso de México)', en Alberto J. Olvera (ed.) *La sociedad civil. De la teoriía a la realidad*, El Colegio de México (Mexico).

—— (2000), 'La modernidad comunitaria', *Desacatos. Revista de Antropología Social*, CIESAS, No. 3, pp.51–61.

Díaz Polanco, Héctor (1997), *La rebelión zapatista y la autonomía*, Siglo Veintiuno Editores (Mexico).

Durán, Leonel (1987), 'El proyecto nacional y las culturas populares: una aproximación', in *México: 75 años de revolución*, Fondo de Cultura Económica\Instituto Nacional e Estudios Históricos de la Revolución Mexicana (Mexico).

Durin, Séverine (2000), 'Acordarse de sus deudas y cumplir con "el" costumbre entre los Wixaritari', paper presented at the colloquium 'Deudas y Desarrollo Rural', Guadalajara, CIESAS, May 2000.

Ebert, Christine (2001), 'Buscando una nueva vida: Liberation through autonomy in San Pedro Chenalhó, 1970–1998', *Latin American Perspectives*, Vol. 28 (2), pp.45–72.

Esping-Andersen, Gosta (1990), *The Three Worlds of Welfare Capitalism*, Polity Press (Cambridge).

Franco, Moisés (1999), 'El debate sobre los derechos indígenas en México', in W.Assies, G. van der Haar y André Hoekema (eds) *El reto de la diversidad*. *Pueblos indígenas y reforma del Estado en América Latina*, El Colegio de Michoacán (Zamora).

Garbett, G. Kingsley (1970), 'The Analysis of Social Situations', *Man*, Vol. 5, pp.214–27.

García Colorado, Gabriel and Irma Eréndira Sandoval (eds) (1998), *Autonomía y derechos de los pueblos indios*, Instituto de Investigaciones Legislativas de la Cámara de Diputados (Mexico).

Gluckman, Max (1958), *Analysis of a Social Situation in Modern Zululand*, Manchester University Press (Rhodes-Livingston Paper No. 28) (Manchester).

Ha fracasado el indigenismo? Reportaje de una controversia (1971), Secretaría de Educación Pública (Mexico).

Hindley, Jane (1995), 'Towards a Pluricultural Nation: The Limits of *Indigenismo* in Article 4', in Rob Aitken, Nickie Craske, Gareth Jones and David Stansfield (eds) *Dismantling the Mexican State?*, Macmillan (London), pp.225–43.

Huntington, Samuel (1996), *The Clash of Civilizations and the Remaking of the World Order*, Simon and Schuster (New York).

Kymlicka, Will (1996), *Ciudadanía multicultural. Una teoría liberal de los derechos de las minorías*, Paidós (Barcelona).

Liffman, Paul (1996), 'Reivindicación territorial y convergencia democrática de los wixáritari (huicholes)', in Jorge Alonso and Juan Manuel Ramírez (comps.) *La democracia de los de abajo en Jalisco*, University of Guadalajara/CIESAS/CIICH-UNAM/Consejo Electoral del Estado de Jalisco (Guadalajara).

——, Beatriz Vázquez and Luz María Macías (1997), 'Práctica ceremonial, tenencia de la tierra y lucha territorial de los Huicholes', in R.I. Estrada Martínez and G. González Guerra (comps.) *Tradiciones jurídicas en comunidades indígenas de México*, Comisión Nacional de Derechos Humanos (Mexico).

Lumholtz, Carl (1904), *El México desconocido. Cinco años de exploración entre las tribus de la Sierra Madre Occidental; en la Tierra Caliente de Tepic y Jalisco, y entre los Tarascos de Michoacán*, Charles Scribner's Sons, 2 vols (New York). (Facsimile edition published by the Instituto Nacional Indigenista, 1986.)

Marshall, T.H. (1964), *Class, Citizenship, and Social Development*, Doubleday (New York).

Marzal, Manuel (1968), *La aculturación de los otomíes del Mezquital*, Masters thesis in Anthropology, Iberoamericana University (Mexico).

—— (1993), *Historia de la antropología indigenista: México y Perú*, Anthropos/Universidad Autónoma Metropolitana-Iztapalapa (Barcelona).

Mitchell, J. Clyde (1983), 'Case and Situation Analysis', *The Sociological Review*, Vol.31, (2), pp.187–211.

Morales Bermúdez, Jesús (1992), 'El Congreso Indígena de Chiapas: Un testimonio', *Anuario 1991*, Instituto Chiapaneco de Cultura, pp.242–370.

Myerhoff, Barbara G. (1974), *Peyote Hunt: The Sacred Journey of the Huichol Indians*, Cornell University Press (Ithaca and London).

Oehmichen, María Cristina (1999), *Reforma del Estado, política social e indigenismo en México, 1988–1996*, Universidad Nacional Autónoma de México–Instituto de Investigaciones Antropológicas (Mexico).

Ong, Aihwa (1999), 'Clash of Civilizations or Asian Liberalism? An Anthropology of the State and Citizenship', in Henrietta Moore (ed.) *Anthropological Theory Today*, Polity Press (Cambridge).

Pakulski, Jan (1997), 'Cultural citizenship', *Citizenship Studies*, 1, pp.73–85.

Plancarte, Francisco (1954), *El problema indígena tarahumara*, Instituto Nacional Indigenista (Memoria, V) (Mexico).

Pozas Arciniega, Ricardo (1976), *Antropología y burocracia indigenista*, Editorial Tlacuilo (Mexico).

Roberts, Bryan (1998), 'Ciudadanía y política social en Latinoamérica', in B. Roberts (ed.) *Ciudadanía y política social (Centroamérica en reestructuración*, Vol. 3), FLACSO\SSRC (San José de Costa Rica).

Rojas, Beatriz (1992), 'Camotlán, entre Jalisco y Nayarit', *Secuencia*, Instituto Mora, No. 22, pp.5–40.

Rojas Cortés, Angélica (1999), 'Escolaridad e interculturalidad. Los jóvenes wixaritari en una secundaria de huicholes', Masters thesis in Social Anthropology, CIESAS Occidente (Guadalajara).

Rojas González, Francisco ([1948] 1998), 'Jículi ba-ba', in *Ensayos Indigenistas*, introduction, edition and notes by Andrés Fábregas Puig, El Colegio de Jalisco (Guadalajara).

Rosaldo, Renato (1997), 'Cultural Citizenship, Inequality, and Multiculturalism', in William V. Flores and Rina Benmayor (eds) *Latino Cultural Citizenship: Claiming Identity, Space, and Rights*, Beacon Press (Boston).

Roseberry, William (1994), 'Hegemony and the Language of Contention' in Gil Joseph and Daniel Nugent (eds), *Everyday Forms of State Formation*: Duke University Press (Durham), pp.355–65.

Sánchez Botero, Esther (1999), 'La tutela como medio de transformación de las relaciones Estado-pueblos indígenas en Colombia', in W. Assies, G. van der Haar and A. Hoekema (eds) *El reto de la diversidad. Pueblos indígenas y reforma del Estado en América Latina*, El Colegio de Michoacán (Zamora).

Sariego, Juan Luis (1998), *El indigenismo en Chihuahua*, Escuela Nacional de Antropología e Historia–Unidad Chihuahua\Fideicomiso para la Cultura México\USA (Chihuahua).

Sieder, Rachel and Jessica Witchell (2001), 'Advancing Indigenous Claims through the Law: Reflections on the Guatemalan Peace Process', in Jane Cowan, Marie Dembour and Richard Wilson (eds), *Culture and Rights*, Cambridge University Press (Cambridge).

Stavenhagen, Rodolfo (1988), *Derecho indígena y derechos humanos en América Latina*, El Colegio de México\Instituto Interamericano de Derechos Humanos (Mexico).

Street, Susan (1990), 'La transformación de un poder sindical: veinte años del SNTE', in G. Guevara Niebla (ed.) *El desafío educativo II*, Fondo de Cultura Económica\Centro de Investigaciones Culturales y Científicas (Mexico).

Taylor, Charles (1995), 'Cross-Purposes: The Liberal-Communitarian Debate', in *Philosophical Arguments*, Harvard University Press (Cambridge, Mass).

Torres Contreras, José de Jesús (1995), 'La organización productiva y las políticas guber-namentales en la zona huichol', *Estudios Jaliscienses*, 19, pp.33–44.

Turner, Bryan S. (1990), 'Outline of a Theory of Citizenship', *Sociology*, 24, pp.189–214.

Van Velsen, Jaap (1967), 'The Extended Case Method and Situational Analysis', in A.L. Epstein (ed.) *The Craft of Social Anthropology*, Tavistock (London).

Villa Rojas, Alfonso (1955), *Los mazatecos y el problema indígena de la cuenca del Papaloapan*, Instituto Nacional Indigenista (Memoria VII) (Mexico).

Villoro, Luis (1998), *Estado plural, pluralidad de culturas*, Paidós/UNAM (Mexico).

Weigand, Phil C. (1992), *Ensayos sobre el Gran Nayar. Entre coras, huicholes y tepehuanos*, CEMCA/INI/El Colegio de Michoacán (Mexico).

Yrigoyen, Raquel (1999), *Pautas de coordinación entre el derecho indígena y el derecho estatal*, Fundación Myrna Mack (Guatemala).

6
Peru: Pluralist Constitution, Monist Judiciary – A Post-Reform Assessment

Raquel Yrigoyen Fajardo

Introduction

In 1993 the Peruvian Constitution was reformed and the International Labour Organisation Convention 169 on Indigenous and Tribal Peoples was ratified by the Peruvian government. A similar process of constitutional reform had occurred in Colombia in 1991, and subsequently took place in Peru in 1993, Bolivia in 1994, Ecuador in 1998 and Venezuela in 1999.[1] This meant that for the first time in the history of the Peruvian republic, the multicultural nature of the nation was formally recognised in the constitution, as was indigenous customary law and a special jurisdiction for its exercise by campesinos and native peoples. With this change, the nineteenth century constitutional ideal of a culturally homogeneous nation-state was abandoned. At the same time, the new Magna Carta parted company with the Kelsenian model of legal monism based on the correspondence between state and law.[2] With the recognition of a multicultural identity and of legal pluralism, the new constitution represented the first step towards the construction of a multicultural state in Peru. However, a preliminary assessment of the seven years since the reform reveals an unsatisfactory record in the implementation of the pluralist principles enunciated in the constitution, particularly in terms of the special jurisdiction for campesinos and native peoples. This has occurred within the broader context of a generalised lack of citizenship rights due to the political authoritarianism of the executive branch and the absence of effective checks and balances.

The example of the *rondas campesinas* and their exercise of 'customary law', explored here, illustrates how the conservative behaviour of the Peruvian

157

judiciary has constituted an enormous brake on legal pluralism as recognised in the 1993 Constitution and ILO Convention 169. In effect, legal pluralism has been repressed by the judiciary in Peru, which has, in turn, endorsed the political authoritarianism of the Executive and failed to act as an independent check on Executive power as stipulated in the law. This stands in marked contrast to developments in Colombia. Despite the fact that the formula for recognition of indigenous customary law and provision for a special jurisdiction is more limited in the Colombian constitution than in its Peruvian counterpart,[3] the Colombian judiciary, and particularly the Colombian Constitutional Court, have developed an important jurisprudence interpreting the 1991 Constitution from a pluralist perspective.[4]

One of the central challenges of the post-constitutional reform phase is to construct a pluralist legal culture which permeates the behaviour of the judiciary. A second challenge of a more global nature relates to political culture: the recognition of the right of indigenous peoples and campesinos to apply their own law and to make law (*iuris dictium*) is only possible within a model of a pluralist society where such peoples and communities are treated as political subjects and not as the objects of policy. Such a shift is essential for the construction of a truly multicultural state.

This chapter aims to make a preliminary assessment of the implementation of the 1993 constitutional reform in Peru with specific reference to the provisions with respect to the recognition of indigenous customary law and the creation of a corresponding special jurisdiction (*jurisdicción especial*). The first section details the different indigenist policies implemented throughout Peruvian history prior to the pluralist model of the 1993 Constitution, considering the ways in which such policies reconfigured the identity of indigenous peoples and campesino communities. A second section examines the content of the 1993 reform, its achievements and limitations with respect to multiculturalism and legal pluralism. The third section analyses the behaviour of the judiciary with respect to the recognition of the special jurisdiction, focusing on the case of the *rondas campesinas*. The conclusion sets out a number of future challenges.

Indigenist policies and the construction of indigenous and campesino identities

Throughout Peruvian history, diverse juridico-political models (summarised below) have been developed to deal with indigenous peoples and cultural diversity.[5] These policies have shaped relations between the state and indigenous peoples, in turn reconfiguring those peoples and their identity.[6]

1. The colonial period: subordination and segregation

During the Colony, a model of segregation was instituted in order to maintain ethnic and racial differences. This was expressed through the existence of differentiated legal regimes and geographical spaces for Peninsulars and

'Indians'. The former lived in *villas de españoles*, whilst the latter were concentrated into *pueblos de Indios*, which, in turn, facilitated the tasks of tribute collection, forced labour and evangelisation for the colonial government. The colonial regime was based on the political subordination and economic exploitation of Indians. This was subsequently legitimised by the elaboration of the ideology of their 'natural inferiority', an ideology which has persisted to the present. On this basis it was argued that Indians lacked sufficient understanding and capacity for self-determination, self-government and the application of natural law; instead, it was maintained, they should be treated as charges by the Spaniards who would be responsible for their evangelisation and control. At the same time their practices and customs (*'usos y costumbres'*) were to be limited by 'human and divine law', reflecting the belief that Indians were, by nature, savages and that their customs required regulation and constraint. Some indigenous authorities were permitted in order to facilitate the governance of the *pueblos de Indios*. Thus it was established that the mayors (*alcaldes*) of these *pueblos* could administer justice in the case of lesser infractions, while more serious cases were passed to the *corregidor español* (a Spanish authority).

2. Independence: assimilation

With the achievement of Independence, led by the *criollo* bourgeoisie, a model of equality before the law amongst all 'citizens' was formally installed and differentiated legal regimes were eliminated, subjecting the entire population to a single written body of law. It was established that only the National Congress could emit laws, that the Executive was exclusively responsible for domestic order and that the judiciary alone had the faculty to administer justice.[7] The cessation of differentiated legal regimes also meant the abolition of the special rights enjoyed by the *pueblos de Indios*, such as the inalienability of their communal lands. This facilitated the dispossession of Indians from such lands and contributed to the growth of the haciendas, property of *criollos* and mestizos. Republican constitutions expressed the assimilationist ideal of constructing a single, culturally homogeneous nation under *criollo* and mestizo leadership, declaring that only their language (Spanish) and religion (Catholicism) were official. In legal terms Indians vanished, leading to the negation of a culturally plural reality. Although different indigenous languages, cultures and legal systems did not totally disappear, they were relegated to a subordinate position.

The ideal of the monopoly of the state on the legitimate exercise of force was not applied in practice, due to the minimal presence of the judiciary throughout the national territory. A kind of alliance developed between the Lima-based bureaucracy and the *hacendados*, which involved the latter exercising de facto control in the rural areas (Cotler 1978). In more remote communities, indigenous law and justice continued to be exercised as part of a broader strategy for cultural survival. The liberal ideal of 'equality before the law' remained a dead letter. The police and the army applied anti-vagrancy laws and laws for road-building service and military service in a discriminatory fashion so that indigenous labour was forcibly displaced to the haciendas, state infrastructural works and the army (the last being responsible for putting down campesino rebellions). The *criollo* and mestizo population tended to concentrate in the cities, whilst indigenous people were relegated to impoverished rural areas.[8]

In the second decade of the twentieth century, due to indigenous demands for land and the emergence of an academic, artistic and political indigenist movement, the 'problem of the Indian' began to be debated in Peru and questions were raised about the lack of legal protection for indigenous people. Indians subsequently reappeared in the law, the 1920 Constitution being the first to recognise indigenous communities and the inalienability of their communal lands. They also reappeared in the 1924 Penal Code which, however, continued to reflect the 'civilising vision' of cultural assimilation. The code characterised indigenous people from the highlands as 'semi-civilised, degraded by servitude and alcohol' and those from the jungle regions as 'savages', declaring them not competent to be legally responsible (as with minors and those judged to be insane) and proposing that they be sent to penal colonies with unlimited sentences until they were 'civilised' (Articles 44 and 45). In this case, cultural differences were recognised and punished.

3. The Republic in the mid-twentieth century: integrationism

In the mid-1940s a movement known as 'integrationism' developed, the aim of which was to move beyond the assimilationist policies in force since Independence and their 'civilising' discourse. Instead these indigenists pursued the 'integration' of indigenous people into the nation and the market as part of a developmentalist vision. They proposed the recognition of indigenous specificities and rights (to land, language, dress, customs and culture), and argued that indigenous people should be helped out of their backward condition. The 'Indian problem' was seen as a problem of socio-economic marginalisation produced by the servile relations of the traditional, feudal economy. The dismantling of this model became a central political priority. However, despite the fact that they recognised specific rights of indigenous people, integrationist policies continued to treat them as political objects, not subjects. For example, the International Labour Organisation's 1957 Convention No. 107 on Indigenous and Tribal Populations established a series of rights for indigenous populations, including recognition of their customary law, but limited these by stating that they should not affect fundamental human rights nor the 'integrationist policies' of individual states towards such populations.

Following a mounting campesino struggle for land during the 1950s and 1960s and a lukewarm agrarian reform law in 1962, an important process of agrarian reform was implemented in Peru under the military government of General Juan Velasco Alvarado.[9] Large haciendas were expropriated and title was given to resident workers through different forms of productive organisation, such as cooperatives (above all on the coast) and campesino groups and communities (principally in the sierra). Within this context the government developed a new regulatory order for communities of Andean descent, changing their name from 'indigenous' to 'campesinos'. This was intended to counter the negative charge associated with the word 'indigenous' that derived from the colonial past. The term 'campesino' was successfully appropriated by the communities and became a marker not only of socio-economic status but also of cultural identity. Part of the pro-campesino discourse of the state included the recognition of Quechua as an official language and the vindication of autochthonous culture. Within an international context that favoured cooperativism and development, campesino communities were legally regulated through a form of internal organisation similar to that of the agrarian reform cooperatives. This resulted in a new system of communal authorities. In addition, the status of ethnic groups in the Amazon jungle region, who had been gradually dispossessed from their land and natural resources by colonists since the era of the rubber boom, was legally regulated. The 1974 Law of Native Communities recognised their territorial rights and even their sub-soil rights (which have been restricted by subsequent norms). However, the law copied the organisational model of the campesino communities, failing to take into account the fact that the Amazonian indigenous communities had different forms of organisation and of land and natural resource use. Thus ethnic groups who had previously cultivated large extensions of land on a discontinuous, seasonal basis were forced to settle in reduced areas delimited and titled for specific communities. Over the years this changed the physiognomy and identity of ethnic groups in the Amazon region, who were recognised by law but fragmented into communities. In national terms, the military's reforms put an end to the oligarchic, landowner model and encouraged the shift of capital into the industrial and other sectors. With the growth of industry and, subsequently, the economic crisis in the countryside that followed the agrarian reform, increasing numbers of indigenous campesinos migrated towards the cities.[10] This also affected indigenous identities.[11]

With respect to judicial reform, the Velasco government adopted a tough line and implemented a series of unprecedented changes. The judiciary, which was politically identified with the old oligarchic order, stubbornly clung to its traditional legal culture and blocked implementation of the agrarian and labour reforms. In response the government created a series of parallel jurisdictions and tribunals staffed by people sympathetic to the reform programme. In addition, the legal right of communities to resolve their internal conflicts was recognised. In the case of the native communities, the 1974 law recognised their right to administer justice for minor cases and offences (similar to the attributions of a justice of the peace);[12] this was later changed by the 1979 Constitution, which reaffirmed legal monism.

The rise of the *rondas campesinas*

By the late 1970s government agencies had dispensed with the pro-campesino discourse, the economic abandonment of the countryside was steadily worsening and the judicial authorities had returned to their traditional bureaucratic routine. Within this context, the northern regions of the country also experienced an increase in widespread cattle rustling and robbery between neighbours.[13] In response to this, a new form of organisation emerged in the northern departments, the so-called *rondas campesinas*.[14] Their original aim was to provide security against robbery, given the weakness and corruption of state authorities, the disappearance of the *ronda* patrols which had existed on the old haciendas (which had occurred as a consequence of the agrarian reform), and the lack of other forms of communal authority. This was an area with very few formally recognised campesino communities. The *rondas* initially consisted of organised night-watch groups, a democratically elected ruling council and general assembly in which all the population participated, this last being the highest local authority. Given their success in controlling cattle rustling, the *rondas campesinas* subsequently began to deal with all kinds of problems and conflicts, extending their functions to include community development activities, local government and co-ordination with the state authorities. The practice of resolving conflicts and problems via general assemblies, the mutual support for the night watch patrol and community projects, and the opening of new spaces of communication and reciprocity became powerful instruments for creating or recreating 'communality'.[15] The demonstration effect of the efficiency of the *rondas campesinas* in combating robbery and solving local conflicts led to their rapid spread to many departments during the late 1970s and 1980s, involving as many as 400,000 local committees.[16] In fact, during the 1980s the *rondero* movement came to constitute the most dynamic campesino movement in the country.

The *rondas* exercise authority within their territory (community, village or hamlet) and, if the cases so require, they coordinate their activities with neighbouring *rondas* in their district or province. They apply restitutive solutions in cases of robbery or cattle rustling, obliging the perpetrators to return the stolen goods, work on behalf of the community and take part in the night-watch patrol. In cases of family, land and other disputes the *rondas* try to address the interests of both parties in a conflict with the aim that the victims receive some kind of reparation or compensation and that the perpetrators are 'reintegrated into the community'. In some cases they also apply physical punishments, but ronderos expressly reject torture, disappearance and capital punishment. As a general rule, more institutionalised *rondas* tend to promote settlements between parties and impose community service instead of physical punishment. Cases which previously took years to process through the courts, and which required significant amounts of time and money from campesino plaintiffs, are now resolved by the *rondas* in a matter or hours in the place where the infraction occurred, and with the presence of the community as a guarantee that the settlements reached will be respected. At the same time the *rondas* have dealt with problems and conflicts previously ignored by the state authorities, such as petty theft, domestic violence, and demands for maintenance in cases where no formal proof of paternity exists.

Given that in many cases the cattle rustlers captured and obliged to do community service and patrol in the *rondas* are connected to local power networks, the relatives or lawyers of these rustlers have denounced the *rondero* authorities for crimes against individual liberty, kidnapping, physical abuse and infractions against the administration of justice. As a result, many *ronda* leaders have been prosecuted in the courts for applying their system of justice. Since their emergence, the *rondas campesinas* have had a complex relationship with the state, which has both recognised and repressed them. At the outset the *rondas campesinas* endeavoured to secure the support of the departmental governor and the local political authorities in order to avoid problems with the police, but towards the end of the 1970s, following a mass mobilisation which was repressed by the army, they turned their attention to demanding a law that recognised their right to adjudicate conflicts.

In response to the crisis of the second phase of military government (1975–79), a constituent assembly was elected and elections subsequently held which led to a return to democratic government in 1980. With respect to the rights of campesino and native communities, the 1979 Constitution reiterated some of the rights recognised during the Velasco period, such as the official recognition of the Quechua and Aymara languages and the legal recognition of the communities and their inalienable rights to land. However, the constitution remained anchored in an integrationalist-paternalist model, treating cultural difference as a question of 'backwardness' and not of diversity. This was illustrated in Article 161, which stated, 'The state respects and protects the traditions of the Campesino and Native communities. It will advance the cultural advancement of their members' (Art. 161 in fine). With respect to the administration of justice, the 1979 Constitution established the 'unity and exclusivity' of the judiciary in the administration of justice, interpreted as removing even the limited rights of native communities to administer justice recognised by the 1974 law.

Immediately after presidential elections were called in May 1980, the guerrilla group Sendero Luminoso rose up in arms against the Peruvian state. The insurgency, and the subsequent army repression, was initially concentrated in the departments of the central-south sierra. The counter-insurgency war later extended to the Amazon jungle and the coastal cities. At the same time, in the northern sierra, the *rondero* movement continued to grow and to lobby for legal recognition.[17] Finally in 1986, as a result of negotiations between the ruling APRA Party, which wished to convert the *rondas* into an auxiliary police force, and the United Left (IU), which preferred them to be independent, Congress passed Law No. 24571 which legally recognised pacific, democratic and autonomous *rondas campesinas*.[18] The law recognised the rights of *rondas* to patrol and to self-defence, but not their right to administer justice, the Congress having maintained that only the judiciary had the right to apply law. Despite the limited recognition of their functions, the new law did put a stop to the majority of police persecution against the *rondas*. In addition, given the principle of organisational autonomy for campesino communities stipulated in the 1979 Constitution, the *rondas* were left with considerable leeway to determine their internal organisation.

During the Aprista government of Alan García (1985–90), the Executive used the mechanism of 'accreditation' mentioned in Law No. 24571 to politically subordinate the *rondas campesinas*. It failed to entirely achieve this, but succeeded in generating considerable tension among campesinos. In 1988 the government emitted an Executive Decree with the aim of co-opting the *rondas* and subjecting them to police control.[19] This was openly rejected by the *ronderos*, who organised marches and meetings to protest against the decree which, ultimately, was never applied. At this time the *rondas* were very strong and were able to organise meetings at departmental and regional level. In addition, they enjoyed the support of the Catholic Church and many other social organisations.

By the end of the 1980s inflation was spiralling towards hyperinflation and the economy was in crisis. Political violence had worsened due to the actions of armed groups and the government's counterinsurgency strategies. The army had begun to incorporate the civilian population into its counterinsurgency tactics, forcing the campesino communities of the central-south sierra to patrol against Sendero Luminoso and to carry out actions against communities which were alleged to sympathise with the guerrillas. In order to legitimise this involvement of the civilian population in army operations, the Executive – and the national press – began to refer to these civil defence groups under military control as *rondas*.

The 1990s: towards a pluralist model?

The 1990s were characterised by the phenomenon of globalisation and the adoption of neoliberal economic models by Latin American countries, including Peru. At the same time, a number of important international changes in indigenist policies occurred as a result of the '500 Years' campaign, the adoption of ILO Convention 169 on Indigenous and Tribal Peoples in Independent Countries in 1989, and the processes of constitutional reform which took place in some 15 Latin American countries (Van Cott 2000a). Included in these changes was the recognition of indigenous peoples, their identity and their collective rights to political participation, both in the affairs that directly affect them and in national policy-making. With these changes, indigenous peoples ceased to be objects of policy and became political actors themselves. Another important feature of a number of constitutional reforms was the recognition of the multicultural nature of the nation-state. This signalled that the right to cultural diversity was no longer a question for 'minorities', but rather a right of all people within a model of 'multicultural citizenship' (Kymlicka 1997). Lastly, the constitutional reforms also included the recognition of so-called customary law and the establishment of special jurisdictions for its exercise. This instituted a model of legal pluralism within the framework, and limits, of international human rights norms.

Both international trends, economic neoliberalism and the legal recognition of multiculturalism and legal pluralism, were played out in Peru. However, in contrast to the efficiency with which neoliberal policies were pursued, the implementation of the recognition of legal pluralism barely began. The pluralist model, based on respect for the autonomy of indigenous peoples and communities, clashed with the political authoritarianism of the Executive and the monist legal culture of the judiciary. In 1990 the first government of Alberto Fujimori was elected, characterised by three features: the so-called 'Fuji-shock' (a series of drastic anti-inflationary measures) in 1990; the breakdown of the constitutional regime with the so-called 'Fuji-golpe' in 1992; and the detention of the leader of Sendero Luminoso in 1993, which contributed to a decline in terrorist activity.

As part of its counterinsurgency strategy, the government developed policies to control the indigenous civilian population through military operations. First Legislative Decree 741 (passed in November 1991) 'legalised' the de facto Self Defence Committees (*Comités de Autodefensa*) created by the previous administration of Alan García. The army then forced the civilian indigenous population in the conflict zones to organise themselves into committees under military command which were armed and obliged to support the armed forces and the police in 'pacification' operations. The government subsequently elaborated a code to regulate the functions of the Self-Defence Committees (Decree 77/DE-92) in November 1992. Finally, in January 1993 it decreed that the *rondas campesinas* should adjust their organisation and functions in line with those of the Self-Defence Committees (Decree No. 002–93-DE/CCFFAA), which formally placed all *rondas campesinas* under the control of the armed forces. This series of decrees, emitted in the first three years of the Fujimori government, established the framework for the instrumental relationship the Executive – and the state – had decided to establish with campesino communities and organisations. Forced military recruitment had traditionally been carried out among indigenous populations in the countryside and impoverished urban barrios. In addition to this, the Fujimori administration institutionalised the involvement of the civilian population in military-style operations against the insurgent forces, thereby violating one of the basic norms of international humanitarian law. Within this context many human rights abuses were committed.

At the same time as the policy of instrumentalising the indigenous campesino population for military ends was implemented, a constitutional reform was discussed and ILO Convention 169 ratified. On the one hand, the constitutional reform included changes dictated by the Executive to increase its relative power, as well as certain features to facilitate the 'anti-terrorist struggle'.[20] However, it also included some of the reforms fought for by progressive sectors that had been implemented in other countries as part of a process of democratic institutionalisation, such as the creation of the figure of the Ombudsman. Finally, in line with the international shifts mentioned above and in response to domestic pressure, the new constitution also incorporated the demand for constitutional recognition of cultural diversity, customary law and a corresponding special jurisdiction.

Various actors played an important part in the recognition of customary law and of the jurisdictional function of communities and *rondas*. An initial inter-sectoral proposal was drawn up in a 1992 workshop between ronderos and judges, organised by a number of institutions, including the Catholic Church (through CEAS, the Comisión Episcopal de Acción Social of the Peruvian Bishops' Conference), the Andean Commission of Jurists and various human rights NGOs. Later, the Forum for Cultural and Legal Pluralism, composed of members of these institutions, worked on a draft article to be included in the new constitution. This was partly based on the Colombian constitutional reform passed in 1991.[21] The Forum lobbied a number of institutions, including the Commission for the Constitutional Reform of the Judiciary, which was already drafting its own proposal. This Commission subsequently incorporated part of the Forum's proposal, encouraged by the Colombian constitutional reform. The Supreme Court did not back the Commission's proposal, but with the support of other sectors it was put forward to the Constituent Assembly. In contrast to the Colombian constitutional reform process, very little discussion about the special jurisdiction took place within the Constituent Assembly. This partly accounts for the way in which it was included in the 1993 Constitution.

As a consequence of criticisms of the ethnocentric vision which underpinned the 1924 Penal Code, the 1991 Penal Code included the formula of 'culturally conditioned error' (Art. 15), which meant that those who transgressed the law by following their culture and customs would be exempt from punishment. The aim of this reform was to overcome the notion of indigenous people as not legally competent, as specified in the 1924 Code. The new Penal Code, as stated in its preamble, aimed to take the cultural diversity of the country into account and to decriminalise cultural difference.[22] The decriminalisation of cultural difference is part of a broader policy of tolerance of difference. A further step in this direction is the recognition of pluralism, characterised by the recognition and protection of cultural diversity by the state, not merely its decriminalisation. The 1991 Penal Code was drafted after several years of debate and within the context of a number of initiatives advanced between 1990 and 1992 aimed at reforming the justice system. This process, however, was frustrated by the 1992 'autogolpe' and was subsequently co-opted by the Executive.[23]

The 1993 Constitution: towards a multicultural state?

The 1993 Constitution abandoned the nineteenth century notion of the nation-state based on the idea that the state should officially represent the cultural hegemony of a single ethnic group and cultural identity. Instead of this monocultural definition, the new text affirmed the multicultural configuration of the nation and established a new relationship between nation and state. The integrationist political model, which had continually valued hegemonic culture as 'superior', 'advanced' and 'civilised', remaining essentially paternalistic (even if it had respected some aspects of other cultures), was dispensed with. As mentioned above, the 1979 Constitution had decreed that 'the state will advance the cultural *advancement* of [the members of campesino and native communities]' (Art. 161 in fine); in contrast, the 1993 Constitution established that 'the state will *respect* the cultural identities of the campesino and native communities' (Art. 89). As part of this new pluralist model, the constitution established the individual right to cultural difference, and the collective right of different cultures and ethnic groups to respect and protection from the state. Article 2.19 states that 'Every person has a right to their cultural and ethnic identity. The state recognises and protects the ethnic and cultural plurality of the nation.' By using the verbs 'recognise' and 'protect', the Peruvian state not only acknowledges the existence of cultural diversity, but also commits itself to protecting this diversity. This obligation covered both reactive dimensions, such as avoiding the criminalisation of cultural difference, and a commitment to advancing proactive measures aimed at strengthening cultural diversity. On the basis of these guiding principles, a new, multicultural institutionality should evolve to strengthen cultural elements such as language, forms of organisation, customs and normative systems. As a corollary of the recognition of cultural plurality, the constitution also officialised indigenous languages, recognised specific rights for campesino and native communities, and customary law and special jurisdiction (campesino and indigenous justice).[24]

Another consequence of the 1993 constitutional reform was that, because cultural diversity was legitimised and guaranteed as a right, the penal system could no longer be used to further the disappearance of diversity by prosecuting people who did not adhere to culturally dominant norms. All cultures now had the right to exist, without prejudicing their right to question and change specific practices of their own based on coercion rather than consensus or which constrain human rights. Respect for cultural diversity implies the decriminalisation of cultural practices which could be construed as punishable acts. In this way, those cultural groups that have forms of marriage, justice, natural resource use or health care different to those presupposed by the Penal Code should not be prosecuted nor threatened with legal prosecution in order that they conform to hegemonic cultural norms. The same principle of respect for cultural diversity should be observed by those who apply campesino or indigenous justice. The legalisation of customary law by the constitutional reform meant that it should no longer be penalised.

Despite its failure to correspond to cultural realities, legal monism has been one of the most fiercely defended ideologies and political positions of legal culture. However, during the last decade of the twentieth century this doctrine was increasingly questioned by alternative conceptions deriving from legal pluralism and the theory of alternative mechanisms for dispute settlement.[25] The 1993 Constitution broke with the model of legal monism by recognising customary law and a corresponding special jurisdiction in line with the recognition of the multicultural nature of the nation. In so doing it established the basis for a multicultural institutionality. The national formula for recognition, inspired by the 1991 Colombian Constitution, states:

> The authorities of the Campesino and Native Communities, with the support of the *rondas campesinas*, shall be able to exercise jurisdictional functions within their territorial ambit in conformity with customary law as long as they do not violate fundamental individual rights. The law establishes forms of coordination between this special jurisdiction and the Justices of the Peace and the other institutions of the judiciary.[26] (Article 149)

The content of this article is considerably broad and complements that of ILO Convention 169 on Indigenous and Tribal Peoples in Independent Countries, which also recognises customary law. The 1993 Constitution recognised the right of campesino and native communities and *rondas campesinas* to exercise jurisdictional functions, apply their own customary law and guaranteed respect for their authorities.[27] In other words, recognition was extended to: a) the normative or regulatory powers of the native and campesino communities and the *rondas*, b) their right to exercise jurisdiction or resolve conflicts, and c) their own institutionality or system of authorities. On the basis of this article not only the legislature has the power to emit norms – communities also have the special right to determine their own forms of self-regulation. Secondly, not only the judiciary has the right to administer justice, rather the jurisdictional attributions of the special or communal justice are also recognised. Finally, not only the Executive has the authority to control order and apply the law; communal authorities and *ronderos* can also do this as part of their customary law.

Customary law consists of a system of norms, values, normative principles, authorities, institutions and procedures which permits peoples and communities to regulate social life, resolve conflicts and organise order within the framework of their own culture and social needs. Such law includes old and new features, autochthonous and adopted elements, but corresponds to the cultural system of those who use it who see it as their own. It also includes the norms by which rules are created or changed. In other words, the recognition of customary law is not the recognition of a static body of rules, but rather of the right of right-holders to create new norms for themselves. The so-called 'special jurisdiction' is a legal jurisdiction (*fuero*) for campesino and native communities and *rondas campesinas* which allows their authorities to exercise legal functions. These functions correspond to those of the national judiciary: that is, to hear, judge and resolve conflicts, to define specific rights and obligations, to order the restrictions of rights (whether through sanctions or restitutive measures), community service, compensation for losses (*daños y perjuicios*) and the confiscation of goods (*disposición de bienes*). This special jurisdiction is not bound by ordinary legislation but rather by customary law, but it must not violate fundamental individual rights.[28] In terms of material competencies, the constitution does not set down any limits on the kind or severity of cases which may be judged within the special jurisdiction. This is in line with ILO Convention 169, which states that such special jurisdiction has the faculty to judge all kinds of cases, however grave the offences. With respect to territorial competencies, the special jurisdiction has full competence within the territorial ambit of the native and campesino communities and the *rondas campesinas*. With respect to whom the special jurisdiction applies to, the constitution does not state that it should only apply to campesinos and natives, mentioning only the territorial criteria. The special jurisdiction could therefore decide cases where the acts in question take place within the territorial ambit of the communities and *rondas*, but which involve non-indigenous, non-community members and people who are not *ronderos*. This addresses a possible loophole whereby non-indigenous individuals could carry out crimes within the communities and later appeal to be judged by state law rather than community law, knowing full well that state justice has limited territorial reach and can be more easily manipulated in their favour than community justice. In any case, both members of the communities and non-community members have the right that their human rights be respected.

The 1993 Constitution came into force after it was ratified in a plebiscite in October of the same year. In November, the Peruvian state ratified ILO Convention 169. On the basis of these two instruments, indigenous peoples and campesino communities gained the right to participate in decisions which directly affected them and in national decision-making processes, the right to differentiated identity and to self-regulation within a framework of autonomy, the only limitation being the stipulation that human rights be respected. However, the authoritarian policies implemented by the Fujimori government and the subordination of campesino and indigenous communities and organisations to military control have blocked the implementation of the constitutional model of pluralism. This has not been challenged by other branches of the state, but rather has been implicitly or explicitly supported by them. Congress has failed to draft a law to establish the coordination between the special jurisdiction and the national legal system, as stipulated in Article 149 of the 1993 Constitution. Neither has it promoted consultation with indigenous peoples on legislative and administrative matters which affect them, as stipulated in Article 6 of ILO Convention 169. The judiciary, hide-bound as a result of the conservatism of a monist legal culture, has not appropriated the pluralist model set down in the 1993 Constitution. At the same time, it has proved incapable of halting the unconstitutional acts of the Executive, due to the increased dependency of the judiciary on the Executive and its precarious institutional nature (more than two-thirds of all judges are provisional appointments).[29] In addition, during the second administration of Fujimori, institutional guarantees to secure the primacy of the constitution over acts of government were weakened with the closure of the Tribunal for Constitutional Guarantees and the controversial withdrawal of Peru from the jurisdiction of the Inter-American Court of Human Rights.

The military instrumentalisation of the campesino and indigenous population directly contradicted the respect and autonomy necessary for the pluralist model set out in the 1993 Constitution to function. In addition, the repressive actions carried out by the army and the police in rural areas or marginal urban barrios were not only aimed at controlling terrorism, but also at containing popular protest against neoliberal economic measures, which generated worsening indices of poverty. In the case of the *rondas campesinas*, the Executive Decree which facilitated their militarisation passed in January 1993 initiated a new stage in relations between the *rondas* and the government, marked by increased intervention and violence. In many regions military commanders forcibly imposed the decree, threatening to detain leaders of the *rondas* for terrorist crimes or imprisoning them for alleged collaboration with Sendero Luminoso. In addition, local political authorities stopped accrediting the *rondas*, as required by Law 24571, assuming that the Executive Decree placing the *rondas* under military command overrode the pre-existing law. At the same time, the judiciary began to issue large numbers of detention orders against *rondero* leaders and bring criminal prosecutions against them, both because of their own monist legal culture and pressure from government agencies. Between 1992 and 1993 more than a hundred detention orders were issued against *ronderos* in the Hualgayoc-Bambamarca province of Cajamarca alone, leading to the imprisonment of many *rondero* leaders and the exodus of others to the cities to avoid capture. This resulted in a general weakening of the *rondas*, a trend which continued throughout the rest of the decade. The government later began to engage in political clientelism by extending credit and implementing public works in the communities. This was institutionalised with a hugely inflated budget through the Ministry of the Presidency, the National Fund for Social Compensation and Development FONCODES (Fondo Nacional de Compensación Social y Desarrollo), the National Food Aid Programme PRONAA (Programa Nacional de Asistencia Alimentaria) and other programmes which aimed to legitimise the government presence in the rural areas. These programmes were designed to ameliorate the impoverishment of rural areas which had resulted from neoliberal policies of structural adjustment.[30]

In some places the *rondas* submitted to military control, in others, such as Bamabamarca, they were effectively neutralised, refusing to submit to the army but left unaccredited by the political authorities and therefore without protection against attempts to bring criminal charges against their leaders.[31] In the case of the *rondas* in Huaraz and Huari, the majority were militarised after they were threatened with being denounced for crimes of terrorism. Only 13 rondero organisations refused to submit to military control, but when they tried to administer justice autonomously they were prosecuted for the crime of exceeding their functions (*usurpación de funciones*) and crimes against individual liberty.[32] Despite the capture of Abimael Guzmán, leader of Sendero Luminoso, in 1993 and the significant reduction in political violence which followed, the government continued to use the counter-insurgency discourse and norms such as the decree militarising the *rondas* in order to control the campesino population. The accusation of terrorism was used on numerous occasions to intimidate campesinos and to constrain protests against the government's economic measures.

Legal pluralism in practice: the judiciary and the *rondas campesinas*

Despite the provisions set out in Article 149 of the 1993 Constitution and in ILO Convention 169, the Peruvian judiciary did not use these norms to advance protection of campesinos' jurisdictional faculties, but instead supported the authoritarian actions of the Executive. The constitutional recognition of customary law and the special jurisdiction was effectively ignored in rulings by the courts, which continued to be guided by a monist logic. Judges have continued to prosecute campesino authorities for applying justice according to their own legal system or law, accusing them of crimes against individual liberty, against the administration of justice and of exceeding their functions.

As illustrated by the legal rulings summarised here,[33] the dominant legal culture in Peru has strongly resisted accepting legal pluralism as specified in Article 149 of the constitution. The cases of *ronderos* criminally prosecuted for 'administering justice' are numerous, and the sentences that follow provide only a few examples.[34] The judiciary does not accept the right of *rondas campesinas* to exercise judicial functions and fails to apply Article 15 of the Penal Code. In only one case of those revised did exercise of customary law by *rondas* not result in prosecution, but the verdict was based on the expiration of the relevant limitation period and not on the application of the constitutional provision.

The case of the *rondas campesinas* of the community of Chalhuayacu is typical of the levels of police violence exercised against the *rondas* and the tacit acceptance of this by the judiciary. A reading of the sentence emitted by the High Court of Ancash (Exp. 276–93, dated 28 August 1999) reveals a highly selective reading of the facts presented in the case. A complete revision of the hearing reveals that the *rondas* applied justice according to their procedures, detaining an alleged cattle rustler in February 1992. Four days later, the public prosecutor – without having carried out any investigation of the case – ordered that the police intervene (in a manner which the sentence refers to only as 'energetic'). What in fact occurred was an armed police raid on the community in the small hours of the morning, which involved breaking down the door of the community centre and demanding the presence of the leaders of the *rondas* in order to arrest them for the crime of kidnapping. The next day, members of the campesino community of Chalhuayacu, together with those of two more communities, went to the police station at Chavín to 'discuss the matter' and arrive at an agreement for reparations, as they had done on previous occasions. According to the declarations, this delegation was of approximately 300 people, including local authorities, women, children and elders. The sentence does not mention that the police killed six people from the communities accused and wounded another 30 (who were later criminally prosecuted) when they approached the police station. As the Human Rights Prosecutor later established, the police tried to cover up the massacre, denouncing the hospitalised victims and other members of the three communities for having carried out 'a terrorist attack'. The Human Rights Prosecutor subsequently established that in fact no terrorist attack had occurred, that the campesinos were unarmed and that the victims had bullet wounds in their backs, sustained when they were running away. The Human Rights Prosecutor denounced the police for the crime of abuse of authority. As a consequence, the charge of terrorism against the campesinos was changed to that of crime against public order. This part of the process was sent to a military tribunal (despite the fact that homicide is a common crime) and the policemen involved subsequently took advantage of the amnesty extended by the government of Fujimori to members of the police and the armed forces who had committed human rights violations as part of the anti-terrorist struggle – this despite the fact that it had been established that in this case no terrorist act had taken place. These events, in which those implicated in abuses appear as the victims, and which were established from the start of the hearing, were not even mentioned in the final ruling. In summary, the sentence covered up the violence carried out by the police against the accused campesinos, which was itself the best argument for the defence of those same campesinos against the charges of attacking and damaging the police station at Chavín. With respect to the charges of kidnapping (crimes against individual liberty and actual bodily harm), the sentence made no reference to the fact that the detention of the alleged cattle rustler by the *ronderos* was part of their 'customary law', decriminalised by the 1991 Penal Code and later legalised by the 1993 Constitution. By the time the final sentence was issued in 1999, some seven years after the events, the statute of limitations for the majority of the charges, including those against individual liberty, actual bodily harm and crimes against public order, had expired. In the case of the charge of damages, the sentence favoured the absolution of the accused due to lack of evidence. However, in the intervening seven years the campesinos in question – and their families – had lived under the threat of criminal prosecution, often with grave personal consequences. The ronderos' defence, based on Article 15 of the Penal Code and Article 149 of the 1993 Constitution, that they were exercising their right to apply customary law, was not even considered by the magistrates.

In the case of the *ronderos* from Huaraz which follows, in both the ruling of the Correctional Tribunal of Huaraz (Exp. 504–96, 27 September 1996), and the sentence of the High Court of Ancash for crimes against individual liberty (Exp. 110–98, 23 November 1998), the judges did not ignore Article 149 of the constitution, but interpreted the special jurisdiction in such a way as to leave it without any substance. The judicial ruling, in effect, nullifies the idea of the special jurisdiction by identifying the exercise of jurisdictional functions by communal authorities as a violation of human rights. The case refers to campesino *ronderos* who detained an alleged cattle rustler and, according to their declarations, made him work for three days in each *ronda campesina* as a sanction imposed by the *rondas*. On the basis of the facts, the judiciary charged them with crimes against individual liberty. The counsel for the defence alleged that the events, which occurred in 1996, were not only not a crime but were in fact validated by Article 149 of the 1993 Constitution. However, the sentence made the following argument:

Although it is true that article 149 of the Political Constitution of the State empowers native and campesino communities, with the support of the *rondas campesinas*, to exercise jurisdictional functions within their territorial ambit in line with customary law when this does not violate basic human rights, in this particular case the right to liberty has been violated, as has been demonstrated by the evidence presented. For this reason the court finds the accused guilty of the crime against individual liberty. (Exp. 110–98, Sentence of the High Court of Ancash, 23 November 1998)

The constitution signals that the limit of the exercise of jurisdictional functions is that of respect for basic human rights. In contrast to the constitutions of Colombia, Bolivia and Ecuador, the Peruvian Constitution has not subordinated the special jurisdiction and indigenous law to the entire constitution or ordinary laws, but states only that they should not violate basic human rights. This limitation is common in all legal systems within the international community. The jurisdictional faculties of the Peruvian judiciary, for example, include forms of restriction of individual liberty, imprisonment and the application of alternatives to incarceration, such as community service. If applied according to established procedures by the competent authority, these restrictions do not constitute a violation of human rights, but rather an exercise of jurisdictional functions. Consequently, curtailment of rights as part of the exercise of jurisdictional functions established in any legal system cannot, a priori, be characterised as violations of human rights. The special jurisdiction also establishes the power to exercise curtailment of rights within the framework of customary law, such as the right to judge, detain, establish sanctions, confiscate goods, mandate community service and other restrictions imposed by community authorities through the legitimate procedures of indigenous communities and peoples.

The sentence does not analyse the jurisdictional functions of the *rondas campesinas*, but simply asserts that the fact that they detained a person and forced them to work constitutes a crime against individual liberty. Yet the very same sentence indicates that these acts were in fact the legitimate acts of *ronda* authorities, referring to the fact that the work carried out was part of 'a sanction imposed by the said organisations'. The acts are acknowledged by the accused, who explain their conduct. This was not an arbitrary, abusive or clandestine act committed by a few *ronderos*, but rather a 'sanction' decided by the *ronda* organisation within their territorial ambit. The sanction of working in the *ronda* patrols, as is well known, is a common punishment applied by the *rondas* and does not constitute a violation of international human rights norms.[35] It is clear that in this case Article 149 of the constitution and Article 9.1 of ILO Convention 169 applied and that the *ronderos* should not have faced criminal prosecution. The sentence does not question the fact that the acts referred to were part of the customary law of the *rondas campesinas*. Therefore, even if it was deemed that these acts were not validated by the constitution because they infringed human rights norms, they should not have been prosecutable offences because Article 15 of the Penal Code exempts those people who have committed such acts in line with their culture or customs from prosecution.

Conclusions and challenges

The content of constitutional reform and its implementation

Some analysts have noted that the constitutional reforms which recognise cultural and legal pluralism in Latin America have occurred within a 'double transition' towards democracy on the one hand and neoliberalism on the other.[36] This second transition towards neoliberalism is indisputable, but while Peru undoubtedly underwent a transition to formal democracy in the 1980s, the 1990s were marked by a shift towards authoritarianism. This situation has changed with the resignation of Fujimori and the installation of a new government in November 2000.

The constitutional reform of 1993 occurred in response to internal and external pressure following Fujimori's 'autogolpe' in 1992. It therefore sought, in the first instance, to re-legitimise the regime and provide it with greater formal attributions. Second, it sought to establish a legal framework for the implementation of neoliberal policies which were not permitted by the statist model set out in the 1979 Constitution. Third, the reform aimed to legalise tougher 'anti-terrorist' policies. In contrast to pluralist constitutional reforms in other countries in the region, where extensive debate, social mobilisation and even indigenous representation in the Constituent Assembly occurred (as in Colombia, Ecuador, Bolivia and Venezuela), in Peru the reform took place with little public debate and in a Constituent Assembly dominated by the governing party. Even though the proposals of some democratic sectors were successfully incorporated, such as the introduction of the figure of the Ombudsman and the articles referring to multiculturalism and legal pluralism, the general framework of the reform was highly undemocratic and provided little opportunity for wider participation. This is not to say that the reform did not represent real social demands with respect to multiculturalism; rather it was not accompanied by any significant social mobilisation, given the repression suffered by the indigenous campesino organisations at that time. The authoritarian context in which the reform occurred also meant that citizens subsequently failed to appropriate or champion the new constitution. It was barely implemented in institutional terms (officials of the judiciary remain unaware of its content even today), yet demands for its observance are almost non-existent.

The situation of the campesino/indigenous movement

In many countries in Latin America the mobilisation and presence of campesino-indigenous organisations has played an important role in securing constitutional reforms which have incorporated ethnic demands. In the Peruvian case, the context of political violence affecting campesino-indigenous communities and organisations, which had exacted a high toll in terms of deaths and displacement, meant the absence of such mobilisation for the reforms of 1993. In response to the presence of armed groups, the military's 'counterinsurgency' strategy at the end of the 1980s and start of the 1990s was based on the militarisation of campesino and indigenous communities and organisations, such as the *rondas*. At the start of 1993, the year of the reform, Fujimori issued the 'pacification decrees' in order to 'legalise' this strategy. This had the effect of immobilising the campesino movement. The autonomous *rondero* movement, the strongest campesino movement in the country during the 1980s, was particularly hard hit, suppressed by military control or punished by the judiciary. Given this wider context, campesino, *rondero* and native-indigenous demands could only be expressed in protected, limited spaces, such as workshops organised by the Catholic Church or other human rights organisations. These organisations attempted to advance their demands through political parties and other mechanisms.

Following the constitutional reform, some campesino *ronderos* invoked the rights recognised in the new constitution in cases where they were charged with exceeding their functions, but in no case were they exonerated by the judiciary. Military control of many rural areas continues today; in others the regime has replaced the civil defence fronts with alternative forms of organisation controlled through neo-clientelist anti-poverty programmes aimed at ameliorating the effects of structural adjustment. In the face of poverty and military control, the reconstitution of the campesino-indigenous movement is likely to be a long process. At the same time such conditions reduce the ability of the campesino-indigenous organisations to mobilise and make it difficult for them to appropriate the more favourable aspects of the reform. In some places workshops are again being organised with the support of the church and NGOs, but these remain highly localised initiatives. With the new government, probably, the situation of indigenous and campesino will change.

Special jurisdiction and the judiciary

The constitutional article recognising legal pluralism in Peru (Article 149) is probably the broadest among all countries in the region which have recognised legal pluralism. The formula allows for special jurisdiction to be exercised within the campesino-indigenous territorial ambit, without limiting the kinds of cases that can be dealt with through customary law, the only restriction being that such procedures should not negatively affect individuals' rights. Formulas employed in other countries include the limitation that customary law should not violate the constitution or ordinary laws (Colombia, Bolivia, Ecuador, Venezuela), which means in effect that the formal space for legal pluralism is very limited. However, the Peruvian judiciary's interpretation of article 149 has meant that, in practice, the Peruvian formula is among the most restricted on the continent. In contrast, the Colombian Constitutional Court's interpretation has gradually overcome the limitations of the more restricted formula for recognition set down in the 1991 Constitution.[37] In Venezuela, even before the 1999 constitutional reform, a number of judicial test cases occurred which, according to René Kuppé, were effectively forms of recognising legal pluralism.[38]

The repression of the *rondero* authorities' attempts to administer their own form of justice has continued within the broader context of restrictions on their autonomy by the executive branch. This has not been challenged by the judiciary, despite the fact that both the 1993 Constitution and ILO Convention 169 expressly recognise customary law and the jurisdictional faculties of campesinos, *ronderos* and natives-indigenous. This is a result of resistance to legal pluralism by a monist and racist legal culture. The judiciary refuses to accept legal pluralism and has also failed to challenge the arbitrary acts of the Executive, this last a direct result of the institutional dependence of the judiciary on the Executive. This was one of the main points on the agenda of the OAS Commission to 'strengthen democracy' in Peru, installed after the highly questioned electoral process of May 2000, and it is also one of the main points on the agenda of the new government. Securing judicial independence and a change in the monist legal culture are two pending challenges for the development of legal pluralism.

Possibilities for the development of legal pluralism in Peru

Multiculturalism and legal pluralism continue to be a reality in Peru, yet despite having been 'constitutionalised', in practice community and *ronda* authorities continue to be penalised for applying autonomous forms of justice. At this moment in time it is not the constitutional order which is at variance with reality on the ground; rather it is the legal model and political practice which are at odds with each other. The regime in place for the last decade had achieved a near-monopoly of power, in the sense that there were almost no counter-balancing forces. It also used to exercise tight social control, to which must be added the disarticulation of the majority of popular organisations in the rural and urban areas. A parallel dismantling has taken place of social welfare provisions (labour rights, inalienability of communal land and so on) and the system of liberal rights and guarantees (the closing of the Constitutional Guarantees Tribunal, restriction of citizenship rights, trial of civilians by military courts, withdrawal of the country from the jurisdiction of the Inter-American Court of Human Rights). The extent of this transformation had been much more far-reaching than in any other Latin American country, save perhaps in Chile under Pinochet.

The implementation of a neoliberal economic model required the suppression of the social demands of impoverished sectors of the population. This continues, in part, through the use of instruments derived from the 'anti-terrorist' struggle. Even though armed opposition movements have declined enormously since 1993, the anti-terrorist legislation remains intact, together with military mechanisms of control over the rural populations. Until the beginning of 2000, over half the country continued to be classified as an 'emergency zone', subject to restriction of constitutional guarantees. Other means of control were instituted through social programmes and forms of clientelism and paternalism emanating directly from the presidency.

It is clear that a pluralist model of governance presupposes the recognition of and respect for indigenous and campesino communities and peoples as subjects, not objects of policy, much less that they should be utilised in government counterinsurgent policies and strategies. Evidently the effective recognition of legal pluralism presupposes respect for the autonomous spheres of decision making of campesino and native communities, *rondas campesinas* and indigenous peoples. A multicultural state is a state where power is decentralised, not concentrated. However, this constituted a clear threat to the authoritarian model of control in place until recently. A regime such as the Fujimori one could only allow very restricted spheres of campesino-indigenous decision-making which did not threaten the prevailing political or economic model. Legislation subsequent to the constitutional reform reflects this spirit.[39]

In summary, overcoming political authoritarianism, reconstructing democratic values and challenging the prevailing economic model which so negatively affects the impoverished majority are factors which could change the situation of the population in general and of the campesino communities and indigenous peoples in particular. At the same time, judicial independence and citizenship rights must be re-established and promoted, and a pluralist legal culture consolidated. These are just some of the challenges which must be met if a multicultural state and the effective recognition of legal pluralism is to be achieved in Peru.

Notes

1. For a comparative analysis of the constitutional reforms in these countries see Yrigoyen Fajardo (2000).
2. Legal monism assumes and proposes that a state should have a single legal system, while legal pluralism assumes that a number of legal systems can exist within the same geo-political space. The identification between the state and a single system of law, originally formulated by Hans Kelsen, is the essence of legal positivism. See Kelsen (1982).
3. The 1991 Colombian Constitution stipulates that customary law cannot violate the constitution or the ordinary laws of the land. The Peruvian Constitution only stipulates that customary law must not violate fundamental individual human rights.
4. See Sánchez Botero (1998).
5. These models are adapted from Marzal (1986).
6. Identity is an inter-subjective phenomenon determined by context: the culture, identity and politico-legal institutions of indigenous peoples have not remained static over the last 500 years but rather have constantly changed. For a useful discussion on shifting cultural identities see Twanama (1992).
7. During the nineteenth and early twentieth centuries some Latin American constitutions allowed mayors to administer justice, an inheritance from the colonial period. This legally endorsed the practice of indigenous justice in indigenous communities and villages.
8. The indigenous, rural population constituted some two-thirds of the Peruvian population during the early decades of the twentieth century.

9. The military coup of General Velasco Alvarado in 1968 opened the way for a series of domestic reforms and the nationalisation of a number of important US-owned companies which had hitherto operated as economic enclaves for the exploitation of natural resources, such as petrol and minerals. Velasco was replaced in 1975 by General Morales Bermudez and the reforms subsequently ground to a halt. During this period the economic situation worsened and the labour and campesino movement created by the reforms was the target of government repression. In the face of pressure from this movement, Morales Bermúdez convened a Constituent Assembly in 1979 and restored the country to democratic rule in 1980.

10. The twin processes of industrialisation and 'modernisation' date from the mid-twentieth century, and resulted in huge migratory shifts which became more acute during the 1970s. In this manner the rural urban balance in Peru changed radically; while in the first half of the twentieth century some two-thirds of the population resided in the countryside, this had dropped to less than one-third by the end of the century.

11. The term 'cholo' dates from the very first rural-urban migration flows and was used, in a pejorative way, to denote ethnically indigenous people who arrived in the cities. Andean migrants in the cities reproduced the cultural and social practices of their villages of origin in the new urban barrios, this constituting the linchpin of their survival strategies. They tended to identify themselves by the name of their village or province of origin. In recent years, however, the words 'cholo' and 'serrano' have been re-appropriated by some people as a form of self-affirmation and vindication of cultural identity. For example, some politicians call themselves 'cholos' or 'serranos' in order to signal their social background and sympathies with a certain ethnic origin.

12. Law of Native Communities, Decree Law No. 20653, of 1974, replaced by Decree Law 22175 in 1978.

13. A substantial part of this rise in cattle rustling was linked to networks of a new commercial bourgeoisie from the coast comprised of former small or medium size landowners in league with truckers, owners of slaughter houses, police and other local authorities.

14. On the *rondas campesinas* see Starn (1999), Yrigoyen Fajardo (1993 and 1998) and Espinoza (1995).

15. When *rondero* campesinos refer to 'my community' this does not necessarily imply that all members of this 'community' share communal lands. They are, however, linked by numerous kinship and reciprocity networks. In these cases the *ronda campesina* is *the* communal organisation, often having assumed the social functions of community organisations in formally recognised campesino communities.

16. Figure calculated by Starn for the 1990s (1998: 18).

17. The organisational strength of the *rondas campesinas* was a factor in the early failures of Sendero Luminoso to penetrate the northern region of the country. The methods of Sendero Luminoso were diametrically opposed to the consensual decision-making processes of the *rondas*.

18. In its first article, Law No. 24571 states: 'Peaceful, democratic and autonomous *rondas campesinos*, whose members are duly accredited before the relevant political authority shall be recognised as organisations aiming to serve the community and contribute to development and social peace without partisan political objectives. In addition, they aim to defend their lands, look after their cattle and other goods, co-operating with the authorities to combat crime. Their statute and internal

organisation are governed by the norms of the campesino communities established in the Constitutional and the Civil Code.'

19. Supreme Decree No. 012–88-IN (18 March 1988) 'Reglamento de Organización y Funciones de las rondas campesinas pacíficas, democráticas y autónomas'.

20. Amongst these, the extension of the death penalty to include the crime of 'sedition and terrorism'.

21. For the complete version of the proposal see 'Pluralidad Cultural y Derechos Étnicos: Propuesta de reforma constitucional' in *Desfaciendo Entuertos*, No. 3–4, 1994.

22. For a more detailed analysis see Yrigoyen Fajardo (1996).

23. An analysis of this process can be found in Belaúnde (1998).

24. Although the 1993 Constitution was an improvement on the 1979 Constitution with respect to the concept of pluralism, in other respects it was a step backwards, in large part because of the introduction of neoliberal policies. For example, it restricted rights to the inalienability of communal lands which had been upheld in previous constitutions. In addition, it reduced the realm in which indigenous languages were treated as official to the areas in which they were spoken, rather than in the country as a whole.

25. In common with other Latin American countries, Peru recognised different mechanisms for alternative dispute resolution as part of a broader process of judicial reform, abandoning the idea of the state as the sole arbiter of social conflict. However, these mechanisms are only legally sanctioned to intervene in certain kinds of cases, defined according to severity and area of law. A compilation of these alternative dispute resolution norms can be found in Ormachea (1998).

26. 'Las autoridades de las Comunidades Campesinas y Nativas con el apoyo de las Rondas Campesinas, pueden ejercer las funciones jurisdiccionales dentro de su ámbito territorial de conformidad con el derecho consuetudinario siempre que no violen los derechos fundamentales de la persona. La ley establece las formas de coordinación de dicha jurisdicción especial con los Juzgados de Paz y con las demás instancias del Poder Judicial.'

27. Some confusion exists regarding the subject of recognition in Article 149. The text itself is not clear, stating 'with the support of the *rondas campesinas*'. Some have interpreted this to mean that only those *rondas* acting as auxiliary organs of campesino and native community authorities are allowed to exercise jurisdictional functions, but not those *rondas* which belong to ordinary communities (which constitute the majority of the *rondas*). An alternative interpretation maintains that the mention of the *rondas*, which are also recognised by their own law, refers to the institution of the *rondas* in general and not to a specific *ronda* belonging to a particular campesino or native community. Given that the campesino and native communities are empowered to act through their own internal authorities in any case, it would not make sense for the Constitution to include special recognition of a specific community organisation.

28. Fundamental individual rights can be understood generally as human rights. In order to establish when a violation of human rights has occurred, the events and the applicable law should be analysed within their socio-cultural context.

29. The Inter-American Commission of Human Rights in its Second Report on the Situation Of Human Rights In Peru states: 'Since 80% of the judges in Peru are provisional, i.e., they do not enjoy the guarantee of stability and may be removed without cause, added to all the other actions limiting rights and freedoms adopted by the Executive and the legislature, the judiciary has seen its autonomy and

independence severely limited ... The "provisional" judges are provided for in the Peruvian Constitution as an exceptional measure and only for filling vacancies, but this exception has become the rule. This high percentage of "provisional" judges has a serious detrimental impact on citizens' right to adequate adminis-tration of justice.' Organization of American States (2000).

30. For an analysis of the regional impact of these policies see Degregori et. al. (1998).
31. Interviews with Víctor Luna, ex-president of the Provincial Federation of *Rondas Campesinas* in Bamabamarca, other *rondero* leaders and their lawyer. Bamabamarca, August 1999.
32. Interview with Teódulo Torres, Director of the Oficina Diocesana de Pastoral Social of the Huaraz diocese and with *ronda* leaders in Huaylas, Huaraz, July 1999.
33. The court rulings summarised here were collected by the Comisión Diocesana de Pastoral Social de Huaraz and by the Comisión Episcopal de Acción Social de la Conferencia Episcopal Peruana. Both institutions have been involved in the defence of campesino *ronderos* for many years. The author also has first-hand experience of the case of the campesino community of Chalhuayacu (Case 1, Annex No.2).
34. The rulings discussed here refer to *rondas campesinas* in formally recognised campesino communities. As mentioned above, considerable ambiguity exists with respect to the Constitution and a conflict of interpretation exists as to whether all the *rondas campesinas* are empowered to exercise jurisdictional functions or whether only *rondas* which belong to formally recognised campesino and native communities are so empowered. In the cases discussed here this problem does not apply as all the *rondas campesinas* in question belong to formally constituted campesino communities.
35. Other types of punishment, such as physical beatings, are more controversial, as are cases when a conflict occurs between individual and collective rights. The Colombian Constitutional Court established that a physical punishment could be lawfully applied within the special jurisdiction, taking into account the severity of the punishment and the context in which it was applied. With due reference to the international jurisprudence on torture, the Court deemed that forms of physical punishment were permissible as long as they did not constitute a violation of the prohibition on torture (Sentence No. T-523/97). The Colombian Court has also established that in the case of a conflict between certain individual rights (such as religious freedom) and the collective right to cultural integrity, the collective right which permits the cultural continuity of the community should prevail. The Court considered that in the case of a conflict between individual and collective rights, the special jurisdiction could not be expected to respect all human rights, but rather a reduced nucleus of fundamental human rights, such as the right to life, the prohibition against slavery and the prohibition against torture. See Sánchez Botero (1998), pp. 321–30. In the case of the *rondas campesinas* discussed here, no such judgment in favour of the special jurisdiction was made.
36. See Van Cott (2000b) and Assies (2000).
37. The Colombian Constitutional Court has deemed that the special jurisdiction is only obliged to respect a minimum core of human rights, with the aim of preserving the collective existence of indigenous peoples. The core definition includes the prohibition on killing, torturing or subjecting someone to slavery. See Sánchez Botero (1998).
38. The Supreme Court of Justice demanded respect for the Piaroas indigenous authorities, constituted 'within piaroa customary law' (ruling of 5 December 1996),

and the Criminal Court of the First Instance in the state of Amazonas maintained that 'effectively, it is through participation that the indigenous minority exercise their rights to their traditions and customs' (ruling of 28 June 1996). See Kuppé (1998).

39. In 1999 a law related to conciliation was passed which allowed communities, *rondas* and other social organisations to resolve their internal conflicts 'taking their customs into account', but this referred only to minor cases and was restricted by the constitution and ordinary legislation, a clear step backwards from that envisaged in Article 149 of the 1993 Constitution.

References

Assies, Willem (2000) 'Indigenous peoples and reform of the State in Latin America' in William Assies, Gemma Van der Haar and Andres Hoekema (eds), *The Challenge of Diversity: Indigenous Peoples and Reform of the State in Latin America*, Thela Thesis (Amsterdam).

Cotler, Julio (1978), *Clases, Estado y Nación en el Peru*, IEP (Lima).

Belaúnde, Javier de (1998), 'Justice, Legality and Judicial Reform', in John Crabtree and Jim Thomas (eds), *Fujimori´s Peru: the Political Economy*, Institute of Latin American Studies, University of London (London), pp.173–91.

Degregori, Carlos Iván et al. (1998), 'Government, Citizenship and Democracy: a Regional Perspective', in John Crabtree and Jim Thomas, *Fujimori's Peru: The Political Economy*, Institute of Latin American Studies, University of London (London), pp.243–61.

Espinoza, Oscar (1995), *Rondas Campesinas y Nativas en la Amazonía Peruana*, CAAAP (Lima).

Kelsen, Hans (1982), *Teoría Pura del Derecho*, EUDEBA (Buenos Aires).

Kuppé, René (1998), 'El Estado actual del Pluralismo Jurídico en Venezuela' in *América Indígena*, Vol. LVIII, No. 1–2.

Kymlicka, Will (1997), *Multicultural Citizenship*, Oxford University Press (New York).

Marzal, Manuel (1986), *Historia de la Antropología Indigenista: México y Perú*, PUCP (Lima).

Organization of American States (2000), *Report on Peru*, 5 April 2000. OEA/Ser.L/V/II.106. Doc. 59 rev. 2 June 2000. The original version of this report is in Spanish; the English version is available at: http://www.cidh.org/countryrep/ Peru2000en/TOC.htm

Ormachea, Iván (1998) *Análisis de la Ley de Conciliación Extrajudicial*, Editorial Cuzco and IPRECON (Lima).

Sánchez Botero, Esther (1998), *Justicia y Pueblos Indígenas de Colombia. La tutela como medio para la construcción del entendimiento intercultural*, Universidad Nacional de Colombia y UNIJUS (Santafé de Bogotá).

Starn, Orin (1999), *Nightwatch: The Politics of Protest in the Andes*, Duke University Press (Durham and London).

Twanama, Walter (1992), 'Cholear en Lima' in *Márgenes-Encuentro y Debate*, Vol.5 (9), pp.206–40.

Van Cott, Donna Lee (2000a), 'Latin America: Constitutional reform and ethnic rights', *Parliamentary Affairs*, pp.41–54.

—— (2000b), *The Friendly Liquidation of the Past. The Politics of Diversity in Latin America*, University of Pittsburgh Press (Pittsburgh).

Yrigoyen Fajardo, Raquel (1993), 'Rural Rondas in Peru' in Mark Findlay and Ugljesa Zvekic (eds), *Alternative Policing Styles*, UNICRI and Kluver Law and Taxation Publishers (Deventer and Boston).

—— (1995), 'De la criminalización de la diferencia cultural a la legitimación constitucional', unpublished MA thesis, Universidad de Barcelona.

—— (1996), 'Control Penal y Diversidad Étnico-cultural' in María del Rosario Diego Díaz-Santos, et al. (eds), *Conflicto Social y Sistema Penal*, COLMEX and the University of Salamanca (Salamanca).

—— (1998), 'Un caso de Pluralidad Jurídica en el Perú: Las rondas campesinas de Cajamarca' in José Luis Domínguez (ed.), *La Joven Sociología Jurídica en España. Aportaciones para una consolidación*, International Institute for the Sociology of Law (Oñati).

—— (2000), 'The Constitutional Recognition of Indigenous Law in the Andean Countries' in William Assies, Gemma van der Haar and Andres Hoekema (eds), *The Challenge of Diversity: Indigenous Peoples and Reform of the State in Latin America*, Thela Thesis (Amsterdam).

7
Recognising Indigenous Law and the Politics of State Formation in Mesoamerica

Rachel Sieder

Introduction

During the 1990s 'pluri-culturalisation' became part of the lexicon of state reform in many Latin American countries, as governments responded to multiple pressures. Indigenous organisations on the ground gained in strength throughout the decade and pressed for recognition of group rights for indigenous peoples. In addition, international organisations such as the UN increasingly advanced indigenous rights as a form of human rights, and a body of international law emerged referring to the specific rights of indigenous peoples. Across the continent governments responded to such developments, to a greater or lesser degree, by adopting a multiculturalist discourse and instituting a series of constitutional and legal reforms to recognise the rights and identities of their indigenous populations.[1]

The reconstruction of the justice system, and the construction of a 'pluricultural rule of law', forms a central part of multiculturalist agendas for state reform throughout the region. Generally this involves proposals to overhaul the existing administration of justice to make it more accessible and less discriminatory for indigenous peoples – for example, through such measures as the provision of legal translators or increasing the coverage and quality of public defence services. It also includes the formal recognition of indigenous customary law (*derecho consuetudinario*). This latter implies the state's acceptance of indigenous peoples' right to resolve conflicts within their communities according to their own legal norms and practices within the broader framework of a multicultural state. Current demands for official recognition of legal pluralism[2] constitute a fundamental challenge to the monist legal traditions of Latin America's liberal republics. Effectively they mean that the state will no longer maintain a monopoly on the production and application of the law. The potential implications of this for existing relations between the state and civil society are far-reaching.

The right of indigenous people to use customary law is set out in ILO Convention 169, the UN Draft Declaration on the Rights of Indigenous Peoples and the Organisation of American States' draft declaration on the rights of indigenous people (Plant 1998, 1999; Dandler 1998). However, while international jurisprudence increasingly recognises the right of indigenous people to use their customary law within the framework of a multicultural state, within individual states the institutional and jurisdictional implications of this recognition remain ill-defined and highly contentious. The question of coordination between indigenous customary law and state law is particularly problematic. In line with ILO Convention 169, most national provisions in Latin America mandate that customary law will only be recognised where it does not conflict with internationally recognised human rights.[3] As an abstract principle this would appear uncontroversial – proponents of a conception of human rights that recognises both individual and group rights maintain that the exercise of the latter should not deny the human rights of individual members of those communities (Kymlicka 1995; Zechenter 1997; Donnelly 1989).[4] Yet provisions limiting the jurisdiction of indigenous customary law to those practices which do not violate human rights raise the difficult issue of who has the authority to decide whether or not a conflict between customary law and individual human rights exists. Who can define a given act as a human rights violation? Can a state which has historically denied or violated rights to certain sectors of the population be trusted with ensuring that their human rights are protected, or with determining when those rights are endangered by local customary practices? And what happens if a government uses the language of universalism – such as citizenship or human rights – in order to abuse minorities or limit their claims to greater autonomy or to a different kind of participation within the nation-state? Many would argue that international human rights law is intended to protect individuals from arbitrary treatment by the state, not by each other, and that government intervention in certain communities on the basis of claims to protect individuals' human rights should be treated sceptically (Nagengast 1997).

Evidently, although internationally recognised norms of human rights are set out in the UN Charter and Covenants, in practice the meaning of 'human rights' is contentious. This is because across the world, universalist discourses and norms of human rights are mobilised around, responded to and utilised by different institutions, groups and individuals in a diversity of political, cultural and socio-economic contexts. Globalisation has meant in effect, as Ann-Belinda Preis has observed, that '[h]uman rights have become "universalised" as values subject to interpretation, negotiation, and accommodation' (1996: 290). They can be understood as a shared site of struggle between contesting visions of 'rights', or as a language in which contesting claims to entitlements and enforcement are played out. Indeed it is precisely because the idea of 'human rights' has such international recognition and force that it is so highly contested. Inevitably, the debate about the nature and content of human rights reflects power inequalities. As Julie Mertus has emphasised, '[t]he process of rights definition and enforcement demonstrates how power is distributed and how relationships are regulated' (1999: 1366–7). Governments and elites routinely attempt to hegemonise human rights discourses, and subordinate groups, in turn, challenge these dominant discourses with alternative proposals. Current struggles across the region to define indigenous rights and human rights and to regulate the relationship between the two reveal much about the power dynamics at play in different contexts and the resources different states can mobilise in response to challenges from below.

Dilemmas over whether and how to recognise indigenous rights to an alternative legal order have been played out in different ways in recent years. I adopt here a comparative historical approach, arguing that current government policies have depended crucially on the ways in which claims for indigenous rights in general have been articulated, and on historical patterns of interaction between indigenous people and the state. The political implications of indigenous claims for official recognition of customary law are explored here by comparing the cases of Mexico – focusing on the state of Chiapas – and Guatemala, both countries where indigenous demands for rights represent a key element in the reconstitution of the political system. During the 1990s both Mexican and Guatemalan elites faced indigenous demands for the recognition of difference on the basis of equality and special rights for indigenous groups – what has been called 'differentiated' or 'ethnic' citizenship (Young 1990, 1995; de la Peña 1999). In Mexico, such developments occurred within the wider context of an uneven and protracted transition from authoritarian government dominated by a hegemonic party towards a multi-party democracy. In Guatemala indigenous demands were articulated not in the context of a transition from authoritarianism to multi-party democracy, but rather through the negotiated settlement to 36 years of armed conflict and, more generally, within the broader context of post-conflict reconstruction.[5] In both countries law became an increasingly important terrain for political contestation as indigenous groups called on international human rights law to challenge the existing political, legal and socio-economic order. The demand for official recognition of indigenous customary norms and practices ('indigenous law') constituted a fundamental part of this challenge. In turn, dominant regional and national elites increasingly turned to the law in an attempt to redraw the boundaries of relations between indigenous people and the state.

An examination of the ways in which indigenous claims for legal autonomy have been articulated, the responses of elites, and the different outcomes in these two cases sheds light on broader processes of state formation and re-composition in the region. In particular it indicates the ways in which changes in the nature of the state provide opportunities for oppositional movements, at the same time as pointing to the comparative abilities and resources of different kinds of states to contain, co-opt or absorb popular demands over time. Such abilities vary over time and place. In part they depend on what Guillermo O'Donnell has referred to as differing degrees of 'embeddedness' of the state: the 'set of social relations that establishes a certain order, and ultimately backs it with a centralised, coercive guarantee, over a given territory' (1999: 135). Throughout much of the twentieth century, the state was far from embedded in Guatemala and Chiapas. The rule of law was largely absent in rural areas, where the poor and disadvantaged remained at the mercy of powerful local economic interests and elites, who tended to colonise municipal and provincial office. In the 1980s in Guatemala, and in the 1990s in Chiapas, state authorities made unprece-dented attempts to extend their authority over indigenous communities in these rural areas, in both instances within the context of counterinsurgency operations which aimed to destroy and disarticulate local challenges to dominant interests. In neither instance did this result in the 'embeddedness' of the state; that is to say the effective rule of law. Rather this trend should be understood as a response to different challenges to dominant elites and their interests.

The intention of this chapter is to provide a historically rooted assessment of current developments with reference to official recognition or non-recognition of indigenous customary law. It examines the ways in which different historical trajectories of state formation in the twentieth century shape the prospects for a multicultural politico-legal order in the twenty-first. In comparing these two cases, a number of questions are considered: first, how have different historical patterns of relations between indigenous peoples and the state shaped contemporary indigenous claims and the responses to them? Second, what role have ideologies of nation-state construction played in these processes? Third, how have indigenous peoples' movements used law to challenge existing political and socio-economic arrangements? And fourth, how have governing elites used the law to respond to indigenous claims?

Revolution and reaction: law in the twentieth century

Throughout the twentieth century the nature of the law and of official policies towards indigenous peoples was markedly different in Mexico and Guatemala. Mexico's state building process after 1920 was broadly inclusionary, emerging from the mass mobilisation of the country's labouring classes during the 1910–20 revolution, it was based on a revolutionary legal order and an ethos of socio-economic redistribution. Article 27 of the 1917 Constitution allowed for the restitution of communal lands of indigenous communities, which had been lost during the Porfiriato.[6] In some parts of the country, such as Chiapas, the strength of conservative elites meant that indigenous people benefited relatively little from the agrarian reform in the first years of the revolution (Harvey 1998; Rus 1994). Yet this changed during the 1930s, when President Lázaro Cárdenas introduced a radical, redistributive land reform. This greatly expanded campesino access to land expropriated from former *haciendas* through the mechanism of the collective, inalienable *ejido*. The legal framework of the revolutionary Mexican State consolidated in the 1930s thus embodied an inclusive concept of citizenship based on socio-economic incorporation of the majority. This included Mexico's indigenous, although they were not recognised as indigenous peoples as such – which would have implied legal recognition of indigenous languages and indigenous forms of political and legal organisation – but rather subsumed into the class-based category of campesino.

The regime also functioned according to a sui generis concept and practice of political inclusion. From the early 1930s the ruling party (Partido Nacional Revolucionario, later PRI) established its hold on power by means of a particularly enduring form of authoritarian clientelism. This was based on a combination of electoral fraud, targeted repression and controlled mobilisation of popular sectors, for example through peasant leagues and trade unions, which were incorporated within the corporatist structures of the PRI. Within the inclusionary dynamic advanced by *Cardenismo*, indigenous communities were afforded a limited and highly conditional communal autonomy, which transformed the very nature of the communities themselves. As Jan Rus has shown for the case of Chiapas, indigenous leaders, similar to other rural caciques, were incorporated as clients of the ruling party through municipal government. 'Traditional' governing structures were remoulded, subordinated and bound to the revolutionary state (Rus 1994), in this way becoming tied to the reproduction and maintenance of the *priista* regime.

Although the historic legitimacy of the revolution was rooted within rural Mexico, the regime developed a marked urban developmentalist bias from the 1940s onwards. Conditions varied across regions, but in general the economic benefits campesinos derived from collective title to land declined as official agricultural and industrial development policies favoured the agro-export sector. The clientelist social pact began to unravel from the 1970s onwards, and autonomous social movements emerged and challenged the dominance of the PRI. Growing numbers of campesinos had no access to land, and the indigenous majority in the southern states became ever more economically marginalised. The introduction of neoliberal economic policies during the 1980s placed further strains on the system, eroding the material benefits and guarantees previously extended by the corporatist system.[7] At the same time the authoritarian clientelism of the PRI faced mounting claims for a multi-party democracy, as independent opposition parties emerged, challenging the PRI on a national scale by the mid-1980s. By the 1990s, the revolutionary legitimacy, which had sustained the *priista* state for so long, had evaporated, leaving a regime that resorted to increasingly authoritarian and coercive means to maintain its hold on power. It was within this context that indigenous demands for political, administrative and legal autonomy became a national political issue, following the 1994 Zapatista uprising.

In contrast to Mexico, Guatemala's state-building process throughout most of the twentieth century was extremely exclusionary, based on a conservative legal order designed to secure benefits for a small ruling oligarchy. Following the 1871 revolution led by Justo Rufino Barrios, the construction of the nation-state came to hinge on the idea of a unitary rule of law. Elites used the ideology of legal equality to pursue assimilationist policies, expropriating indigenous lands and removing the special protections for indigenous peoples extended by conservative regimes and the Catholic Church, so facilitating their ever-greater exploitation as cheap labour for plantation-based agro-export agriculture. Prior to 1944, dominant elites did not attempt to mobilise indigenous people as clients of political parties, but rather relied on an increasingly powerful army to exert control by force. During the 1930s official anti-communism meant state repression of workers' movements and legal restrictions on popular mobilisation. Citizenship was highly restricted and did not extend to the labouring majority. However, the limited presence of the state in many remote rural areas of the country did permit a considerable degree of de facto autonomy for indigenous communities and their traditional authorities, which were not linked to dominant forms of rule as they were in Mexico.

It was only during the reformist period between 1944 and 1954 that an attempt was made to incorporate indigenous people into the political and socio-economic order. This was principally as campesinos, beneficiaries of a redistributive agrarian reform introduced in 1952 (Handy 1994; García Añoveros 1981; Gleijeses 1991). In addition, the constitution promulgated in 1945 recognised a series of collective rights for indigenous groups and communities, such as inalienable rights over communal lands.[8] Indigenous men were given the vote and political parties and trade unions linked to the revolutionary regime organised throughout the country, incorporating certain groups and individuals in indigenous communities into national structures of governance. However, such trends towards greater inclusion were almost completely reversed after the reformist regime was overthrown in 1954. During the 1960s and 1970s the politico-legal order became increasingly restrictive in an attempt to suppress growing popular demands for land and better rural wages. Political rights were limited by electoral fraud and state violence, and civil rights systematically violated. This culminated in the all-out war against indigenous people, which took place in the context of the army's counterinsurgency campaign against the Unidad Revolucionaria

Nacional Guatemalteca (URNG) in the early 1980s (ODHAG 1998; CEH 1999). During the previous 30 years state neglect had in practice provided a considerable degree of de facto autonomy for indigenous authorities at communal level, but in the aftermath of the violence indigenous communities were systematically transformed (Manz 1988; Carmack 1988; Wilson 1995). 'Traditional' community structures such as *cofradías* and councils of elders were destroyed or subordinated to the counterinsurgency. Instead military commissioners (local appointees who acted as 'link-men' between the communities and the army), paramilitary civil patrol chiefs and municipal and auxiliary mayors presided over local conflict resolution.[9] In addition, the fact that so many indigenous people were co-opted by the army as auxiliary paramilitary forces exacerbated local divisions and gave them a particularly lethal edge.

In 1985 an army-led transition installed an elected civilian government, but political parties remained weak and fragmented and civil society still subject to high levels of state violence. Only towards the end of the decade did civil opposition groups emerge, most to demand an end to human rights violations. Greater political liberalisation during the 1990s combined with international developments to permit the emergence of an indigenous rights movement (Bastos and Camus, 1995; Warren 1998). This movement increasingly articulated its demands through the framework of the peace negotiations between the government and the URNG. A comprehensive peace settlement, negotiated in consultation with representatives of civil groups, was concluded in December 1996, raising the possibility of building a more inclusive political and socio-economic order and improving observance of human rights. In contrast to Mexico, where the struggle for indigenous rights centred on demands for greater autonomy from an increasingly illegitimate regime, in Guatemala the articulation of indigenous demands for greater inclusion and cultural rights took place in a context of post-conflict reconstruction following massive state violence against the civilian population.

State-building policies: *indigenismo* and assimilation

Different historical representations of indigenous peoples within the discursive constructions, or 'imaginaries', of the modern nation-state are a significant factor influencing the spaces available to indigenous peoples in the contemporary *re*-making of those states. In other words, ideational legacies as well as socio-economic and political factors shape the ways in which challenges of claims for indigenous inclusion and equality with difference are made and met today. State-building ideologies in twentieth century Mexico were harnessed to include different groups within the revolutionary hegemony, or – in Mexican anthropologist Manuel Gamio's famous phrase – to *'forjar patria'* (Gamio 1960). The notion of *mestizaje*, a projected national identity which combined the Spanish legacy with Mexico's pre-hispanic indigenous heritage, included indigenous people in the nation-state at a symbolic and discursive level at the same time as it advanced their eventual disappearance. This was articulated through the official ideology of *indigenismo*, which promoted a range of paternalistic developmentalist policies, the ultimate aim of which was to secure the assimilation of indigenous peoples into a *mestizo* identity by modernising or 'Mexicanising' them (Knight 1990). Under Lázaro Cárdenas, the revolutionary state began to sponsor *indigenismo* across Latin America as a means to incorporate indigenous people into the domestic market and extend the benefits of welfare policies to the indigenous peasant sector.[10] In 1948 the Instituto Nacional Indigenista (INI) was set up and in 1951 it established its first regional development programme in San Cristóbal de las Casas, Chiapas, promoting an integrationist approach through such mechanisms as bilingual education programmes and the inclusion of indigenous *promotores* in health programmes.

Although *indigenismo* ultimately aimed to secure the disappearance of distinct ethnic identities, in practice it signified a certain official acceptance of cultural differences and sanctioned a limited, de facto communal autonomy, which permitted the persistence of customary authorities and legal practices (*usos y costumbres*) at local community level.[11] However, this limited autonomy was highly dependent on the revolutionary state, linked as it was to the PRI's co-option of indigenous caciques as a mechanism of political control. Indigenous people were in effect clients of the revolutionary state; municipal governments could be elected according to customary mechanisms but candidates had to be registered with a political party.[12] Indigenous autonomy was officially tolerated when it suited the interests of the PRI, and throughout the 1970s and 1980s the 'tradition' of indigenous communities was frequently invoked to legitimate the arbitrary rule of caciques. The use of violence against contenders to the traditionalist caciques' power, for example through witchcraft murders or expulsions, were not legally prosecuted by the state, which argued such matters were 'customary' legal practices and as such internal to indigenous communities. Such a political logic explains why little official action was taken against the caciques of San Juan Chamula in Chiapas who, since 1972, forcibly expelled over 20,000 Protestants in the name of preserving tradition (Nash 1995: 21).

During the 1980s and 1990s opponents of the arbitrary rule of *priista* traditionalists who argued for a new relationship between indigenous peoples and the state increasingly challenged the official ideology of *indigenismo*. Such groups frequently built alliances with opposition parties, the PRD and the PAN, threatening the PRI's monopoly on power. Although during the 1980s state indigenist institutions changed their discourse from explicit assimilationism to 'participatory indigenism', programmes remained paternalistic in nature. During the late 1980s a number of new institutions were established to mediate indigenous peoples' demands and representation in the state, such as the Secretaría de Atención a los Pueblos Indígenas (SEAPI) and the Consejos Indígenas Estatales (CIE), set up under the presidency of Carlos Salinas. As in other areas, as independent challenges to the PRI emerged, the official response was to direct funding to compete with or defuse independent groups. Yet this strategy began to unravel after 1994, when the Zapatista movement internationalised the critique of official *indigenismo*, appealing to global concepts of indigenous rights, human rights and democracy to challenge the ways in which the indigenous population had hitherto been incorporated into the Mexican nation-state. As George Collier notes, a symbolic and conceptual shift occurred in the 1990s, when 'for the first time, indigenous collective rights were being treated as distinct from citizenship rights or general human rights, and thus deserving of separate legal recognition' (2000: 24).

In Guatemala, in contrast to Mexico, no ideological constructs of national identity or community that included the indigenous majority developed in the twentieth century. The plantation economy depended on forced indigenous labour and the dominant *criollo* and ladino identities were based on racist exclusion.[13] Official policies towards indigenous people favoured cultural assimilation, which effectively translated into the eradication of indigenous languages and culture. Within the framework of revolutionary nationalism during the 1944–54 October revolution, the social reform agenda of the Arévalo and Arbenz administrations led them to view the 'ethnic question' as a problem of backwardness and under-development. Instead of forcible assimilation, the reformers aimed to gradually integrate the indigenous population by improving their material conditions and providing them with some special protections. However, the Instituto Indigenista Nacional, founded in 1945, rejected any notion of cultural pluralism, aiming instead to promote an 'homogeneous nationality' (González Ponciano 1998: 25).

During the 1944–54 period indigenous men were integrated into revolutionary political parties and trade unions, but after 1954 political control was secured by time-honoured methods of force rather than by co-option or symbolic inclusion. The strength of official anti-communist doctrine translated into increasingly militarised forms of government. Together with a new wave of agro-export development in the 1960s that provoked land loss and increased out-migration, this severely constrained communal autonomy. Indigenous authorities continued to exist and some developed links with political parties of the extreme right, such as the Movimiento de Liberación Nacional (MLN), but in the main they were not co-opted into governing structures by ruling elites. Attempts at mass mobilisation grew and were increasingly met with repression.[14] The guerrilla movement that developed during the 1970s incorporated many indigenous people into its ranks and moved away from the earlier class-reductionism of the Guatemalan left. However, despite a vigorous debate on the 'ethnic-national question', in practice the revolutionary vanguard treated indigenous people primarily as the foot soldiers of the revolution and not as ethnically differentiated subjects.[15] The state-orchestrated violence unleashed by the army in the early 1980s deployed a deliberate and targeted policy of genocide in key guerrilla strongholds, and throughout the rest of the country subordinated the indigenous population to a new counterinsurgent political order (CEH 1999). It was not until the army-led transition to elected government that cultural pluralism received any official recognition. The constitution passed in 1985 was the first ever to recognise the multicultural nature of the Guatemalan nation-state. Articles 66–70 recognised that 'Guatemala is formed by different ethnic groups [including] indigenous groups of Mayan origin' and committed the state to 'recognise, respect and promote their forms of life, customs, traditions, forms of social organisation ... language and dialects'. Yet these were largely formalistic recognitions and did not lead to any significant changes in state policy or secondary legislation. In fact the autonomy of indigenous communities to use customary law was significantly reduced by the 1985 Constitution. Previously *alcaldes municipales* had exercised the functions of *jueces de paz*, meaning that in predominantly indigenous municipalities indigenous mayors and *alcaldes auxiliares* in the surrounding villages could resort to customary legal practices to resolve local conflicts. However, Article 203 of the new constitution clearly stated that the judicial function was reserved exclusively for state tribunals.

Indigenous movements in the 1990s: the strategic use of law

During the 1990s the struggle for indigenous rights in Chiapas became part of the wider struggle of many Mexicans to become citizens of a meaningful democracy as opposed to clients of the *priista* state. Indigenous organising built on the strength of the heterogeneous indigenous movement which had developed throughout different regions of the country in the 1970s and 1980s criticising state *indigenismo* and calling for a different, more just and less paternalistic treatment of indigenous peoples. The 1994 Zapatista uprising made ethnic claims a national, rather than a regional or local concern, linking indigenous rights to issues of democracy and citizenship. As has been widely observed, the roots of the rebellion lay in economic globalisation and the neoliberal restructuring package first introduced by the De la Madrid administration in 1982, which had abolished constitutional provisions for collective land-holding and eroded the limited historical benefits awarded by the Mexican state to rural inhabitants. More local concerns pointed to a rejection of the venality of local politicians and indigenous caciques co-opted into the PRI who had used the banner of 'tradition' to justify their pact with dominant elites. In opposition to rule by the 'traditionalist' caciques, many marginalised sectors within indigenous communities – such as women – began to refashion and reclaim 'tradition' in order to advance their own demands for greater participation and independence.[16] Within this highly politicised context, indigenous 'culture' and the right to define 'tradition' became highly contested, both between indigenous groups and the state and within indigenous communities themselves.[17]

In addition to questioning the new economic order and demanding the restitution of collective land rights, the Chiapas rebellion raised the question of regional autonomy, representing a fundamental challenge to existing federal arrangements. Whereas previously limited autonomy had been granted to local indigenous communities by a paternalist state, a range of indigenous organisations now began to demand a redrawing of the political map involving greater municipal and regional autonomy and a change in the relationship between municipal, state and federal governments.[18] Questions relating to recognition of indigenous customary law were inextricably bound up with these demands for new forms of political organisation and territoriality, which implied independence from the PRI. While a considerable degree of autonomy for justice administration in indigenous communities had long existed in practice, customary law was closely linked to the official justice system. Local indigenous authorities dealt with minor disputes via procedures that aimed to conciliate the parties, but serious crimes were generally remitted to the state courts. However, after 1994 a number of indigenous communities opposed to the PRI and sympathetic to the EZLN (and often aligned with the PRD) rejected any form of cooperation or collaboration with state authorities. Instead they declared themselves to be 'multi-ethnic autonomous municipalities' and insisted on their international legal rights to select their own authorities and exercise their customary legal practices. By 1997 parallel governing bodies had been set up in dozens of municipalities throughout Chiapas in direct opposition to traditional *priista* forms of rule (Eber 2001; Mattiace 2001). These parallel structures resolved conflicts between EZLN militants and sympathisers, while those remaining loyal to the PRI made recourse to the officially recognised authorities. By 1997 these autonomous municipalities were increasingly the targets of government counterinsurgency operations. Indigenous authorities were imprisoned and state authorities fomented paramilitary operations against those claiming autonomy, leading to increased violence and displacement (López Monjardin and Rebolledo Millán 1999).

In Guatemala the struggle for indigenous rights throughout the 1990s was less about a desire to move from client to citizen status than it was about claims for respect for cultural difference and inclusion within a reconfigured nation-state. The national indigenous movement grew in strength during the early 1990s and in May 1994 the Coordinating Body of Mayan Organisations of Guatemala (COPMAGUA) presented a proposal on the identity and rights of indigenous peoples to the Civil Society Assembly (ASC), a consultative body empowered to present proposals to the parties to the peace negotiations. This document referred to the political, economic, social and cultural rights of Guatemala's indigenous peoples and included a call for the constitutional recognition of their right to use customary law. In contrast to Mexico, demands for land were part of the indigenous rights agenda but tended to be subordinated to appeals for respect for cultural differences, such as language, law and spirituality.[19] The question of indigenous autonomy was discussed at length in the ASC, but Mayan activists were unable to secure the backing of the URNG and civil groups for proposals for regional autonomy for ethno-linguistic communities (conceived of as an intermediate level of government, between the municipal and the national).[20] The revised proposal accepted by the ASC in July 1994 made no reference to the question of autonomy linked to territory. Instead it vaguely defined autonomy in terms of indigenous peoples' right to decide their destiny as peoples – a weak formula that had little or no implications for existing arrangements for municipal and national representation. The Agreement on the Rights and Identity of Indigenous Peoples (AIDPI), signed by the government and the URNG in March 1995, included commitments to increase indigenous peoples' access to justice by developing bilingual state justice and to constitutionally recognise indigenous customary law and incorporate it into the national judicial system. However, the AIDPI left unspecified questions of territorial jurisdiction, coordinating mechanisms between state law and customary law, and other questions relating to the implementation of the broad commitment to recognition.

At a local level, the revival of 'customary' legal practices throughout different parts of the country during the 1990s and the promotion of 'Mayan law' by certain Mayan organisations drew on the language of historical continuity and tradition. In practice, however, such 'imagining of tradition' represented an attempt by local and national indigenous activists to reconstruct communities and rebuild identities in the wake of an armed conflict which had left over 200,000 dead and a million displaced. Often those indigenous communities which defended most strongly their right to use 'traditional' mechanisms of conflict resolution were those that had been most uprooted by the war, such as the returned refugees and internally displaced. Customary law was applied by a variety of community-based institutions, including *consejos de ancianos* (many of which were reconstituted under the auspices of the pro-indigenous wing of the Catholic Church), *alcaldes auxiliares* and *comites pro-mejoramiento* – these last imposed by the militarised state during the 1980s and appropriated during the 1990s as spaces for more autonomous community decision-making. The revival of indigenous customary law was also a response to the manifest inability of the state legal system to meet popular demands for justice and conflict resolution in the context of rising common crime. Although the 1985 Constitution specified that only justices of the peace and the courts had legal attributions, less than half the municipalities in the country had a *juzgado de paz* at the end of the armed conflict. Higher courts were all concentrated in the departmental capitals. Rather than representing a claim for political autonomy against local domination and co-option by the state (as in Chiapas), in Guatemala recourse to customary law had more to do with post-conflict reconstruction, rebuilding local and national identities and filling in the gaps left by a weak and notoriously inefficient state judicial system.

Official recognition of customary law – theory and practice

The emergence of a more articulated opposition to the PRI's traditional modes of interaction with indigenous communities generated a series of constitutional, legal and political changes during the 1990s. The 1991 reform of the federal Penal Procedures Code recognised the right of indigenous people to a translator and to the use of customary law inside their communities, stating that state justice system should establish coordination mechanisms with customary justice (González Galván 1994: 100). Indigenous claims for recognition of customary law were accepted in principle by government ratification of ILO Convention 169 in 1990 and by the reform of the Penal Procedures Code in 1991. In 1992, Article 4 of the Mexican Constitution was reformed, officially recognising for the first time the ethnically plural nature of the nation. However, the reformed Article 4 effectively subordinated indigenous legal practices to state law, leaving government authorities with a wide margin to decide what could and could not be recognised as 'custom'.[21] The February 1996 San Andrés Larrainzer Accords on Indigenous Culture and Rights, negotiated between the government and the Ejército Zapatista de Liberación Nacional (EZLN), confirmed the right of indigenous communities to use traditional authorities and customary law to settle internal conflicts. They also promised political representation of indigenous peoples in regional and national legislatures and stipulated the right of indigenous communities to use customary law. Yet the implementation of these commitments proved highly contested, conflictive and incomplete. The Zedillo government manoeuvred to reduce the scope of indigenous autonomy set out in the accords, alleging that the original proposals would conflict with the existing federal model and the rights to property guaranteed by the constitution. An indigenous rights law was eventually approved by Congress in 2001. However, in contrast to the law drawn up by the consultative peace commission (Comisión de Concordia y Pacificación, COCOPA) on the basis of the 1996 agreements, this was a unilateral initiative of the Executive that restricted indigenous autonomy to the municipal level.[22] In Chiapas, the state constitution was reformed by the state governor in July 1999 without consultation with indigenous organisations. The resulting formula to recognise indigenous communities was ambiguous and did not recognise indigenous peoples as subjects of rights.

Official concessions to demands for recognition of customary law are undoubtedly the result of indigenous struggle, but they can also be explained as part of attempts by the PRI and local elites to keep indigenous communities from allying with opposition parties.[23] As Shannon Speed and Jane Collier have shown (2000), in Chiapas the PRI increasingly used the new legal framework to repress practices within indigenous communities that contested the party's dominance. Under current constitutional arrangements, the federal courts are charged with resolving alleged conflicts between customary law and individuals' constitutional rights. Judicial authorities allied with the PRI have argued that certain customary sanctions applied by indigenous authorities, such as detentions, obligatory community service or public beatings (*azotes*), violate both the Mexican Constitution and the Universal Declaration of Human Rights. In particular, Articles 13–22 of the constitution, if rigorously applied, provide the grounds for pursuing prosecutions against local indigenous authorities for 'usurping' the functions of the legally appointed judiciary.[24] ILO Convention 169, ratified by the Mexican government in 1989, clearly states that intercultural mechanisms – such as mixed tribunals including judges and members of the community in question – should be established to decide on cases where a conflict between customary law and human rights is alleged. Such mechanisms have never been created in Mexico and some fear that even if they were they would still be manipulated.[25] During the 1990s both the federal and state government increasingly adopted the discourse of universal human rights in order to limit the power of indigenous authorities claiming greater autonomy and political independence. While multiculturalist state policies have undoubtedly opened up new spaces for contesting traditional legal and political arrangements, they can also be understood as attempts by dominant elites to devise a new form of 'governmentality' to re-establish their political hegemony or as a new means of assimilation and co-option.

In Guatemala the 1996 Peace Accords between the government of Guatemala and the Unidad Nacional Revolucionaria Guatemalteca (URNG) promised constitutional recognition of indigenous customary law together with the development of a pluri-cultural justice system which would include a greater role for alternative forms of dispute resolution in general. The Accord on the Identity and Rights of Indigenous Peoples (AIDPI), signed in March 1995, stated that indigenous communities would have the right to use customary norms, providing these did not conflict with the fundamental rights set out in the constitution and in international human rights law. In March 1996, despite concerted opposition from powerful economic elites, Congress ratified ILO Convention 169.[26] In 1998 the Commission for Strengthening Justice, created by the Peace Accords, also recommended constitutional recognition of customary law and the elaboration of a law to establish mechanisms of coordination between state law and customary law (Comisión de Fortalecimiento de la Justicia 1998).

Yet in the wake of the peace settlement, proposals put forward by COPMAGUA for constitutional reform to recognise a special jurisdiction for customary law were ignored by the PAN administration of Alvaro Arzú (1996–2000), which opposed any reform of Article 203 (stating that only state courts could exercise legal jurisdiction). In September 1997 Congress passed a series of amendments to the 1994 Penal Procedures Code which aimed to promote greater use of alternative dispute resolution mechanisms, such as conciliation and mediation. The original proposal recognised indigenous peoples' right to exercise their customary law, as demanded by indigenous activists. However, in the event this clause was vetoed in Congress and instead a new form of 'community court' (*Tribunal Comunitario*) was introduced.[27] Rather than recognising existing community-level institutions and practices for dispute resolution, what this measure in effect did was to superimpose a new, officially sanctioned form of 'community court' in a few indigenous municipalities with negligible prior consultation with the communities concerned.[28]

A comprehensive proposal for constitutional reform was subsequently drafted between the different political parties represented in Congress, effectively renegotiating the commitments set out in the Peace Accords. The issue of recognition of customary law again proved a major point of contention. Conservative elites within the powerful private sector association CACIF (Comité Coordinador de Asociaciones Agrícolas, Comerciales, Industriales y Financieras) raised fears that recognition of indigenous authorities and legal norms and procedures would lead to 'one law for indigenous people and another law for everyone else'. They predicted that recognition would mean special privileges for Indians, discrimination against ladinos, abuses of human rights, the end of the rule of law and even the balkanisation of Guatemala. In the end the government, bound by the conditionality of international donor funds which tied aid disbursement to implementation of the peace agreements, agreed a weak and somewhat ambiguous formula for recognition of customary law with the other parties in Congress.[29]

In the event, even this revised proposal for recognition was not adopted. The 1985 Constitution stated that any constitutional reforms had to be approved by popular referendum. The conservative right mobilised their supporters to vote 'no', using scaremongering tactics which focused particularly on the supposed dangers of multiculturalism and of recognising customary law, for example pointing to lynchings of suspected criminals in rural areas as examples of indigenous 'customary law'.[30] The indigenous movement lacked leverage within the political parties and the organisational capacity to mobilise voters. Neither the governing PAN nor the URNG made sufficient efforts to secure support for a 'yes' vote. In May 1999 the package of 50 reforms approved by Congress was rejected on an electoral turnout of 18 per cent, blocking the constitutional recognition of legal pluralism and indigenous rights promised by the peace agreements for the foreseeable future.[31] Attempts to reform the judicial system continued to advance the increased use of alternative dispute mechanisms, but the contentious issue of customary law was effectively dropped from the political agenda. Indigenous communities and authorities continue to practise customary dispute resolution de facto, but their international right to do so remains unrecognised by the Guatemalan state.

Conclusions

At the start of the twenty-first century a developing international jurisprudence is increasingly affirming the right of indigenous people to use their traditional norms and practices to solve disputes within their communities. But what indigenous people across Latin America claim today is not so much a return to 'traditional law', but rather the redress of historical injustices and the legitimate power to regulate their own affairs. Such challenges imply a revision of the nation-state as historically configured in the region and demand a rethinking of the rule of law and issues of political autonomy, participation and representation. The central challenge remains how to balance indigenous peoples' demands for greater autonomy to regulate their own affairs with their claims for greater inclusion in the nation-state.

The comparative historical approach adopted here has focused on different trajectories of state formation and reform and through a comparison of two cases has attempted to indicate the ways in which these have shaped indigenous demands for recognition of legal pluralism and the official responses to them. In Chiapas, traditions of clientelist authoritarianism and co-option of indigenous actors and communities meant the PRI long recognised the right of indigenous communities to 'traditional law' (or *usos y costumbres*) in practice, as long as those communities remained loyal to the ruling party. Indeed this was a mechanism integral to maintaining the dominant party's control over rural areas. It is this form of 'tradition' that has increasingly been challenged by new indigenous movements, whose demands for official recognition of customary law are part of wider and more explicit claims for greater political autonomy. As indigenous communities changed, becoming less defined by narrow geographic boundaries and asserting their political independence from the PRI, so the state intervened in new ways, this time under the banner of human rights and multiculturalism. Government policies in the 1990s can thus be understood as an attempt on the part of dominant elites to re-calibrate mechanisms of co-option and control within the context of neoliberal adjustment. The adoption of multiculturalism as an official ideology and regulatory framework was facilitated by historical traditions of state-formation in Mexico. These included the comparatively strong presence of the official party in rural areas, the nation-building ideology of *indigenismo*, and a practice of flexible engagement on the part of dominant elites. Government authorities may have embraced customary law and multiculturalism, but in fact these were deployed as a means to maintain the hegemony of dominant elites. The de jure recognition of customary law extended in the 1990s provided justification for intervening in indigenous communities to suppress 'unacceptable' aspects of customary law on the grounds that they violate human rights. Nonetheless, such attempts to quash indigenous claims for autonomy and internal self-determination have not been altogether successful.

Authoritarian rule in Guatemala has traditionally been of a non-clientelist, highly exclusive and violent nature. Attempts in the twentieth century to include indigenous peoples as campesinos within a less inequitable socio-economic order were quashed. This has ultimately meant that contemporary indigenous claims for greater inclusion and for recognition of customary law are more difficult for dominant elites to accommodate. Although indigenous authorities and legal practices have long existed at the margins of state law, they have never been formally incorporated within the governing apparatus of the state, and institutionalised links between indigenous authorities and the party system have not been a feature of contemporary politics. In addition, traditions of extreme racism and the systematic negation of indigenous people in Guatemalan discourses of nation-building have meant that the contemporary adjustment to multiculturalism is highly contested and problematic. Certain sectors of the civilian and military elites did shift their positions throughout the peace negotiations, realising that the discourse of multiculturalism could provide a means to legitimate state power in the post-war period. However, the powerful business sector – which remains reliant on the exploitation of indigenous labour for agro-exports – continues to resist any attempt to formally recognise even limited indigenous autonomy and rights, insisting on a unitary rule of law in order to defend its historical privileges. The indigenous movement is comparatively weak, lacking allies within the political parties and increasingly subject to internal divisions in the wake of the peace process. In the absence of an effective state or rule of law, indigenous communities continue to strengthen their customary norms and practices de facto, particularly as militarised forms of control have gradually receded. Yet as long as these remain unrecognised by the state they cannot constitute a clear alternative to local control by non-indigenous authorities and political parties.

It has been argued here that claims for the official recognition of the right of indigenous peoples to use their own norms and practices to regulate their affairs affect existing relations between the state and civil society in different ways in different contexts during different historical conjunctures. While the formal recognition of legal pluralism by certain Latin American governments in the 1990s undoubtedly represents an advance for indigenous organisations, the incorporation of customary law into official legality can also be understood as a new form of governmentality. In other words, legal recognition of indigenous norms and practices – subject to national and international human rights norms – represents a way in which ruling elites map out new territories and communities, extending their control to areas formerly beyond their reach or currently beyond their control. Yet such an exercise cannot be understood merely as an extension of power from the top down: it also signals the manner in which the state itself is becoming increasingly porous as the boundaries between state and society change. New forms of legality and 'tradition' are emerging in what is an increasingly plural and transnationalised international context (Santos 1995). Indigenous movements call on the international human rights regime to counterbalance the power of the state, transnationalising debates about legal pluralism ever further. In addition, the weaknesses of judicial systems throughout Latin America and international donor preferences for strengthening alternative forms of dispute resolution constitute another means by which spaces for indigenous law are being strengthened, even when governments continue to block recognition of indigenous peoples' right to exercise it. Such factors will continue to shape and reshape the nature of the legal order and of state–society relations in the future.

Notes

1. Constitutional provisions concerning indigenous peoples were passed in Guatemala (1985), Nicaragua (1986), Brazil (1988), Colombia (1991), Ecuador (1998), Mexico (1992), Paraguay (1992), Argentina (1994), Bolivia (1994), Peru (1993) and Venezuela (1999).

2. Much contemporary research on legal pluralism focuses on the imbrication of different legal orders in a given field, territory or space, and is concerned with the ways in which the legal ideas and processes of subordinate groups are constrained and shaped by dominant legal frameworks. Legal pluralism should therefore be understood not as a plurality of separate and bounded cultural systems, but rather as a plurality of continually evolving and interconnected processes enmeshed in wider power relations. For discussions of legal pluralism see Merry (1988, 1992, 1997); Moore (1978, 1986); Griffiths (1986); Hooker (1975); Starr and Collier (1989); Fuller (1994); Santos (1987), Benda-Beckmann (1997).

3. Yrigoyen provides a useful comparison of the different provisions for recognition of customary law in the Andean countries (1999a: 76–82).

4. Kymlicka's idea of external protections and internal restrictions has been particularly influential. He argues that a liberal theory of rights should recognise collective rights in the sense of external protections (that is, protection of the group from external threat or dominance). However, it cannot justify the restriction of the individual human rights of members of the collectivity in the name of the group (Kymlicka 1995).

5. Liberalisation in Guatemala occurred in the mid-1980s, when the army orchestrated a transition to restricted multi-party democracy; the broader process of democratisation was linked to the peace negotiations during the 1990s. See Azpuru (1999); on the military see Schirmer (1998).

6. Alan Knight observes that the pace of the reform process was slow; by 1930 only 9 per cent of Mexico's land (by value) had been transferred to *ejidal* – communal – farms. However, he also notes that the change in social relations between landlords and peasants prompted by the *agrarista* legislation was more far-reaching than indicated by the figures alone (1991: 242–3).

7. Yashar has argued that this dismantling of corporate privileges is one of the major factors explaining the emergence of indigenous movements in Latin America (Yashar 1998).
8. Jim Handy has detailed the conflict over communal lands within highland Maya communities generated by the 1952 Agrarian Reform Law (Handy 1994, esp. Chapter 6).
9. Prior to the introduction of the 1985 Constitution, municipal mayors (*alcaldes*) exercised judicial functions as justices of peace (*jueces de paz*).
10. The Instituto Indigenista Interamericano was created in 1940 after the Congress of Pátzcuaro, sponsored by Cárdenas.
11. For an excellent analysis of the relationship between the Mexican state and indigenous customary law see Nader (1980).
12. The stipulation that indigenous authorities elected by customary practices should also be registered with a political party was ended in the state of Oaxaca in 1995. As of March 2001 it remained in force in Chiapas, although the 1996 San Andrés Accords call for reforms to the constitution to recognise the right of indigenous people to compete for public office independently of political parties. See Hernández Navarro (1999); Harvey (1999).
13. González Ponciano argues that notions of 'whiteness' and 'Indianness' have dominated constructions of race and ethnicity in Guatemala, playing a key role in maintaining the hegemony of a small elite. According to this view, dichotomous analyses of Guatemala as divided into indigenous and ladinos, combined with internalised notions of white superiority on the part of the mestizo population, have prevented the emergence of *mestizaje* as a unifying discourse (González Ponciano 2000).
14. The Instituto Indigenista was reconstituted with an explicitly anti-communist logic, but its activities were limited (González Ponciano 1998: 36–8).
15. For a seminal contribution to the Ejercito Guerrillero de los Pobres' (EGP) position on Mayan autonomy and the 'national-ethnic question' see Payeras (1997).
16. Hernández and Garza examine in detail the claims of indigenous women, who wish to change certain *usos y costumbres* they consider detrimental to their interests. See Hernández and Garza (1997).
17. As anthropologists have repeatedly emphasised in recent years, 'culture' is not an essence, a bounded entity or an unproblematic expression of group identity, but is rather determined historically, socially and politically by negotiation, struggle and conflict.
18. Significant differences exist within the indigenous movement over the kind of autonomy project that should be advanced. The EZLN and the San Andrés Accords emphasised municipal and state level autonomy, while other organised indigenous groups favoured regional autonomy, contemplating an additional level of government, alongside the existing municipal, state and federal level, through which indigenous peoples could exercise greater control over natural resources.
19. This was a reflection both of the fear engendered by the state's genocidal response to indigenous demands for land and better wages in the 1970s and of the left's unwillingness to 'ethnicise' the land question.
20. Guatemala is divided administratively into departments. However, departmental governors continue to be non-elected presidential appointments and there are no departmental assemblies.
21. The revised version of Article 4 stated: 'La Nación mexicana tiene una composición pluricultural sustentada originalmente en sus pueblos indígenas. La Ley protegerá

y promoverá el desarrollo de sus lenguas, culturas, usos, costumbres, recursos, formas específicas de organización social, y garantizará a sus integrantes el efectivo acceso a la jurisdicción del Estado. En los juicios y procedimientos agrarios en que aquéllos sean parte, se tomarán en cuenta sus prácticas y costumbres jurídicas en los términos que establezca la Ley.' The important point here is that in the amended article, indigenous cultures rather than indigenous peoples are assigned legal recognition – the collective rights demanded by indigenous peoples were not specified. For a full critique of the constitutional reform see Hindley (1995), Harvey (1999).

22. The law sent by the governing PAN to the National Congress in March 2001 contained elements of the COCOPA draft law, but did not recognise the legal status of indigenous peoples, their rights to land, territory and extensive autonomy, nor their right to extra-municipal association. It remained subject to ratification by a majority of state congresses.

23. See Hernández Navarro on the experience of the state of Oaxaca, where the PRI eventually supported reform of state law regarding customary practices for selected municipal officials in order to keep indigenous communities from allying with the PAN and the PRD (Hernández Navarro 1999).

24. Article 13 states that no one can be judged by particular laws (*leyes privativas*); article 14 establishes that no one can be denied their liberty without a prior trial; Article 16 prevents home arrests without a detention order; and Article 19 limits detentions without charges to three days.

25. Given the PRI's historical abilities of co-optation, such fears are perhaps justified. Notes from discussions, Diplomado de Antropología Jurídica, CIESAS, San Cristóbal de las Casas, Chiapas, December 1999.

26. The Constitutional Court ruled that the ILO Convention was not incompatible with the 1985 Constitution, as certain groups had alleged.

27. Even the original proposal, while stating that indigenous customary law constituted an alternative mechanism for the solution of criminal cases, insisted that it should not violate constitutional or international human rights guarantees. It also proposed that all customary rulings should be validated by a judge within the state judiciary (Ramirez, Solorzano and Caxaj 1999).

28. Five pilot community courts were established in 1998. Each had three 'justices of the peace' (*jueces de paz*); local, bilingual candidates appointed by the Supreme Court following consultation with community authorities. The judges were only permitted to use customary norms and practices if these were in line with the Penal Procedures Code. In addition, all the auxiliary staff in the courts was non-indigenous, appointed by the CSJ. Nonetheless, the pilot courts appeared to have had some success in providing greater access to bilingual conflict resolution *in situ*, in some places coordinating their efforts with traditional and municipal authorities. However, in practice they dealt with all kinds of cases, including family conflicts, which were not within their legal remit, raising the possibility that they could be accused of exceeding their functions. See Ramirez, Solorzano and Caxaj (1999); Murga Armas (1999). A similar mechanism was introduced by the Chiapas state governments in 1998, the so-called 'indigenous courts of peace and conciliation', apparently with much less public acceptance than in Guatemala. See Collier (1999).

29. In effect while the proposal supported the creation of a special jurisdiction for customary law, it did not explicitly mandate recognition of indigenous authorities as judicial authorities. It also insisted that parties had to voluntarily submit to

customary resolutions, and stipulated that decisions reached in customary forums could not affect the interests of third parties. For a detailed analysis of the proposal, see Yrigoyen (1999b: 25–7).
30. Mob lynchings of suspected criminals increased in the wake of the peace settlement – between 1996 and 2000 some 635 attacks occurred, 185 of which resulted in fatalities. Most analysts agree this is a consequence of the acute militarisation and violence experienced throughout the country during the 1980s (MINUGUA 2000).
31. For discussion of the referendum and its implications see Arnson (1999).

References

Arnson, Cynthia (ed.) (1999), 'The Popular Referendum (*Consulta Popular*) and the Future of the Peace Process in Guatemala', Working Paper No.241, Woodrow Wilson Center Latin American Program (Washington DC).

Azpuru, Dinorah (1999), 'Peace and Democratization in Guatemala: Two Parallel Processes', in Cynthia Arnson (ed.), *Comparative Peace Processes in Latin America*, Woodrow Wilson Center and Stanford University Press (Washington DC and Stanford), pp.97–125.

Banton, Michael (1996), 'International Norms and Latin American States' Policies on Indigenous Peoples', *Nations and Nationalism*, Vol.2 (1), pp.89–103.

Bastos, Santiago and Manuela Camus (1995), *Abriendo Caminos: las organizaciones mayas desde el Nobel hasta el Acuerdo de derechos indígenas*, FLACSO (Guatemala).

Benda-Beckmann, Franz (1997), 'Citizens, Strangers and Indigenous Peoples: Conceptual Politics and Legal Pluralism', *Law and Anthropology*, Vol.9, pp.1–42.

Burguete Cal y Mayor, Aracely (coord.) (1999), *México: Experiencias de Autonomía Indígena*, International Working Group on Indigenous Affairs (IWGIA) (Copenhagen).

Cancian, Frank (1992), *The Decline of Community in Zinacantán: Economy, Public Life, and Social Stratification, 1960–1987*, Stanford University Press (Stanford).

Carmack, Robert (ed.) (1998), *Harvest of Violence: Guatemala's Indians in the Counterinsurgency War*, University of Oklahoma Press (Norman).

CEH (Comisión de Esclarecimiento Histórico) (1999), *Guatemala: Memoria del Silencio*, United Nations (Guatemala).

Collier, George (2000), 'Zapatismo Resurgent: Land and Autonomy in Chiapas', in *NACLA: Report on the Americas*, Vol.XXXIII, No.5, pp.20–5.

Collier, Jane F. (1999), 'Two Models of Indigenous Justice in Chiapas, Mexico: A Comparison of State and Zinacanteco Visions', unpublished draft paper.

Comisión de Fortalecimiento de la Justicia (1998), *Una Nueva Justicia para la Paz: Resumen Ejecutivo del Informe Final de la Comisión de Fortalecimiento de la Justicia*, Magna Tierra editores (Guatemala).

Dandler, Jorge (1998), 'Indigenous Peoples and the Rule of Law in Latin America: Do they have a Chance?' in Juan E. Mendez, Guillermo O'Donnell and Paulo Sergio Pinheiro (eds), *The (Un)Rule of Law and the Underprivileged in Latin America*, University of Notre Dame Press (Notre Dame).

De la Peña, Guillermo (1999), ' Territorio y ciudadanía étnica en la nación globalizada', *Desacatos: Revista de Antropología Social*, Vol.1. CIESAS (Mexico), pp.13–27.

Díaz-Polanco, Héctor (1994), 'La rebelión de los más pequeños. los zapatistas y la autonomía', *Boletín de Antropología Americana*, December, pp.85–103.

—— (1995) 'La rebelión de los indios zapatista y la autonomía', in Noam Chomsky et al. (eds), *Cinco ensayos sobre la realidad mexicana*, Txalaparta (Navarra).

Donnelly, Jack (1989), *Universal Human Rights in Theory and Practice*, Cornell University Press (Ithaca).

Eber, Christine (2001), '*Buscando una nueva vida*: Liberation Through Autonomy in San Pedro Chenalhó, 1970–1998', *Latin American Perspectives*, Vol.28 (2), pp.45–72.

Franco Mendoza, Moisés (2000), 'The Debate Concerning Indigenous Rights in Mexico', in Willem Assies, Gemma van der Haar and André Hoekema (eds), *The Challenge of Diversity: Indigenous Peoples and Reform of the State in Latin America*, Thela Thesis (Amsterdam), pp.57–75.

Fuller, Chris (1994), 'Legal Anthropology – Legal Pluralism and Legal Thought', *Anthropology Today*, Vol.10 (3), pp.9–12.

Gamio, Manuel ([1916] 1960), *Forjando Patria*, Editorial Porrúa (Mexico).

García Añoveros (1981), *La Reforma Agraria de Arbenz en Guatemala*, Ediciones Cultura Hispanica de Cooperación Iberoamericana (Madrid).

Gleijeses, Piero (1991), *Shattered Hope: The Guatemalan Revolution and the United States, 1944–1954*, Princeton University Press (Princeton).

González Galván, Jorge Alberto (1994), 'La condición jurídica del Indio', in Mario Melgar Adalid, José Francisco Ruiz Massieu and José Luis Soberanes Fernández (coords), *La rebelión en Chiapas y el derecho*, UNAM (Mexico).

González Ponciano, Jorge Ramón (1998), '"Esas sangres no están limpias". El racismo, el Estado y la Nación en Guatemala (1944–1997)', *Anuario 1997*, Centro de Estudios Superiores de México y Centroamérica, Tuxla Gutiérrez (Chiapas).

—— (2000), 'Anthropology in Guatemala after the Peace Agreement', paper read at Latin American Studies Association meeting, Miami, 16–18 March.

Griffiths, John (1986), 'What is Legal Pluralism?' *Journal of Legal Pluralism and Unofficial Law*, No.24, pp.1–55.

Handy, Jim (1994), *Revolution in the Countryside: Rural Conflict and Agrarian Reform in Guatemala, 1944–1954*, University of North Carolina Press (Chapel Hill and London).

Harvey, Neil (1998) *The Chiapas Rebellion: The Struggle for Land and Democracy*, Duke University Press (Durham NC).

—— (1999), 'Resisting Neoliberalism, Constructing Citizenship: Indigenous Movements in Chiapas', in Wayne A. Cornelius, Todd A. Eisenstadt and Jane Hindley (eds), *Subnational Politics and Democratisation in Mexico*, Center for US–Mexican Studies, University of California (San Diego), pp.239–65.

Hernández, Aida and Anna María Garza (1997), 'En torno a la ley y la costumbre: problemas de antropología legal en los Altos de Chiapas' in Rosa Isabel Estrada Martínez and Gisela González Guerra (eds), *Tradiciones y costumbres jurídicas en comunidades indígenas de México*, Comisión Nacional de Derechos Humanos (Mexico).

Hernández Navarro, Luis (1999), 'Ethnic Identity and Politics in Oaxaca' in Wayne A. Cornelius, Todd A. Eisenstadt and Jane Hindley (eds), *Subnational Politics and Democratisation in Mexico*, Center for US–Mexican Studies, University of California (San Diego), pp.13–73.

Hindley, Jane (1996), 'Towards a Pluricultural Nation: *Indigenismo* and the Reform of Article 4', in *Dismantling the Mexican State*, edited by Rob Aitken, Nikki Craske, Gareth A. Jones and David E. Stansfield (eds), Macmillan Press (London and Basingstoke), pp.225–43.

Hooker, M.B. (1975), *Legal Pluralism: An Introduction to Colonial and Neo-Colonial Laws*, Clarendon Press (Oxford).

Joseph, Gilbert M. and Daniel Nugent (eds) (1994), *Everyday Forms of State Formation: Revolution and the Negotiation of Rule in Modern Mexico*, Duke University Press (Durham NC).

Knight, Alan (1990), 'Racism, Revolution and *Indigenismo*: Mexico, 1910–1940' in Richard Graham (ed.), *The Idea of Race in Latin America, 1870–1940*, Cambridge University Press (Cambridge).

—— (1991), 'The Rise and Fall of Cardenismo, *c*.1930–*c*.1946', in Leslie Bethell (ed.), *Mexico Since Independence*, Cambridge University Press (New York).

Kymlicka, Will (1995), *Multicultural Citizenship*, Clarendon Press (Oxford).

López Monjardin, Adriana and Dulce María Rebolledo Millán (1999), 'Los municipios autónomos zapatistas', in *Chiapas*, No.7, Universidad Nacional Autónoma de México (Mexico), pp.115–34.

Manz, Beatriz (1988), *Refugees of a Hidden War: The Aftermath of Counterinsurgency in Guatemala*, State University of New York Press (Albany).

Mattiace, Shannan L. (2001), 'Regional Renegotiations of Space: Tojolabal Ethnic Identity in Las Margaritas, Chiapas', *Latin American Perspectives*, Vol.28 (2), pp.73–97.

Merry, S. Engle (1988), 'Legal Pluralism', *Law and Society Review*, Vol.22, pp.869–96.

—— (1992), 'Anthropology, Law and Transnational Processes', *Annual Review of Anthropology*, Vol.21, pp.357–79.

—— (1997), 'Legal Pluralism and Transnational Culture', in R. Wilson (ed.), *Human Rights, Culture and Context*, Pluto Press (London), pp.28–48.

Mertus, Julie (1999), 'From Legal Transplants to Transformative Justice: Human Rights and the Promise of Transnational Civil Society', *American University International Law Review*, Vol.15 (5), pp.1335–89.

MINUGUA (2000), 'Informe de Verificación. Los linchamientos: un flagelo contra la dignidad humana', consult at www.minugua.guate.net

Moore, Sally Falk (1978), *Law as Process: An Anthropological Approach*, Henley (London) and Routledge and Kegan Paul (Boston).

—— (1986), *Social Facts and Fabrications: Customary Law on Kilimanjaro, 1880–1980*, Cambridge University Press (New York).

Murga Armas, Jorge (1999), 'Análisis del funcionamiento de los Juzgados de Paz Comunitarios. Reformas al Código Procesal Penal', draft document, PNUD (Guatemala).

Nader, Laura (1980), *Harmony Ideology, Justice and Control in a Zapotec Mountain Village*, Stanford University Press (Stanford).

Nagengast, Carole (1997), 'Women, Minorities, and Indigenous Peoples: Universalism and Cultural Relativity', *Journal of Anthropological Research*, Vol.53, pp.349–69.

Nash, June (1995), 'The Reassertion of Indigenous Identity: Mayan Responses to State Intervention in Chiapas', *Latin American Research Review*, Vol.30 (3), pp.7–41.

ODHAG-Oficina de Derechos Humanos del Arzobispado de Guatemala (1998). *Guatemala: Nunca Más*, ODHAG (Guatemala).

O'Donnell, Guillermo (1999), 'On the State, Democratization, and Some Conceptual Problems: A Latin American View with Glances at Some Postcommunist Countries', in *Counterpoints: Selected Essays on Authoritarianism and Democratization*, University of Notre Dame Press (Notre Dame IN), pp.133–57.

Payeras, Mario (1997), *Los pueblos indígenas y la revolución guatemalteca: ensayos étnicos 1982–1992*, Magna Tierra/Luna y Sol (Guatemala).

Plant, Roger (1998), 'Indigenous Rights and the Guatemalan Peace Process: Conceptual and Practical Challenges', in R. Sieder (ed.), *Guatemala After the Peace Accords*, Institute of Latin American Studies (London).

—— (1999), 'Los derechos indígenas y el multiculturalismo latinoamericano: lecciones del proceso de paz en Guatemala', *Diáologo*, No.9, FLACSO (Guatemala).

Preis, Ann-Belinda S. (1996), 'Human Rights as Cultural Practice: An Anthropological Critique', *Human Rights Quarterly*, Vol.18, pp.286–315.

Ramirez, Luis, Justo Solorzano and Mario Caxaj (1999), 'Informe: Tribunales Comunitarios', INECIP, Guatemala, draft document, unpaginated.

Rus, Jan (1994), 'The "Comunidad Revolucionaria Institucional"; the Subversion of Native Government in Chiapas, 1936–1968', in Gil Joseph and Daniel Nugent (eds), *Everyday Forms of State Formation: Revolution and the Negotiation of Rule in Modern Mexico*, Duke University Press (Durham), pp.265–300.

Santos, Boaventura De Souza (1987), 'Law: A Map of Misreading. Toward a Post-Modern Conception of Law', *Journal of Law and Society*, 14 (3), pp.279–302.

—— (1995), *Toward A New Common Sense: Law, Science and Politics in the Paradigmatic Transition*, Routledge (New York).

Schirmer, Jennifer (1998), *The Guatemalan Military Project: A Violence called Democracy*, University of Pennsylvania Press (Philadelphia).

Speed, Shannon and Jane F. Collier (2000), 'Limiting Indigenous Autonomy in Chiapas, Mexico: The State Government's Use of Human Rights', *Human Rights Quarterly*, Vol.22, pp.877–905.

Stamatopoulou, Elsa (1994), 'Indigenous Peoples and the United Nations: Human Rights as a Developing Dynamic', *Human Rights Quarterly*, Vol.16, pp.58–81.

Starr, June and Jane Collier (1989), *History and Power in the Study of Law: New Directions in Legal Anthropology*, Cornell University Press (Ithaca and London).

Stavenhagen, Rodolfo (1996), 'Indigenous Rights: Some Conceptual Problems', in Elizabeth Jelin and Eric Hershberg (eds), *Constructing Democracy: Human Rights, Citizenship and Society in Latin America*, Westview Press (Boulder).

Stephen, Lynn and George Collier (1997), 'Reconfiguring Ethnicity, Identity and Citizenship in the Wake of the Zapatista Rebellion', *Journal of Latin American Anthropology*, Vol.3 (1), pp.2–13.

Urban, Greg and Joel Sherzer (eds) (1991), *Nation-States and Indians in Latin America*, University of Texas Press (Austin).

Van Cott, Donna Lee (ed.) (1994), *Indigenous Peoples and Democracy in Latin America*, Inter-American Dialogue/St Martin's Press (New York).

—— (1998), 'Latin American Constitutions and Indigenous Peoples', unpublished draft table.

Warren, Kay (1998), *Indigenous Movements and their Critics: Pan-Mayan Activism in Guatemala*, Princeton University Press (Princeton).

Wilson, Richard (1995), *Mayan Resurgence in Guatemala: Q'eqchi' Experiences*, University of Oklahoma Press (Norman).

Yashar, Deborah (1998), 'Contesting Citizenship: Indigenous Movements and Democracy in Latin America', *Comparative Politics*, Vol.31 (1), pp.23–42.

Young, Iris Marion (1990), *Justice and the Politics of Difference*, Princeton University Press (Princeton).

—— (1995), 'Polity and Group Difference: a critique of the ideal of universal citizenship' in Ronald Beiner (ed.), *Theorizing Citizenship*, New York State University Press (Albany, New York).

Yrigoyen, Raquel (1999a), *Pautas de Coordinación entre el Derecho Indígena y el Derecho Estatal*, Fundación Myrna Mack (Guatemala).

—— (1999b), 'El debate sobre el reconocimiento constitucional del derecho indígena en Guatemala', draft document.

Zechenter, Elizabeth M. (1997), 'In the Name of Culture: Cultural Relativism and the Abuse of the Individual', *Journal of Anthropological Research*, Vol.53, pp.319–47.

8
Latin America's Multiculturalism: Economic and Agrarian Dimensions

Roger Plant

This chapter examines some economic and agrarian dimensions of Latin America's multicultural challenge. Given that the impetus for state reform is coming from the indigenous movement, the main emphasis is on issues of indigenous rights and development. Yet the move for multi-ethnicity, multiculturalism and multilingualism (the 'three Ms') clearly embraces more than indigenous peoples alone. A feature of the constitutional reforms of the 1990s, notably in Colombia and Ecuador, has been to extend to certain rural black communities the special collective land rights that had previously been recognised only for indigenous peoples. The growing recognition of differentiated rights over land and related natural resources, based at least in part on factors of ethnic origin and historically based patterns of land and resource use, has as yet unforeseen consequences for Latin America. If such trends were to extend to Brazil, for example, the implications would be immense. The concept of differentiated citizenship, and its implications for land and resource rights, would take off on a new and more complex plane.

In brief, some problem areas and challenges can be posed as follows.

Much of the normative work on indigenous peoples focuses on the concept of *separate space* for indigenous peoples. This can be legal and political space, physical space, and perhaps even cultural space. With the growing interest in legal pluralism, most analysts are keen to pinpoint the dichotomies between 'national' and indigenous systems of law, rather than to examine where they overlap and complement each other. With regard to political space, a strong interest is the mechanisms for local and regional autonomy through the empowerment of representative indigenous institutions. In some countries, however, there has been some emphasis on national mechanisms for ensuring indigenous involvement in planned reforms. With regard to physical space, indigenous demands are seen as relating to their territorial rights, under an autonomous and protective legal regime, and also the greatest possible degree of control over natural resource management.

The language of the contemporary indigenous rights movement encapsulates these approaches. *Autonomy, self-determination, self-government, self-development* and *territorial control* are some of the terms that spring to mind. All of this is a reaction against the assimilationist tendencies of the 'national integration' period of the mid-twentieth century. Many indigenous communities derived material advantage when they traded an 'indigenous' for a 'campesino' identity in the land reforms of Bolivia and Peru, or when the indigenous corporate community enjoyed some political patronage in Mexico and Peru. But this was at the cost of cultural identity. Indigenous institutions might be left alone at the local level. But the promotion of specifically indigenous values was never part of national policy.

Yet today's reality, at least in the countries with the largest proportions of indigenous peoples, is of cultural differences in *shared space*. It is usually only in the Amazon lowlands that indigenous peoples exercise some control over large and contiguous territorial areas. Even in these regions, there are conflicts with settler colonists, cattle-ranchers, forestry companies and increasingly the energy multinationals. Bolivia's 1996 commitment[1] to vest title over some 10 million hectares of land in the hands of indigenous groups has been bogged down by the presence of third-party colonists and large forestry concessions within the claimed indigenous areas. Ecuador's paper titles for indigenous communities,[2] in theory also covering millions of hectares, do not reflect land control on the ground for the simple reason that the areas have never been properly demarcated. There are similar problems in the *comarcas* of Panama's Darien and other regions, and in Brazil's indigenous reserves. And Colombia's Amazon land titling efforts,[3] wonderful on paper, have been torpedoed by the civil conflict and narcotics interests. Despite all this, there can be some realistic hope that Amazon Indians will achieve the territorial base on which they can construct a sustainable form of economic self-development.

In most of the Andean and Mesoamerican highlands, the situation is markedly different. Whatever the legal arrangements (communal tenure, private or informal tenure) the reality is of small individual plots, growing landlessness, and increasing out-migration on a seasonal or permanent basis. Moreover, the past decade has seen renewed efforts to dismantle corporate agrarian structures. As during nineteenth century liberalism, free-market reformers have identified the traditional indigenous communities as an obstacle to greater agricultural productivity. Land privatisation in such countries as Ecuador,[4] Mexico[5] and Peru[6] has admittedly been voluntary; requiring the approval of a certain number of assembly members before land can be parcelled individually. In these regions the implications of a territorial approach, or one based on indigenous autonomies, have to be examined critically. As will be seen later there have been recent attempts to apply territorial concepts to Andean regions, for fiscal and administrative purposes. But the economic and agrarian realities are ones of unequally shared space, with long-standing discrimination against indigenous communities with regard to land and resources, and in some cases access to market opportunities and institutions.

New juridical figures are being created with implications for the *campesinos indígenas* in the temperate highlands of the Andes and Mesoamerica. There are such fiscal-cum-political entities as the Indigenous Territorial Entities of Colombia's 1991 Constitution, or the Indigenous Territorial Circumscriptions of Ecuador's 1998 Constitution. Panama has created some sizeable new *comarcas* embracing temperate as well as tropical regions, the most significant being the Ngobe-Bugle (Guaymi) territory recognised in 1997. An intriguing feature of the Bolivian highlands is the efforts of some Aymara and Quechua communities to reconstitute their traditional *ayllus*, availing themselves of the new 1996 land reform law which allows for the titling of *Tierras Comunitarias de Origen* (Original Community Lands) in both highland and lowland areas. In the first months of the year 2000 Quechua indigenous communities from the Potosí highlands filed a claim over no less than 2.5 million hectares of land.

Where all this will lead is far from clear. The territorial entities provided for in the Colombian and Ecuadorean constitutions have not yet seen the light of day. In the Colombian case, the requisite regulations had still not been adopted almost ten years later. But ethnicity is a potential factor in the decentralisation initiatives now gathering pace throughout Latin America. Demands can be for a high degree of administrative autonomy, as in the case of the 'Pluri-Ethnic Autonomous Regions' proposed by Mexico's Zapatistas after the 1994 Chiapas uprising. More moderate proposals can be for a restructuring of social services along ethnic or linguistic lines. This approach was taken in the Indigenous Agreement signed as part of the Guatemalan peace process,[7] in which the government undertook to regionalise the administration of educational, health and cultural services of indigenous peoples on the basis of linguistic criteria. As with other efforts to promote indigenous rights and indigenous legal systems, there will be tensions over the degree of autonomy entailed. The new political structures set out in some recent reforms can recognise specifically indigenous entities. This can be the case of broader-based entities, such as the Panamanian *Comarcas*, or smaller and more local-level units, such as the *Distritos Municipales Indígenas* (Indigenous Municipal Districts) provided for in Bolivia's popular participation laws after 1994. The latter might be seen more correctly as an exercise in national integration, which aims to build in part on traditional social structures. Some indigenous activists claim that the central recognition of new indigenous structures actually serves to undermine their own *ayllu* movement.

A further feature, linked to the indigenous rights momentum, has been the growing interest in the concept of *indigenous development*. Indigenous and pro-indigenous activists are formulating their own concepts of 'ethno-development' or 'development with identity'. The concept enjoys wide support among the international donor community, with the multilateral development banks and some overseas governments now keen to target their development assistance specifically at indigenous communities and other ethnic minorities. Some governments are now formulating broad-based indigenous development plans. In Bolivia a government bureaucracy seeks to implement these. Ecuador has a quasi-official Council for Indigenous Development, though in this case headed by indigenous officials, and with the participation of the main indigenous organisations. Guatemala has its indigenous development fund (FODIGUA), headed by a government-nominated indigenous person, though expected to work in close collaboration with indigenous organisations.

All of this raises the question of urban-based indigenous peoples, and what the concept of 'indigenous development' might mean for them. Over recent years there has been a steady movement of indigenous peoples to urban areas, both to the capital cities and to other towns. While they tend to maintain close relations, including trading networks, with their communities of origin, they are particularly likely to see their problems in terms of discrimination vis-à-vis other urban population groups. Participation in markets, both national and international, will be a key area of concern. There has been a tendency to promote indigenous industrial and marketing associations, and even indigenous chambers of commerce. It remains to be seen whether initiatives of this kind are effective ways of breaking down the barriers to greater market participation.

The manner in which concepts of 'indigenous development' and the 'indigenous economy' are now taken forward will be issues of vital importance for the future configuration of multicultural and multi-ethnic societies in Latin America. This – and the articulation between the political/juridical and the economic aspects of multiculturalism – are the main themes addressed in this chapter. A key question is the circumstances in which the concept of an 'indigenous economy', rather than indigenous participation in a national or even international economy, makes analytical sense. To deal with these questions, highly complex in some countries, requires a focus on demographic factors, poverty trends, normative indigenous rights, and also issues of definition.

Such analysis can also help determine when issues of indigenous development and economic participation can be addressed from a local and community perspective, and when they must be seen as national concerns. This depends on realities of territorial control and land security, patterns of discrimination, on such demographic issues as the growing indigenous presence in urban areas, and also the strength and attitudes of the indigenous organisations themselves. In Ecuador and Guatemala indigenous issues are clearly of major importance in national economic agendas, as well as cultural and political ones. In Mexico many advocates would like indigenous issues to be part of a truly national reform agenda, but have not as yet succeeded in achieving this. In Bolivia there have been similar failures for rather different reasons. In Peru, attempts to determine a national agenda on economic and agrarian issues is only incipient, and there are many doubts that it will ever take off.

Issues of indigenous identity, and their economic implications

Latin America's indigenous population is generally estimated at some 40 million people altogether, or approximately 8 per cent of the total. In some countries, as in Argentina and Brazil, they comprise small minorities of less than 1 per cent of the national population. In others, such as Bolivia and Guatemala, by some estimates they comprise more than half the national population.

A precise identification of indigenous peoples has always been beset by problems, in Latin America as elsewhere, because of the diverse criteria used. Some national statistics refer to objective criteria such as dress and language. Others, including new international standards, place more emphasis on the retention of traditional cultural institutions and practices, as well as on the important issues of 'self-perception' and 'self-definition'. Others have also referred to certain functional criteria for identifying indigenous peoples, including a close attachment to ancestral territories and natural resources, or primarily subsistence-oriented production.[8]

Various efforts have been made to classify indigenous peoples by their type of economic or agrarian activity. Most people tend to draw a broad distinction between the mostly peasant farmers of Mexico, Central America and the Andes, with their lengthy history of contact with the remainder of national societies, and the Indians of lowland South America, who have traditionally remained more isolated, and tend to combine agriculture with other subsistence activities. It has been argued for example that the latter category need special protection and specific supporting strategies because, unlike the peasant indigenous peoples who need mostly land and agricultural support, they need territories conceived in an ecologically integrated way (Gnerre 1990). Yet it is also clear that indigenous groups can display very different characteristics within the same country. Colombia's National Department of Planning distinguishes between the four major categories of: indigenous tribal population with sporadic contacts; indigenous tribal population with stable contacts; indigenous tribal population with a peasant economy; and the indigenous peasant population.[9]

Yet a key question now has to be faced. Is a particular economic system, or a particular relationship with the land and environment, at the heart of being defined or identified as indigenous? Urban-based intellectuals often lead today's indigenous movements in Latin America. And an important feature of Latin America's recent socio-economic development has been the increasing presence in urban areas of people who, by the criterion of ethnic origin, could define themselves as indigenous.

Indigenous peoples can be accorded a special status either because of their own wishes and aspirations, for purposes of protection, or indeed for reasons of exploitation and discrimination. During the Spanish colonial period indigenous peoples were marked out for purposes of tribute and compulsory labour. After independence there were drawn-out conflicts between political liberals (who wished to introduce equality of rights for all within the liberal state, and to do away with a separate economic regime for indigenous peoples) and political conservatives (who basically aimed to maintain racial segregation).

It was during the late nineteenth century, when liberal economic and social policies brought the greatest de facto pressure on indigenous lands and communities in the more populated areas, that the concept of *indígena* or *indio* began to be seen as a biological rather than a fiscal category. Left without any protection or a special status, indigenous peoples increasingly provided the cheap and servile labour in the new agricultural export sector. The general association of the very concept of indigenous with poverty can probably be dated to this period, which also saw concerted efforts to stamp out indigenous cultural identities.

The early twentieth century then saw new approaches, and a reaction against the excesses of nineteenth century liberalism. A watershed was clearly the Mexican revolution and its social legislation and reforms, which subsequently had a strong effect throughout the continent. A key aspect of Mexican revolutionary philosophy, rather than to provide a separate or 'protective' status for indigenous peasants and workers, was to seek a new, syncretic nationalism by incorporating indigenous culture and institutions within the new society. Thus the *comunidad indígena* was recognised as a legal entity, and there were provisions for the restitution to indigenous communities of lands over which they could prove unlawful dispossession. But in practice there was no difference between the regime of the indigenous communities and that of the *ejidos* used as the model for land distribution to all land reform beneficiaries. In both cases there were prohibitions on land alienation and mortgaging.

The mid-twentieth century periods of agrarian reformism, some with clear socialist inspiration, led to some well-known complexities over national identity. Some reformist governments promoted communal or collective farming systems among peasant farmers of largely indigenous origin, while deliberately and often successfully breaking down their sense of a separate indigenous identity. Examples are Bolivia and Peru, where natives of the tropical lowlands tend to define themselves as indigenous, while Aymara-

and Quechua-speaking peasant farmers have tended at least until now to reject this identification.

Moreover, there can be a particularly strong sense of indigenous identity in countries where there is almost no communal agriculture today, such as Guatemala. In Guatemala, where the indigenous communities as territorial entities were broken up by liberal land tenure reforms, there is now a resurgent sense of Mayan consciousness. Each of Guatemala's Mayan ethnic groups tends to have a triple sense of identity, first as a K'iche or Pokomchi or Kakchiquel, second as a Mayan, and third as a Guatemalan national. Yet the vast majority of Guatemalan Indians are farming small private plots, some with registered title, others under more customary forms of ownership.

Official definitions of the term 'indigenous' have thus changed over time. The same can be said for the perceptions of the people who define themselves as indigenous. As the indigenous movement now gains momentum throughout Latin America, the complexities over identity are as strong as ever. The days of overt prejudice are largely gone, together with most of the coercive rural labour systems that affected mainly indigenous and black populations. The pendulum now appears to be swinging the other way, in that there can be a definite economic advantage in self-definition as indigenous, further stimulated by international development approaches. Definitions can still be based on diverse criteria, all of which have their implications for addressing relations between indigenous peoples and the state. Biological criteria of descent from pre-Columbian peoples still provide the entry point for territorial and autonomy claims, on the grounds that land rights were never extinguished to the colonial power. Difficulties can arise when the maintenance of a particular lifestyle, or a particular relationship with the land and environment, is considered as a 'functional' criterion for determining whether or not a person or community should be recognised as indigenous. Indigenous peoples certainly have their own cultural values, often involving a spiritual relationship with the land, which can be an important part of their overall identity. Yet problems arise if they are expected by outsiders and policy-makers to behave in a certain way, eschewing modernisation and locking themselves into a subsistence economy in accordance with the more romanticised notions of indigenous lifestyles. This point will be discussed further below, when recent land and territorial claims are considered.

Normative issues of indigenous development: ILO Convention No. 169 and its implications

Normative developments, such as the emerging international instruments on indigenous rights, are of obvious relevance here. While other international standard on indigenous identity and rights are currently in draft form, such as those of the United Nations and the Organisation of American States, the most important instrument for practical purposes is the Indigenous and Tribal Peoples Convention No. 169 adopted by the International Labour Organisation in 1989. Under ILO procedures, its Conventions have force of domestic law in the member states that choose to ratify them. Convention No. 169 it has now been ratified by ten Latin American countries, including the five with the largest numbers and proportions of indigenous peoples (Bolivia, Ecuador, Guatemala, Mexico and Peru). The other signatories are Argentina, Colombia, Costa Rica, Honduras and Paraguay. Indigenous peoples are increasingly using this Convention to air their grievances internationally. Between 1996 and 1999, representations were submitted in Bolivia, Mexico and Peru, alleging failure to observe the Convention on issues pertaining mainly to land rights and consultation procedures.

The Convention has been widely interpreted, with some analysts seeing it as an instrument promoting autonomy and self-determination. In the view of the ILO itself, as observed by its main supervisory body last year, '[o]ne of the fundamental precepts of this Convention is that a relationship of respect should be established between indigenous and tribal peoples and the States in which they live, a concept which should not be confused with autonomy or political and territorial independence from the nation State'.[10] The ILO has studiously avoided any reference to autonomy and self-determination, insisting that such political aspects are the exclusive competence of the United Nations.

Apart from its strong provisions on land and resource rights, arguably the most significant aspects of Convention No. 169 are its requirements on consultation and participation (Articles 6 and 7). Governments are to consult indigenous peoples 'through appropriate procedures and in particular through their representative institutions, whenever consideration is being given to legislative or administrative measures which may affect them directly'; to 'establish means by which these peoples can freely participate, to at least the same extent as other sectors of the population, at all levels of decision-making in elective institutions and administrative and other bodies responsible for policies and programmes which concern them'; and 'establish means for the full development of these peoples' own institutions and initiatives, and in appropriate cases provide the resources necessary for the purpose'. Under Article 7, indigenous peoples are to

> have the right to decide their own priorities for the process of development as it affects their lives, beliefs, institutions and spiritual well-being and the lands they occupy or otherwise use, and to exercise control, to the extent possible, over their own economic, social and cultural development. In addition, they shall participate in the formulation, implementation and evaluation of plans and programmes for national and regional development that may affect them directly.

Taken together, these are fairly strong requirements. They try to find the balance between indigenous self-development, construed as control over their local and community affairs, and participation in all aspects of national life and planning (including law reform) which could have an impact on indigenous livelihoods. But in some of the Andean countries like Peru – where there are no truly representative indigenous organisations in the highlands, and issues of indigenous identity remain highly complex – these conditions may not be easy to fulfil.

Yet without a national mechanism in which indigenous peoples nominate their own representatives, such consultative procedures run the risk of being merely *pro forma*. At the national level, governments can establish mechanisms for formal consultation and participation. Private and multinational companies too, now under greater pressure from their shareholders back home not to infringe indigenous rights, can engage in rudimentary consultations with local indigenous groups in the project area without engaging in dialogue with more representative indigenous bodies. Thus consultation procedures have now become a critical issue in policy dialogue between indigenous peoples and states. Different modalities are also discussed further below.

Demographic and poverty concerns

The issues can be summarised quite briefly. Trends in indigenous poverty are described in some detail in another chapter in this volume,[11] and need not be repeated here. In brief, from regression analyses in a number of countries it is clear that structural patterns of indigenous poverty, using conventional economic indicators, have been deteriorating over the past two decades. For analysts of agrarian and agrarian reform processes in Mesoamerica and the Andes, statistical findings have to come as no surprise. The generalised increase in commercial agriculture has led to increasing demand for seasonal agricultural labour, in many countries provided mainly by impoverished indigenous families. While countries such as Guatemala were bypassed altogether by the redistributive land reform process, in others including Colombia, Ecuador and Mexico it ground to a halt without dealing with the massive backlog of land claims from indigenous and other peasant families. A classic example was Chiapas, where aggressive expansion of commercial agriculture took place at the expense of indigenous communities, in a violent atmosphere, and where some semi-feudal labour practices remained widespread. Similar processes could be seen in parts of Guatemala during the civil conflict. In almost all countries the absence of reformist programmes, and also the gradual reduction of state support programmes, inevitably undermined the communities. There is evidence that indigenous communities, once such an important provider of staple food for the cities, may be earning as little as a quarter of their incomes from agriculture (the importance of these statistics depends of course on how much of their produce they would expect to sell in local and other markets) (Plant 1998; Psacharopoulos and Patrinos 1994).

There is also abundant evidence of growing indigenous participation in distant labour migrations, such as the mass movements from southern to northern Mexico, the international migrations from Bolivia to Argentina, or Guatemala through Mexico to the USA, and others (Gómez and Klein 1993). Indigenous growing poverty in the cities, as mentioned above, has been amply documented.

There are also some potentially positive aspects to these trends. Indigenous entrepreneurship is growing, in various forms of transport and other markets. Some classically entrepreneurial indigenous peoples, such as the Guatemalan K'iche, are continually trying to penetrate new markets and break down the discriminatory obstacles to their wider market participation.

Land and territorial claims: experience of the 1990s

In the 1990s, the pendulum has been swaying in different directions. On paper, indigenous peoples in the tropical lowlands have been the 'winners' of the more recent titling laws and programmes, and the *campesinos indígenas* often the 'losers', if territory has been the issue at stake. Bolivia, Brazil, Colombia, Ecuador and Peru all have strong commitments to title many millions of hectares in the names of indigenous communities. In practice, rather little has happened to render this indigenous land ownership effective, and to sort out conflicting claims of land ownership and possessions between indigenous peoples and third-party colonists. Bolivia appears furthest down the road in doing this, since a major programme to title over 10 million hectares of indigenous lands got under way in 1998.[12] Peru has had an effective programme in some regions, indigenous organisations such as the Ashaninka often taking the lead in titling their own land areas with external support (Garcia Hierro, Hvalkof and Gray 1998). Colombia's titling programmes look good on paper, though indigenous land security has been completely undermined by the civil conflict in parts of the Amazon.

In the highlands by contrast, the juridical figure of the *Comunidad Indígena* has been under attack in the 1990s. The special protection against market forces for indigenous agrarian communities – the famous 'four Is' of *inalienable, indivisible, imprescriptible* and *inembargable*, has been questioned by governments and the international financial institutions, who see these as a drain on agricultural efficiency. Seeing lack of market integration rather than market forces as the problem, these agencies tend to see individual and freely disposable land titles as the passport to credit and progress, and a fast track out of indigenous poverty. Mexico, Peru and Ecuador have all to some extent followed this route, though with some reconsideration following widespread indigenous opposition to liberalising land reforms. Dismantling *ejidos*, indigenous or peasant communities is seen as a voluntary process, requiring the approval or a certain percentage of indigenous assembly members before land sales can occur.

Indigenous land rights have generally been safeguarded in the new constitutions. Moreover, special laws concerning the titling of indigenous lands have also been adopted in some countries. Attention is being given to indigenous control over renewable, and occasionally non-renewable, resources within their land and territorial areas.

Consistent with the constitutional trends, most national secondary legislation continues to promote collective land titling for indigenous peoples. In some countries, rather than have laws of national coverage, governments have dealt with specific geographical areas of the country or with specific ethnic groups. This has been the case, in one way or another, of Bolivia, Ecuador, Panama and Peru. In Bolivia and Ecuador, presidential or other decrees at first stipulated the titling of specific indigenous lands, in the early 1990s. In Panama, the rights of different indigenous groups have continued to be dealt with under separate legislation. And in Peru, while some agrarian legislation has been of national coverage, one land titling law was adopted specifically for coastal regions where commercial agriculture is most in evidence. Bolivia's 1996 land reform law actually provides for different land tenure regimes for different parts of the country, as well as differentiating by type of agriculture and by the ethnic identity of different farmers.

A feature of the past decade has been the willingness of governments to enter into direct negotiations with indigenous peoples' organisations, concerning land and territorial rights among other issues. Some of the major titling initiatives in the tropical lowlands have come in response to demonstrations and protests by indigenous organisations, as in the case of Bolivia and Ecuador in the early 1990s. More recently, indigenous land rights have been part of the agenda of peace processes in the countries that have been affected to some degree by armed conflict.

The recognition of indigenous ownership of sometimes-vast territorial areas has raised complex issues of control over, and management of, strategic natural resources. Many Latin American governments had awarded large timber concessions within areas of traditional indigenous habitation. Moreover, the past decade has seen a huge increase in energy development, particularly hydrocarbons, in tropical Latin America. There has been substantial international investment in the oil and gas potential of Brazil, Bolivia, Colombia, Ecuador and Peru, among other countries. This has led to prolonged negotiations between indigenous peoples and governments concerning control over resource and energy development, including profit-sharing arrangements.

Furthermore, environmental concerns have caused governments to establish ministries or other agencies for the environmental, sometimes assuming responsibilities for the titling and management of forest lands. National parks, protected areas and biosphere reserves have been widely created – at times with the assistance of the multilateral development banks – often overlapping the areas of indigenous habitation. At times such areas have been created within the territorial areas already titled to indigenous communities, creating overlapping land claims and potential conflict.

Despite the law reforms, there have been few major programmes to title and demarcate the lands claimed by indigenous peoples. Under the ILO's Convention No. 169, governments are obliged to take the necessary steps not only to identify the lands which indigenous peoples traditionally occupy, but also to guarantee effective protection of their rights of ownership and possession. Moreover, governments shall take measures to prevent the unauthorised intrusion upon, or use of, the lands of indigenous peoples.

A serious problem has been the presence of non-indigenous settlers in the lands adjudicated to indigenous peoples. Where title had been issued to indigenous peoples over large and contiguous territorial areas, a major challenge has been to sort out the competing claims to the land, and to determine the priorities for granting compensation to either indigenous or non-indigenous land occupants.

The concept of special land rights for non-indigenous ethnic groups has been pioneered in Colombia, where since the mid-1990s, there has been an active INCORA programme to title Afro-Colombian lands in the Pacific (INCORA 1998; Hoffman 1999). The programme has its origins in the demands of the Afro-Colombian communities protesting against plans for a large timber concession within their traditional habitat. Their organisation ACIA pressed successfully for an 800,000 hectare Area of Special Management, with black participation in natural resource management including control and surveillance of the zone. This can be seen as the first step towards general recognition of collective territorial rights. After the enactment of Law 70 of 1993 – which recognised the right to collective land titles for black communities in select environmental regions including the Pacific – a significant programme of collective titling was undertaken by the Colombian land reform agency INCORA. Some 23 titles had been issued altogether by January 1999, covering 1.2 million hectares and benefiting some 13,000 families.

An important feature of the past decade has been the growing capacity of indigenous peoples to carry out their own land demarcation and titling programmes. Backed by extensive international funding and technical support, organisations have developed considerable technical expertise to back up their undisputed knowledge of terrain and boundaries. And this indigenous involvement has had an impact beyond the titling process itself, often leading to greater participation in the political process in the local regions concerned. As a result of these efforts, indigenous and also black peoples' organisations have now elaborated their own proposals for local development.

Indigenous rights and development: participatory mechanisms at different levels

In some countries, indigenous peoples are becoming a significant force in national development policies. An obvious example is Ecuador, the Andean country with the strongest unified indigenous movement representing highland and lowland regions. CONAIE has always taken a truly national perspective on development issues, successfully challenging a new privatising land reform bill in 1994, and conducting a series of indigenous mobilisations against national economic policies. Moreover, Ecuador probably has the most developed structures for representing indigenous interests before national legislative and planning bodies. After an unsuccessful experience with a national office and then secretariat of indigenous affairs, Ecuador created its National Planning Council of Indigenous and Black Peoples (CONPLADEIN, later replaced by CODENPE) in 1997. Headed by an indigenous person with ministerial rank, this had the objectives of implementing the concept of a multicultural nation in all aspects including national, regional and local development planning. Ecuador's Indigenous Parliament is also highly active. It is a moot point whether these participatory structures have played any role in raising the level of indigenous consciousness on national economic development concerns.

Guatemala represents a different approach. Government proposals to create an official entity for indigenous affairs met with little interest from the rapidly growing indigenous organisations after the mid-1990s. The Congressional Commission of Indigenous Affairs has been a weak entity, serving the ruling party's interests. The government-sponsored Indigenous Development Fund (FODIGUA) has similarly displayed little dynamism or vision, mainly funding micro-level projects at the community level. But the 1995 Indigenous Accord under Guatemala's peace process established a unique mechanism of the *Comisiones Paritarias* (Joint Commissions), empowered to negotiate a series of laws and administrative reforms with the government in order to give effect to the multiple commitments of the Peace Accords. The Indigenous Accord also provides in the longer term for a series of participatory mechanisms at local, regional and national levels. Their structure and modus operandi is to be defined by one of the Joint Commissions.

In Bolivia, the other country with a majority indigenous population, the popular participation process after 1994 promised much. Decentralisation, together with new fiscal arrangements, offered the prospect of more involvement by indigenous institutions, organised on their own terms, in municipal management and planning. Indigenous Municipal Districts were created as a new administrative entity to allow more indigenous participation in municipal affairs. Yet the structure could also lend itself to a vertical approach, with the government using the new structures for patronage and the channelling of funds. In effect, the Bolivian government has aimed to implement its indigenous development policies through its Vice Ministry of Indigenous Affairs (VAIPO), tapping international resources for its programmes. Though an indigenous parliament exists, and VAIPO has its consultative group on indigenous affairs, there is no evidence that broader development policies are being concerted with indigenous organisations. The exception is the programme for the ordering and titling of *Tierras Comunitarias de Origen* (TCOs) in Eastern Bolivia, for which there appears to be a degree of concertation between VAIPO, the land reform agency INRA, and the CIDOB organisation of lowland indigenous peoples.

Panama has exemplified a more localised approach to indigenous development, based on territorial autonomy. Despite the obvious strength of the Kuna and Ngobe-Bugle indigenous peoples, and the favourable autonomy arrangements within the *comarcas*, there has been no national legislation on indigenous issues. Each of the *comarcas* is established by separate law, and contains its own by-laws. Quite recently however, new structures were established to address the national perspectives of indigenous development. A National Council for Indigenous Development was created by the Presidency of the Republic in January 2000. It remains to be seen how effective the new structure will be, in placing indigenous concerns on national economic and social agendas (IGWIA 2000).

The indigenous economy and development: future challenges

Visions of an indigenous economy can be unduly romantic, still applying outdated concepts of the enclosed corporate community. Indigenous production systems can be widely portrayed as subsistence-oriented. In practice, indigenous peoples have always participated extensively in national markets, usually as the providers of staple food for the cities. The more creative are now trying to penetrate niche international markets, through tropical products, wood products, or even competing with commercial producers through their own coffee cooperatives. Latin America's indigenous cannot yet compete with the Canadian Dene, running their own airline. But there is no reason to believe they wish to be consigned to a traditional subsistence economy.

Thus the important thing is to distinguish between the traditional aspects of resource management, and indigenous participation in the wider economy. One needs also to determine the circumstances in which it makes sense to target finance specifically at indigenous peoples.

The entry point for targeted assistance should arguably be the existence of historically based discrimination, and the need to combat it. Discrimination is evident in land access, access to financial institutions, participation in labour markets, and usually access to public services. There is also discrimination against indigenous languages and communications, spirituality and sometimes dress. Affirmative action measures to combat such discrimination are always likely to prove controversial, given the perceptions of reverse discrimination; and also the risk that, in communities or regions where the indigenous and non-indigenous landless or peasantry may be equally resource poor, any ethnic favouritism can increase social polarisation. Where local or regional development is concerned it makes more sense to target support at the geographical areas where poverty is greatest (where there is likely to be a high incidence of indigenous population) rather than on the specific grounds of ethnic affiliation. But where indigenous poverty is to be found alongside non-indigenous affluence, as can be the case in areas of settler colonisation and also some urban areas, ethnic targeting of assistance can make more practical sense.

In the lowlands there are now considerable opportunities for targeted assistance to title indigenous lands, to ensure careful demarcation and land ordering, and to help these communities devise long-term strategies of economic management. Little funding has so far been available for the land ordering and titling programmes. And if the opportunities are not taken, colonists and commercial entrepreneurs will continue to move in and consolidate their situation. Indigenous organisations also need to be further empowered to undertake technical work, and to negotiate with the energy sector multinationals. A state presence is also needed, to monitor any agreements. These seem to be the classic areas where indigenous peoples' development plans, broken up into specific areas, are justified.

Outside the tropical lowlands, the nature of the challenges and opportunities for promoting indigenous development are clearly different. When indigenous communities do not control (or have much chance of controlling in the foreseeable future) a large and contiguous territorial area on which to base their cultural integrity and development, then it makes little sense to perceive of an indigenous economy or development independently from the wider economy and society.

One problem has been the extreme positions taken by policy-makers, on either the desirability of indigenous market participation or the obstacles to it. One position – first evident in nineteenth century liberalism, and second in the liberal economic thought of recent years – has aimed to stimulate market participation by removing any restrictions on the free operation of indigenous land markets. The other extreme has put all its emphasis on protection, aiming to protect indigenous peoples from the market forces that could lead to pernicious encroachment on their traditional lands and lifestyles.

The reality is that most of Latin America's indigenous communities have generally sought a high degree of *external* market participation, while maintaining *internal* land tenure arrangements that can act as a defensive mechanism against encroachment by outsiders. External participation has been in labour markets and trading networks, and in many countries indigenous peasant farmers have also provided much of the staple food supply for urban populations. Internally, their land use and production arrangements can be quite complex. There can be widespread perceptions that indigenous communities have based their economy on collective forms of production, organised through communal work institutions rooted in archaic traditions. Yet these perceptions – and the policy implications deriving from them – are gradually being dispelled, as more is known about the reality of indigenous agrarian systems. In the mid-1970s for example, the World Bank's land reform policy had recommended that communal tenure systems be abandoned in favour of freehold titles and the subdivision of the commons. In contrast, a recent paper by the World Bank's leading land tenure specialists questions these earlier assumptions, now recognising that communal tenure systems can be more cost-effective than formal title. Recent proposals are to award property rights to communities, which then decide on the most suitable tenure arrangements (Deininger and Binswanger 1999).

In practice, virtually no indigenous societies in Latin America base their production on communal labour. Whether in peasant-based indigenous societies adapted to the highland ecologies, or in lowland horticulturist and extractivist communities, production tends to be planned and executed by individual family units. Each family owns its produce on an individual basis, and may manage its own marketing. In the Andean and Central American highlands, indigenous communities have internally subdivided their lands into individually owned plots, registered and affirmed by the Community Councils. Indeed consolidating these units through decentralised titling arrangements, using traditional institutions and practices, makes eminent sense on economic, social and cultural grounds. It can prove one of the most effective ways of giving practical meaning to the concept of local autonomy.

Can useful distinctions be drawn between local, regional and national dimensions of indigenous and state relations, in the search for more genuinely multi-ethnic but also more equitable societies? Does this depend on the indigenous percentage of the overall population? On patterns of indigenous participation in the economy, including past and present discrimination? On the themes addressed? Or on the ideological composition and approaches of the indigenous pressure groups, for example between the *culturalista* and *popular* indigenous tendencies?

Ideally, the multi-ethnic challenge should be seen as a truly national reform agenda. It has its more and less radical interpretations, on an expanding scale. Indigenous peoples may have some very localised short-term demands. Panama's *comarcas* and their authorities might be able to manage their own affairs quite effectively, with limited state input. The same could be said for some of the Amazon territorial entities, as long as the state fulfils its duty of negotiating fair terms with multinationals, and providing some support to indigenous enterprises as applicable. These seem to be the more classic examples of indigenous self-development.

At the other end of the spectrum is the paradigmatic peace process in Guatemala. There, because of the historical legacy (both economic and social discrimination and the brutal legacy of the civil conflict with the destruction of traditional institutions), as well as demographic factors (the sharing of physical space between ethnic groups, the huge Mayan presence in Guatemala City), almost nothing can be treated as a local issue. A fascinating aspect of Guatemala's Indigenous Agreement is that, although heavily influenced by such international indigenous rights instruments as the ILO's Convention 169, it goes way beyond them. It is also an exploratory exercise in novel nation-building, suggesting that a new concept of the nation can be constructed on Guatemala's rich cultural legacy. Potentially, the further development of the peace process could lead to a fundamental rethinking of all institutions. Bilingual intercultural education would be complex in a small country of so many languages, but it should certainly involve the rewriting of the national curriculum. Political participation mechanisms could lead to some remarkable new institutions of representative democracy. But the real crunch will always be forms of economic opportunity for the country's indigenous peoples, on or off the land. And these issues can only be tackled at the national level.

Yet looking through the continent, it is difficult to detect anything like a consensus 'indigenous view' on the agrarian question in today's economic environment. Finding the balance between the multiple land use restrictions of the agrarian socialist era (themselves a restriction on indigenous autonomy) and the outright attack on the indigenous community is the conceptual challenge for the future. This in itself will not solve the massive problems of extreme poverty now facing indigenous communities in the Central American and Andean highlands. The indigenous community, under present patterns of land shortage and environmental erosion, remains more of a social construct than an economically viable entity. It is important to consolidate these communities in all aspects, reinforcing their political structures and capacities for conflict resolution, because these strengthen the cultural identity of indigenous peoples as well as providing economic survival strategies of last resort. But the consolidation of genuinely multicultural and multi-ethnic societies must have a broader economic underpinning, and this has to reach out beyond the community level. Decisions have to be taken at the national level, with the active involvement of the indigenous parliaments, development councils and other participatory structures that are now being set up throughout the continent. The exact degree of preferential treatment and market access is beyond the scope of this chapter. It could be mass investments in bilingual education, quotas in education and public service, seed money for indigenous enterprises, preferential pricing policies, support for eco-tourism and many other options. But if the economic basis of discrimination is not tackled head on, Latin America's early experiments in multiculturalism may be in for a rocky ride.

Notes

1. National Law of the Agrarian Reform Service, Law No. 1715, 18 October 1996.
2. Amazonian titles for indigenous peoples in Ecuador have been issued by decree without any specific legal framework. The substantive agrarian legislation is the 1994 Law of Agrarian Development, which provides that state land can be adjudicated free of charge to indigenous and Afro-Ecuadorian peoples, and also to *montubias* (coastal peasants) that have held such lands in their ancestral possession.
3. Colombia's 1991 Constitution provides for ample recognition of indigenous land rights, as well as special land rights for Afro-Colombian Pacific and riverine communities. Law 160 of 1994 is the main legal instrument for agrarian law and policy. It provides for amplification of existing indigenous *resguardos*, including those of colonial origin, in accordance with need.
4. Ecuador's 1994 Law of Agrarian Development, while respecting indigenous forms of ownership, permits the *comunas* to change their form of land use through parcelling or conversion into a cooperative or other juridical personality.
5. Mexico's new Agrarian Law was adopted in early 1992, shortly after liberalising reforms to Article 27 of the Mexican Constitution had spelled an effective end to redistributive land reforms. The Agrarian Law sets out the procedures under which the tenurial status of either the *ejidos* or the *comunidades indígenas* can be altered upon a majority vote by their members.
6. Law No. 26505 of 1995, commonly known as the *Ley de Tierras* or Lands Law, specifies the conditions under which various categories of land can be opened up to the market, or sold by the state to private investors. In *sierra* and *selva* areas, where the Peasant and Native Communities for peoples of indigenous extraction are located, any rental, sale or mortgaging of communal lands requires the vote of two-thirds of the members of the community's general assembly.
7. Agreement on the Identity and Rights of Indigenous Peoples, signed between the government of Guatemala and the URNG, Mexico City, 31 March 1995.
8. These are two of the six functional criteria identified by the World Bank, for example, in its Operational Directive 4.20 on indigenous peoples.
9. Cited in Roque Roldan Ortega, 'La Cuestión Indígena en Colombia', unpublished manuscript prepared for International Labour Organisation, Bogotá, September 1997.
10. *Report of the Committee of Experts on the Application of Conventions and Recommendations*, Report 111 (Part 1A), International Labour Conference, 87th Session, 1999.
11. See Chapter 9 by Shelton Davis, referring also to earlier World Bank studies on indigenous poverty and development.
12. With support from the Danish Development Agency (DANIDA), the government of Bolivia has embarked on a major programme to title at least 16 *Tierras Comunitarias de Orígen* (Original Community Land areas), covering several millions of hectares, in the eastern lowlands. The National Agrarian Reform Agency (INRA) has had responsibility for the technical aspects of land ordering and titling, while the government agency responsible for indigenous affairs (VAIPO) has been given the task of determining the socio-economic and spatial needs of indigenous communities. Though the methodologies have been criticised quite extensively by indigenous organisations, it was estimated that several of the communities would receive their titles in the course of the year 2000. For more information see Plant and Hvalkof 2001. For a critical account, see: *Titulación de Tierras Indígenas:*

un balance a dos años de la promulgación de la Ley INRA, Revista de Debate Social y Jurídico, Jan–April 1999, No. 6, Centro de Estudios Jurídicos e Investigación Social, Santa Cruz, Bolivia.

References

Deininger, Klaus and Hans Binswanger (1999), 'The Evolution of the World Bank's Land Policy: Principles, Experience and Future Challenges', *The World Bank Research Observer*, Vol.14 (2), August.

Garcia Hierro, Pedro, Soren Hvalkof and Andrew Gray (1998), *Liberation through Land Rights in the Peruvian Amazon*, International Work Group for Indigenous Affairs (IWGIA), Document No. 90 (Copenhagen).

Gnerre, Maurizio (1990), 'Indigenous Peoples in Latin America', International Fund for Agricultural Development (Rome), (Working Paper No. 20 prepared for IFAD report on The State of World Poverty).

Gómez, Sergio and Emilio Klein (eds) (1993), *Los Pobres del Campo: el Trabajador Eventual*, FLACSO/PREALC (Santiago).

Hoffman, Odile (1999), 'Titling Collective Lands of the Black Communities in Colombia, between Innovation and Tradition' in Willem Assies, Gemma van der Haar and Andre Hoekama (eds), *The Challenge of Diversity: Indigenous Peoples and Reform of the State in Latin America*, Thela Thesis (Amsterdam), pp.123–36.

IGWA (2000), *The Indigenous World, 1999–2000*, IGWIA (Copenhagen).

INCORA (1998), *Tierras de las Comunidades Negras*, Instituto Colombiano de Reforma Agraria (Bogotá).

Plant, Roger (1998), *Issues in Indigenous Poverty and Development*, Technical Study, Inter-American Development Bank (Washington DC), December.

—— and Soren Hvalkof (2001), *Land Titling and Indigenous Peoples*, Inter-American Development Bank (Washington DC).

Psacharopoulos, George and Harry Patrinos (1994), *Indigenous People and Poverty in Latin America*, World Bank (Washington DC).

Report of the Committee of Experts on the Application of Conventions and Recommendations (1999), Report 111 (Part 1A), International Labour Conference, 87th Session.

Roldan, Ortega Roque (1997), 'La Cuestión Indígena en Colombia', unpublished manuscript prepared for International Labour Organisation (Bogotá), September.

Titulación de Tierras Indígenas: un balance a dos años de la promulgación de la Ley INRA, Revista de Debate Social y Jurídico, January–April 1999, No.6, Centro de Estudios Jurídicos e Investigación Social (Santa Cruz, Bolivia).

9
Indigenous Peoples, Poverty and Participatory Development: The Experience of the World Bank in Latin America[1]

Shelton H. Davis

Introduction

Indigenous peoples have historically been the poorest and most excluded social sectors in Latin America. They have not only faced acute discrimination in terms of their basic rights to their ancestral property, languages, cultures and forms of governance, but also in terms of access to basic social services (education, health and nutrition, water and sanitation, housing, and so on) and the essential material conditions for a satisfying life. These conditions of extreme poverty and material deprivation – what might be best described as a denial of the fundamental social citizenship rights of indigenous peoples – are widespread throughout Latin America and have recently come to the attention of international development agencies, such as the World Bank, the Inter-American Development Bank and the various bilateral development agencies. The denial of the basic social citizenship rights of indigenous peoples have also been a growing concern of scholars, journalists and others concerned with social conditions in Latin America.[2]

In the aftermath of the national protests and aborted military coup that led to the resignation of Ecuadorian president Jamil Mahaud in January 2000, for example, the *Washington Post* carried an article entitled 'Indians Showed Political Muscle in Ouster of Ecuadorian Leader'. While the article focused upon the increasing power of the indigenous movement to influence national politics in Ecuador, it also highlighted the increasing economic poverty and social marginalisation of that sector of the population. Noting that over 90 per cent of the country's 12.4 million people had some Indian blood, it stated that the 10 per cent of the population that are white control over 50 per cent of the nation's wealth. Annual per capita income in Ecuador, according to the *Washington Post*, stood at $1600, but among Indians it is had stagnated at about $250. 'Indians generally', the article stated, 'inhabit Ecuador's highlands, the least developed area of the country, with the fewest enterprises, the lowest level of public services and the deepest sense of alienation.'[3] *New York Times* reporter Larry Rohter writing from the highland town of Latacunga in the aftermath of the late January political changes made similar observations. Rohter noted that the one-third of the Ecuadorian population that is Indian and which resides mainly in the rural highlands are treated as 'second class citizens, deprived of economic and educational opportunities, with their languages and cultures ridiculed for even longer than Ecuador has been a nation'. The economic crisis of the late 1990s has been particularly damaging for the indigenous population. Between 1998 and 2000 inflation rates rose to 60 per cent, the country's currency lost 67 per cent of its value against the dollar in 1999 and another 20 per cent during the month of January 2000. One expert was cited as claiming that during the 1990s a 'process of pauperisation' had occurred in the countryside that had particularly affected the well-being of the indigenous population. Indian leaders, interviewed by Rohter in the Latacunga marketplace, complained that their 'villages were the last to receive electricity, water, telephones, and sewers', that the terms of trade for their products (mainly potatoes and other agricultural commodities) had worsened. They also noted that, as a result of the government's austerity measures, successive administrations had reduced support for bilingual education in Quechua and other indigenous languages.[4]

At least two investigations carried out by the World Bank in the months previous to the January 2000 protests corroborated in much more systematic fashion these journalistic accounts of increasing social and economic deprivation among Ecuador's large indigenous population. The first was a qualitative study called *Consultations with the Poor in Ecuador*, elaborated in preparation for the World Development Report 2000 and carried out by a team of Ecuadorian social researchers contracted by the Poverty Reduction and Economic Management Department at the World Bank and released in August 1999. The report noted that studies conducted by the World Bank in 1995 and the United Nations Development Programme in 1996 demonstrated a clear tendency towards an increase of the impoverished population in both rural and urban areas of Ecuador. They also indicated that Ecuador has one of the highest indices of wealth concentration in Latin America, that areas of high concentration of poverty are correlated with areas inhabited by indigenous and Afro-Ecuadorian populations, and that growing frustration among the poor population has led to increased juvenile delinquency, gangs and urban violence. Based upon household interviews with poor men and women, as well as a series of focus group discussions with local officials and organisations working with the rural and urban poor, the report found increasing pauperisation and a decline in well-being as a result of the country's persistent financial, economic and political crises. It also encountered a lack of faith in the efficiency of government institutions and services, and general malaise among the poor population in terms of the capacity of the state to respond to the country's crisis and to provide basic health, educational and other social services.[5]

A second report, prepared in November 1999 by the Human and Social Development Group of the World Bank's Latin America and Caribbean Region, was entitled *Crisis, Poverty and Social Services in Ecuador*. The report noted that Ecuador had entered its current crisis with some of the worst inequalities and lowest per capita income in the Latin America region. Ecuador's already high levels of poverty and income inequality have worsened in recent years; the number of poor increased by almost 19 per cent between 1995 and 1998. Over the same period, the Gini coefficient of income inequality increased from 0.54 to 0.58 and the bottom fifth of the population's share of total consumption decreased from 5.3 to 4.3 per cent. Poverty is particularly extreme in rural areas, among the indigenous population and among children, especially those who live in extended households. Particularly troublesome, according to the November 1999 report, were the effects of both natural disasters (El Niño phenomena) and the 'unprecedented macroeconomic crisis' which have increased the vulnerability of the poor population, especially pregnant women and children. Even more worrying was the government's incapacity to respond to the crisis. As a result of shrinking public resources, the report forecasted that social sector expenditures in 1999 would decline by 15 per cent in health and 21 per cent in education from what they had been in 1998. 'The Government', the report concluded,

faces stark choices and cruel trade-offs. Poverty and inequality have increased since 1995 and continue to worsen. In the short-term, the poor and vulnerable groups require improved protection from declining incomes. In the medium-term, both social protection and basic social services need strengthening. If inequality and poverty are to decline in the future, the poor will require significantly improved access to basic health and education services of higher quality.[6]

While the Ecuadorian situation is particularly dramatic as a result of the continuing economic and financial crisis, the situation of poverty is generalised among indigenous peoples throughout Latin America. Across the region, indigenous peoples live in conditions of extreme poverty, are systematically excluded from access to basic social services, and are not being provided with the conditions to take advantage of the new opportunities provided by globalisation and the opening up of their respective national economies. This chapter examines some recent studies of indigenous poverty in Latin America, the new models of 'participatory development' being introduced in response, some of the political obstacles in the way of implementing these models, and a number of the future challenges posed in the struggle against indigenous poverty. While the chapter draws heavily upon the experience of the World Bank, some of the comments made may also reflect those of other international agencies involved in promoting the social and economic rights of indigenous peoples in Latin America.[7]

Indigenous peoples, poverty and social capital

In 1994, two World Bank economists, George Psacharopoulos and Harry Patrinos, published a study entitled *Indigenous People and Poverty in Latin America: An Empirical Analysis*.[8] The study, based upon an analysis of household survey data from four countries (Bolivia, Guatemala, Mexico and Peru), found that indigenous people were more likely than any other social group of a country's population to be poor. A person was considered to be 'poor' in the Psacharopoulos and Patrinos study if his or her income was less than $2 per day. While the incidence of poverty is high throughout Latin America, it was found to be particularly severe and deep among indigenous families. This was the case whether they lived in remote rural areas or on the fringes of the region's growing cities, and no matter how they were identified (by language, self-identification, place of residence, and so on). In Bolivia, where data was derived from an urban household survey, more than half of the sampled population (52.6 per cent) was poor, but nearly two-thirds (64.3 per cent) of the indigenous population was poor. In Guatemala, over 65.6 per cent of the sampled population was poor compared with 86.6 per cent of the indigenous population. In Peru, 79.0 per cent of the indigenous population was poor as compared to 49.7 per cent of the non-indigenous population; while in Mexico 80.6 per cent of the indigenous population was poor as compared to only 17.9 per cent of the non-indigenous population.[9]

These poverty statistics were correlated with a striking lack of access to essential social services. For example, in Peru, indigenous people were more likely to become ill than non-indigenous people, but much less likely to have access to or consult a physician. Perhaps as a result of poor initial health conditions or neglected treatment, the duration and severity of illness were greater among the indigenous population. The proportion of indigenous people hospitalised in Peru was almost twice that of the Spanish-speaking population. Although the average cost of both hospitalisation and medicine was less for indigenous people, only 57 per cent of indigenous people purchased medicine for their illnesses, as compared to 81 per cent of the non-indigenous population. The Psacharopoulos and Patrinos study also indicated that a strong correlation exists between lack of schooling, being indigenous and being poor. The indigenous population possesses considerably less schooling at all levels from primary education through secondary school and universities. The comparative statistics on literacy and schooling between indigenous and non-indigenous persons are particularly revealing. In Guatemala, the majority of indigenous people (most of them speakers of Mayan languages in their homes) have no formal education and of those who do, the majority have only primary education. On average, indigenous people have only 1.3 years of schooling and only 40 per cent are literate. Mayan-speaking children, if they do attend school, are more likely to repeat grades at the primary level and are more likely to drop out of school altogether. In Bolivia, the schooling levels of indigenous individuals are approximately three years less, on average, than those for non-indigenous individuals. The differences are even greater for indigenous girls, suggesting that they are the most disadvantaged group in Bolivian society. In Peru, non-indigenous individuals have 20 per cent more education than do indigenous individuals. Not only is the indigenous population less educated and less literate than the Spanish-speaking population, but it also lags behind in terms of training. Differences in educational levels of indigenous and non-indigenous individuals are substantial. Only 40 per cent of indigenous heads-of-households have education in excess of primary schooling. In contrast, 41 per cent of Spanish-speaking heads-of-households have some secondary school education, and 22 per cent have some post-secondary education. However, only 6 per cent of indigenous heads-of-households have some post-secondary education. Finally, in Mexico, access to formal education for Indians has expanded in recent years but educational levels remain significantly higher in areas with non-indigenous as compared to indigenous populations. Illiteracy continues to be a serious problem in some federal states, especially those such as Chiapas that have relatively large numbers of indigenous inhabitants. The rate of illiteracy increases for both males and females as the percentages of indigenous population rises. The disparity, however, is greatest in the female sub-sample where the illiteracy rate is more than four times greater in the 'high' indigenous *municipio* category than in the 'low' one. In addition, the gender disparity in the illiteracy rate increases as the indigenous percentage of *municipios* increases. Overall, school enrolment rates are much higher in non-indigenous areas than in indigenous ones.[10]

Beyond implications for the economic welfare of the indigenous individuals and families involved, the Psacharopoulos and Patrinos study argued that these statistics indicated a series of lost opportunities for the national economies in terms of the development and use of these countries' human capital. Economic and educational policy-makers, the authors concluded, could help indigenous people to improve their general household incomes and economic opportunities by strengthening their human capital. Policies to reduce the educational gaps between indigenous and non-indigenous persons, such as bilingual education programmes that are demonstrated to decrease significantly school drop-out and grade repetition rates and to improve student achievement, could make a large dent in earnings potential and lead to a considerable decline in poverty among indigenous peoples. They could also contribute to the wider productive performance of the region's national economies and lower the social tensions in their polities.[11]

Since the publication of the Psacharopoulos and Patrinos study, the World Bank has financed several other studies that deepen our understanding of the nature and scope of indigenous poverty in Latin America. One of these studies was a national poverty assessment in Peru, which compared household survey data on income, consumption and access to human services among poor Peruvian families (both urban and rural and disaggregated by region) from 1994 and 1997. This was a period in which there was relatively robust economic growth in Peru, and in which poverty rates – especially severe consumption poverty – showed a decline from 19 to 15 per cent. Yet poverty among speakers of indigenous languages, and especially in the sierra and Amazon regions, was found to have increased rather than decreased during this period. The Peru poverty assessment found that the native-language speaking, indigenous population was 29 per cent more likely to be poor than the Spanish-speaking population in 1997, as compared to 24 per cent in 1994. School attendance figures for children from native-language speaking families were significantly below the national average, and children from indigenous families were found to be more than twice as likely to be malnourished as children from non-indigenous families. In 1997, nearly 60 per cent of the extreme poor in Peru were native language speakers. In other words the native-speaking Peruvian population had been 'left behind' by the economic growth and welfare changes that had taken place in the country between 1994 and 1997.[12] A second study carried out in Panama (a relatively high per-capita income country) in 1997 found that, while comprising only 8 per cent of the country's total population, indigenous peoples made up 19 per cent of the country's poor and 35 per cent of the extreme poor. Poverty rates, which in some indigenous areas were as high as 95 per cent, were particularly severe among the Ngobe-Bugle (the largest indigenous group in Panama), followed by the Embera-Wounan, and the Kuna. They were also correlated with high malnutrition rates among children, and lack of access to basic services such as schools, health clinics, water and sanitation, electricity and other basic services.[13]

As part of the Panama poverty assessment, a special survey called the Social Capital Qualitative Survey (SCQS) was carried out in order to identify and measure the social capital among both rural and urban poor communities. Following the approach of political scientist Robert Putnam, social capital was defined in the SCQS as 'features of social organisation such as trust, norms and networks, that can improve the efficiency of society by facilitating coordinated action'. One of the major findings of this study was that 'social capital' (as measured by the presence of various forms of community organisations and associations, both traditional and modern) was much higher in rural indigenous communities than in other poor communities, whether they were rural or urban. This strong tendency to form community associations, the report argued, was one of the major assets of the indigenous communities. This could serve as a critical factor in combating poverty among indigenous peoples if combined with sound social policies and a willingness of government to work with indigenous organisations and communities to raise their incomes and productive capacities.[14]

In summary, there is nothing inevitable about the poverty faced by indigenous peoples. Large-scale investments in education targeted at indigenous people and tailored to their specific linguistic and cultural characteristics could play a significant role in equalising the income-generating characteristics of indigenous and non-indigenous populations and improve their productive success in both market and non-market activities. At the same time, investments in the strengthening of the social capital of indigenous organisations and communities could play an important role in revitalising what have become moribund rural economies. The combination of increased investments in human and social capital, based upon new participatory methodologies and a respect for indigenous cultures and identities, lies at the heart of current strategies to combat poverty among indigenous peoples. In the remainder of this chapter, I shall highlight some of the lessons learned by the World Bank in promoting such indigenous development in Latin America. At the same time, I shall describe some of the obstacles, many of them political in nature, in the way of such development, and the challenges that the World Bank and other multilateral institutions face in their future operational activities and investments in attempting to alleviate poverty and promote economic development among the region's large indigenous population.

Participatory approaches to indigenous development

Perhaps one of the major lessons of the past decade is the recognition on the part of international development agencies that indigenous peoples need to be provided with the enabling conditions, technical skills and financial resources to participate actively in the planning and implementation of their own development. This idea of indigenous or 'self-development', sometimes referred to as 'ethno-development' or 'development with identity', is recognised in and is a central tenet of the International Labour Organisation (ILO) Convention 169 concerning Indigenous and Tribal Peoples in Independent Countries. Article 7 of ILO Convention 169, for example, states that 'the peoples concerned shall have the right to decide their own priorities for the process of development as it affects their lives, beliefs, institutions and spiritual well-being and the lands they occupy or otherwise use, and to exercise control, to the extent possible, over their own economic, social and cultural development'. The same article goes on to state that, 'In addition, they shall participate in the formulation, implementation and evaluation of plans and programmes for national and regional development which may affect them directly.'[15]

When the World Bank drafted its Indigenous Peoples Policy in the early 1990s (Operational Directive 4.20, issued in September 1991), it had in mind these provisions of the ILO Convention. The Operational Directive states that 'The Bank's policy is that the strategy for addressing the issues pertaining to indigenous peoples must be based on the *informed participation* [italics in original] of the indigenous people themselves.' Such participation, the Operational Directive goes on to state, shall include 'identifying local preferences through direct consultation, incorporation of indigenous knowledge into project approaches, and appropriate early use of experienced specialists as core activities for any project that affects indigenous peoples and their rights to natural and economic resources'.[16] Other parts of the same directive call for the preparation of Indigenous Peoples Development Plans (IPDPs) for any World Bank-financed project that affects indigenous peoples. These plans should be prepared in a 'culturally appropriate' manner and be 'based on full consideration of the options preferred by the indigenous peoples'. They should take into account 'local patterns of social organisation, religious beliefs and resource use' and 'should support production systems that are well adapted to the needs and environment of the indigenous peoples'. Mechanisms should be included in such plans for the 'participation by indigenous peoples in decision making throughout project planning, implementation and evaluation', and where indigenous peoples have their own representative organisations these should be used as 'channels for communicating local preferences'. The directive also mentions the willingness of the World Bank to provide technical assistance 'to strengthen relevant government institutions or to support development initiatives taken by indigenous peoples themselves'.[17]

Since the issuing of this policy directive, nearly 100 World Bank-financed projects have been identified as affecting indigenous peoples in the Latin America and Caribbean Region.[18] This constitutes about one-sixth of the regional project investment portfolio for the period 1992 and 1999. The vast majority of these projects are in the Environment area (many of these are Global Environmental Facility-funded projects in the biodiversity conservation area), in the Rural and Social Development fields (approximately 48.5 per cent of the identified projects), or in Human Development (approximately 30.3 per cent of identified projects in the fields of education, health, and social protection). Interestingly, some of the more conventional World Bank-financed projects in transport, electric power and energy, mining and industry no longer form a major part of the regional investment portfolio affecting indigenous peoples. This is especially the case as the private, rather than the public sector in Latin America increasingly assumes financing of these projects. The portfolio analysis also shows that the largest number of World Bank-financed projects affecting indigenous peoples are in Central America (30.9 per cent) and Bolivia, Paraguay and Peru (24.7 per cent). Somewhat smaller numbers of projects exist in Brazil (11.3 per cent), Colombia, Ecuador and Venezuela (11.3 per cent), Mexico (10.3 per cent), Argentina, Chile and Uruguay (7.2 per cent), and the Caribbean (4.1 per cent, mainly in Belize and Guyana). As for the types of interventions included in these projects, 52 per cent have been identified as having special IPDPs or strategies for indigenous peoples as required under Operational Directive 4.20. Some 17.3 per cent have some type of mechanism for indigenous peoples' participation, but no formal development plan or strategy. Another 10.2 per cent have a special indigenous component (such as a land regularisation component) financed under the project. Another 9.2 per cent are 'stand-alone' Indigenous Peoples Development Projects, and 11.2 per cent have no specified intervention on behalf of indigenous peoples.

The so-called Indigenous Peoples Development Projects are perhaps the major innovation of the World Bank's Latin American and Caribbean Region in the past few years. These projects, which are prepared and implemented directly with indigenous peoples organisations and communities, began with the preparation and financing of two natural resources management projects: a Community Forestry Project in the southern state of Oaxaca in Mexico and the Sierra Natural Resources Management Project in Peru. They were followed by the preparation and financing, in cooperation with the International Fund for Agricultural Development (IFAD), of the Ecuador Indigenous and Afro-Ecuadorian Peoples Development Project (PRODEPINE is the acronym used for the project in Ecuador). Recently, the World Bank has also approved what is called a 'Learning and Innovation Loan' (LIL) for an Indigenous and Afro-Peruvian Peoples Development Project in Peru and similar projects of this type are currently under preparation in Bolivia and Argentina and being considered in Panama and Honduras.[19] Almost all of these projects contain components or mechanisms by which small-scale productive, natural resources management, or social infrastructural projects proposed by indigenous organisations, cooperatives or community groups are financed under the project loan.

Several lessons have emerged from these early experiences in promoting and investing in indigenous people's development in Latin America. Perhaps, the most important of these is that it is nearly impossible for multilateral institutions to support the economic development of indigenous peoples at the community level without an adequate national policy framework that recognises the existence of indigenous peoples, their collective land rights, and their unique linguistic and cultural characteristics. For such initiatives to be effective, national policy frameworks also need to provide for some degree of autonomy for indigenous peoples and their organisations in terms of their participation in local development planning and decision-making.

Fortunately, as a result of the political initiatives of indigenous peoples themselves, there has been a virtual legal revolution in many Latin American countries in terms of the constitutional recognition of the rights of indigenous peoples and, in some countries, those of other traditionally excluded or marginalised ethnic groups, such as people of Afro-Latin American descent.[20] In some countries, such as Bolivia and Colombia, indigenous peoples have also benefited from more general processes of democratisation and decentralisation, with increasing amounts of central government development resources being allocated to local-level indigenous councils, municipal governments and communities for purposes of physical infrastructure and social investment in the often remote areas where indigenous peoples live.[21]

Second, the World Bank and other multilateral institutions have found it necessary to invest heavily in strengthening the capacity of indigenous organisations and communities to plan and manage their own development initiatives. The idea of such pre-investment in capacity strengthening arose from discussions that indigenist specialists at the World Bank, the Inter-American Development Bank, the International Fund for Agricultural Development and the Fondo Indígena in La Paz had with several leaders of indigenous organisations at the time of the launching of the International Decade for the World's Indigenous People in 1993. Beginning in 1994, the World Bank, in collaboration with the Fondo Indígena and Chile's National Corporation of Indigenous Development (CONADI), assisted in the organisation of the first of these training and capacity-strengthening courses with a group of Mapuche indigenous organisations in the southern city of Temuco and later with a group of Aymara and Atacameno indigenous organisations in the northern city of Arica. Subsequent training courses were held in Bolivia, Mexico, Ecuador, Nicaragua, Honduras, Argentina, Guatemala, Colombia and Panama. These courses were financed by a regional Institutional Development Fund (IDF) grant facility at the World Bank and a Swedish Government Trust Fund administered by the World Bank's Environment Department. The training courses were usually organised as partnerships between government agencies responsible for indigenous affairs or social development and indigenous organisations. The content of the courses focused upon specific themes, such as the philosophy of indigenous or ethno-development, methods of project preparation and implementation, basic accounting and project management skills, project monitoring and evaluation, forestry and natural resources management, and the legal rights of indigenous peoples. The trainers or facilitators for such courses often came from indigenous organisations themselves, and attempts were made in several cases to field-test the lessons learned in such courses through hands-on experiences in indigenous communities. To date, two evaluations have been conducted of the overall training programme, both of which indicate strong demand and reception on the part of the participating indigenous leaders and organisations, as well as important lessons learned by participating government agencies.[22]

The World Bank has financed several other studies that deepen our understanding of the nature and scope of indigenous poverty, supporting indigenous organisations on a joint footing with government agencies in the preparation, management and evaluation of project activities.[23] Perhaps, the major experience that the World Bank has had to date with such joint decision-making bodies between indigenous organisations and government agencies is represented by the Project Coordinating Committee (*Comité de Gestión*) set up during the preparation of the Ecuador Indigenous and Afro-Ecuadorian Peoples Development Project. The Coordinating Committee contained three representatives of indigenous and Afro-Ecuadorian organisations and three representatives of the Ecuadorian government, as well as an Executive Coordinator – in this case an indigenous professional – representing the Project Technical Unit. Working out the ground rules of the Project Coordinating Committee and ensuring the autonomy of the Project Technical Unit were among the major challenges of this project. Recent experience indicates that the early thought and negotiation time given to such joint decision-making procedures proved crucial in respect of the capacity of this project to withstand various national political changes that have taken place in Ecuador over the past few years.[24]

At the same time, in both this and other Indigenous Peoples Development Projects, methodologies have had to be developed for ensuring indigenous participation at the regional and local levels within countries. For example, in all of the stand-alone Indigenous Peoples Development Projects (including the forestry and natural resource management projects in Mexico and Peru), regional indigenous organisations – many of them organised as cooperatives or other types of indigenous farmer organisations – play an important role in managing funds, providing technical assistance, and mobilising local communities for purposes of economic development, natural resources management and other community-based activities. At the local level, new participatory diagnostic and planning techniques have been developed for ensuring that indigenous communities actually participate in and take ownership of the local-level development process. It has been found in other World Bank-financed projects that such community participation and ownership contribute to transparency and accountability in the use of project funds and provide the necessary social basis for the sustainability of project activities at the local level after such project funding ends.[25]

Two additional points are also worthy of mention in relation to these initial projects addressed specifically to the development priorities and needs of indigenous peoples. One is the relatively limited amount of attention placed to date on the participation of indigenous women in these World Bank-financed projects. In part, this lack of gender sensitivity in project design has resulted from the traditional gender biases of international and national development agencies and programmes, as well as from the dominance of men in the leadership positions of many of the most influential indigenous peoples organisations in Latin America. However, given the key role that indigenous women play in the transmission of indigenous languages and cultures, as well as the more limited access of indigenous girls to primary and secondary education in many Latin American countries noted above, more attention needs to be paid to gender issues in all aspects of project design, implementation and evaluation. In this regard, it is noteworthy that the recently approved Indigenous and Afro-Peruvian Peoples Development Project contains specific performance indicators for measuring the number of indigenous and Afro-Peruvian women and women's organisations that are actively involved in project implementation. The aforementioned Ecuador Indigenous and Afro-Ecuadorian Development Project is also financing a special study of how to more strategically incorporate a gender perspective into all aspects of project activities.[26]

A second and final point concerns the role that indigenous knowledge and culture has played in these projects. While the World Bank specialists who have assisted in the preparation of these projects are aware of the need to strengthen indigenous cultures and identities as part of the development process, only limited operational attention has been addressed to these issues in project design. In some projects funds have been set aside for the financing of community and inter-community cultural activities such as handicraft promotion, festivals and fairs, the identification of archaeological and historical sites, the production of audio-visual materials by indigenous artists and communication specialists, indigenous radio productions, and the like. However, much of this cultural promotion to date has been done in an ad hoc fashion and techniques have yet to be developed for assessing either the state of cultural resources and knowledge within indigenous communities or for measuring the effects of development interventions on cultural assets and identities. Much more work also needs to be done on the intellectual property rights of indigenous communities in order to ensure the protection of their cultural and historical patrimony in the face of growing commercial interests and the expanding global economy. Work in these cultural areas is fundamental if the whole notion of 'ethno-development' or 'development with identity' is to become a reality rather than merely a form of discourse for mobilising resources on behalf of indigenous organisations and communities.[27]

The politics of indigenous participation

In preparing and accompanying the implementation of these new Indigenous Peoples Development Projects, specialists in the World Bank and other multilateral institutions have become more aware of the complex political (as opposed to purely operational or technical) factors which influence attempts to promote greater participation of indigenous peoples in the development process. These political factors, in turn, affect the capacity of the World Bank and other multilateral institutions to truly influence the processes of poverty reduction in rural and indigenous areas of Latin America. As historically discriminated against and socially excluded populations, indigenous peoples have largely been at the losing end of the development process. Most national development policies and programmes tend to exploit indigenous land and labour for the enrichment of other social groups or regions and seldom take into account the cultural needs and aspirations of indigenous peoples themselves. Even when attempts are made to provide for indigenous participation and to give indigenous organisations and communities some degree of control over development programmes and resources, powerful political and economic interests can subvert the original intent of such programmes, creating in their wake social frustration, turmoil and resistance on the part of the so-called beneficiaries.

Even prior to the release of Operational Directive 4.20, when the World Bank was financing several regional development projects in lowland South America which contained so-called 'indigenous peoples components', some experiences indicated that the implementation of the new policy based upon a more participatory approach to development would face political problems and conflicts. One of the earliest examples of these problems was the history of the Indigenous Peoples Component of the Bolivia Eastern Lowlands Natural Resources Management and Agricultural Development Project, approved by the World Bank's Board of Directors in 1990.[28] The purpose of the Indigenous Peoples Component of this project was to provide land tenure security and other services to several Ayoreo and Chiquitano Indian communities in the Eastern Lowlands of Bolivia, particularly in a new area of agricultural colonisation and soy bean cultivation in the department of Santa Cruz. Originally prepared in a highly participatory manner by the regional Indian federation (CIDOB) in collaboration with a non-Indian technical assistance group (APCOB), the Indigenous Peoples Component sought to increase the capacity of the recently contacted and increasingly pauperised Ayoreo communities to determine their own development priorities. It intended to do so by strengthening the development planning capacity of a newly created regional Ayoreo organisation. From the outset, however, implementation problems were encountered. These resulted not from any technical inadequacies of the design of the Indigenous Peoples Component, but rather were due to the regional political context in which the project was embedded.[29] The precipitating event for these problems was a protest march by CIDOB calling for more indigenous control over forestry resources in the Eastern Lowlands. Carried out in the aftermath of another highly publicised protest over forest concessions by indigenous organisations in the Beni region, a dispute broke out between CIDOB and CORDECRUZ, the regional development corporation which served as the implementing agency for the overall project. In the midst of the dispute, representatives of

CORDECRUZ publicly denounced CIDOB in the regional and national press and called for the transfer of the administration of the Indigenous Peoples Component to its own institution rather than, as in the project description and loan agreement with the World Bank, keeping it under the control of CIDOB. A series of highly charged meetings between representatives of CIDOB and CORDECRUZ, the World Bank Project Manager and indigenous specialists took place. These attempted to resolve these differences – some of which had a history even prior to the protest march over the forest concessions – between the regional Indian federation and the regional development corporation. In the end, however, CORDECRUZ assumed control of the indigenous component. In the aftermath of the unsuccessful negotiations, the entire design of the component was changed with more control given to a new implementing unit in the regional development corporation and with the Indian federation playing a minor role in its implementation. At the same time, the Ayoreo formed into different factional groups, some of them allied with CIDOB and others with CORDECRUZ, and this led to internal disputes and accusations within the Ayoreo communities about misuse of funds and over access to resources and services provided under the component. A detailed description and analysis of the history of the Eastern Lowlands Indigenous Peoples Component written by one of the key actors in the original design of the component paints a picture of false hopes, frustrated plans and generalised social disruption all carried out in the name of regional development, sustainable resource management and indigenous participation.[30]

Even where governments have a rhetorical commitment to social participation on the part of indigenous and other rural populations, state agencies may also attempt to use such participation in order to co-opt rural and indigenous organisations into broader national or provincial political processes. As is well known, processes of decentralisation in Latin America have had a mixed record, providing both greater autonomy in development decision-making and resource control to local governments, NGOs and community organisations, while at the same time providing opportunities for more clientelistic relations on the part of provincial, departmental or municipal authorities. This is particularly true in federal systems such as exist in Argentina, Brazil and Mexico, where elected state-level or provincial governments now play an important role in the allocation of development funds and resources. In some countries where opposition political parties have begun to gain a stronger foothold in the countryside, decentralised development assistance can be used to either capture or marginalise indigenous and other rural organisations. One of the major challenges faced by international development agencies committed to both decentralisation and social participation is how to ensure that development resources and services are allocated in a transparent and efficient fashion for purposes of poverty alleviation without being used for electoral and other political purposes. In almost all cases where World Bank and other multilateral development agency funds are dispersed through decentralised mechanisms (for example, the recent generation of Social Investment and Municipal Funds in Mexico and Central America) the possibility exists of such political capture and co-optation. Neither are indigenous organisations, which in many countries have recently become a significant force in local municipal and national elections, immune from such political capture, nor are they protected from being marginalised or excluded from development assistance if they maintain an autonomous stance vis-à-vis the larger political and electoral system.[31]

Politics may also play an important role in the relations among indigenous organisations at the national level, as well as in the relations between these organisations and local indigenous communities. In most Latin American countries today a diversity of indigenous organisations exists, some of them organised into secondary regional organisations and national-level federations or confederations. A number of these organisations are also linked internationally to sub-regional and international bodies, such as the Coordinating Body of Indigenous Organisations of the Amazon Basin, COICA, or the former World Council of Indigenous Peoples and the various hemispheric networks set up to protest the 500th anniversary of Columbus's 'discovery' of the Americas or to participate in the International Decade of the World's Indigenous People. The social roots of these various indigenous organisations differ greatly in terms of their geographical (highland versus lowland), ethnic (large versus smaller ethnic and linguistic groups), religious (Catholic and evangelical) and political (syndicalist, left-wing political party, and so on) affiliations. They also differ in terms of their leadership styles, modes of organisation, and degree of participation and representation of local affiliates or communities. Such organisational diversity, within a context of national and local electoral politics, by its very nature creates problems of political competition and these can easily be reflected in struggles for control over development programmes and resources. Much of the drama of recent politics in Ecuador, for example, has been acted out on a smaller and albeit more limited scale in the struggle for control by different indigenous organisations, or factions within such organisations, of the World Bank and IFAD-financed PRODEPINE project. Much of the effort of the World Bank and IFAD task team responsible for the supervision of the project has needed to deal with the implications of these political differences among the indigenous organisations for the efficient functioning of the project.[32]

Finally, it has become clear from experience that some of the recent World Bank-funded projects which have tried to link the concerns of indigenous and Afro-Latin American organisations and communities may have exacerbated rather than reduced inter-ethnic tensions and rivalries. This has been the case, for example, in the initial implementation stages of the Colombia Natural Resources Management Project, one of the first natural resources management projects funded by the World Bank after the issuing of Operational Directive 4.20. Responding to the demands of both Afro-Colombian and indigenous organisations, the World Bank has been supporting a collective land titling programme for both indigenous and black communities along the Pacific Coast as part of a broader forestry and natural resources management project. The collective land titling programme is based upon new legislation arising from the 1991 reforms in the Colombian Constitution and during the preparation stage it included fairly systematic social and legal assessments of the land tenure situation of both indigenous and black communities in the Pacific Coast region. It also included funding for the setting up of a series of Regional Committees organised by the government's Social Solidaridad Network (*Red de Solidaridad Social*) in order to create consensus between the various government agencies participating in the Natural Resources Management Programme – the Environment, Interior Affairs and Agricultural Ministries, the latter including the Agrarian Reform and Colonisation Institute – and the participating indigenous and black organisations over the nature of the land surveying and titling processes.[33] As the land titling programme was initiated, inter-ethnic conflicts began to emerge between the indigenous and black organisations. Many of the black organisations felt excluded because earlier government agrarian reform programmes had recognised and titled indigenous reserves (*resguardos*) without taking into account the land and natural resource rights of black communities. At the same time, following the passage of a new law recognising the collective land rights of black communities along the Pacific Coast (Law 70 of 1993), indigenous organisations felt marginalised and unattended by the regional agrarian reform authorities. As survey teams started to demarcate lands claimed by black communities, indigenous communities began to protest that their own lands were being invaded and that they were not being taken into account in the survey operations. Finally, after numerous meetings and protest letters to the project authorities, the agrarian reform institute and the World Bank, an Action Plan was formulated to respond to the land titling needs of both the indigenous and black communities and changes were made in the regional agrarian reform authorities. Recent evaluations indicate that these initial problems of inter-ethnic conflict within the collective land titling process are now being resolved. However, some of these problems could have been avoided had the project authorities and the World Bank staff responsible carried out a more realistic assessment of the potential conflicts between the various ethnic and racial groups along the Pacific Coast. The project would have also benefited from more up-front social analysis of how national and regional politics, including the escalation of violence in the area, could potentially have affected the land titling programme proposed for the region.

In many World Bank project documents, politics is seen as a 'risk' which can determine the success or failure of a Bank-funded investment operation. Increasingly, however, social development specialists in the World Bank are seeing such political factors not only as risks (in a conventional investment banking sense) but as the institutional contexts in which development operations by their very nature take place. While the Bylaws of the World Bank do not permit its staff to intervene in the political processes of the countries where it provides assistance, there is no reason why institutional factors of a political nature should not be analysed and taken into account in the design of World Bank-funded operations. This is especially true of projects which are intended to benefit the poor, and where there is an increasing commitment on the part of the World Bank and other multilateral development agencies to government transparency and accountability and the participation of the poor in development operations. One would expect in the future that such institutional assessments, taking into account the broader political context in which development interventions occur, will be a standard aspect of international assistance programmes including – where appropriate – those programmes dealing with indigenous peoples, Afro-Latin Americans and other traditionally poor and socially excluded groups.

Challenges for the future

In this chapter I have provided a broad overview of the current work being done by the World Bank in supporting the participation of indigenous peoples and their organisations in development projects in Latin America. I have argued that this must be seen within the broader framework of the poverty reduction work of the World Bank, and its attempts to improve both the human and social capital of the indigenous poor. Much of this work is based on the premise that indigenous peoples, if provided with adequate capacity-strengthening, technical assistance and financial resources, can become the central actors in a self-managed process of economic development. This is especially true in those countries where there are strong indigenous organisations at the national, regional and local levels who are taking the lead in defining their own agendas for purposes of development. At the same time, I have stressed that these efforts to promote indigenous development are not without their own challenges and problems. These include, among others, the need for more active participation on the part of indigenous women in all aspects of development planning, the need for greater focus on the role of indigenous knowledge and cultures (including issues of intellectual property rights) within the local-level development process, and the need to assess more realistically the political obstacles and challenges to such self-managed development. In essence, the past decade – which opened with the Rio Conference on Environment and Development, the 500 Years of Resistance Movement, and the launching of the International Decade of the World's Indigenous People has been one of great learning both for indigenous peoples and for the various international donor agencies which have attempted within their own spheres of influence to provide them with support. What, though, are the future challenges posed for these agencies as they enter the new millennium?

First, I think there will probably be much greater attention in the years ahead on the development needs and priorities of both rural indigenous communities (mainly farming and agro-pastoral communities in the highland regions and recently sedentarised, horticultural, hunting and fishing communities in the tropical lowlands) and to those of the growing numbers of urban-dwelling indigenous populations. Although official statistics are lacking, it is noteworthy that recent studies in the Andean region and Mexico indicate that the urban indigenous population may – as a result of displacement and migration from the countryside – be growing much more rapidly than the rural indigenous population. While birth rates among indigenous peoples in rural areas remain relatively high, there has also been a corresponding out-migration of indigenous peoples from rural to urban areas over the past two or three decades. In the cities indigenous people often settle together in enclaves with others persons from their home villages or regions. They also often establish new types of associations, which create linkages and flows of people, resources and symbolic meanings and identities between the countryside and the city. Specialists in the World Bank's Latin America and Caribbean Region's Social Development Unit, working in collaboration with various regional scholars, are beginning to analyse these urban trends among the hemisphere's indigenous population. They are also seeking operational ways of dealing with questions relating to poverty reduction, urban service delivery, and the resurgence of indigenous ethnic identity in many of Latin America's cities, especially in the Mesoamerican and Andean regions.[34]

A second challenge, which will need much more attention in the years ahead, is how to improve the entrepreneurial capacity and competitiveness of indigenous businesses, whether they are collectively, family or individually owned. Some recent experiences indicate that indigenous businesses or productive organisations, such as cooperatives, have been able to respond to new opportunities provided by increasing commercial openness and globalisation. Witness, for example, the rise in recent demand in Western Europe and North America for organic coffee, much of it grown and marketed by indigenous farmer organisations in Latin America. There are also examples of indigenous businesses or productive organisations having suffered from increased competitiveness, such as the sudden rise and then decline in markets for indigenous artisan products in places such as Otavalo in Ecuador. The ability of indigenous businesses to take advantage of globalisation and not be undermined by it will in large measure depend upon the capacity of these organisations to improve their own entrepreneurial and managerial skills and to adapt to new circumstances and opportunities. These include the increasing use of the Internet and other modern information technologies for purposes of trade and commerce. Many indigenously owned businesses in Canada and the United States are making this adaptive transition and in the future one would expect greater attention given to building up the entrepreneurial and other capacities of indigenous businesses on the part of both indigenous organisations and international agencies working in Latin America.[35]

Thirdly, there will need to be much more cooperation among international agencies, including joint planning and finance, if the support of indigenous development initiatives are to be effective in achieving the goals of reducing poverty and promoting self-managed development. For a number of years the World Bank has formed part of a network of international agencies concerned with indigenous development issues in Latin America. These agencies include the Inter-American Development Bank, the International Labour Organisation, the International Fund for Agricultural Development, the Pan-American Health Organisation, and the Fondo Indígena. After a period of inactivity a second meeting of representatives of this Inter-Agency Working Group was held in Washington at the Inter-American Development Bank in March 1999 and a follow-up meeting was held in Costa Rica in May 2000. For the first time, joint training initiatives are being organised by these institutions. In April 2000, for example, the World Bank, the Inter-American Development Bank and the Pan-American Health Organisation sponsored a two-day technical workshop in Washington on 'Indigenous Peoples and Social Sector Projects in Latin America'. The workshop brought together agency project personnel working in the human and social development areas with government ministry representatives and various regional specialists, including a number of indigenous professionals, working in the fields of indigenous education, health and social protection. The purposes of the workshop were to exchange experiences and develop guidelines based upon such experiences for more effectively delivering culturally appropriate education, health and social protection services to indigenous communities.

Lastly, much more attention will need to be devoted in the years ahead to measuring the actual impact of internationally financed development initiatives on the lives of indigenous peoples and their communities. As the current efforts in the area of self-managed or ethno-development go beyond concept and rhetoric to project design and implementation, it will be necessary to evaluate the performance and impacts of such efforts both in terms of their capacity to reduce the current widespread poverty which exists among indigenous peoples and to assess how effective such programmes are in promoting self-managed and sustainable processes of development, especially at the community level. Many of the standard methods of monitoring and evaluation, as well the indicators used to track and measure the impact of development projects, may not necessarily be relevant in indigenous communities where there is much greater concern with issues of social and cultural disruption (especially among indigenous youth) and the spiritual and ecological balance of their communities. A major challenge in the years ahead will be for specialists working in international agencies to develop new social development indicators which take into account the great cultural, linguistic and ethnic diversity which still exists in Latin America, but which is threatened by past and current models of economic development. Only by factoring such cultural diversity into our models of development, including in our ways of measuring economic performance and social progress, can we expect to create a world free of poverty and social exclusion – one in which indigenous peoples can continue to maintain their ethnic identities and cultures, but have the same social citizenship rights as other members of their respective national societies.

Notes

1. The views expressed in this chapter are solely those of the author and should not be attributed to the World Bank, its Board of Directors or its Member Countries. The author would like to thank the various members of the Institute of Latin American Studies workshop for their comments on the original paper, many of which have been included in the current version.
2. The denial of the social and economic rights of indigenous peoples, and their relation to what is called 'social citizenship' in the growing literature on democratisation in Latin America, is taken from Marshall (1964).
3. See Buckley (2000).
4. See Rohter (2000).
5. CEPLAES-World Bank Poverty Group (1999).
6. Human and Social Development Group, Latin America and the Caribbean Region, World Bank (1999).
7. See, for example, the paper by Roger Plant in this volume, as well as Plant (1998).
8. Psacharopoulos and Patrinos (1994). The World Bank published a Spanish translation of this study in 1999.
9. The measurement of poverty in general, and indigenous poverty in particular, is a highly polemical issue. National censuses, if they contain questions on ethnicity, often do not capture the relatively large size of indigenous populations. Living standards surveys, supported by the World Bank and other international agencies, have relatively limited understanding of indigenous economies and cultures and may overlook or underestimate what might be termed the 'hidden sources of income' (sharing among extended family members, off-farm employment, remittances from migrant family members, and so on) of indigenous households. Some attempts have been made to remedy these methodological problems through combining various sources of data (national censuses, household and community surveys, use of spatial data, and so on), but the problems remain significant in terms of both statistical reliability and cultural biases. For some discussion, see the papers presented at the special symposium on 'geographical targeting and poverty alleviation' in *The World Bank Economic Review*, Volume 14, Number 1, January 2000.
10. Psacharopoulos and Patrinos (1994).
11. The World Bank and other donor agencies are currently financing several indigenous education programmes, in countries such as Bolivia, Guatemala, Mexico and Peru. For further background, see Davis and Patrinos (1996). On recent educational reforms in Latin America and the Caribbean and the role of World Bank and other multilateral financing, see World Bank Group (1999).

12. See World Bank (1998) and World Bank (1999a). The usage of 'native language speakers' as a substitute for 'indigenous peoples' may significantly underestimate the size and socio-economic status of the indigenous population in Peru, especially of those persons from the Sierra region who have migrated to the Coastal region and to Lima and in the process taken on Spanish as the language of their households, while at the same time maintaining their regional or indigenous identities. For background, see the interesting discussion in Lourdes Gallardo (2000).

13. World Bank (1999b).

14. See Junho Pena and Lindo-Fuentes (1998). Work of a similar nature has been carried out in Andean countries and tends to corroborate the role of social capital in rural poverty alleviation strategies among indigenous peoples. On the latter, see Bebbington and Carroll (2000). The work by Robert Putnam referred to in this paragraph is Putnam et al. (1993).

15. See International Labour Organisation Convention 169, Article 7.

16. See World Bank, Operational Directive 4.20, and Paragraph 4.

17. Operational Directive 4.20. Citations from paragraphs 14 (a), 14 (d), 14 (e), 15 (d) and 12. Background on the evolution of the World Bank's policy on Indigenous Peoples is contained in Davis (1993). See also Kingsbury (1999).

18. For the evolution of the implementation of Operational Directive 4.20 in the Latin America and Caribbean Region, see Partridge and Uquillas with Kathryn Johns (1996) and Uquillas and Davis (1997).

19. Along with these investment operations, the World Bank's Latin America and Caribbean Region has financed the preparation of several country-level profiles or national diagnoses of indigenous peoples' development policies and experiences, and two independent reviews of the experiences in indigenous development of other funding agencies and indigenous organisations. For the latter, see Iturralde and Krotz (1996) and Montgomery Roper, Frechione and DeWalt (1997).

20. On the general background to recent constitutional and other legal reforms, see Van Cott (1994) and Dandler (1999).

21. The construction of rural roads, schools, health clinics, water and sewage systems has increased significantly in many countries in recent years.

22. See Uquillas, Martinez, Gigler and Condori (1998) and Uquillas and Aparicio Gabara (1999).

23. For general discussions of these new participatory approaches to development in World Bank-financed operations, see World Bank (1995).

24. For background, see Van Nieuwkoop and Uquillas (2000).

25. A growing amount of literature, much of it in the form of operational manuals, has been produced recently on participatory planning in indigenous communities. See especially the 1998 *Manual de Planificación Participativa en Areas Indígenas: Lineamientos y Bases Metodológicas Para La Formulación de Planes Distritales de Desarrollo Indígena* published in La Paz by the Bolivian Ministry of Sustainable Development and Planning in collaboration with the Indigenous Confederation of the Oriente, Chaco and Amazon Regions of Bolivia (CIDOB) and the Forestry, Trees and Rural Communities Programme of FTPP-FAO and CERES.

26. The recently approved Peruvian: Indigenous and Afro-Peruvian Peoples Development Project is noteworthy in this regard as it was prepared in collaboration with a new Technical Secretariat for Indigenous Affairs (SETAI) in the Ministry for Women and Human Development (PROMUDEH) and was based on the recommendations of regional consultations with leaders of indigenous organ-

isations in both the Sierra and Amazon regions in which there was strong participation by indigenous women.

27. For background on this topic, see Kleymeyer (1994).
28. For background on these early World Bank-financed indigenous peoples
    components, many of them having to do with Amerindian land regularisation, see
    Wali and Davis (1992).
29. See the brief description of the political conflict surrounding the Eastern Lowlands
    Amerindian component in Davis and Soeftestad (1995), p.15.
30. See Heijdra (1997).
31. On the relations between decentralisation and indigenous and other peasant
    organisations in the specific context of recent rural development programmes in
    Mexico, see Fox (1994 and 1996).
32. On these issues of internal power struggles among indigenous organisations and
    the relation of such organisations to state-level institutions and ideologies, see
    Andolina (1999).
33. For background on the Afro-Colombian movement along the Pacific Coast, see
    Villa (1996). On the land-titling programme for black communities in the region,
    see Vargas Sarmiento (1999).
34. For background, see the two-volume edition edited by Hirabayashi and Altamirano
    (1991). The World Bank has completed an investigation of recent social and
    cultural trends relating to urban indigenous populations in Peru and is currently
    working on a similar investigation in Mexico.
35. Several very interesting case studies of the varying responses of indigenous
    production organisations to changing national and international economic
    contexts are contained in Iturralde and Krotz (1996). The World Bank, as part of
    a new Competitiveness Project in Guatemala, is considering ways of increasing
    the entrepreneurial capacity of indigenous businesses and productive organisa-
    tions, especially through the providing of technology and training in new Internet
    technologies in the Altiplano region.

References

Andolina, Robert James (1999), 'Colonial Legacies and Plurinational Imaginaries:
    Indigenous Movement Politics in Ecuador and Bolivia', unpublished PhD dissertation
    Faculty of the Graduate School, University of Minnesota.
Bebbington, Anthony J. and Thomas F. Carroll (2000), *Induced Social Capital and
    Federations of the Rural Poor*, The World Bank, Social Capital Initiative Working Paper
    No. 19, Social Development Family, Environmentally and Socially Sustainable
    Development Network (Washington DC).
Buckley, Stephen (2000), 'Indians Showed Political Muscle in Ouster of Ecuadorian
    Leader', *Washington Post*, 27 January.
CEPLAES-World Bank Poverty Group (1999), *Consultations with the Poor in Ecuador*,
    World Bank, Poverty Reduction and Economic Management Department
    (Washington DC).
Dandler, Jorge (1999), 'Indigenous Peoples and the Rule of Law in Latin America: Do
    They Have a Chance?' in Juan E. Mendez, Guillermo O'Donnell and Paulo Sergio
    Pinheiro (eds), *The (Un)Rule of Law and the Underprivileged in Latin America*, University
    of Notre Dame Press (Notre Dame), pp.116–51.

Davis, Shelton H. (1993), 'The World Bank and Indigenous Peoples', paper prepared for a panel discussion on Indigenous Peoples and Ethnic Minorities at the Denver Initiative Conference on Human Rights, University of Denver Law School, Denver Colorado, 16–17 April. Reprinted in Lydia van de Fliert (ed.) (1994), *Indigenous Peoples and International Organizations*, Bertrand Russell House (Nottingham).

Davis, Shelton H. and Lars T. Soeftestad (1995), *Participation and Indigenous Peoples*, Social Development Papers, No. 9, Environmentally and Socially Sustainable Development Network (Washington DC).

Davis, Shelton H. and Harry Anthony Patrinos (1996), 'Investing in Latin America's Indigenous Peoples: The Human and Social Capital Dimensions', in *Proceedings of the Seminar on Indigenous Peoples, Production and Trade*, Copenhagen, Nordic Council of Ministers, pp.69–80.

Fox, Jonathan (1994), 'Targeting the Poorest: The Role of the National Indigenous Institute in Mexico's National Solidarity Programme', in Wayne Cornelius, Ann Craig and Jonathan Fox (eds), *Transforming State-Society Relations in Mexico: The National Solidarity Strategy*, University of California at San Diego, Center for U.S.–Mexican Studies (La Jolla).

Fox, Jonathan and Josefina Aranda (1996), *Decentralization and Rural Development in Mexico: Community Participation in Oaxaca's Municipal Funds Programme*, University of California at San Diego, Center for U.S.–Mexican Studies (La Jolla).

Gallardo, Maria Lourdes (2000), 'The Alleviation of Social Exclusion of the Indigenous Communities in Peru: The Impact of the Social Investment Fund', Master's thesis in Public Administration, Cornell University, Ithaca, New York.

Heijdra, Hans (1997), *Participación y Exclusión Indígena en el Desarrollo: Banco Mundial, CIDOB y El Pueblo Ayoreo en el Proyecto Tierras Bajas del Este de Bolivia*, Pueblos Indígenas de Las Tierras Bajas de Bolivia, Vol. 6 (Santa Cruz).

Hirabayashi, Lane and Teofilio Altamirano (eds) (1991), 'Indigenismo urbano', *América Indígena*, Volume LI, Nos 2–4, 1991.

Human and Social Development Group, Latin America and the Caribbean Region, World Bank (1999), *Crisis, Poverty and Social Services in Ecuador* (Washington DC) (draft document).

Iturralde, D. and E. Krotz (eds) (1996), *Desarrollo Indígena: Pobreza, Democracia y Sustentabilidad*, Fondo Para el Desarrollo de los Pueblos Indígenas de América Latina y El Caribe (La Paz).

Junho Pena, Maria Valeria and Hector Lindo-Fuentes (1998), *Community Organization, Values and Social Capital in Panama*, The World Bank, Central America Country Management Unit, Latin America and Caribbean Region (Washington DC).

Kingsbury, Benedict (1999), 'Operational Policies of International Institutions as Part of the Law-Making Process; The World Bank and Indigenous Peoples', in Guy S. Goodwin-Gill and Stefan Talmon (eds), *The Reality of International Law: Essays in Honour of Ian Brownlie*, Clarendon Press (Oxford), pp.323–42.

Kleymeyer, Charles David (ed.) (1994), *Cultural Expression and Grassroots Development: Cases from Latin America and the Caribbean*, Lynne Rienner Publishers (Boulder, Colorado).

Manual de Planificación Participativa en Areas Indígenas: Lineamientos y Bases Metodológicas Para La Formulación de Planes Distritales de Desarrollo Indígena (1998), Bolivian Ministry of Sustainable Development and Planning in collaboration with the Indigenous Confederation of the Oriente, Chaco and Amazon Regions of Bolivia

(CIDOB) and the Forestry, Trees and Rural Communities Programme of FTPP-FAO and CERES (La Paz).

Marshall, T.H. (1964), *Class, Citizenship and Social Development*, University of Chicago Press (Chicago).

Montgomery Roper, J., John Frechione and Billie R. DeWalt (1997), *Indigenous People and Development in Latin America: A Literature Survey and Recommendations*, University of Pittsburgh, Latin American Monographs and Document Series, No. 12 (Pittsburgh).

Partridge, William L. and Jorge E. Uquillas with Kathryn Johns (1996), 'Including the Excluded: Ethnodevelopment in Latin America', in *Poverty and Inequality in the Latin America and Caribbean Region, World Bank Latin American and Caribbean Studies* (Washington DC);

Plant, Roger (1998), *Issues in Indigenous Poverty and Development*, Inter-American Development Bank, Sustainable Development Department, Indigenous Peoples and Community Development Unit, Technical Study (Washington DC).

Psacharopoulos, George and Harry Anthony Patrinos (eds) (1994), *Indigenous Peoples and Poverty in Latin America: An Empirical Analysis*, World Bank (Washington DC).

Putnam, Robert with Robert Leonardi and Raffaella Nanetti (1993), *Making Democracy Work: Civic Traditions in Modern Italy*, Princeton University Press (Princeton).

Rohter, Larry (2000), 'Bitter Indians Let Ecuador Know Fight Isn't Over', *New York Times*, 27 January.

Uquillas, Jorge E. and Shelton H. Davis (1997), 'El Banco Mundial y Los Pueblos Indígenas de América Latina', in Lydia van de Fliert (ed.), *Guia Para Pueblos Indígenas*, Comisión Nacional de Derechos Humanos (Mexico).

Uquillas, Jorge E., Juan Martinez, Soren Gigler and Norma Condori (1998), *Participatory Training of Indigenous Peoples in Latin America: Progress Report on a World Bank-Supported Capacity Building Initiative*, Environmentally and Socially Sustainable Development Department, Latin America and Caribbean Region, The World Bank (Washington DC).

Uquillas, Jorge E. and Teresa Aparicio Gabara (1999), *Strengthening Indigenous Organizations in Latin America: The Cases of Colombia and Guatemala*, Environmentally and Socially Sustainable Development Department, Latin America and Caribbean Region, The World Bank (Washington DC).

Van Cott, Donna Lee (ed.) (1994), *Indigenous Peoples and Democracy in Latin America*, St. Martin's Press (New York).

Van Nieuwkoop, Martien and Jorge E. Uquillas (2000), *Defining Ethnodevelopment in Operational Terms: Lessons from the Ecuador Indigenous and Afro-Ecuadorian Peoples Development Project*, Latin America and Caribbean Region Sustainable Development Working Paper No. 6 (Washington DC).

Vargas Sarmiento, Patricia (1999), *Construcción Territorial en el Chocó: Volumen 1, Historias Regionales*, Ministerio de Cultura and Instituto Colombiano de Antropología (Bogota).

Villa, William (ed.) (1996), *Comunidades Negras: Territorio y Desarrollo, Propuestas y Discusión*, Special Issue of the Revista *Esteros*, Editorial Endymion (Medellin).

Wali, Alaka and Shelton H. Davis (1992), *Protecting Amerindian Lands: A Review of World Bank Experience with Indigenous Land Regularization Programmes in Lowland South America*, Latin America and Caribbean Region, Environment Department, Technical Paper (Washington DC).

World Bank (1995), *World Bank Participation Sourcebook*, Environment Department Papers, Participation Series No. 019 (Washington DC).

—— (1998), *Peru: Poverty Comparisons*, Latin America and Caribbean Region (Washington DC).

—— (1999a), *Poverty and Social Developments in Peru, 1994–1997* (Washington, DC).

—— (1999b), *Panama Poverty Assessment: Priorities and Strategies for Poverty Reduction*, Human Development Department, Latin America and Caribbean Region (Washington DC).

World Bank Group (1999), *Educational Change in Latin America and the Caribbean*, Human Development Network, Latin America and the Caribbean Region (Washington DC).

10
The Excluded 'Indigenous'?
The Implications of Multi-Ethnic
Policies for Water Reform in Bolivia[1]

Nina Laurie, Robert Andolina and Sarah Radcliffe

Introduction

Recent legislative changes throughout Latin America have produced a swathe of new laws that include multicultural agendas (Stavenhagen 1996). These laws cover a range of areas, including good governance, constitutional reform, decentralisation and resource management. The main objective of multi-ethnic policies is usually to achieve social inclusivity. However, as Lopez's (1993) study of the evolution of the terms 'pluri-cultural', 'multi-ethnic' and 'pluri-national' in Ecuador during the indigenous uprisings of 1990 and 1992 illustrates, specific terminology emerges as the result of strategic representations made by different groups about particular events and debates. This chapter examines how such processes of representation are becoming important in the context of specific development projects and indicates how the representation of people as 'indigenous' or not indigenous – regardless of the validity of these labels – shapes the outcome of the application of new laws.

Funding opportunities are affected by classifications of groups of people as indigenous or not, and by the representations of specific components of development projects as 'productive', 'sustainable' and 'participatory'. Transnational actors greatly influence the representations involved in legislative and funding processes, as they create discourses of who 'indigenous' people are and what their role in development planning and project execution should be. These actors help shape the context for and imple-mentation of new resource laws by helping to construct the international and national policy environment in which these laws are passed. Donor organisations such as the World Bank currently label indigenous people as 'social capital', untapped human resources that need to be brought into the decision-making processes associated with development planning. Conceptualisations of indigenous people as social capital places them firmly in the nexus between participatory development approaches (which planners are increasingly using to target poverty alleviation) and liberalisation policies. As a result, key donor organisations now have indigenous people's units in their policy-making teams as a matter of course. These units promote multi-ethnic interests across funding and policy sectors and produce guidelines for 'mainstreaming' indigenous issues in development planning.

Bolivia is a country where the promise of large-scale modernisation still drives funding agendas as well as popular imaginaries of what development goals and projects should be. This continues to be the case even though it is widely accepted that modernisation is patchy in its outreach in the Andes. This chapter examines recent development trajectories in Bolivia and analyses what happens to supposedly inclusionary multi-ethnic policies when they implement water and land reform, part of a wider set of liberalisation policies that have been operating in the country since 1985. We argue that current negotiations over constructions of indigeneity[2] and the inclusiveness of land and water reform must be placed in the context of what Kearney and Varese (1995) call the 'post development era' in Latin America. They argue that the 'post development era' provides an opportunity for identities to be reconstructed in non-dichotomous terms, in ways that are neither wholly modern nor traditional.[3] Below we extend this argument to focus on the spatialities of development and indigenous identities. In particular, we suggest that indigenous identities are being constructed as neither completely urban nor rural. Our approach raises questions about what it means to be, or be defined as, indigenous in Bolivia and what implications these definitions have for modernising or neoliberal development strategies. We analyse the effects of these constructions on the everyday politics of meeting demands and achieving development goals, focusing on recent responses to land and water reform in the department of Cochabamba. Two case studies are examined, the *'Coordinadora de Defensa del Agua y de la Vida'* (The Coordinator for the Defence of Water and Life) and the Raqaypampa Ch'aky project, which is part of a wider local indigenous development plan.

The first section of the chapter provides the background to the recent Bolivian neoliberal reforms concerning water and land. It shows how the new laws attempt to accommodate two seemingly divergent world-views: one that emphasises collective rights (defined largely in terms of indigenous and campesino collective rights) and the other that focuses on commercialisation and private, individual ownership. The second and third sections outline the two case studies and illustrate how key players have engaged with the state and different transnational actors[4] in contrasting ways. The fourth, concluding section identifies the similarities and differences between the two case studies and attempts to explain these differences in the context of shifting 'post-development' identities.

Clashing views? 'Indigenous' actors, the state and the negotiation of liberalisation

In many parts of the world when indigenous livelihoods come under threat, tensions emerge over the negotiation of development trajectories. In the Andes, where relationships with land and water structure social and religious life, the commodification and commercialisation of land and water have become significant points of conflict in the context of wider decentralisation and liberalisation policies. Debates over the commercialisation of water and land are currently bringing clashing worldviews into high relief in the Andes. On the one hand, new national laws are establishing mechanisms through which 'dynamic' land and water markets can be created and confusion over existing patterns of land ownership clarified, while on the other, Andean cosmologies maintain that such resources cannot be owned by anyone.

> The neoliberal vision of land distribution is based on the concept that 'the land belongs to those who have the money to buy it' and that the land is an object like any other commodity that you can buy and sell. We think that to consider land an object is irrational – it may make sense to other people but not to us ... Is land just something to exploit for profit? The Aymara, Quechua, Guaraní cultures would say the opposite. We live together with the land. There is complementarity between people and land. (Guaraní leader quoted in Benton 1999: 76)

Similar arguments are made about water: 'Water is a living and fertile being. Without water there is not life' (Gerbandy and Hoogendam 1998: 60).[5]

Since the early 1990s, fundamental changes have occurred in state jurisdiction and territorial control in Bolivia, a result of decentralisation policies guided by the combined rhetoric of economic liberalisation, social inclusion and poverty alleviation. This fusion of different policy objectives was not necessarily the direct policy of the state. However, throughout the decade indigenous and campesino movements won many concessions from the government, in turn strengthening this trend. In addition, as elsewhere in Latin America, the international donor community supported such a combined approach. So when neoliberal reforms were first introduced in Bolivia in 1985 under the Paz Estensorro regime, dialogue with and occasional accommodation of indigenous-campesino interests was a necessary and sometimes obligatory element of policy making. In particular, the World Bank has promoted the campesino-indigenous agenda under the rubric of neoliberal development planning in Bolivia. According to the Bank's head of rural development in Bolivia, the institution invests more per capita in Bolivia than in any other country and recently Bolivia has joined a small number of countries acting as pilot cases for innovations in development planning. This approach reflects a recent wider shift in the way in which the Bank is tackling poverty-focused policy making through more participatory methods (see Robb 1999) and its explicit policy of promoting indigenous interests as part of wider social development goals.[6] The Bank's approach targets institutional strengthening activities in a range of rural communities, including indigenous districts that produce local development plans (World Bank 1998).

Multi-ethnic pressure on neoliberal visions and the inclusion of multicultural notions of development within neoliberal packages has led to a series of specific policies in Bolivia which afford a degree of representation to formerly excluded groups. Through *Participación Popular* (Popular Participation) – a set of decentralisation policies introduced by the Sánchez de Lozada government (1993–97) – the state has handed over funds[7] and local decision-making to *alcaldías* (local councils). It has also recognised the representation of a range of social organisations, from urban block communities to indigenous groups and campesino unions. These organisations can become OTBs (base territorial organisations) and apply for collective legal identity (*personería jurídica*). Despite significant achievements in putting multiculturalism into practice, tensions have emerged around the rhetoric of inclusivity and neoliberal change. In particular, conflict has occurred over land and water reform. Indigenous and campesino pressure on the government during the legislative stage, together with the participatory nature of the implementation process, has meant that indigenous people have gained access to land titling in order to register ancestral lands and have modified key elements of sewerage and drinking water reform.

New resource legislation: land and water

Under the 1996 Law of the Instituto Nacional de Reforma Agraria, commonly referred to as the 'Ley INRA' or INRA Law, individual and collective land titles can be applied for once *personería jurídica* has been obtained. As an extension to the 1952 Agrarian Reform Law, the INRA Law was intended to clarify complex issues of ownership as much land in Bolivia is not registered and titling is contested by a number of individuals and communities. Under the new legislation many indigenous groups claimed state recognition for ancestral land based on titles granted during the Spanish Viceroy. However, subsequent governments have not respected these titles, leaving such lands and their inhabitants open to exploitation.

After the land reform of 1952, both collective campesino and individual land titles existed in rural areas. By the 1980s, indigenous lowland groups came to perceive land titling as important in order to protect their land from commercial exploitation by loggers and petroleum companies, among others.

In the highlands where existing land tenure is often contested, the state decided that new titling was needed in order to ensure that ownership was clarified so that land could be sold if so desired. More rigorous titling procedures were also needed to ensure that community land was not broken down into small plots that could become unsustainable in the face of population pressure. Pressure from campesino and indigenous groups during the negotiations over the INRA Law meant that indigenous and original or ancestral communities (*comunidades originarias*) secured the possibility of asserting collective rights to legal land tenure. All land claims are administered through a '*saneamiento*' (clearing) process, which establishes the history of land tenure before titles are granted. There are two forms of *saneamiento* relevant to campesino and indigenous communities. '*Saneamiento simple*' is a process designed to allot individual and community titles to campesino communities. A more complex process is required in order to obtain an indigenous and *originario* (ancestral) land title in the form of a TCO (*Tierra Comunitaria de Origen* – original communal territory). According to Benton (1999) these lands are:

> [G]eographic spaces that constitute the habitat of indigenous peoples and original communities, to which they have traditionally had access and where they maintain and develop their own forms of economic, social and cultural organisation, in a way that ensures their survival and development. Such lands cannot be broken up, mortgaged or sold and are not subject to tax. (Benton 1999: 88)

Some of these lands are more easily identifiable than others, reflecting the differentiated influence of the colonial and republican state. Indigenous jurisdiction[8] in many lowland and some highland areas has remained fairly intact over time.

While the negotiations which led up to the INRA Law were highly contested by indigenous groups,[9] many indigenous leaders seized the unexpected opportunities created under the new law to mobilise communities into claiming TCO status. This was particularly marked among lowland groups, with the first TCOs being granted to the Chiquitano and Ayoreo peoples in November 1999. While the main campesino union, the CSUTCB, initially refused to entertain thoughts of working within the framework of this new law (Andolina 1999; Condo 1998), many donors were not as resistant. The Danish governmental bilateral aid organisation DANIDA, for example, chose to invest heavily in INRA and VAIPO (the Vice-Ministry for Indigenous and Original Peoples) after 1996 in order to fund the processing of TCO claims. Their pro-indigenous approach supported indigenous participatory planning by providing funding for community consultation and for indigenous mappers to participate in boundary drawing.[10]

Despite all the interest that the INRA Law has generated among international donors and local activists, tensions have continued. The implementation of the new law has been extremely slow, and the granting of TCO status especially tardy.[11] Furthermore, the INRA Law has not only failed to deliver land titles within a reasonable time frame, but has also left untouched the related and complex issue of scarce water resources. Such resources are coming under increased competition in areas like the Lake Titicaca region where greater population pressure is occurring (Benton 1999), and in the Cochabamba valley where increased urbanisation and water scarcity is producing desertification. Some of the semi-arid altiplano areas of the Cochabamba department also have intense water problems, which generate much concern when new development priorities are negotiated with local, national and international funders. In such areas the state, through INRA, has not only failed to offer solutions to the complex question of water rights but has greatly complicated the relationship between land and water. Although land and water are interconnected, they have been dealt with separately in the new legislation. One set of laws refers to land reform (INRA) and de-centralisation (Popular Participation) and another relates to water (separating irrigation and sewerage and drinking water). The land laws were passed in the mid-1990s, whereas as of August 2000 only one of the water laws had been passed.

In lowland areas water has been clearly identified by indigenous organisations such as CIDOB (Confederación Indígena Del Oriente Boliviano) as part of a wider set of specifically indigenous rights that lowland groups have sought to protect in the face of threats from mining, logging, petroleum exploitation and genetic patenting. Thus, protection of lowland indigenous rights has been closely linked to an environmental agenda and the need for a legislative framework that can channel transnational and national private capital. This overtly indigenous and environmental context contrasts with highland areas, where water has been linked to rural development agendas and managed communally as part of extensive collective labour systems, many of which date back to pre-conquest times. Water rights are seen as part of customary law, which recognises *usos y costumbres* (existing uses and customs). These arrangements are key to structuring social life in indigenous *ayllus* (Gerbrandy and Hoogendam 1998) and are also important to agricultural production on former hacienda lands where water is managed through collective organisation based within the structure of the campesino unions. Members of communities are obliged to take part in collective infrastructural works and use irrigation water allocated to them in particular time slots (Bustamante and Gutiérrez 1999; Gutiérrez 1998). If they do not use their allocation, then the governing committee or association removes their rights to water. These indigenous campesino forms of water management have also been adopted in more recent contexts. For example, large-scale donor-led[12] irrigation projects in Bolivia and elsewhere increasingly engage with notions of Andean irrigation (*riego andino*) to ensure that projects are participatory and sustainable (Gandarillas et al. 1994; Sánchez et al. 1994). This participation not only requires community labour as co-financing, but also establishes water committees and associations along seemingly 'traditional' lines in order to ensure equal distribution of water and the long-term maintenance of the network. In peri-urban areas, water associations and committees often operate among neighbours who share costs and pay fines when they do not participate in collective activities. In highland regions therefore, indigenous approaches to water have incorporated changing social demands and development contexts.

As with the INRA Law, the various water law projects produced by a variety of ministries met with persistent opposition from indigenous and campesino groups who were keen to protect the '*usos y costumbres*' associated with water. Tensions over water sector reform peaked when the Ley 2029 de Servicios de Agua Potable y Alcantarillado Sanitario (Law 2029 of Potable Water and Sewerage Services) was introduced in October 1999. Indigenous and campesino organisations felt that many of the issues that had been resisted in previous proposals for an irrigation law (a *ley de aguas*) had been unfairly added into this law. While the decision to postpone passing the irrigation law had been taken in order to allow further discussion, the Ley 2029 had been passed through Congress with virtually no consultation in an attempt to 'steamroll' opposition. As a result there was much confusion about exactly what the different water laws referred to and specifically concerning what was already law and what remained under discussion. An interview with the CIDOB spokesperson on water in October 1999, days after the publication of the 2029 Law, highlighted the fact that the new laws were producing confusion:

> There are three laws, the Municipalities Law, which has to do with water because it passes through its jurisdiction as a public utility, the 2029 Law, which refers to 'sewerage' [in the title], but which has a lot more to do with water and the other law which is the blessed law for water resources [the irrigation law]. (Interview CIDOB Assembly, 30 October 1999)[13]

Under the new Municipalities Law local government was granted the power to give water concessions for 30 years, but under the 2029 Law a new national water regulator was created in order to grant concessions to national or transnational companies for 40 years. These laws created confusion over jurisdiction and lengths of concessions, but more importantly left unclear how the two new laws related to the irrigation law still under discussion.

The following sections focus on two examples of how the inclusionary nature of neoliberal reforms in water and land can unravel when new laws are implemented in specific contexts. In Bolivia problems are occurring not only because land and water are dealt with by distinct sets of laws which are not always compatible at a local level, but also because the new multicultural contexts for the liberalising laws has set up specific opportunities for the representation of 'indigenous' identities. Here the focus of analysis is on the role that indigenous and rural representations play in the negotiating processes relating to these water and land conflicts. Both cases indicate how particular grass-roots activists construct water and land rights as part of an indigenous heritage. The case studies show how grass-roots activists question the fixed nature of indigenous and non-indigenous categories, as well as the role that 'indigenous' actors are currently given in participatory planning. Each case highlights the role that the state and transnational actors play in defining who and what can be constructed as indigenous and in what environments. Both examples are drawn from the department of Cochabamba. The first refers to a proposal for a micro-irrigation project in Raqaypampa, a semi-arid region in the south-east of the department. It involves debates over the individual land titling for small pieces of land required for the irrigation project and the clashes between these and the TCO claims of the indigenous communities involved. The second addresses reactions to the introduction of new water laws and a water concession granting an international consortium the right to manage the Cochabamba City water utility. It refers to a broader coalition of interests which involves protecting established water *usos y costumbres*, but which also raises issues relating to the collective land titling of campesino lands in a small number of communities in the Misicuni valley where a dam is due to be built. There are marked similarities between the rural communities discussed. Both the Misicuni and Raqaypampa communities are Quechua-speaking and are currently undergoing educational reform through the promotion of intercultural and bilingual education programmes.[14] These state-sponsored programmes seek to strengthen cultural identity amongst different ethnic groups in Bolivia (Albó 1999). With regard to land tenure, the two communities have similar histories. Both areas are comprised of ex-hacienda lands and, as such, currently have a complex set of land titles including individual and collective titles as well as large tracts of land where titles have been lost or where there is confusion over ownership. Both communities have been granted OTB status through their union structures as campesino communities.

Our analysis examines the role which representations of inhabitants as 'indigenous', 'campesino' and 'rural people' play in constructing viable negotiating platforms in contests over the application of the new laws. We assess the success of specific representations in negotiations with the state and transnational actors before relating this success to the emergence of 'post-development indigenous identities'. We argue that the subjectivities and bargaining platforms available to the actors in each case study were constrained by the contradictions inherent in the confused policy framework within which they were obliged to act. Although, to some extent, the legislation exists in order for groups of people to assert collective rights as indigenous people, 'access' to these rights depends on the representations made of self and others in the implementation of new laws and the classifications of particular demands as legitimate rights.

The Raqaypampa story

The Raqaypampa example highlights a fundamental contradiction in the socially inclusive rhetoric of neoliberal land and water policies in Bolivia. The INRA Law indirectly opened up new opportunities for communal titles, for indigenous communities to frame a discussion of human rights as collective rather than individual rights and to speak in spiritual terms about 'resources' such as water and land. However, when land is discussed in relation to the implementation of specific development projects the language of private ownership and commodification often prevails. The case of Raqaypampa indicates the fundamental differences that exist between the neoliberal origins of the INRA Law – designed to create a market for land – and the inclusive additions to the law that have been won by indigenous and campesino protest. In this particular case these divergent interests can only be held in check by bureaucratic gerrymandering, which in turn undermines the legitimacy of processes of participation and *saneamiento* themselves.

Well known in Bolivia for its highly politicised Quechua identity, Raqaypampa suffers from extreme gullying and soil erosion in the production of maize and potatoes on the high plateau. Its political profile has been enhanced through links with CENDA, a national NGO that receives funding from a variety of international sources and works with Andean cosmologies to conceptualise and implement agricultural change. The relationship between CENDA and the Raqaypampa leadership highlights the important role that national and regional NGOs can play in promoting notions of Andean cosmology in rural development.[15] Their approach 'seeks to preserve the common resources of the community and minimise internal economic differentiation' (Kearney and Varese 1995: 212). Common resources include water and land, as well as 'cultural' resources such as distinctive music and clothing.

Under the opportunities created by *Participación Popular*, communities in Raqaypampa sought OTB status by obtaining *personería jurídica* through union structures. In 1999, on the basis of this legal identity, the *Central* – a collection of several large unions operating in the Raqaypampa region – devised a local indigenous development plan (*Plan Indígena*), drawing on participatory planning. This conceptualised the area as an indigenous district that would be able to compete for decentralised funds without having to go through the local municipality. This plan was the first Indigenous District Plan to be produced under the new decentralised policies of *Participación Popular*. Although the success of indigenous plans in obtaining decentralised funds has been questioned (see Van Cott in this volume), the Raqaypampa plan was heralded by many governmental and international agencies as an exemplar of the way in which *Participación Popular* was able to stimulate grass-roots participation in regional and local planning, especially of previously excluded indigenous populations. With the widescale participation of community members assisting in the collection of oral histories and statistical data, all community members were involved in the prioritisation of development goals through a series of general assemblies among the local unions. Thus, as far as the World Bank and other funding agencies were concerned, the plan exemplified best practice in grass-roots participatory planning. These same participatory measures also supported the Raqaypampa claim for TCO status, as the community was required to show that land was organised and worked communally and that the claim for TCO status was the result of a collective community decision. Under the recent education reform laws, most areas applying for TCO status would also be expected by the state to participate in bilingual/intercultural education as indigenous communities. The Raqaypampa plan highlighted three key areas for development: the promotion of indigenous teachers and an indigenous curriculum following the agricultural calendar; the *saneamiento* of land as a TCO; and the provision of more irrigation water. One particular irrigation scheme focused on the development of a network of small lagoons where each lagoon would provide approximately five families with water during times of scarcity.

From indigenous plan to the Cha'ky Project

Launched in August 1999 at a festival of Raqaypampan music held in Cochabamba, the plan quickly came to the attention of the Fondo de Desarrollo Campesino (FDC – Rural Development Fund) and the PDCR (Programme for Rural Community Development), the main organisation involved in institutional strengthening for participative planning under *Participación Popular*, funded largely by the World Bank. With the successful launch of the indigenous plan and the high profile it soon achieved, the PDCR suggested that the lagoons project could be funded through the new small grants scheme of the FDC. This scheme allows any community with OTB status to apply directly to the Fund for small grants without requiring co-funding. It formed part of the state's wider decentralisation mission, but specifically encouraged indigenous peoples to define their own development projects. This proposal became known as the Ch'aky Project.

When the PDCR and FDC offer of funding was initially made there was much concern in Raqaypampa about the fact that water issues were being advanced before education and, more importantly, before land *saneamiento* had taken place. Another concern expressed at various community meetings was the initial scale of implementation. Pressure came from the FDC and the PDCR to start construction at once and to complete 211 lagoons in 23 communities before the rainy season. This was to ensure that funding could be channelled during one budgetary year. Indigenous villages preferred the option of constructing lagoons in one area on a trial basis and to link their construction with obtaining land titling as a TCO. The *Central* members who represented the leaders of the local unions decided to negotiate with the World Bank, the main funder of the PDCR. Their assumption was that the World Bank would have more sway over the bureaucratic demands of national agencies than they themselves would. They also hoped that the World Bank could pressure INRA to ensure that land *saneamiento* would be completed before the water project commenced. There was an underlying assumption that the World Bank had substantial power over state organisations and that its rhetoric of promoting pro-indigenous and decentralising policies could be used to the advantage of grass-roots indigenous organisations. CENDA played an important role in suggesting that the community enter into dialogue with the World Bank in order to secure land titling as a TCO. Like the *Central* leaders, the NGO was also concerned about the scale of the project and its departure from what it saw as 'Andean' experimentation. CENDA was also wary of the possible long-term effects of large influxes of money on community dynamics and cohesion.

The *Central* invited the Bolivian World Bank director of rural development to visit Raqaypampa. At this meeting, they were keen to assert their freedom to advance the project in keeping with what they called the 'Andean way', to experiment with lagoons on a small scale before implementing the project across the whole region. They were also keen to ensure that finance for the Ch'aky Project would not divide the community. There was concern about the fact that one of the five main *sub-centrales* (a collection of smaller union groupings that make up the larger *Central*) was not represented in the project proposal because its land was not suitable for lagoons. The *Central* leaders felt that experimentation over a longer period of time would provide an opportunity for all the *sub-centrales*, including the one that would not benefit directly, to come to terms with the project. CENDA emphasised that institutional strengthening of the campesino unions (especially the *Central*) as representative indigenous organisations was one of the key aims of the *Plan Indígena* and that causing division between *sub-centrales* would make this goal unachievable. CENDA also suggested that starting on a smaller scale would involve less investment and would therefore prevent any tensions emerging around the sudden influx of large amounts of money into the community.

When the meeting was finally held between the funders, the community leaders, the CENDA agronomist who had designed the project and two CENDA board members, the negotiations took a turn that the Raqaypampa leaders had not anticipated. Although the meeting took place in the PDCR offices in Cochabamba and not in Raqaypampa (due to the time constraints of those travelling from La Paz), the Raqaypampa leadership were able to achieve most of their specific aims. They negotiated a smaller project to commence in the one *sub-central* that they had decided to prioritise as a trial project. While funding would not be available from the FDC small grants for the remaining lagoons, the donors agreed that Raqaypampa could submit a further project for the lagoons in the remaining *sub-centrales* through the normal FDC channels. Instead of the usual requirement for financial co-funding it was agreed that the contribution of local labour would be sufficient. This shift in demands for co-funding represented a departure from usual FDC practice and was particularly championed by the World Bank representative, thereby confirming the influence that multilateral donors can have on national bureaucracies. However, despite these apparent successes, the manner in which these negotiations took place and the issues raised concerning the consolidation of the rights of Raqaypampa's inhabitants to consolidate collective land holding through the legislative claim for TCO status, threatened to undermine their role as actors in the participatory planning process. When the community leaders stated that they wanted to secure TCO status before starting the lagoons project, the World Bank representative said that the Bank had no power over INRA and no money to finance TCO claims. He refused to address the issue of land *saneamiento*. However, despite assertions about not wanting to be involved in *saneamiento* issues, much of the discussion that followed focused on possible mechanisms to secure land ownership over the specific pieces of land where the lagoons were to be built.

These discussions and the debate they generated point clearly to the types of problems that can arise with the introduction and implementation of new legislation that indirectly separates land and water issues. Community leaders were initially reticent to discuss whether the land where the lagoons were to be located was privately owned because they emphasised that they were in the process of applying for TCO status and communal land titles, hence their desire to link the Ch'aky Project to *saneamiento*. As the CENDA agronomist who designed the project stated:

> The issue is that there has to be a title now. [However,] this has to be put in the context of the fact that the community has already entered into an internal process over *saneamiento*. They have decided to go for a TCO so therefore there has been discussion [over this]. Historically water doesn't belong to anyone it belongs to God. (Field notes from donor meeting with Raqaypampa community, 15 December 1999, Cochabamba)[16]

The final resolution of the situation in Raqaypampa was that '*actas*' (written minutes) would be signed to demonstrate agreement that the land and water rights were to be relinquished to the Ch'aky Project. These *actas* would mean that where the land needed for the lagoons already belonged to the community, these collective rights to land would be relinquished to the lagoons project. In cases where the lagoon was to be built on land that was owned by an individual, the *actas* indicated that those individuals had relinquished any claim to this land and given it to the lagoons project. This solution was suggested by the World Bank representative, even though it was later agreed by those at the meeting that everyone knows that '*actas*' have no real legal value.

Project representation and funding

The tensions reflected in the Raqaypampa compromise were further underlined by the issue of finance for the project and the representations made of the project components in order to secure funding in the first place. Here the purpose of the lagoons was crucial. The lagoons were described in the indigenous plan and in the funding application as 'productive' projects, and therefore cast by the Raqaypampa community and the CENDA agronomist involved in producing the documentation as 'modernising projects' designed to increase output for the market. Discussion in Raqaypampa among the *sub-centrales* and in the meeting in Cochabamba made it clear, however, that no one (not the donors, the NGO or the Raqaypampa leaders and community members) really believed that they were productive projects designed directly to improve crop production. They were framed as such in the indigenous plan and the funding applications in order to fulfil the requirements of the state's *Fondo de Desarrollo Campesino*. In reality, all parties at the meeting agreed that the lagoons would only influence production indirectly. Their main role was to provide drinking water for livestock and to serve as a source of water security in times of scarcity. They were therefore part of wider support for existing livelihoods rather than irrigation projects designed to improve crop production. Despite these obvious differences in project aims, all parties adopted the language of production in order to discuss funding. Such collusion over the legitimacy of specific language illustrates the types of compromises involved in the everyday politics of meeting demands and achieving development goals.

The Raqaypampa example begs the question of whether it is not possible simply to rethink the categories under which rural development is conceptualised so that actors do not have to mediate between seemingly 'traditional' and 'modern' goals. It is not enough to introduce new laws that provide opportunities for indigenous groups to assert their claims for land as collective human rights if the aims of such laws are undermined by the fact that development projects are framed within a context of private ownership. Such implementation issues point to problems associated with the staggered introduction of new laws. Land laws were drawn up by the state and negotiated by indigenous-campesino groups before a complete set of water laws was passed. In particular the INRA Law was passed before discussions concerning a new irrigation law (*ley de aguas*) were completed. Such a law could have establish guidelines for the operation of development projects within the context of collective water rights and established *usos y costumbres*. The types of contradictory representation of projects and indigenous interests generated by the lack of a legislative focus on the relationship between water and land is likely to produce longer-term problems. The acceptance of the dominance of the language of production implies that collective rights, Andean cosmologies and agricultural practices are in fact subordinate to individual ownership and modernising discourses. The transnational and national funding agencies, however, seem to assume that, by being complicit with such misrepresentations, indigenous actors are automatically going to continue in a relationship of good faith with the development agencies concerned. Yet this is not always the case and, as the following case study suggests, multiple representations of indigenous interests can be mobilised as part of wider resistance movements, with the consequence that these mobilisations often work better for some groups than for others.

The Cochabamba water uprisings (November 1999–April 2000)

Led by an umbrella organisation the *Coordinadora de Defensa del Agua y de la Vida* (The Coordinator of the Defence of Water and Life), the Cochabamba water uprisings were a response to state liberalisation of the Bolivian water sector. However, unlike the Raqaypampa case, support for indigenous rights was not spearheaded by NGOs, rural campesino or indigenous organisations, but by a city-based movement that succeeded in uniting cross-sector interests by mobilising powerful representations of access to water as collective rights based on existing uses and customs (*usos y costumbres*). The state's introduction of the new water and sewerage law (2029 Law) in October 1999 without prior consultation with civil society was widely criticised by indigenous and campesino groups nationally. In the city of Cochabamba the response was particularly strong, as the new law coincided with a massive increase in water tariffs and proposals to monitor private wells associated with a new water concession granted by the state.[17] The threat that the new law and well monitoring measures posed for existing *usos y costumbres* played a key role in the success of the Cochabamba water campaign. Recourse to a language of *usos y costumbres* invoked a seemingly untouchable set of inherited rights with their basis in customary law and Andean spirituality. The campaign eventually led to amendments to the 2029 Law, which included the recognition of *usos y costumbres* as well as the withdrawal of the transnational water consortium Aguas de Tunari from Cochabamba. The legislative recognition of *usos y costumbres* represented the first legal legitimation, under neoliberal reform, of indigenous collective water rights in Bolivia. The Cochabamba water campaign was a call for the defence of cultural heritage by a diverse set of interest groups, united by a seemingly common idea of how cultural practices are threatened by market forces. This type of politics had resonance with wider state rhetoric of a 'multi-ethnic' Bolivia expressed in Popular Participation and the bilingual/intercultural education reform and was thus difficult for the state to repudiate. By adopting such a language, not only was the campaign attempting to include the interests of peri-urban/rural irrigators and well owners, but it was also mobilising a powerful historical, indigenous imagery concerning water.

Given the long-standing problem of water scarcity in the Cochabamba valley, the issue of private wells was extremely controversial throughout the campaign. Many access points for water in the poorer areas of the city had been established over the years by water cooperatives and associations using Andean communal labour systems as individuals contributed their own finance and labour. Historically any attempt to regulate wells has met with collective resistance, as Crespo's analysis of the 1994–95 water conflicts on the outskirts of the city illustrates (Crespo and Halkyer 1999).

Representing a campaign: protecting cultural heritage

The Cochabamba water uprising manifested itself in marches, roadblocks and public demonstrations that were reported in the international press and on CNN news. By early February 2000 the movement had gathered momentum, and a peaceful march programmed for 4 February met with a strongly militarised reaction from the government which set the scene for later clashes culminating in large-scale civil unrest throughout the department and in rural areas by April.

The most important aspect of the Cochabamba water campaign was the fact that it united rural and urban interests under one banner with its focus on protecting *usos y costumbres*. While urban and rural interests have long since been fused in El Alto, La Paz, due to the large presence of Aymara-based politics in the city, this has not been the case in Cochabamba. Here rural and urban interests have largely remained separate. For example, while the well-known protests by *cocaleros* from the Chapare converged on Cochabamba as the regional capital throughout the 1990s, these uprisings did not engage the urban public to any great extent, with the exception of key NGOs and union movements.

The rural-indigenous representations of the Cochabamba water campaign were made strongly by the *Coordinadora* during the uprisings, which started on 11 January and led to the first large protest uniting 20,000 people in the main plaza. During these uprisings a series of roadblocks on the outskirts of the city stopped the through traffic from La Paz and Santa Cruz for various days and a number of roadblocks also appeared in the rural areas of the department, blocking the main road over long distances. While the blockades on the La Paz side of the city were the most numerous,[18] on the Santa Cruz road at Quintanilla (Kilometre 8) blockades were also very strong. Here, several independent peri-urban water cooperatives came together to defend the private wells and water channels they had constructed on individual household plots using communal labour. This history of collective action, together with an efficient system of fines (*multas*) for anyone who did not participate in group activities, made these organisations very strong. However, these actors were protecting their rights as domestic consumers in peri-urban areas rather than as collective 'rural' producers, and the wells they were protecting were private drinking water rather than irrigation. Yet despite an emphasis on drinking water and the location of the water cooperatives on the outskirts of the city, the language used by these groups was one of collective rights that invoked Andean rural imagery and history. This use of collective symbolism was evident in the remarks made by one woman at the Quintanilla roadblock in November 2000:

> Water is an inheritance from our ancestors and we are going to defend it with our lives. The law has been passed, [but] what we want is to repeal it … because it's as if they are touching a nerve with the water. We have let other companies become the owners of our petroleum, mines and even our politics and all of that. Now all of that is contaminated. Everything has reached here and all of us have let them. But now the water is like they have touched a nerve and we are not going to let it happen because we are women and we are going to fight no matter where we have to with our lives. (Interview: Quintanilla roadblock, 6 November 1999)[19]

By the time of the January uprising, language defending cultural heritage and collective rights was at the forefront of the campaign. On the first day of the protest in Quintanilla on 11 January posters appeared saying 'Water is ours' and identifying five key demands. These demands focused on increases in tariffs, the privatisation of private wells which 'we have built ourselves in urban and rural areas' (thereby highlighting the urban-rural nature of the campaign) and the lack of public consultation over the Aguas de Tunari contract. However with the arrival of the members of the *Coordinadora* mid-way through the same morning, a second similar poster appeared with additional wording. The new demands focused specifically on the protection of '*usos y costumbres*' and demanded the repeal of the 2029 Law. A key feature of the second poster was the augmentation of the main title: 'Water is ours' with the phrase 'Pachamama, Woracocha and Tata Dios gave it to us to live, not to do business with'. Of the other headings that followed, the first and largest section was devoted to repealing the 2029 Law. Under this heading respect was demanded for the rights of drinking water committees and cooperatives with their 'uses and customs'. This language cemented the representation of the campaign as a struggle to gain recognition for the role of Andean cosmologies in water management and to assert collective 'indigenous' rights to water.

Exclusion and 'indigenous' representations

These indigenous-rural discourses were, however, to some extent exclusionary. The focus on *usos y costumbres* and the process of fore-grounding the interests of well owners for reasons of 'rural heritage' sidelined other groups. In particular, it left little room for identifying the needs of those people who were not able to appeal to notions of rurality/indigeneity. Originally, one of the powerful arguments for privatising the Cochabamba municipal water company was the claim that it would facilitate more water connections in the poorest sector of the city, a hilly area populated by recent migrants (see Laurie and Marvin 1999). Here there is poor access to ground water and few wells, so water cooperatives and irrigation groups are less common. Despite the fact that connecting more people to the water network in these areas was one of the main justifications for seeking outside investment in the municipal water company, Aguas de Tunari were not interested in augmenting new connections in the short term. Their priority was to increase output in the existing network.[20] However, the focus on rural identities and *usos y costumbres* in the water campaign meant in practice that the poorest members of society – who had no existing access to water other than that bought from expensive tankers and whose interests could only be constructed as urban – were sidelined. The only support given to the interests of these poor urban groups by the *Coordinadora* was through the water campaign's focus on retaining the Misicuni project. This was a proposal for a large multiple dam project (Hydro Electricity Power (HEP), irrigation water, and drinking water) that for many years had been linked to regionalist agendas. It was seen by many as the way to kick-start industrial development in the region and as the solution to water scarcity (Laurie and Marvin 1999). In response to widespread support for the Misicuni dam in the Cochabamba region, the state had negotiated the construction of the project as a requirement of the water concession granted to Aguas de Tunari. However, as Aguas de Tunari was the only contender for the concession, the company was able to negotiate very favourable terms. Specifically, they were able to reduce the size of the dam to be built and ensure that the initial land acquisition and costly tunnel construction for the dam would be carried out by a public company, the Empresa Misicuni.

These circumstances set up a series of tensions in the water campaign that underlines the fact that rights are structured by differences of class, ethnicity and location. The relationships between land and water and the construction of a rural-indigenous platform via a focus on *usos y costumbres* in the Cochabamba water campaign indicate that the successful definition and protection of indigenous rights is influenced by uneven processes of representation. The 'rights' of those with no access to water were being recognised by supporting Misicuni's likely future role in increasing water supplies. However, this support threatened the 'rights' of the urban middle classes already connected to the urban water system who were demanding a reduction in tariffs. This was difficult to achieve because Aguas de Tunari claimed that increases were needed to pay for the Misicuni dam.

A final twist in the analysis of 'rights' is that the *Coordinadora*'s support for Misicuni further called into question the nature of the 'rural' and 'indigenous' interests in the campaign. An emphasis on the Misicuni dam did not take into consideration the rights of Quechua-speaking campesinos living in the eight rural communities which would be flooded by the dam. Their interests were not represented at all by the protesters. Nor were they of any interest to Aguas de Tunari, which relied on the state (via the Empresa Misicuni) to deliver their lands to the company in readiness for the construction of the reservoir. In the event, the Empresa Misicuni secured access to these lands through careful use of the INRA Law. While, in theory, with its sixfold classification of land holdings, the INRA Law defends the lands of campesinos and *pueblos originarios*, in practice the protection given to land registered as TCOs is often greater than that afforded to campesino lands. In addition, both these sets of collective land titling can be bypassed by the state in particular circumstances, as there is a clause stating that land can be requisitioned if it is needed for public use. The use of INRA definitions of campesino residential and smallholdings (*El solar campesino, La pequeña propiedad*), meant that the Misicuni land could be expropriated by the state and compensation paid (Article 58).

The Empresa Misicuni employed a full-time lawyer to deal with the paperwork of first establishing OTB status for the different rural unions and later going through the *saneamiento* process. They applied for collective land titles as campesino communities on ex-hacienda lands, despite the fact that some of the leaders were not in agreement with the titling process. INRA and campesino union representatives involved in the negotiations suggested that existing land titling was confusing, as individual and collective titles were already held for the same pieces of land. They also suggested that there were some arguments to be made in favour of classifying the land as a TCO on the basis that the community worked the land collectively and took decisions through 'indigenous' leaders and institutions recognised by the communities.[21] If the lands had been classified as *tierras comunitarias de orígen*, this process would have become far more complicated. Despite the obvious rural interests of these campesinos, the ambiguity over *saneamiento* and extensive discussions with the Empresa Misicuni, their interests were not represented in the *Coordinadora*.

Conclusions

The Cochabamba and the Raqaypampa case studies have much in common. Both are seen as exemplary grass-roots initiatives engaging with 'collective rights' under purportedly new multicultural legislative provision and political culture. The Raqaypampa indigenous development plan has been trumpeted by governmental and donor organisations as a highly successful example of indigenous involvement in development planning, while the Cochabamba *Coordinadora* has been heralded as a role model for collective action based on supporting existing customs in resisting transnational and state neoliberal agendas.[22] Despite these apparent successes, the rights and identities available to the actors in each case study were constrained by the contradictions inherent in the policy framework within which they were obliged to act.

The successful mobilisation of indigenous and campesino applications of rights under multicultural or pro-indigenous legislative frameworks is fragmented and uneven. The opportunities available to the Raqaypampa leaders as indigenous activists, while limited, appear more diverse than those available to the campesinos in the Misicuni valley. Despite the similarities between the two rural communities, marked differences exist with regard to the proposed classification of land tenure under INRA. In Misicuni, the members of the communities that will be displaced have taken out communal titles as campesinos, whereas the Raqaypampa communities have opted to apply for TCO status. Raqaypampa is likely to be the first TCO in the highlands of the department,[23] whereas the communal land title for Misicuni has largely been negotiated between INRA and the Empresa Misicuni in order to facilitate the sale of land to the water company. Several of the Misicuni leaders claimed that they have not been happy with the land titling process and yet, despite this, no attention was given to their situation by the *Coordinadora*'s wider water campaign in Cochabamba. Thus legislative provisions for indigenous territorial rights notwithstanding, in the Misicuni case these rights have been subordinated to commercial interests. Despite the similarities between the two communities, no one from INRA or from the Empresa Misicuni officially promoted the idea that the Misicuni communities could apply for TCO status, even though their lands already fall within the jurisdiction of the Tunari National Park. The role of these community members within the debate has mostly been a passive one as the paperwork has been led by INRA and the Empresa Misicuni. This is in stark contrast to Raqaypampa, where questions concerning project implementation from a community well known for its politicised Quechua identity brought the World Bank's head of rural development and high ranking members of the PDRC from La Paz for discussions with 'indigenous' leaders and a national NGO.

The contrasting situations in Raqaypampa and Misicuni demonstrate that the political culture surrounding pro-indigenous people's rights in practice is one that relies mostly upon representations of indigenous-ness, rather than on established criteria, self-determination and/or self-identification (in spite of what the legislation might suggest). While it is important that new legislative provision seeks to support collective indigenous rights in keeping with ILO Convention 169, the next main challenge facing states such as Bolivia is the application of these new laws. This is particularly important given the context of donor conceptualisations of indigenous peoples as potential social capital coupled with neoliberal economic policies that attempt to create 'dynamic' resource markets. Despite pro-indigenous clauses in the Ley INRA, in practice these policies and approaches often promote private ownership while denying some 'indigenous' groups full political autonomy and potentially harming their collective interests.

Despite the apparent success of the Raqaypampa indigenous platform when compared with the limited impact of a Misicuni campesino agenda, both these sets of actors had fewer bargaining positions than those used by members of peri-urban water cooperatives and associations involved in the Cochabamba water debate. These groups were successfully able to draw together collective and private interests across the divide of rural-urban identities and win major concessions through the water campaign, including the withdrawal of Aguas de Tunari and the rewriting of key articles in the 2029 Law. The state's rhetoric of a pro-multi-ethnic Bolivia allowed these peri-urban dwellers to locate themselves on the border between 'traditional' and 'modern' identities. In a political culture that allows the re-vindication of indigenous-ness, they were able to claim collective rights to existing 'uses and customs' embracing and validating recent forms of social organisation associated with new water projects, semi-private domestic water sources, and pre-conquest collective irrigation practices.

While the language and imagery of cultural heritage used by water associations and cooperatives was a successful representation in terms of strategy, its links with rurality were tenuous and to some extent exclusionary. These actors used notions of *usos y costumbres* to defend interests that involved the collective construction of wells and infrastructure on private land for domestic consumption and reproduction. In contrast, no arguments based on identities as indigenous people, rural peasants or recent rural migrants were made in favour of the urban poor in the southern zone. The success of the campaign's 'rural-urban' platform therefore marginalised the unconnected urban poor who, according to Laserna (2000), are likely to suffer most from the failure to reach an agreement with Aguas de Tunari. The mobilisation of fragmented representations of indigenous-campesino and rural-urban interests thus has its losers and winners.

A number of factors explain the differences between the subjectivities mobilised in the two case studies. First, the INRA Law becomes confusing when implemented. To date, there have been very few titles issued. Those that have been granted belatedly have all been in lowland areas, reflecting in part the high level of political institutionalisation of indigenous demands among lowland groups as well as national imaginaries of where the indigenous live. In many quarters it is assumed that the concept of TCOs is not really suitable for upland areas because land ownership is confused and land and water are in short supply. Also the use of the terms 'indigenous' and *'originario'* are contested by the strong presence of the campesino movement since the 1952 revolution.[24] Many highland communities questioned whether or not to apply for TCO status, especially given the fact that the CSUTCB (the national campesino confederation) is still wary of INRA. In Raqaypampa, while there was much discussion about whether or not to work with this particular aspect of state legislation, the decision was finally taken to follow through with land titling. Thus, land *saneamiento* as a TCO in Raqaypampa was an important political decision that was cemented in the *Plan Indígena*. However, where does such a conceptualisation of indigenous-ness linked to land leave other groups, such as rural-urban migrants, peri-urban dwellers and semi-nomadic groups in the lowlands?

Answers to this question in part lay with the definition of indigenous and *originario* used and constructed through the water and land reform debates. The fact that few people question the appropriateness of the terms for lowland groups, nomadic or otherwise, reflects long-standing essentialist ideas about space and indigeneity in Bolivia. These ideas construct the indigenous as being those who are not only 'rural', but also 'remote and far away', reflecting a historical geographical imaginary of the nation which casts the *Oriente* as a vast open space, a backwater in need of conquering (Velasco Canelas 1999). These essentialised assumptions about space, distance and engagement with the state are also seen in the different treatment of the Misicuni and Raqaypampa Quechua communities and rural and urban dwellers. Raqaypampanians are cast as the 'real indigenous', whereas the Misicuni communities are seen as incomers.[25] Peri-urban dwellers can mobilise hybrid identities, whereas the disconnected poor, with no access to water, are fixed as 'urban' – despite the fact that many of them are recent rural migrants who identify with a Quechua identity.

While Kearney and Varese's focus on post-development does not explain why these inequalities exist, their analysis does explain the emergence of diversity:

> More and more indigenous people are being drawn into post development conditions of production and reproduction. It is in such contexts that indigenous identities are not only destroyed but also recreated. That is to say, these contexts both destroy and preserve traditional social and cultural forms, even more notable, post development conditions also stimulate and support the emergence of forms of indigenous identity that are strictly speaking neither modern nor traditional. Indeed, one of the most notable characteristics of the contemporary era is the collapse of the distinction between modern and traditional. (Kearney and Varese 1995: 216–17)

Despite this focus on the new post-development conditions structuring identity, it is not enough merely to highlight increased diversity, but rather to focus on the processes that produce different positions and possible inequalities. Here the issue of essentialised cultural markers remains pertinent, even though the lines of discrimination may have shifted to some extent under the new state rhetoric of multi-ethnicity. On the one hand, the Raqaypampa land claim seems to rest on cultural issues – in particular the INRA officers point to the distinctive clothes worn by the Raqaypampanians as setting them apart from other campesinos, such as those living in Misicuni or even in the city. These markers have become a form of cultural capital, which allows the Raqaypampa inhabitants to position themselves favourably within certain contexts, even if negotiation processes with funders are not always entirely participatory. It is also no coincidence that the Raqaypampa *Plan Indígena* was launched at a music festival celebrating new songs from the region, thereby reaffirming the link between cultural representation and indigeneity. However, on the other hand, the Cochabamba peri-urban dwellers, with their successful mobilisation of a language of '*usos y costumbres*' represent an important challenge to such fixed ideas of indigenous identity. It is important to recognise that their mobilisation of *usos y costumbres* crosses dichotomies of modern–traditional and urban–rural, despite the fact that the promotion of these identities in specific contexts may generate new exclusions for other factions of the urban poor.

The conditions structuring identities in Bolivia are changing under the specific multi-ethnic political context generated by state legislation and transnational discourses promoting pro-indigenous agendas in participatory development planning. Nevertheless, not everyone is benefiting to the same extent. Listening to the voices of the emerging excluded during the application of the new multi-ethnic policies represents the next main challenge in the development of pro-indigenous, socially inclusive development practices.

Notes

1. The research for this chapter is drawn from a wider Economic and Social Research Council (ESRC) project 'Now we are all Indians: Transnational Indigenous Communities in Ecuador and Bolivia'.
2. Notions about who and what can be classified as indigenous.
3. The post-development era is characterised by the fact that visions of modernisation still drive development agendas in attempts to fulfil the enlightenment dream, despite the fact that this dream is frustrated by the ways in which relations of production and reproduction are structured by colonial relationships of dependency. Social movements and alternative development visions must engage with this complex set of relationships and realities (see Escobar 1992).
4. Both donor organisations shaping the policy environment and private companies investing in newly liberalised land and water markets.
5. 'El agua es un ser vivificante y fecundante. Sin agua no hay vida'.
6. Specifically, in Bolivia the Bank has funded a small grants scheme through the *Fondo Campesino* that is designed to stimulate participatory planning. It allows communities to apply for funding for projects of less than $30,000 without having to search for co-funding from municipal government, and reflects wider Bank support for decentralisation and participatory rural investment projects (World Bank 1997, 1998).
7. Dunkerley (1998) indicates how the Bolivian municipal budget increased by $150 million between 1990 and 1996. This increased budget represented more than 30 per cent of total public expenditure.

8. Indigenous jurisdiction is understood as the exercise of indigenous authority within a specific territory according to custom.

9. There were two major marches on La Paz in 1996 by thousands of campesinos and indigenous people focusing specifically on the INRA Law (see Condo 1998).

10. While DANIDA has funded the technical side of mapping and TCO work has witnessed some very innovative projects allying state cartographers, consultants and indigenous mappers (*técnicos indígenas*), approximately 20 of the original 26 claims are still waiting to be dealt with, despite being on the list since 1996. DANIDA has been highly critical of both the administrative backlog and the mathematical formulae used to estimate the spatial needs (*necesidades espaciales*) of indigenous groups. Interviews with DANIDA consultants and staff, 28 August 1999, 7 October 1999.

11. The slow processing of claims is of even more concern, given the fact that INRA is only scheduled to operate until 2006, by which time all land titles are supposed to be registered.

12. The leading proponent of this form of rural development in Bolivia is the German bilateral aid organisation GTZ, which has invested heavily in projects, training programmes for engineers and institutions (both academic centres and government institutions such as the National Programme for Irrigation PRONAR).

13. '[H]ay tres leyes, la ley de municipios que tiene que ver con el agua, que pasa su dominio como utilidad pública, la ley 2029, que lógicamente dice, saneamiento básico pero que tiene que ver mucho mas con el agua, y la otra ley, que es la bendita ley del recurso agua.'

14. While established in Bolivian legislative and state practices, intercultural and bilingual education programmes are not uniformly implemented in all areas. Many peri-urban areas or rural areas close to large cities with bilingual populations do not provide intercultural education.

15. Together with the community, CENDA has systematised data collection on indigenous agriculture in an attempt to document what Scott (1976) terms the moral economy of the peasant, in relation to the efficiency of Andean land management and the introduction of innovation. CENDA has documented experiments with indigenous forms of alternative technology over a number of years. The community's relationship with the NGO has sought to show how indigenous agricultural practices have resisted colonisation through what Kearney and Varese (1995) describe as the 'economic rationality of a social philosophy' rather than the individualism of market-based economies.

16. 'El tema es que hay que tener título ya, hay que ponerlo en el contexto de que la comunidad ya ha entrado en un proceso interno sobre saneamiento, han decidido TCO, entonces hay una discusión. El agua por historia no pertenece a nadie, pertenece a dios.'

17. The tariff increases in January 2000 were scheduled to raise prices, in some cases by up to 300 per cent, and the concession granted allowed the water consortium to control the construction of new wells in their area of jurisdiction. It also permitted the company to charge those people who were already connected to the sewerage system through the installation of meters in private drinking water and irrigation wells.

18. There is a recent history in this area of militancy around water (see Crespo and Halkyer 1999) and in Quillacollo/Vinto the *regantes* – irrigators – are very well organised.

19. 'El agua es una herencia de nuestros antepasados y lo vamos a defender con nuestras vidas, el decreto ya está, lo que queremos es que se derogue ... es como si nos estuvieran tocando nuestro tuétano con el agua, hemos permitido que de nuestro petróleo se adueñen otras empresas, las minas, incluso hasta la política y todo eso, y ya esta contaminado todo eso, a nosotros nos han llegado todo, y todos nos hemos dejado, pero el agua es como nuestro tuétano que nos han tocado y no lo vamos a permitir, porque somos mujeres y vamos a pelear y donde sea, con nuestras vidas.'

20. Interview Aguas de Tunari, 25 November 1999.

21. Interviews and conversations with those closely involved in these negotiations indicated that discussions had taken place between community representatives and INRA and within INRA internally over a potential TCO claim. These discussions, however, were subsequently abandoned.

22. Its actions have been copied elsewhere. For example, a *Coordinadora del Agua y de la Vida* was created in La Paz in February 2000 uniting 17 organisations *'para sumarse a la heroica lucha de la Coordinadora de Cochabamba'* (*Los Tiempos* 18 February 2000).

23. Interview with INRA director Cochabamba, 9 December 99.

24. Interview with DFID advisor, La Paz 28 August 1999.

25. Interviews with Departmental INRA offices 6 November 1999; 9 December 1999. The term is used to summarise a set of descriptions given of these people in the interviews. It was suggested that they lived 'too' close to the city and that their livelihoods in part depended on this proximity. It was implied that these people could not necessarily trace a long history of family residence in the area because the land is an ex-hacienda (as is Raqaypama where no such distinction is made to suggest that they cannot be classified as indigenous).

References

Albó, X. (1999), *Iguales Aunque Diferentes*, Ministerio de Educación, UNICEF and CIPCA (La Paz).

Andolina, R. (1999), 'Colonial Legacies and Plurinational Imaginaries: Indigenous Movement Politics in Ecuador and Bolivia', unpublished PhD dissertation, University of Minnesota.

Benton J. (1999), *Agrarian Reform in Theory and Practice: A Study of the Lake Titicaca Region of Bolivia*, Ashgate (Aldershot).

Bustamante, R. and Z. Gutiérrez (1999), 'Usos y costumbres en la gestión de riego; caos u orden en la gestión de agua para riego' in P. Hoogendam, *Aguas y Municipios*, Plural Editores (La Paz), pp.163–89.

Condo F. (1998), *La Marcha del Siglo, Testimonio de Román Loayza y Modesto Condori. Marcha de las naciones originarias El Tiempo del Instrumento Político*, Ediciones Alkamari (La Paz).

Crespo, C. and R. Halkyer (1999), *Conflictos Ambientales (dos Casos: Agua y Territorio)*, CERES (Cochabamba).

Dunkerley, J. (1998), 'The 1997 Bolivian Elections in Historical Perspective', *Occasional Papers ILAS* (London).

Escobar, A. (1992), *Encountering Development. The Making and Unmaking of the Third World*, Princeton University Press (New Jersey).

Gandarillas, A. et al. (1994), *Dios Da el Agua ¿Que Hacen los Proyectos?* Hisbol/PRIV (La Paz).

Gerbrandy, G. and P. Hoogendam (1998), *Aguas y Acequias. Los Derechos al Agua y la gestión Campesina de Riego en los Andes Bolivianos*, Plural Editores (La Paz).

Gutiérrez, Z. (1998), 'La Práctica de la distribución de agua en distintos sistemas de riego' in G. Gerbrandy and P. Hoogendam, *Aguas y Acequias. Los Derechos al Agua y la gestión Campesina de Riego en los Andes Bolivianos*, Plural Editores (La Paz), pp.99–348.

Kearney, M. and S. Varese (1995), 'Latin America's Indigenous Peoples: Changing Identities and Forms of Resistance' in S. Halesbsky and R. Harris (eds), *Capital, Power and Inequality in Latin America*, Westview Press (Boulder), pp.207–31.

Laserna, R. (2000), 'Aguas o muerte. Venceremos? Puntos de Vista', *Los Tiempos* 10 March 2000.

Laurie, N. and Marvin, S. (1999), 'Globalisation, Neo-Liberalism and Negotiated Development in the Andes: Water Privatisation and Regional Identity in Cochabamba', *Environment and Planning*, Vol.31, pp.1401–15.

Lopez, Ana (1993), 'La Demanda Indigena de la Pluriculturalidad y Multietnicidad: El Tratamiento de la Prensa', in Diego Cornejo (ed.), *Los Indios y el Estado-Pais. Pluriculturalidad y Multietnicidad en el Ecuador. Contribuciones al Debate*, Abya Yala (Quito), pp.21–59.

Marvin, S. and N. Laurie (1999), 'An Emerging Logic of Urban Water Management in Cochabamba, Bolivia', *Urban Studies*, Vol.36 (2), pp.341–57

'Nace una Coordinadora del Agua y la Vida en La Paz', *Los Tiempos*, 18 February 2000.

Robb, C. (1999), *Can the Poor Influence Policy? Participatory Poverty Assessments in the Developing World*, World Bank (Washington DC).

Sánchez, L., D. Tuchschneider and P. Zutter (eds) (1994), *¿Del Paquete al Acompañamiento?* Hisbol/PRIV (La Paz).

Scott J. (1976), *The Moral Economy of the Peasant Rebellion and Subsistence in Southeast Asia*, Yale University Press (New Haven).

Stavenhagen, R. (1996), 'Indigenous Rights: Some Conceptual Problems' in E. Jelin and E. Hershberg (eds), *Constructing Democracy: Human Rights, Citizenship and Society in Latin America*, Westview Press (Boulder), pp.141–59.

Velasco Canelas, R. (1999), 'Propuestas para dialogar sobre identidades construidas'. Paper presented at *'Seminario Andino, Conflictos y Políticas Interculturales: Territorio y Educación'*. CEIDES/CESU/CENDA, Universidad Mayor de San Simón, Cochabamba, 20–22 October 1999.

'Water War in Bolivia', *The Economist*, 12 February 2000, p.66.

World Bank (1997), 'World Bank Supports Government Decentralisation in Bolivia'. News release no. 98/1432/LAC, 5 August 1997.

—— (1998), 'World Bank Finances Participatory Rural investment Projects in Bolivia'. News release no. 97/1764/LAC, 13 May 1998.

Index